English Lessons Through Literature
Level 4

Kathy Jo DeVore

www.barefootmeandering.com
veritas • gnaritas • libertas

Copyright © 2014 by Kathy Jo DeVore. The eBook version may be printed for the use of one household and may not be resold. The print version may not be reproduced.

Scripture quotations taken from the New American Standard Bible®, Copyright © 1960, 1962, 1963, 1968, 1971, 1972, 1973, 1975, 1977, 1995 by The Lockman Foundation. Used by permission.

Clipart images Copyright © GraphicsFactory.com

liberis meis

Table of Contents

Introduction 11
Level 4 Literature List 17
1. Introduction to the Thesaurus 19
2. Parts of Speech: Nouns 22
3. Literary Analysis 27
4. Parts of Speech: Verbs 30
5. How to Write a Condensed Narrative 34
6. Condensed Narrative: Anansi and Nothing 38
7. Parts of Speech: Pronouns 40
8. The Sentence 45
9. Descriptive Writing 51
10. The Four Types of Sentences, Part 1 55
11. Parts of Speech: Adjectives; Articles 59
12. Condensed Narrative: Why the Lizard Moves His Head 63
13. The Four Types of Sentences, Part 2 64
14. Linking Verbs; Predicate Nominatives 68
15. Literary Analysis 73
16. Adjectives That Tell Which One and Whose 75
17. Predicate Adjectives 78
18. Condensed Narrative: Why We See Ants Carrying Bundles 82
19. Helping Verbs 84
20. Plurals with -f and -fe 87
21. Descriptive Writing 93
22. Direct Objects 96
23. Plurals with -o 101
24. Amplified Narrative: The Fox and the Grapes 105
25. Nouns as Adjectives 107
26. Diagramming Interrogative Sentences 110
27. Literary Analysis 115

28. Compound Subjects and Predicates 118

29. Quotations 123

30. Amplified Narrative: The Bundle of Sticks 126

31. Diagramming Imperative Sentences 129

32. Parts of Speech: Adverbs 132

33. Descriptive Writing 139

34. Adverbs That Tell How and When 141

35. Adverbs That Tell Where and How Often 145

36. Amplified Narrative: The Leap at Rhodes 149

37. Adverbs That Tell to What Extent 151

38. Writing an Outline 155

39. Literary Analysis 159

40. The Paragraph 162

41. Point of View 166

42. Point of View Narration: The Humble Bee's Nest 170

43. Phrases and Clauses 173

44. Parts of Speech: Conjunctions 179

45. Descriptive Writing 185

46. Parts of Speech: Interjections; Nouns of Direct Address ... 188

47. Appositives 195

48. Point of View Narration: A Frog's Life 198

49. Commas in a Series 200

50. Writing an Outline 204

51. Literary Analysis 209

52. Homonyms 213

53. Parts of Speech: Prepositions 218

54. Point of View Narration: The Greedy Stranger 222

55. Object of the Preposition 224

56. Diagramming Prepositions 228

57. Descriptive Writing 235

58. Prepositions and Adverbs 238

59. Slant Narratives 242

60. Slant Narrative: The Ants and the Grasshopper 246

61. Noun and Pronouns Cases 248

62. Pronoun Cases: Correct Usage 252

63. Literary Analysis 257

64. Interrogative Adverbs 260

65. The Principal Parts of the Verb 264

66. Slant Narrative: The Town Mouse and the Country Mouse 268

67. The Infinitive; Verb Properties: Person 270

68. Verb Properties: Number 273

69. Descriptive Writing 279

70. Verb Properties: Tense 282

71. Properties of Nouns and Pronouns 289

72. Slant Narrative: The Hare and the Tortoise 294

73. Collective Nouns 297

74. Subject-Verb Agreement 302

75. Literary Analysis 307

76. Comparatives 310

77. Superlatives 314

78. Scientific Narration: Snow 317

79. Irregular Verbs 319

80. Tenses: Negatives and Questions 324

81. Descriptive Writing 329

82. To Be 332

83. To Do and To Go 337

84. Scientific Narration: Silk 341

85. To See and To Come 343

86. To Have 348

87. Literary Analysis 353

88. Other Irregular Verbs 356

89. Subordinate Conjunctions 363

90. Scientific Narration: Sound 367

91. Compound Sentences 370

92. Review: Phrases and Clauses. 376

93. Descriptive Writing 381

94. Complex Sentences 384

95. Indirect Objects. 389

96. Historical Narration: Hieroglyphics 394

97. Review: Compound and Complex Sentences 396

98. Commas After Introductory Elements 401

99. Literary Analysis 405

100. Relative Pronouns 408

101. A Poem and a Fable 413

102. Historical Narration: The Nile Valley. 416

103. Sit and Set 419

104. Lie and Lay 424

105. Descriptive Writing 429

106. Well and Good. 432

107. A Poem and a Fable 436

108. Historical Narration: Greek Life 438

Exercise Answers. 441

Appendix A: Memory Work 470

Appendix B: Correct Use of Words 473

Appendix C: Diagramming Reference 476

Appendix D: Additional Writing Lessons for Older Students. 483

Appendix E: Eleanor of Aquitaine 488

Introduction

English Lessons Through Literature has three lessons per week for thirty-six weeks. This is a total of 108 lessons per year.

Level 4 is intended for 4th grade and up. Level 5 is intended for 5th grade and up. It is the first of a two-volume set which is intended for use before high school. Either level could be used for older children as well. I would advise Level 4 first for children who do not have a very strong background in grammar. If you are doing Level 4 with older students, please see Appendix D: Additional Writing Lessons for Older Students.

It is best to transition children gently into doing new things. In writing, this means that first we talk, then we write. *English Lessons Through Literature* includes oral lessons in some levels so that students can practice new concepts without the stress of having to write the answers. Oral lessons in early levels will then be written lessons in the following level.

Literature

The literature suggested in this book is in the public domain in the United States, and the full text of each story and book can be found online. Most are also available as audio books, and children who are reading well can read the book themselves rather than using the books as read-alouds.

I do recommend reading the literature prior to the lesson. The examples and the copywork almost always come from the reading selection from that day. We like to read it the day before so that written lessons can begin without delay on the lesson day.

Since most of the examples and part of the daily copywork come directly from the literature, reading the literature is an important component of this program. However, there is certainly room to skip books that the child does not like, and it is up to the parents to determine whether or not a recommended resource is right for their family. My homeschooling motto has long been: Use the curriculum; don't let the curriculum use you. I recommend the motto more highly than I recommend any of the literature selections in this book.

Lessons and Exercises

If your child has already covered some of the concepts in this book, use the lesson as a review by having him tell what he knows on the subject. Instead of reading the lesson on nouns, say, "Tell me everything you know about nouns." Afterwards, you can skim the lesson and see if he's left out any pertinent information. Prompt him for that information ("What do you know about abstract and concrete nouns?"), or go over that portion. In this way, he practices narration, he makes the information his own by telling it himself, and—in some cases—he may be reminded that he doesn't know or remember as much as he thinks he does. We often believe that since "we've been over this a hundred times," that means we know the subject. The student who can give you the lesson instead of reading it truly does.

English Lessons Through Literature narrations should be in addition to the oral narrations in other areas such as history and science. At this age, I recommend beginning to include written narrations from those subjects as well. You can start with just one per week, and work up from there.

The writing lessons follow a two-week repeating pattern.

Day 1: The model story for the next two weeks (six lessons) is in this lesson. The student reads and orally narrates the new model story.
Day 2: The student has a playing with words copia exercise, or he outlines the new model story.
Day 3: The student has either a literary analysis or descriptive writing exercise.
Day 4: The student has a playing with sentences copia exercise.
Day 5: The student has a commonplace book entry from the model story.
Day 6: The student writes the written narration from his outline.

I love using real sentences from real books for the lessons and exercises. They are far more interesting, which means children are far more likely to be engaged by the material. Copywork selections are only altered to change outdated punctuation and/or spelling when necessary. Lesson examples are often shortened—some of those old authors really knew how to write a paragraph into a sentence. Some sentences are simplified for diagramming.

When I check over the exercises with my children, I do not do so with red pencil in hand. Instead, we look at the work together, and I point out mistakes which he then corrects. I believe working with real sentences, even modified ones, can be a little harder than manufactured sentences. But I also believe that there's more value in working through the exercises to discover the correct answers.

English Lessons Through Literature includes a moderate number of exercise sentences to practice the concepts presented in the lessons. However, some children require more practice with grammatical concepts than others. Rather than fill each level with an excessive number of exercises, I chose to create a free download full of worksheets which can be used with any level for extra practice. The sentences are all taken from *The Wonderful Wizard of Oz* as most children will have a basic familiarity with that story, one way or another. You can find a link to the practice worksheets on my website: www.barefootmeandering.com/bookstore.html.

Prepared Dictation

Like copywork, dictation is a form of studying grammar, spelling, and the mechanics of writing. However, dictation requires children to take a more active role and actually study and think about the material, as opposed to passively taking it in through copywork. For this reason, dictation should not begin until third or fourth grade, depending on readiness.

Dictation is for children who write easily. A child who is still struggling with reading or penmanship should just continue with copywork. However, children who type can type their dictations instead. This simplifies the process for children who hate writing.

In prepared dictation, children type or write a passage after studying it for five to ten minutes. Without this preparation, the exercise is not a teaching exercise; it is a test. In *Home Education*, Charlotte Mason went further, describing dictation without preparation as "a fertile cause of bad spelling" (241).

I know that dictation can sound like a huge, time consuming exercise, especially with multiple children. It's not. We do prepared dictation twice a week, on the "off" days from grammar. Each of my boys studies his exercise for about 10 minutes. He chooses, sometimes with my help, two or three words to analyze. A passage should not have more than three or four unknown words to be studied. He adds these to his Spelling Journal, writing each word with a space between the syllables, which helps him to analyze each word syllable by syllable. The Spelling Journal organizes words according to phonogram or spelling rule, and it is a free download on my site.

Dictations may be written or typed. My boys type their dictations. The spelling and grammar checks are turned off in our word processing program, and we increase the font size to 20+ points so that I can read over their shoulders. I read the exercises while each boy takes his turn at the keyboard. I stand behind them so that I can make sure they don't make any mistakes.

English Lessons Through Literature includes two dictation exercises each week. Sources include the literature, poems, and Bible verses. If you prefer, choose dictation exercises from history, science, or free reading.

Watch as the child writes to catch mistakes immediately. Mistakes imprint on a child's mind just as correctly written material does, and this confusion is difficult to correct, as some of us have found while using poor spelling programs which ask children still learning the basics to proofread something. In *Home Education*, Charlotte Mason writes:

> Once the eye sees a misspelt word, that image remains; and if there is also the image of the word rightly spelt, we are perplexed as to which is which. Now we see why there could not be a more ingenious way of making bad spellers than 'dictation' as it is commonly taught. Every misspelt word is an image in the child's brain not to be obliterated by the right spelling. It becomes, therefore, the teacher's business to prevent false spelling, and, if an error has been made, to hide it away, as it were, so that the impression may not become fixed (242).

Commonplace Book

A commonplace book is a book for copying poetry, passages from literature, and other writings or information. A simple composition book can be used for this purpose.

Each narration story has a commonplace book exercise, a passage from the story to copy. Children can also begin to add to the commonplace book from other reading: history, science, literature, or free reading. My children choose their own passages to copy, passages which speak to them in some way. For my oldest son, it's often something philosophical or political. For my second son, it's usually something funny.

In Level 5, the commonplace book completely replaces copywork. In Level 4, however, copywork suggestions are still given. If you want to transition to the commonplace book, then I recommend giving the child a choice each day. He can either do the scheduled copywork, or he can choose a passage that he enjoyed from another book.

Picture Study

Charlotte Mason recommended having the child look at the picture without interruption for several minutes, then putting the picture away and having the child describe the picture. It is, in essence, a picture narration. Afterwards, bring the picture back out and see if he notices anything else. This is not art criticism, though. It is learning to attend to detail and to form a love and appreciation for art.

Each artist has six paintings studied with new paintings added every other week, so you have a full twelve weeks to enjoy each artist and to include additional activities if desired. For example, you could read a children's biography of the artist and view some of his additional works. More paintings can often be found at http://www.wikipaintings.org/, or just do an internet search for the artist's name.

All pictures of paintings in this book are, by necessity, black and white. Color copies of the paintings are provided on my site at no cost for your convenience. These can be printed so that you can display the picture for the two weeks between new paintings. In the past, we have also used the pictures as backgrounds on my computer. However, my oldest son did tell me once that it was strange seeing a particular painting without the icons.

Memory Work and Reference Pages

Memory work is an important part of this program. The student cannot properly analyze a sentence when he doesn't remember the difference between a verb and an adverb, or a phrase and a clause, or if he can't remember which verbs are linking verbs. When it comes to learning the basics of any subject, vocabulary is king.

At the back of the book, there are pages that have all the definitions and lists to learn from this book to make it easy to learn and review the information. New material should be read three times every lesson day, or daily, until it is learned. Newly learned material should be reviewed regularly at first, perhaps once a week. Material which has been learned for a longer time should be reviewed every month to six weeks, but if it stops being automatic, it goes back to the frequent review.

There are more than one hundred poems in this book. My suggestion is to select a poem, preferably one the child enjoys, and begin to memorize it. When he has memorized it, move on to a new one.

Appendix B has sentences to read, if desired, for correct use of words. The purpose is akin to that of copywork in that it is intended to imprint certain grammatical concepts into the child's mind just through repetition. Saying these sentences aloud regularly will help the correct forms to "sound" right to our children and to ourselves. My advice is to read these sentences approximately once a week for the school year.

Diagramming reference pages are also included in Appendix C.

Third Person Singular Pronouns

I wish the English language had a gender-neutral third person singular pronoun acceptable for people. I use the masculine because it's what I grew up with and I'm too old to like change. It is at least as correct as the feminine form and, as the mother of four boys, the feminine sounds odd to me in reference to children; I still call my daughter "son" more often than not. And using the plural with a singular antecedent, which is becoming more common, is simply incorrect.

Level Four

Level 4 Literature List

All the literature selections suggested herein are in the public domain in the United States of America and are probably available at your local library. The complete texts can also be found online from Project Gutenberg (www.gutenberg.org) and/or the Baldwin Project (www.mainlesson.com). Most are available as audio books, and free audio book versions may be found online from LibriVox (www.librivox.org).

The Book of Dragons by E. Nesbit

Black Beauty by Anna Sewell

Ozma of Oz by L. Frank Baum

"The Reluctant Dragon" by Kenneth Grahame
"The Reluctant Dragon" is part of the book *Dream Days* by Kenneth Grahame on Gutenberg.org. It is also available commercially as an illustrated book.

Heidi by Johanna Spyri

Tanglewood Tales by Nathaniel Hawthorne

1. Introduction to the Thesaurus

- The Book of Dragons, Chapter 1

Like the dictionary, the **thesaurus** is a book of words. But while the purpose of the dictionary is to define words, the purpose of the thesaurus is to help you find the best word for your writing.

The thesaurus includes both **synonyms** and **antonyms**. Synonyms are words which have the same or similar meanings, while antonyms have opposite meanings.

In *The Book of Dragons*, young Lionel apologizes to the Prime Minister for **vexing** him.

"Well, I'm sorry if I've vexed you," said Lionel. "Come, let's kiss and be friends."

Roget's Thesaurus at www.thesaurus.com lists both synonyms and antonyms for the word **vex**.

Synonyms: afflict, agitate, annoy, displease, disquiet, disturb, embarrass, exasperate, gall, infuriate, irk, irritate, offend, peeve, perplex, rile, torment.

Antonyms: aid, appease, calm, comfort, delight, ease, help, make happy, please, quiet, soothe.

Look at how we could change that sentence with this information.

"Well, I'm sorry if I've agitated you," said Lionel.

"Well, I'm sorry if I've exasperated you," said Lionel.

"Well, I'm sorry if I didn't help you," said Lionel.

"Well, I'm sorry if I didn't appease you," said Lionel.

Within the lists above, we have shades of meaning. The synonyms do not mean exactly the same thing, and the antonyms are not perfect opposites. Using the thesaurus, we can find the best word to express the exact meaning we want to convey. The thesaurus can also help us to vary our word choice so that we are not using the same words over and over again.

Today, get acquainted with the thesaurus. Look up a few words, and find different ways to say them.

New Feet Within My Garden Go

By Emily Dickinson

New feet within my garden go,
New fingers stir the sod;
A troubadour upon the elm
Betrays the solitude.
New children play upon the green,
New weary sleep below;
And still the pensive spring returns,
And still the punctual snow!

Writing: Oral Narration

A model story is one which you will be using as a model for your own writing. When you get a new model story, you will read it and give an oral narration of it. Over the following five lessons, you will have other exercises with the model story, finally producing a written narration from it.

Read your new model story below, and then give your instructor an oral narration of it.

Anansi and Nothing

From *West African Folk-Tales* by William H. Barker

Near Anansi's miserable little hut there was a fine palace where lived a very rich man called Nothing. Nothing and Anansi proposed, one day, to go to the neighboring town to get some wives. Accordingly, they set off together.

Nothing, being a rich man, wore a very fine velvet cloth, while Anansi had a ragged cotton one. While they were on their way Anansi persuaded Nothing to change clothes for a little while, promising to give back the fine velvet before they reached the town. He delayed doing this, however, first on one pretext, then on another—till they arrived at their destination.

Anansi, being dressed in such a fine garment, found no difficulty in getting as many wives as he wished. Poor Nothing, with his ragged and miserable cloth, was treated with great contempt. At first he could not get even one wife. At last, however, a woman took pity on him and gave him her daughter. The poor girl was laughed at very heartily by Anansi's wives for choosing such a beggar as Nothing appeared to be. She wisely took no notice of their scorn.

The party set off for home. When they reached the cross-roads leading to their respective houses the women were astonished. The road leading to Anansi's house was only half cleared. The one which led to Nothing's palace was, of course, wide and well made. Not only so, but his servants had strewn it with beautiful skins and carpets, in preparation for his return. Servants were there, awaiting him, with fine clothes for himself and his wife. No one was waiting for Anansi.

Nothing's wife was queen over the whole district and had everything her heart could desire, Anansi's wives could not even get proper food; they had to live on unripe bananas with peppers. The wife of Nothing heard of her friends' miserable state and invited them to a great feast in her palace. They came, and were so pleased with all they saw that they agreed to stay there. Accordingly, they refused to come back to Anansi's hut.

He was very angry, and tried in many ways to kill Nothing, but without success. Finally, however, he persuaded some rat friends to dig a deep tunnel in front of Nothing's door. When the hole was finished Anansi lined it with knives and broken bottles. He then smeared the steps of the palace with okro to make them very slippery, and withdrew to a little distance.

When he thought Nothing's household was safely in bed and asleep, he called to Nothing to come out to the courtyard and see something. Nothing's wife, however, dissuaded him from going. Anansi tried again and again, and each time she bade her husband not to listen. At last Nothing determined to go and see this thing. As he placed his foot on the first step, of course he slipped, and down he fell into the hole. The noise alarmed the household. Lights were fetched and Nothing was found in the ditch, so much wounded by the knives that he soon died. His wife was terribly grieved at his untimely death. She boiled many yams, mashed them, and took a great dishful of them round the district. To every child she met she gave some, so that the child might help her to cry for her husband. This is why, if you find a child crying and ask the cause, you will often be told he is "crying for nothing."

Commonplace Book

With your instructor's approval, add the passage below to your commonplace book, or choose your own passage from a work of fiction. This can be from either school reading or free reading.

> When the people in the town saw the Dragon fly off after the Hippogriff and the King, they all came out of their houses to look, and when they saw the two disappear, they made up their minds to the worst, and began to think what they would wear for Court mourning.

Dictation

> At last came a Saturday when the Dragon actually walked into the Royal nursery and carried off the King's own pet Rocking Horse. Then the King cried for six days, and on the seventh he was so tired that he had to stop. He heard the Blue Bird singing among the roses and saw the Butterfly fluttering among the lilies, and he said, "Nurse, wipe my face, please. I am not going to cry any more."

2. Parts of Speech: Nouns

• The Book of Dragons, Chapter 2

Definition: A noun is the name of a person, place, thing, or idea.

Nouns are naming words. Everything and everybody has a name, and all of those names are nouns. Some nouns are the names of people, like **Princess Mary Ann**, a little **girl**, and **Tom**, the gardener's **boy**. Some words name places, like **castle**, **Zoological Gardens**, and **Rotundia**. Some words name things, like **pet** and **rhinoceros**, two words we thankfully don't normally see together. And some words name ideas, like **wickedness** and **love**.

Look at the following passage from *The Book of Dragons*. The underlined words are all nouns.

> What with the elephant, and the Princess's affection, and the knowledge that the very next day he would receive the *History of Rotundia*, beautifully bound, with the Royal arms on the cover, Tom could hardly sleep a wink. And, besides, the dog did bark so terribly. There was only one dog in Rotundia—the kingdom could not afford to keep more than one.

In this sentence, we have a person: Tom. We have places: kingdom and Rotundia. We have things: elephant, *History of Rotundia*, arms, cover, wink, and dog. And we have ideas: affection and knowledge. All of these words are nouns.

Nouns can be either **common** or **proper**. Common nouns like **girl** and **boy** could refer to any child at all, but **Princess Mary Ann** and **Tom** refer to very specific children. There are many **kingdoms**, but no other like **Rotundia**. There are many **elephants** in the world, but only **Fido** is six inches tall and can fit in your pocket. Common nouns are general; proper nouns are specific and point out an individual person, place, thing, or idea. Proper nouns are always capitalized.

Some authors capitalize nouns that aren't ordinarily capitalized. For instance, the animal names in Aesop are always capitalized. We have stories about the Tortoise and the Hare, and even the Ants and the Grasshopper. He used the common names as if they were the proper names for his characters. If the author treats a noun as a proper noun by capitalizing it, I also treat it as a proper noun in the exercises.

You'll be learning the definitions for all the parts of speech as well as lists of important material. It is important to know this information well.

The Fairy in Winter

By Walter De La Mare

There was a Fairy—flake of winter—
Who, when the snow came, whispering, Silence,
Sister crystal to crystal sighing,
Making of meadow argent palace,
Night a star-sown solitude,
Cried 'neath her frozen eaves, "I burn here!"
Wings diaphanous, beating bee-like,
Wand within fingers, locks enspangled,
Icicle foot, lip sharp as scarlet,
She lifted her eyes in her pitch-black hollow—
Green as stalks of weeds in water—
Breathed: stirred.
Rilled from her heart the ichor, coursing,
Flamed and awoke her slumbering magic.
Softlier than moth's her pinions trembled;
Out into blackness, light-like, she flittered,
Leaving her hollow cold, forsaken.
In air, o'er crystal, rang twangling night-wind.
Bare, rimed pine-woods murmured lament.

How Mushrooms First Grew

From *West African Folk-Tales* by William H. Barker

Long, long ago there dwelt in a town two brothers whose bad habits brought them much trouble. Day by day they got more deeply in debt. Their creditors gave them no peace, so at last they ran away into the woods. They became highway robbers.

But they were not happy. Their minds were troubled by their evil deeds. At last they decided to go home, make a big farm, and pay off their debts gradually.

They accordingly set to work and soon had quite a fine farm prepared for corn. As the soil was good, they hoped the harvest would bring them in much money.

Unfortunately, that very day a bushfowl came along. Being hungry, it scratched up all the newly planted seeds and ate them.

The two poor brothers, on arriving at the field next day, were dismayed to find all their work quite wasted. They put down a trap for the thief. That evening the bushfowl was caught in it. The two brothers, when they came and found the bird, told it that now all their debts would be transferred to it because it had robbed them of the means of paying the debts themselves.

The poor bird—in great trouble at having such a burden thrust upon it made a nest under a silk-cotton tree. There it began to lay eggs, meaning to hatch them and sell the young birds for money to pay off the debts.

A terrible hurricane came, however, and a branch of the tree came downs. All the eggs were smashed. As a result, the bushfowl transferred the debts to the tree, as it had broken the eggs.

The silk-cotton tree was in dismay at having such a big sum of money to pay off. It immediately set to work to make as much silk cotton as it possibly could, that it might sell it.

An elephant, not knowing all that had happened, came along. Seeing the silk cotton, he came to the tree and plucked down all its bearings. By this means the debts were transferred to the poor elephant.

The elephant was very sad when he found what he had done. He wandered away into the desert, thinking of a way to make money. He could think of none.

As he stood quietly under a tree, a poor hunter crept up. This man thought he was very lucky to find such a fine elephant standing so still. He at once shot him.

Just before the animal died, he told the hunter that now the debts would have to be paid by him. The hunter was much grieved when he heard this, as he had no money at all.

He walked home wondering what he could do to make enough money to pay the debts. In the darkness he did not see the stump of a tree which the overseers had cut down in the road. He fell and broke his leg. By this means the debts were transferred to the tree-stump.

Not knowing this, a party of white ants came along next morning and began to eat into the tree. When they had broken it nearly to the ground, the tree told them that now the debts were theirs, as they had killed it.

The ants, being very wise, held a council together to find out how best they could make money. They decided each to contribute as much as possible. With the proceeds one of their young men would go to the nearest market and buy pure linen thread. This they would weave and sell and the profits would go to help pay the debts.

This was done. From time to time all the linen in stock was brought and spread out in the sunshine to keep it in good condition. When men see this linen lying out on the ant-hills, they call it "mushroom," and gather it for food.

Writing: Copia, Playing with Words

Part of writing is developing what the ancient Greeks called copia, which means an abundance of words and phrases. The writing exercises are meant to help you develop copia, so in addition to writing narrations, you'll also be playing with words and sentences so that you'll learn a variety of ways to say things.

Take each of the following words from your model story and look them up in the thesaurus. Give two or three different ways to say each word.

garment, scorn, wounded, miserable, rich

Exercise

Review memory work. This can be an oral exercise. Find the nouns in this passage. Which nouns are proper nouns, and which are common?

> "Come, little birthday present," he said tenderly. "The dragon will be so pleased. And I'm glad to see you're not crying. You know, my child, we cannot begin too young to learn to think of the happiness of others rather than our own. I should not like my dear little niece to be selfish, or to wish to deny a trivial pleasure to a poor, sick dragon, far from his home and friends."

Commonplace Book

With your instructor's approval, add the poem below to your commonplace book, or choose your own poem.

> There was a Fairy—flake of winter—
> Who, when the snow came, whispering, Silence,
> Sister crystal to crystal sighing,
> Making of meadow argent palace,
> Night a star-sown solitude,
> Cried 'neath her frozen eaves, "I burn here!"

Dictation

Hebrews 13:7-8

Remember those who led you, who spoke the word of God to you; and considering the result of their conduct, imitate their faith. Jesus Christ is the same yesterday and today and forever.

Young Women Picking Fruit by Mary Cassatt

Picture Study

1. Read the title and the name of the artist. Study the picture for several minutes, then put the picture away.

2. Describe the picture.

3. Look at the picture again. Do you notice any details that you missed before? What do you like or dislike about this painting? Does it remind you of anything?

3. Literary Analysis

- The Book of Dragons, Chapter 3

Writing: Literary Analysis

This should be an oral exercise.

With your instructor's approval, choose a story from *The Book of Dragons*, or one of the other books you're currently reading, and answer the following questions.

If you could trade places with one of the characters, which one would it be, and why?

It's important to tell why you feel this way. Give examples from the story. For instance, don't say that you liked a character because he was nice. Instead, give an example from the story that shows that he was nice. For example, consider the two men in yesterday's fable who wanted to pay back their debts. Were they good men? If I wanted to write about that fable, I might say one of the following sentences.

> I think the two men were trying to be good. They stopped thieving and started farming to pay back their debts.

> I think the men were still bad. They said they wanted to pay back their debts, but when they bushfowl ate their crop, they claimed that the debts they had run up were now his.

Wee Willie Winkie

By William Miller

Wee Willie Winkie rins through the town,
Up-stairs and doon-stairs, in his nicht-gown,
Tirlin' at the window, cryin' at the lock,
  "Are the weans in their bed?—for it's now ten o'clock."

Hey, Willie Winkie! Are ye comin' ben?
The cat's singin' gay thrums to the sleepin' hen,
The doug's speldered on the floor, and disna gie a cheep;
But here's a waukrife laddie that winna fa' asleep.

Onything but sleep, ye rogue! Glow'rin' like the moon,
Rattlin' in an airn jug wi' an airn spoon,
Rumblin' tumblin' roun' about, crowin' like a cock,
Skirlin' like a kenna-what—wauknin' sleepin' folk.

Hey, Willie Winkie! The wean's in a creel!
Waumblin' aff a body's knee like a vera eel,
Ruggin' at the cat's lug, and ravellin' a' her thrums,—
Hey, Willie Winkie!—See, there he comes!

Wearie is the mither that has a storie wean,
A wee stumpie stoussie that canna rin his lane,
That has a battle aye wi' sleep before he'll close an ee;
But a kiss frae aff his rosy lips gies strength anew to me.

Origin of the Difference in Modes of Life Between Hottentots and Bushmen

From *South-African Folk-Tales* by James A. Honey

In the beginning there were two. One was blind, the other was always hunting. This hunter found at last a hole in the earth from which game proceeded and killed the young. The blind man, feeling and smelling them, said, "They are not game, but cattle."

The blind man afterwards recovered his sight, and going with the hunter to this hole, saw that they were cows with their calves. He then quickly built a kraal (fence made of thorns) round them, and anointed himself, just as Hottentots (in their native state) are still wont to do.

When the other, who now with great trouble had to seek his game, came and saw this, he wanted to anoint himself also. "Look here!" said the other, "you must throw the ointment into the fire, and afterwards use it." He followed this advice, and the flames flaring up into his face, burnt him most miserably; so that he was glad to make his escape. The other, however, called to him: "Here, take the kirri (a knobstick), and run to the hills to hunt there for honey."

Hence sprung the race of Bushmen.

Exercise

Review memory work. This can be an oral exercise. Find the nouns in this passage. Which nouns are proper nouns, and which are common?

> "We must go and look," said Harry boldly. "You shall wear a dragonproof frock, made of stuff like the curtains. And I will smear myself all over with the best dragon poison, and—"
>
> Effie clasped her hands and skipped with joy and cried: "Oh, Harry! I know where we can find St. George!"

Commonplace Book

With your instructor's approval, add the passage below to your commonplace book, or choose your own passage from a work of non-fiction. This can be from the Bible, a biography, or one of your history or science books.

> Then they joined hands and set out to walk to St. George's Church. As you know, there are many St. George's churches, but fortunately they took the turning that leads to the right one, and went along in the bright sunlight, feeling very brave and adventurous.

4. Parts of Speech: Verbs

• The Book of Dragons, Chapter 4

Definition: A verb is a word that shows action or a state of being.

Verbs are what we do. They show action. Can you **speak, hop, listen,** and **talk**? These are all action verbs. If you can do it, it's a verb. Look at the following sentences from *The Book of Dragons*. The action verbs are underlined. Notice that I use a double underline for verbs.

The fairy spears of light <u>twinkled</u> and <u>gleamed</u>.

George <u>kicked</u> his boots against the fencing.

Some actions are invisible. Can you **love, wonder,** and **believe**? Of course you can, but no one can see these actions. What two invisible action verbs are in the sentence below?

Very few people know this, though you would think they could tell it by the ice in the jugs of a morning.

In the sentence above, the two invisible action verbs are **think** and **know**. Although you can do these things, the action cannot be seen by others. Can you think of other invisible action verbs?

Not all verbs show action. Some verbs merely show that something or someone exists. We call these verbs **state of being verbs**.

The state of being verbs are: am, are, is, was, were, be, being, been.

I am. You are. He is. These sentences show existence, not action, but they are still verbs. Often, they are used to answer questions.

Is it the North Pole? It is.

Were the children naughty to go there? They were.

If I Had But Two Little Wings

By Samuel Taylor Coleridge

If I had but two little wings
  And were a little feathery bird,
To you I'd fly, my dear!
But thoughts like these are idle things
And I stay here.

But in my sleep to you I fly:
  I'm always with you in my sleep!
The world is all one's own.
And then one wakes, and where am I?
All, all alone.

Thunder and Anansi

From *West African Folk-Tales* by William H. Barker

There had been a long and severe famine in the land where Anansi lived. He had been quite unable to obtain food for his poor wife and family. One day, gazing desperately out to sea, he saw rising from the midst of the water, a tiny island with a tall palm tree upon it. He determined to reach this tree—if any means proved possible—and climb it, in the hope of finding a few nuts to reward him. How to get there was the difficulty.

This, however, solved itself when he reached the beach, for there lay the means to his hand, in the shape of an old broken boat. It certainly did not look very strong, but Anansi decided to try it.

His first six attempts were unsuccessful—a great wave dashed him back on the beach each time he tried to put off. He was persevering, however, and at the seventh trial was successful in getting away. He steered the battered old boat as best he could, and at length reached the palm tree of his desire. Having tied the boat to the trunk of the tree—which grew almost straight out of the water—he climbed toward the nuts. Plucking all he could reach, he dropped them, one by one, down to the boat. To his dismay, every one missed the boat and fell, instead, into the water until only the last one remained. This he aimed even more carefully than the others, but it also fell into the water and disappeared from his hungry eyes. He had not tasted even one and now all were gone.

He could not bear the thought of going home empty-handed, so, in his despair, he threw himself into the water, too. To his complete astonishment, instead of being drowned, he found himself standing on the sea-bottom in front of a pretty little cottage. From the latter came an old man, who asked Anansi what he wanted so badly that he had come to Thunder's cottage to seek it. Anansi told his tale of woe, and Thunder showed himself most sympathetic.

He went into the cottage and fetched a fine cooking-pot, which he presented to Anansi—telling him that he need never be hungry again. The pot would always supply enough food for himself and his family. Anansi was most grateful, and left Thunder with many thanks.

Being anxious to test the pot at once, Anansi only waited till he was again seated in the old boat to say, "Pot, pot, what you used to do for your master do now for me." Immediately good food of all sorts appeared. Anansi ate a hearty meal, which he very much enjoyed.

On reaching land again, his first thought was to run home and give all his family a good meal from his wonderful pot. A selfish, greedy fear prevented him. "What if I should use up all the magic of the pot on them, and have nothing more left for myself! Better keep the pot a secret—then I can enjoy a meal when I want one." So, his mind full of this thought, he hid the pot.

He reached home, pretending to be utterly worn out with fatigue and hunger. There was not a grain of food to be had anywhere. His wife and poor children were weak with want of it, but selfish Anansi took no notice of that. He congratulated himself at the thought of his magic pot, now safely hidden in his room. There he retired from time to time when he felt hungry, and enjoyed a good meal. His family got thinner and thinner, but he grew plumper and plumper. They began to suspect some secret, and determined to find it out. His eldest son, Kweku Tsin, had the power of changing himself into any shape he chose; so he took the form of a tiny fly, and accompanied his father everywhere. At last, Anansi, feeling hungry, entered his room and closed the door. Next he took the pot, and had a fine meal. Having replaced the pot in its hiding-place, he went out, on the pretence of looking for food.

As soon as he was safely out of sight, Kweku Tsin fetched out the pot and called all his hungry family to come at once. They had as good a meal as their father had had. When they had finished, Mrs. Anansi—to punish her husband—said she would take the pot down to the village and give everybody a meal. This she did—but alas! In working to prepare so much food at one time, the pot grew too hot and melted away. What was to be done now? Anansi would be so angry! His wife forbade every one to mention the pot.

Anansi returned, ready for his supper, and, as usual, went into his room, carefully shutting the door. He went to the hiding-place—it was empty. He looked around in consternation. No pot was to be seen anywhere. Some one must have discovered it. His family must be the culprits; he would find a means to punish them.

Saying nothing to any one about the matter, he waited till morning. As soon as it was light he started off towards the shore, where the old boat lay. Getting into the boat, it started of its own accord and glided swiftly over the water—straight for the palm tree. Arrived there, Anansi attached the boat as before and climbed the tree. This time, unlike the last, the nuts almost fell into his hands. When he aimed them at the boat they fell easily into it—not one, as before, dropping into the water. He deliberately took them and threw them over-board, immediately jumping after them. As before, he found himself in front of Thunder's cottage, with Thunder waiting to hear his tale. This he told, the old man showing the same sympathy as he had previously done.

This time, however, he presented Anansi with a fine stick and bade him good-bye. Anansi could scarcely wait till he got into the boat so anxious was he to try the magic properties of his new gift. "Stick, stick," he said, "what you used to do for your master do for me also." The stick began to beat him so severely that, in a few minutes, he was obliged to jump into the water and swim ashore, leaving boat and stick to drift away where they pleased. Then he returned sorrowfully homeward, bemoaning his many bruises and wishing he had acted more wisely from the beginning.

Writing: Copia

Take the following sentence and play with it. Remember that the point is not necessarily to make the sentence better. The point is to play with the sentence and make it different. Make a new sentence with a change from each of the following categories. For the first category, change the grammar in one of the ways listed. For the second category, use synonyms or antonyms. New categories and different types of changes will be added as you learn more.

> The wife of Nothing heard of her friends' miserable state and invited them to a great feast in her palace.

1. Change the grammar.
   - Change the nouns from common to proper and vice versa. You can make up names for this exercise if you want.
   - Change the nouns from singular to plural and vice versa.

2. Use synonyms and antonyms.
   - Substitute synonyms.
   - Say the opposite thing using antonyms.

Exercise

Review memory work. This can be an oral exercise. Find the verbs in this passage.

> "Tumble for your life!" cried George, and he fell down at once, because it is the only way to stop. Jane fell on top of him—and then they crawled on hands and knees to the snow at the edge of the slide—and there was a sportsman, dressed in a peaked cap and a frozen moustache, like the one you see in the pictures about Ice-Peter, and he had a gun in his hand.

Commonplace Book

With your instructor's approval, add the passage below to your commonplace book, or choose your own passage from a work of fiction. This can be from either school reading or free reading.

> "Well, well," said he, "here's a whole Arctic expedition thrown away! I shall have to go home and fit out another. And that means a lot of writing to the papers and things. You seem to be a singularly thoughtless little girl."

Dictation

> All around the Pole, making a bright ring about it, were hundreds of little fires, and the flames of them did not flicker and twist, but went up blue and green and rosy and straight like the stalks of dream lilies.
> Jane said so, but George said they were as straight as ramrods.

5. How to Write a Condensed Narrative

• The Book of Dragons, Chapter 5

Today you'll learn how to write a condensed narrative. A condensed narrative is also called a **summary**. When you write a summary, you leave out all the details and only include the most important information.

Read the following story.

Tit for Tat

From *West African Folk-Tales* by William H. Barker

There had been a great famine in the land for many months. Meat had become so scarce that only the rich chiefs had money enough to buy it. The poor people were starving. Anansi and his family were in a miserable state.

One day, Anansi's eldest son—Kweku Tsin—to his great joy, discovered a place in the forest where there were still many animals. Knowing his father's wicked ways, Kweku told him nothing of the matter. Anansi, however, speedily discovered that Kweku was returning loaded, day after day, to the village. There he was able to sell the meat at a good price to the hungry villagers. Anansi immediately wanted to know the secret—but his son wisely refused to tell him. The old man determined to find out by a trick.

Slipping into his son's room one night, when he was fast asleep, he cut a tiny hole in the corner of the bag which Kweku always carried into the forest. Anansi then put a quantity of ashes into the bag and replaced it where he had found it.

Next morning, as Kweku set out for the forest, he threw the bag, as usual, over his shoulder. Unknown to him, at each step, the ashes were sprinkled on the ground. Consequently, when Anansi set out an hour later he was easily able to follow his son by means of the trail of ashes. He, too, arrived at the animals' home in the forest, and found Kweku there before him. He immediately drove his son away, saying that, by the law of the land., the place belonged to him. Kweku saw how he had been tricked, and determined to have the meat back.

He accordingly went home—made a tiny image and hung little bells round its neck. He then tied a long thread to its head and returned toward the hunting-place.

When about half-way there, he hung the image to a branch of a tree in the path, and hid himself in the bushes near by—holding the other end of the thread in his hand.

The greedy father, in the meantime, had killed as many animals as he could find, being determined to become rich as speedily as possible. He then skinned them and prepared the flesh—to carry it to the neighboring villages to sell. Taking the first load, he set off for his own village. Half-way there, he came to the place where the image hung in the way. Thinking this was one of the gods, he stopped. As he approached, the image began to shake its head vigorously at him. He felt that this meant that the gods were angry. To please them, he said to the image, "May I give you a little of this meat?" Again the image shook its head. "May I give you half of this meat?" he then inquired. The head shook once more. "Do you want the whole of this meat?" he shouted fiercely. This time the head nodded, as if the image were well pleased. "I will not give you all my meat," Anansi cried. At this the image shook in every limb as if in a terrible temper. Anansi was so frightened that he threw the whole load on the ground and ran away. As he ran, he called back, "Tomorrow I shall go to Ekubon—you will not be able to take my meat from me there, you thief."

But Kweku had heard where his father intended to go next day—and set the image in his path as before. Again Anansi was obliged to leave his whole load—and again he called out the name of the place where he would go the following day.

The same thing occurred, day after day, till all the animals in the wood were killed. By this time, Kweku Tsin had become very rich—but his father Anansi was still very poor. He was obliged to go to Kweku's house every day for food.

When the famine was over, Kweku gave a great feast and invited the entire village. While all were gathered together, Kweku told the story of his father's cunning and how it had been overcome. This caused great merriment among the villagers. Anansi was so ashamed that he readily promised Kweku to refrain from his evil tricks for the future. This promise, however, he did not keep long.

A story has a beginning, a middle, and an end. Can you identify the beginning, middle, and end of today's story?

> Beginning: A great famine was in the land, and meat was scarce.

> Middle: Kweku found a place where there were still many animals. His father, Anansi, tried to trick Kweku into telling him where the animals were, but Kweku instead tricked Anansi and kept his secret.

> End: Kweku gave a great feast when the famine was over and told the story of how he had overcome his father's cunning.

Notice that in our condensed version, I've left out all the details about Anansi's trickery, and how Kweku overcame it. These details make the story more interesting, but they are unnecessary in a summary.

When we put the parts together as a paragraph, we have a condensed narrative, or a summary paragraph. The original story was almost two pages, but the summary is only a few sentences long.

A great famine was in the land, and meat was scarce. Kweku found a place where there were still many animals. His father, Anansi, tried to trick Kweku into telling him where the animals were, but Kweku instead tricked Anansi and kept his secret. Kweku gave a great feast when the famine was over and told the story of how he had overcome his father's cunning.

The Star-Spangled Banner

By Francis Scott Key

O! Say, can you see, by the dawn's early light,
  What so proudly we hailed at the twilight's last gleaming—
Whose broad stripes and bright stars, through the perilous fight,
  O'er the ramparts we watched were so gallantly streaming!
And the rocket's red glare, the bombs bursting in air,
Gave proof through the night that our flag was still there;
O! Say, does that star-spangled banner yet wave
O'er the land of the free, and the home of the brave?

On that shore dimly seen through the mists of the deep,
  Where the foe's haughty host in dread silence reposes,
What is that which the breeze, o'er the towering steep,
  As it fitfully blows, now conceals, now discloses?
Now it catches the gleam of the morning's first beam,
In full glory reflected now shines on the stream;
  'Tis the star-spangled banner; O long may it wave
O'er the land of the free, and the home of the brave!

And where is that band who so vauntingly swore
  That the havoc of war and the battle's confusion
A home and a country should leave us no more?
  Their blood has washed out their foul footsteps, pollution.
No refuge could save the hireling and slave
From the terror of flight, or the gloom of the grave;
And the star-spangled banner in triumph doth wave
O'er the land of the free, and the home of the brave.

O! Thus be it ever, when freemen shall stand
  Between their loved homes and the war's desolation!
Blest with victory and peace, may the heav'n-rescued land
  Praise the power that hath made and preserved us a nation.
Then conquer we must, for our cause it is just,
And this be our motto—"In God is our trust":
And the star-spangled banner in triumph shall wave
O'er the land of the free, and the home of the brave.

Exercise

Review memory work. This can be an oral exercise. Find the verbs in this passage.

> The stuff in the cauldron boiled up in foaming flashes of yellow and blue and red and white and silver, and sent out a sweet scent, and presently the witch poured it out into a pot and set it to cool in the doorway among the snakes.

Writing: Commonplace Book

Add the passage below from your model story to your commonplace book.

> Nothing, being a rich man, wore a very fine velvet cloth, while Anansi had a ragged cotton one. While they were on their way Anansi persuaded Nothing to change clothes for a little while, promising to give back the fine velvet before they reached the town. He delayed doing this, however, first on one pretext, then on another—till they arrived at their destination.

Dictation

Use the first stanza of today's poem for dictation.

6. Condensed Narrative: Anansi and Nothing

- The Book of Dragons, Chapter 6

Write "Anansi and Nothing" as a condensed narrative, or summary. Remember, just include the main content of the story and leave out unnecessary details. What is the beginning, the middle, and the end of "Anansi and Nothing"?

Down-Adown-Derry

By Walter De Le Mare

Down-adown-derry,
Sweet Annie Maroon,
Gathering daisies
In the meadows of Doone,
Hears a shrill piping,
Elflike and free,
Where the waters go brawling
In rills to the sea;
Singing down-adown-derry.

Down-adown-derry,
Sweet Annie Maroon,
Through the green grasses
Peeps softly; and soon
Spies under green willows
A fairy whose song
Like the smallest of bubbles
Floats bobbing along;
Singing down-adown-derry.

Down-adown-derry,
Her cheeks were like wine,
Her eyes in her wee face
Like water-sparks shine,
Her niminy fingers
Her sleek tresses preen,
The which in the combing
She peeps out between;
Singing down-adown-derry.

Down-adown-derry,
Shrill, shrill was her tune:—
"Come to my water-house,
Annie Maroon:
Come in your dimity,
Ribbon on head,
To wear siller seaweed
And coral instead";
Singing down-adown-derry.

"Down-adown-derry,
Lean fish of the sea,
Bring lanthorns for feasting
The gay Faërie;
'Tis sand for the dancing,
A music all sweet
In the water-green gloaming
For thistledown feet";
Singing down-adown-derry.

Down-adown-derry,
Sweet Annie Maroon
Looked large on the fairy
Curled wan as the moon
And all the grey ripples
To the Mill racing by,
With harps and with timbrels
Did ringing reply;
Singing down-adown-derry.

"Down-adown-derry,"
Sang the Fairy of Doone,
Piercing the heart
Of Sweet Annie Maroon;
And lo! When like roses
The clouds of the sun
Faded at dusk, gone
Was Annie Maroon;
Singing down-adown-derry.

Down-adown-derry,
The daisies are few;
Frost twinkles powdery
In haunts of the dew;
And only the robin
Perched on a thorn,
Can comfort the heart
Of a father forlorn;
Singing down-adown-derry.
Down-adown-derry,
There's snow in the air;
Ice where the lily
Bloomed waxen and fair;
He may call o'er the water,
Cry—cry through the Mill,
But Annie Maroon, alas!
Answer ne'er will;
Singing down-adown-derry.

Editing

- Did you meet the goal of this writing exercise?

7. Parts of Speech: Pronouns

- The Book of Dragons, Chapter 7

Definitions:
A pronoun is a word used in the place of a noun.
An antecedent is the noun that a pronoun replaces in a sentence.

We use pronouns so that we don't have to keep using the same noun over and over again. The noun replaced by a pronoun is called the antecedent. Consider the following sentence from *The Book of Dragons* which has had its pronouns removed.

> Sabrinetta's name was Sabrinetta, and Sabrinetta's grandmother was Sabra, who married St. George after St. George had killed the dragon, and by real rights all the country belonged to Sabrinetta.

With its pronouns, the sentence is much easier to read.

> <u>Her</u> name was Sabrinetta, and <u>her</u> grandmother was Sabra, who married St. George after <u>he</u> had killed the dragon, and by real rights all the country belonged to <u>her</u>.

In the sentence above, the antecedent for the pronoun **her** in each case is **Sabrinetta**. The antecedent of the pronoun **he** is **St. George**. Notice, though, that the sentence has a mix of nouns and pronouns. If you use too many pronouns, the antecedent may not be clear, and you may end up wondering if Sabra married St. George or the dragon.

Different pronouns are necessary for speaking about different people. We use first person pronouns when we speak of ourselves. I can speak only of myself and use the singular form, or I can speak of myself and others with the plural form. The first person pronouns are: I, me, my, mine, we, us, our, ours.

We use second person pronouns to refer to the person to whom we are speaking. Singular and plural pronouns are the same in the second person. The second person pronouns are: you, your, yours.

We use third person pronouns to refer to people and things which we are discussing. The third person pronouns are: he, him, his, she, her, hers, it, its, they, them, their, theirs.

The Bee Is Not Afraid of Me
By Emily Dickinson

The bee is not afraid of me,
I know the butterfly;
The pretty people in the woods
Receive me cordially.
The brooks laugh louder when I come,
The breezes madder play.
Wherefore, mine eyes, thy silver mists?
Wherefore, O summer's day?

Writing: Oral Narration

Read your new model story below, and then give your instructor an oral narration of it.

Why the Lizard Continually Moves His Head Up and Down
From *West African Folk-Tales* by William H. Barker

In a town not very far from Anansi's home lived a great king. This king had three beautiful daughters, whose names were kept a secret from everybody except their own family. One day their father made a proclamation that his three daughters would be given as wives to any man who could find out their names. Anansi made up his mind to do so.

He first bought a large jar of honey, and set off for the bathing-place of the king's daughters. Arrived there, he climbed to the top of a tree on which grew some very fine fruit. He picked some of this fruit and poured honey over it. When he saw the princesses approaching he dropped the fruit on the ground and waited. The girls thought the fruit dropped of its own accord, and one of them ran forward to pick it up. When she tasted it, she called out to her sisters by name to exclaim on its sweetness. Anansi dropped another, which the second princess picked up—she, in her turn, calling out the names of the other two. In this fashion Anansi found out all the names.

As soon as the princesses had gone Anansi came down from the tree and hurried into the town. He went to all the great men and summoned them to a meeting at the King's palace on the morrow.

He then visited his friend the Lizard, to get him to act as herald at the Court next day. He told Lizard the three names, and the latter was to sound them through his trumpet when the time came.

Early next morning the King and his Court were assembled as usual. All the great men of the town appeared, as Anansi had requested. Anansi stated his business, reminding the King of his promise to give his three daughters to the man who had found out their names. The King demanded to hear the latter, whereupon Lizard sounded them on his trumpet.

The King and courtiers were much surprised. His Majesty, however, could not break the promise he had made of giving his daughters to the man who named them. He accordingly gave them to Mr. Lizard. Anansi was very angry, and explained that he had told the names to Lizard, so that he ought to get at least two of the girls, while Lizard could have the third. The King refused. Anansi then begged hard for even one, but that was also refused. He went home in a very bad temper, declaring that he would be revenged on Lizard for stealing his wives away.

He thought over the matter very carefully, but could not find a way of punishing Lizard. At last, however, he had an idea.

He went to the King and explained that he was setting off next morning on a long journey. He wished to start very early, and so begged the King's help. The King had a fine rooster, which always crowed at daybreak to waken the King if he wished to get up early. Anansi begged that the King would command the rooster to crow next morning, that Anansi might be sure of getting off in time. This the King readily promised.

As soon as night fell Anansi went by a back way to the rooster's sleeping-place, seized the bird quickly, and killed it. He then carried it to Lizard's house, where all were in bed. There he quietly cooked the rooster, placed the feathers under Lizard's bed, and put some of the flesh on a dish close to Lizard's hand. The wicked Anansi then took some boiling water and poured it into poor Lizard's mouth, thus making him dumb.

When morning came, Anansi went to the King and reproached him for not letting the rooster crow. The King was much surprised to hear that it had not obeyed his commands.

He sent one of his servants to find and bring the rooster to him, but, of course, the servant returned empty-handed. The King then ordered them to find the thief. No trace of him could be found anywhere. Anansi then cunningly said to the King: "I know Lizard is a rogue, because he stole my three wives from me. Perhaps he is the thief." Accordingly, the men went to search Lizard's house.

There, of course, they found the remnants of the rooster, cooked ready to eat, and his feathers under the bed. They questioned Lizard, but the poor animal was unable to reply. He could only move his head up and down helplessly. They thought he was refusing to speak, so dragged him before the King. To the King's questions he could only return the same answer, and his Majesty got very angry. He did not know that Anansi had made the poor animal dumb. Lizard tried very hard to speak, but in vain.

He was accordingly judged guilty of theft, and as a punishment his wives were taken away from him and given to Anansi.

Since then lizards have always had a way of moving their heads helplessly backward and forward, as if saying, "How can any one be so foolish as to trust Anansi?"

Exercise

Review memory work. This can be an oral exercise. Find the pronouns in this passage. What is the antecedent of each pronoun?

> It only came out for a minute, but she saw it quite plainly, and she said to herself: "Dear me, what a curious, shiny, bright-looking creature! If it were bigger, and if I didn't know that there have been no fabulous monsters for quite a long time now, I should almost think it was a dragon."

Commonplace Book

With your instructor's approval, add the passage below to your commonplace book, or choose your own passage from a work of fiction. This can be from either school reading or free reading.

> "I wish it had not been in such a hurry to get back into the wood," said Sabrinetta. "Of course, it's quite safe for me, in my dragon-proof tower; but if it is a dragon, it's quite big enough to eat people, and today's the first of May, and the children go out to get flowers in the wood."

Dictation

The little white Princess always woke in her little white bed when the starlings began to chatter in the pearl gray morning. As soon as the woods were awake, she used to run up the twisting turret-stairs with her little bare feet, and stand on the top of the tower in her white bed-gown, and kiss her hands to the sun and to the woods and to the sleeping town, and say, "Good morning, pretty world!"

8. The Sentence

• The Book of Dragons, Chapter 8

> Definition: A sentence is a group of words that expresses a complete thought.

To be a sentence, a group of words must express a complete thought. To express a complete thought, a sentence must have two parts. The first part of the sentence is called the **subject**, and it tells who or what the sentence is about. The second part is called the **predicate**, and it tells what the subject is (state of being verb) or is doing (action verb).

Complete Subject	**Complete Predicate**
And now the cockatrice	stirred it with his tail

Above, you can see the **complete subject** and the **complete predicate** of a sentence from *The Book of Dragons*. The complete subject includes all the words which tell who or what the sentence is about. The complete predicate includes all the words that tell what the subject is or is doing.

The sentence also has a **simple subject** and a **simple predicate**. The simple subject is the main word—a noun or pronoun—which tells who or what the sentence is about. The simple predicate is the main word—a verb— which tells what the subject is or is doing.

Who is this sentence about? The **cockatrice**. What is he doing? He **stirred**. The simple subject of the sentence is **cockatrice**, and the simple predicate is **stirred**.

We can draw a word picture, called a **diagram**, to show the parts of a sentence. We start with a long line divided in half. On the left hand side, we write the simple subject. On the right hand side, we write the simple predicate.

| cockatrice | stirred |

Name the simple subject and simple predicate from each of the following sentences.

So the cockatrice began.

And Edmund ate his eggs and his turnover.

He told the boys at school about the cockatrice.

When you do your exercises, you will double underline the simple predicate and underline the simple subject. Label each part of speech: nouns N, proper nouns PN, pronouns PRO, and verbs V. If a part of speech is more than one word, make arms stretched out to include the whole thing, like this: ———PN———. Then you will diagram the simple subject and the simple predicate of each sentence.

          n   v
So the <u>cockatrice</u> <u><u>began</u></u>.

        pn   v
And <u>Edmund</u> <u><u>ate</u></u> his eggs and his turnover.

 pro v
<u>He</u> <u><u>told</u></u> the boys at school about the cockatrice.

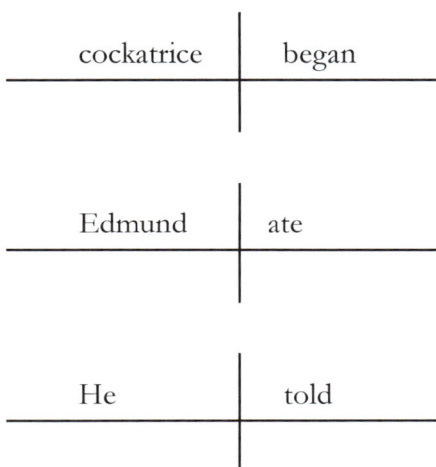

If—

By Rudyard Kipling

If you can keep your head when all about you
Are losing theirs and blaming it on you;
If you can trust yourself when all men doubt you,
But make allowance for their doubting too;
If you can wait and not be tired by waiting,
Or being lied about, don't deal in lies,
Or being hated, don't give way to hating,
And yet don't look too good, nor talk too wise;

If you can dream—and not make dreams your master;

If you can think—and not make thoughts your aim,
If you can meet with Triumph and Disaster
And treat those two impostors just the same;
If you can bear to hear the truth you've spoken
Twisted by knaves to make a trap for fools,
Or watch the things you gave your life to, broken,
And stoop and build 'em up with worn-out tools;

If you can make one heap of all your winnings
And risk it on one turn of pitch-and-toss,
And lose, and start again at your beginnings
And never breathe a word about your loss;
If you can force your heart and nerve and sinew
To serve your turn long after they are gone,
And so hold on when there is nothing in you
Except the Will which says to them: 'Hold on!'

If you can talk with crowds and keep your virtue,
Or walk with Kings—nor lose the common touch,
If neither foes nor loving friends can hurt you,
If all men count with you, but none too much;
If you can fill the unforgiving minute
With sixty seconds' worth of distance run,
Yours is the Earth and everything that's in it,
And—which is more—you'll be a Man, my son!

Why White Ants Always Harm Man's Property

From *West African Folk-Tales* by William H. Barker

There came once such a terrible famine in the land that a grain of corn was worth far more than its weight in gold. A hungry spider was wandering through the forest looking for food. To his great joy he found a dead antelope.

Knowing that he would not be allowed to reach home in safety with it, he wrapped it up very carefully in a long mat and bound it securely.

Placing it on his head, he started for home. As he went, he wept bitterly, telling every one that this was his dead grandfather's body. Every one he met sympathized heartily with him.

On his way he met the wolf and the leopard. These two wise animals suspected that this was one of Spider's tricks. They knew that he was not to be trusted. Walking on a little way, they discussed what they could do to find out what was in the bundle.

They agreed to take a short cut across the country to a tree which they knew Cousin Spider must pass. When they reached this tree they hid themselves very carefully behind it and waited for him.

As he passed the place they shook the tree and uttered frightful noises. This so frightened Mr. Spider that he dropped his load and ran away.

The two gentlemen opened the bundle and, to their great joy, discovered the flesh of the antelope in it. They carried it off to their own home and began to prepare supper.

When Mr. Spider recovered from his fear he began to wonder who could have been at the tree to make the noises. He decided that his enemies must be Wolf and Leopard. He made up his mind he would get his meat back from them.

He took a small lizard and filed his teeth to fine, sharp points. He then sent him to spy upon the wolf and leopard—by begging fire from them. He was to get the fire and quench it as soon as he left their cottage. He could then return and ask a second time. If they asked him questions, he must smile and show his teeth.

The lizard did as he was told, and everything turned out just as Spider had expected. Wolf and Leopard eagerly asked the lizard where he had had his teeth filed so beautifully. He replied that "Filing Spider" had done it for him.

Wolf and Leopard discussed the matter and decided to have their teeth filed in the same way. They could then easily break the bones of their food.

Accordingly, they went to the house of the disguised spider and asked him to make their teeth like Lizard's. Spider agreed, but said that, to do it properly, he would first have to hang them on a tree. They made no objection to this.

When he had them safely hung, Spider and his family came and mocked them. Spider then went to their cottage and brought away the body of the antelope. The whole village was invited to the feast, which was held in front of the two poor animals on the tree. During this festival every one made fun of the wolf and leopard.

Next morning White Ant [Termite] and his children passed the place on their way to some friends. Mr. Leopard begged them to set him and his friend free. White Ant and his family set to work, destroyed the tree and set them at liberty. Leopard and Wolf promised the ants that on their return they would spread a feast for them.

Unfortunately, Spider heard the invitation and made up his mind to benefit by it. On the third day (which was the very time set by the wolf and leopard) Spider dressed up his children like the ants. They set out, singing the ants' chorus, in order to deceive Leopard.

Wolf and Leopard welcomed them heartily and spread a splendid feast for them, which the spiders thoroughly enjoyed.

Soon after their departure the real ants arrived. The two hosts, thinking these must be Spider and his family, poured boiling water over them and killed them all except the father.

White Ant, on reaching home again, in great anger, vowed that he would never again help any one. He would take every opportunity to harm property. From that day to this white ants have been a perfect pest to man.

Writing: Copia, Playing with Words

Take each of the following words from your model story and look them up in the thesaurus. Give two or three different ways to say each word.

king, daughter, stated, surprised, explained

Exercise

Review memory work. This can be an oral exercise. Find the pronouns in this passage. What is the antecedent of each pronoun?

> Now, one day Edmund made a new lantern out of something chemical that he sneaked from the school laboratory. And with it he went exploring again to see if he could find the things that made the other sorts of noises.

Copy each sentence below. Double underline the predicate, and underline the subject. Label the part of speech of each Noun, N; Proper Noun, PN; Pronoun, PRO; Verb, V. Diagram the simple subject and simple predicate from each sentence.

The next moment Edmund turned a corner.

He told him about mines and treasures and geological formations.

He pointed out of the window.

Commonplace Book

With your instructor's approval, add the poem below to your commonplace book, or choose your own poem.

> If you can talk with crowds and keep your virtue,
> Or walk with Kings—nor lose the common touch,
> If neither foes nor loving friends can hurt you,
> If all men count with you, but none too much;
> If you can fill the unforgiving minute
> With sixty seconds' worth of distance run,
> Yours is the Earth and everything that's in it,
> And—which is more—you'll be a Man, my son!

Dictation

Matthew 4:4

But He answered and said, "It is written, 'Man shall not live on bread alone, but on every word that proceeds out of the mouth of God.'"

Mother and Child by Mary Cassatt

Picture Study

1. Read the title and the name of the artist. Study the picture for several minutes, then put the picture away.

2. Describe the picture.

3. Look at the picture again. Do you notice any details that you missed before? What do you like or dislike about this painting? Does it remind you of anything?

9. Descriptive Writing

- Black Beauty, Chapter 1

Today we're going to look at a descriptive passage. A descriptive passage is one which describes a person, place, thing, idea, or event. The author creates a picture with words.

The descriptive passage we'll be looking at is the beginning of *Black Beauty*. In this passage, Black Beauty describes the first home he can remember.

Since a descriptive passage paints a word picture, you should be able to draw a picture from a good description. Try to draw a picture of your own from the first paragraph of *Black Beauty* before looking at the example on the next page. The point is not to create a perfect picture, so don't worry if you don't draw well. The point is to draw a representation of what's described in the passage. Later on, this picture will help you to write your own description about Black Beauty's memory.

> The first place that I can well remember was a large pleasant meadow with a pond of clear water in it. Some shady trees leaned over it, and rushes and water-lilies grew at the deep end. Over the hedge on one side we looked into a plowed field, and on the other we looked over a gate at our master's house, which stood by the roadside; at the top of the meadow was a grove of fir trees, and at the bottom a running brook overhung by a steep bank.

The description doesn't tell us which side the master's house is on and which side the field is on. It doesn't tell us exactly where the pond is located, or which end is the deep end. However, it still gives us enough details so that we can have a general idea of the layout of the meadow that Black Beauty remembers.

If you need to keep up with details sometimes, and you don't want to draw a picture, you can also make a few notes with words instead.

- A large meadow
- Pond in meadow with shady trees along one side, and rushes and water lilies at the deep end
- Plowed field on one side
- Master's house on the other side by the road
- Grove of fir trees at the top of the meadow
- Running brook with a steep bank at the bottom of the meadow

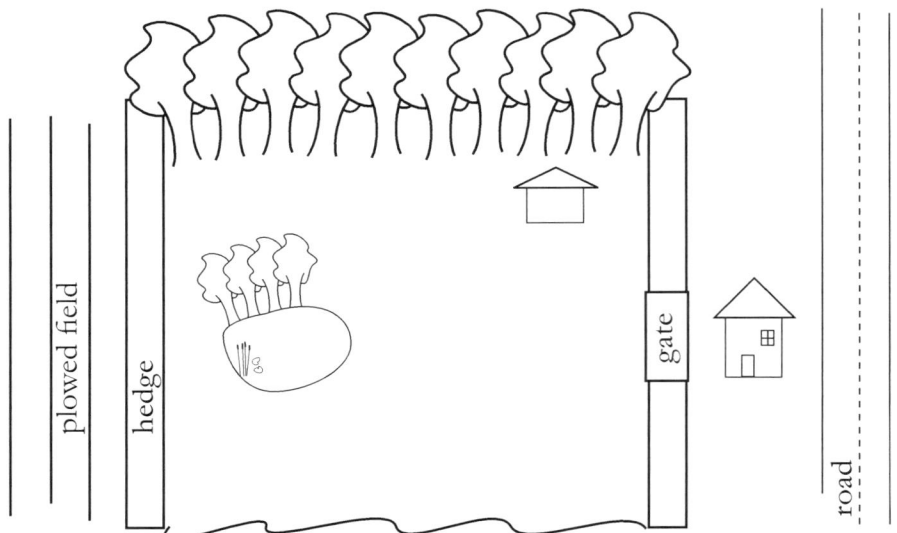

Writing: Descriptive Writing

Read the passage below and write a narration from it. Notice the words that Anna Sewell uses to create a word picture. Use your picture to remember the details of the meadow. This passage describes not only the meadow, but also some of Black Beauty's early memories.

Black Beauty

    The first place that I can well remember was a large pleasant meadow with a pond of clear water in it. Some shady trees leaned over it, and rushes and water-lilies grew at the deep end. Over the hedge on one side we looked into a plowed field, and on the other we looked over a gate at our master's house, which stood by the roadside; at the top of the meadow was a grove of fir trees, and at the bottom a running brook overhung by a steep bank.

    While I was young I lived upon my mother's milk, as I could not eat grass. In the daytime I ran by her side, and at night I lay down close by her. When it was hot we used to stand by the pond in the shade of the trees, and when it was cold we had a nice warm shed near the grove.

    As soon as I was old enough to eat grass my mother used to go out to work in the daytime, and come back in the evening.

    There were six young colts in the meadow besides me; they were older than I was; some were nearly as large as grown-up horses. I used to run with them, and had great fun; we used to gallop all together round and round the field as hard as we could go. Sometimes we had rather rough play, for they would frequently bite and kick as well as gallop.

The Village Blacksmith

By Henry Wadsworth Longfellow

Under a spreading chestnut-tree
  The village smithy stands;
The smith, a mighty man is he,
  With large and sinewy hands,

And the muscles of his brawny arms
  Are strong as iron bands.

His hair is crisp, and black, and long;
  His face is like the tan;
His brow is wet with honest sweat,
  He earns whate'er he can,
And looks the whole world in the face,
  For he owes not any man.

Week in, week out, from morn till night,
  You can hear his bellows blow;
You can hear him swing his heavy sledge,
  With measured beat and slow,
Like a sexton ringing the village bell,
  When the evening sun is low.

And children coming home from school
  Look in at the open door;
They love to see the flaming forge,
  And hear the bellows roar,
And catch the burning sparks that fly
  Like chaff from a threshing-floor.

He goes on Sunday to the church,
  And sits among his boys;
He hears the parson pray and preach,
  He hears his daughter's voice
Singing in the village choir,
  And it makes his heart rejoice.

It sounds to him like her mother's voice,
  Singing in Paradise!
He needs must think of her once more,
  How in the grave she lies;
And with his hard, rough hand he wipes
  A tear out of his eyes.

Toiling,—rejoicing,—sorrowing,
  Onward through life he goes;
Each morning sees some task begin,
  Each evening sees it close;
Something attempted, something done,
  Has earned a night's repose.

Thanks, thanks to thee, my worthy friend,
  For the lesson thou hast taught!
Thus at the flaming forge of life
  Our fortunes must be wrought;
Thus on its sounding anvil shaped
  Each burning deed and thought.

A Jackal and a Wolf

From *South-African Folk-Tales* by James A. Honey

Jackal and Wolf went and hired themselves to a man to be his servants. In the middle of the night Jackal rose and smeared Wolf's tail with some fat, and then ate all the rest of it in the house. In the morning the man missed the fat, and he immediately accused Jackal of having eaten it. "Look at Wolf's tail," said the rogue, "and you will see who is the thief." The man did so, and then thrashed Wolf till he was nearly dead.

Exercise

Review memory work. This can be an oral exercise. Find the pronouns in this passage. What is the antecedent of each pronoun?

> There were six young colts in the meadow besides me; they were older than I was; some were nearly as large as grown-up horses. I used to run with them, and had great fun; we used to gallop all together round and round the field as hard as we could go. Sometimes we had rather rough play, for they would frequently bite and kick as well as gallop.

Copy each sentence below. Double underline the predicate, and underline the subject. Label the part of speech of each word. Noun, N; Proper Noun, PN; Pronoun, PRO; Verb, V. Diagram the simple subject and simple predicate from each sentence.

> He gave us good food, good lodging, and kind words.

> My mother always took him to the town.

> We trotted up nearer to see what went on.

Commonplace Book

With your instructor's approval, add the passage below to your commonplace book, or choose your own passage from a work of non-fiction. This can be from the Bible, a biography, or one of your history or science books.

> "I hope you will grow up gentle and good, and never learn bad ways; do your work with a good will, lift your feet up well when you trot, and never bite or kick even in play."
> I have never forgotten my mother's advice; I knew she was a wise old horse, and our master thought a great deal of her. Her name was Duchess, but he often called her Pet.

Editing

• Did you meet the goal of this writing exercise?

• Look at your word choice. Is there a good mixture of nouns and pronouns? Is the antecedent of each pronoun clear?

10. The Four Types of Sentences, Part 1

- Black Beauty, Chapters 2-3

There are four types of sentences, and today we'll discuss two of them.

1. A declarative sentence makes a statement. It ends with a period.

To declare means to state or announce something. The purpose of a declarative sentence is to give information.

> She never would go to that part of the field afterward.

2. An interrogative sentence asks a question. It ends with a question mark.

To interrogate means to ask questions. You may have read or seen a story in which criminal suspects were **interrogated** by law enforcement. The purpose of an interrogative sentence is to ask for information.

> "What hare?" I said.

We can change sentences from one type to another. Look at the example sentences above from *Black Beauty*. Can you make the first one a question, and the second one a statement? You might need to change a word or two to make it work.

Here's a way that we could change each of those sentences.

> Would she ever would go to that part of the field afterward?

> "That hare," I said.

When the sentence type changes, the meaning of the sentence also changes. The sentence type helps to give meaning to the sentence.

The Ruin

By Walter De La Mare

When the last colors of the day
Have from their burning ebbed away,

About that ruin, cold and lone,
The cricket shrills from stone to stone;
And scattering o'er its darkened green,
Bands of the fairies may be seen,
Chattering like grasshoppers, their feet
Dancing a thistledown dance round it:
While the great gold of the mild moon
Tinges their tiny acorn shoon.

Why Spiders Are Always Found in the Corners of Ceilings

From *West African Folk-Tales* by William H. Barker

Egya Anansi was a very skillful farmer. He, with his wife and son, set to work one year to prepare a farm, much larger than any they had previously worked. They planted in it yams, maize, and beans—and were rewarded by a very rich crop. Their harvest was quite ten times greater than any they had ever had before. Egya Anansi was very well pleased when he saw his wealth of corn and beans.

He was, however, an exceedingly selfish and greedy man, who never liked to share anything—even with his own wife and son. When he saw that the crops were quite ripe, he thought of a plan whereby he alone would profit by them. He called his wife and son to him and spoke thus: "We have all three worked exceedingly hard to prepare these fields. They have well repaid us. We will now gather in the harvest and pack it away in our barns. When that is done, we shall be in need of a rest. I propose that you and our son should go back to our home in the village and remain there at your ease for two or three weeks. I have to go to the coast on very urgent business. When I return we will all come to the farm and enjoy our well-earned feast."

Anansi's wife and son thought this a very good, sensible plan, and at once agreed to it. They went straight back to their village, leaving the cunning husband to start on his journey. Needless to say he had not the slightest intention of so doing.

Instead, he built himself a very comfortable hut near the farm—supplied it with all manner of cooking utensils, gathered in a large store of the corn and vegetables from the barn, and prepared for a solitary feast. This went on for a fortnight. By that time Anansi's son began to think it was time for him to go and weed the farm, lest the weeds should grow too high. He accordingly went there and worked several hours on it. While passing the barn, he happened to look in. Great was his surprise to see that more than half of their magnificent harvest had gone. He was greatly disturbed, thinking robbers had been at work, and wondered how he could prevent further mischief.

Returning to the village, he told the people there what had happened, and they helped to make a rubber-man. When evening came they carried the sticky figure to the farm, and placed it in the midst of the fields, to frighten away the thieves. Some of the young men remained with Anansi's son to watch in one of the barns.

When all was dark, Egya Anansi (quite unaware of what had happened) came, as usual, out of his hiding-place to fetch more food. On his way to the barn, he saw in front of him the figure of a man, and at first felt very frightened. Finding that the man did not move, however, he gained confidence and went up to him. "What do you want here?" said he. There was no answer. He repeated his question with the same result. Anansi then became very angry and dealt the figure a blow on the cheek with his right hand. Of course, his hand stuck fast to the rubber. "How dare you hold my hand!" he exclaimed. "Let me go at once or I shall hit you again." He then hit the figure with his left hand, which also stuck. He tried to disengage himself-by pushing against it with his knees and body, until, finally, knees, body, hands, and head were all firmly attached to the rubber-man. There Egya Anansi had to stay till daybreak, when his son came out with the other villagers to catch the robber. They were astonished to find that the evil-doer was Anansi himself. He, on the other hand, was so ashamed to be caught in the act of greediness that he changed into a spider and took refuge in a dark corner of the ceiling lest any one should see him. Since then spiders have always been found in dark, dusty corners, where people are not likely to notice them.

Writing: Copia

Take the following sentence and play with it. Remember that the point is not necessarily to make the sentence better. The point is to play with the sentence and make it different. Make one new sentence from each of the following categories.

> He first bought a large jar of honey, and set off for the bathing-place of the king's daughters.

1. Change the grammar.
   - Change the nouns from common to proper and vice versa.
   - Change the nouns from singular to plural and vice versa.
   - Change the sentence type.

2. Condense the sentence.

3. Use synonyms and antonyms.
   - Substitute synonyms.
   - Say the opposite thing using antonyms.

Exercise

Review memory work. Find the pronouns in this passage. What is the antecedent of each pronoun?

> When I was four years old Squire Gordon came to look at me. He examined my eyes, my mouth, and my legs; he felt them all down; and then I had to walk and trot and gallop before him. He seemed to like me, and said, "When he has been well broken in he will do very well."

Copy each sentence below. Double underline the predicate, and underline the subject. Label the part of speech of each word. Noun, N; Proper Noun, PN; Pronoun, PRO; Verb, V. Diagram the simple subject and simple predicate from each sentence.

> My master sent me for a fortnight to a neighboring farmer's.

> I galloped to the further side of the meadow.

> My master often drove me in double harness with my mother.

Commonplace Book

With your instructor's approval, add the passage below to your commonplace book, or choose your own passage from a work of fiction. This can be from either school reading or free reading.

> When I was four years old, Squire Gordon came to look at me. He examined my eyes, my mouth, and my legs; he felt them all down; and then I had to walk and trot and gallop before him. He seemed to like me, and said, "When he has been well broken in he will do very well."

Dictation

> Before I was two years old, a circumstance happened which I have never forgotten. It was early in the spring; there had been a little frost in the night, and a light mist still hung over the woods and meadows. I and the other colts were feeding at the lower part of the field when we heard, quite in the distance, what sounded like the cry of dogs.

11. Parts of Speech: Adjectives; Articles

• Black Beauty, Chapter 4

Definition: An adjective is a word that modifies a noun or a pronoun. Adjectives tell what kind, how many, which one, and whose.

Adjectives point out and describe nouns and pronouns. Do you ever have an apple for a snack? Do you like your apple **big** or **small**? Do you prefer **red** or **green**? Do you like your apple **juicy** or **dried**? All of the bold words are adjectives which tell us more about the apple.

Look at the following sentence from *Black Beauty*. The underlined words are adjectives.

The <u>first</u> stall was a <u>large</u> <u>square</u> one, shut in behind with a <u>wooden</u> gate; the others were <u>common</u> stalls, <u>good</u> stalls, but not nearly so <u>large</u>.

Adjectives tell what kind, how many, which one, and whose. Today, we're discussing **what kind** and **how many**.

Adjectives that tell **what kind** are descriptive in nature. What kind of ball? The **red**, **striped**, **bouncy** ball, or the **hard**, **heavy**, **bowling** ball? What kind of pet? The **large**, **furry** dog, or the **bald**, **scaly** lizard? Adjectives tell **what kind**.

What kind of stall did Beauty have? One which was **large** and **square**. The others were **common** stalls, **good** but not as **large**. Using adjectives, the author tell us more about Beauty's new home.

Adjectives also tell **how many**. Numbers are adjectives that tell how many, but we have other words which describe an amount of something as well, such as **plenty**, **some**, **several**, **few**, and **much**. **None** is also an adjective that tells **how many**.

But I need only describe the stable into which I was taken; this was very roomy, with <u>four</u> good stalls.

He gave me <u>some</u> very nice oats, he patted me, spoke kindly, and then went away.

Articles are the most common adjectives that you will see.

The articles are a, an, the. Articles are adjectives.

The is the definite article, while **a** and **an** are called indefinite articles. **The** is specific in nature, while **a** and **an** are non-specific in nature. In other words, "a book" may refer to any book at all, but "the book" implies a specific book. **A** is used before words which begin with a consonant, and **an** is used before words which begin with a vowel.

An adjective is diagrammed by placing it on a diagonal line below the noun or pronoun which it modifies.

The kindly groom patted me.

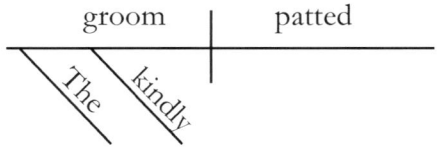

The Nightingale

By William Cowper

A nightingale, that all day long
Had cheered the village with his song,
Nor yet at eve his note suspended,
Nor yet when eventide was ended,
Began to feel, as well he might,
The keen demands of appetite;
When, looking eagerly around,
He spied far off, upon the ground,
A something shining in the dark,
And knew the glow-worm by his spark;
So, stooping down from hawthorn top,
He thought to put him in his crop.
The worm, aware of his intent,
Harangued him thus, right eloquent:
   "Did you admire my lamp," quoth he,
   "As much as I your minstrelsy,
You would abhor to do me wrong,
As much as I to spoil your song;
For 'twas the self-same power divine,
Taught you to sing and me to shine;
That you with music, I with light,
Might beautify and cheer the night."
The songster heard his short oration,
And warbling out his approbation,
Released him, as my story tells,
And found a supper somewhere else.

Anansi the Blind Fisherman

From West African Folk-Tales by William H. Barker

Anansi, in his old age, became a fisherman. Very soon after that his sight began to fail. Finally, he grew quite blind. However, still being very strong, he continued his fishing—with the help of two men. The latter were exceedingly kind to him, and aided him in every possible way. They led him, each morning, to the beach and into the canoe. They told him where to spread his net and when to pull it in. When they returned to land they told him just where and when to step out, so that he did not even get wet.

Day after day this went on, but Anansi—instead of being in the least grateful to them—behaved very badly. When they told him where to spread his net, he would reply sharply, "I know. I was just about to put it there." When they were directing him to get out of the boat, he would say, "Oh, I know perfectly well we are at the beach. I was just getting ready to step out."

This went on for a long time, Anansi getting ruder and ruder to his helpers every day, until they could bear his treatment no longer. They determined when opportunity offered to punish him for his ingratitude.

The next day, as usual, he came with them to the beach. When they had got the canoe ready, they bade him step in. "Do you think I am a fool?" said he. "I know the canoe is there." They made no answer, but got in and patiently pulled toward the fishing-place. When they told him where to spread his net, he replied with so much abuse that they determined, there and then, to punish him.

By this time the canoe was full of fish, so they turned to row home. When they had gone a little way they stopped and said to him, "Here we are at the beach." He promptly told them that they were very foolish—to tell him a thing he knew so well. He added many rude and insulting remarks, which made them thoroughly angry. He then jumped proudly out, expecting to land on the beach. To his great astonishment he found himself sinking in deep water. The two men rowed quickly away, leaving him to struggle.

Like all the men of that country he was a good swimmer, but, of course, being blind, he was unable to see where the land lay. So he swam until he was completely tired out—and was drowned.

Exercise

Review memory work. Copy each sentence below. Double underline the predicate, and underline the subject. Label the part of speech of each word. Noun, N; Proper Noun, PN; Pronoun, PRO; Verb, V; Adjective, ADJ; Article, ART. Diagram each sentence.

Handsome Merrylegs turned.

The colt spoke.

Ill-tempered Ginger snapped.

Writing: Commonplace Book

Add the passage below from your model story to your commonplace book.

> When he saw the princesses approaching, he dropped the fruit on the ground and waited. The girls thought the fruit dropped of its own accord, and one of them ran forward to pick it up. When she tasted it, she called out to her sisters by name to exclaim on its sweetness.

Dictation

Use part of today's poem for dictation.

12. Condensed Narrative: Why the Lizard Moves His Head

- Black Beauty, Chapters 5-6

Write "Why the Lizard Moves His Head" as a condensed narrative, or summary. Remember, just include the main content of the story and leave out unnecessary details. What is the beginning, the middle, and the end of the story?

Sleepyhead

By Walter De La Mare

As I lay awake in the white moonlight
I heard a faint singing in the wood,
"Out of bed,
Sleepyhead,
Put your white foot, now;
Here are we
Beneath the tree
Singing round the root now."
I looked out of window, in the white moonlight,
The leaves were like snow in the wood—
"Come away,
Child, and play
Light with the gnomies;
In a mound,
Green and round,
That's where their home is.
"Honey sweet,
Curds to eat,
Cream and frumenty,
Shells and beads,
Poppy seeds,
You shall have plenty."
But, as soon as I stooped in the dim moonlight
To put on my stocking and my shoe,
The sweet shrill singing echoed faintly away,
And the grey of the morning peeped through,
And instead of the gnomies there came a red robin
To sing of the buttercups and dew.

Editing

- Did you meet the goal of this writing exercise?

- Look at your word choice. Is there a good mixture of nouns and pronouns? Is the antecedent of each pronoun clear?

13. The Four Types of Sentences, Part 2

• Black Beauty, Chapter 7

You've learned about the first two types of sentences. Can you remember what they are?

1. A declarative sentence makes a statement. It ends with a period. The purpose of a declarative sentence is to give information.

2. An interrogative sentence asks a question. It ends with a question mark. The purpose of an interrogative sentence is to ask for information.

Today, we'll be discussing the last two types of sentences.

3. An exclamatory sentence shows sudden or strong feeling. It ends with an exclamation mark.

To exclaim means to cry out suddenly. The purpose of an exclamatory sentence is to show that sudden or strong feelings are involved.

"How good that mash was!"

4. An imperative sentence gives a command or makes a request. It ends with a period.

An **imperator** was a Roman general. Do you know what generals do? They give commands! The purpose of an imperative sentence is to get someone to do something.

"Come along, lassie, come along."

Sometimes, a sentence seems to be both an exclamatory and an imperative sentence, like this one:

"Stand still, stand still!"

It gives a command, but it also shows sudden or strong feeling. Since it ends with an exclamation mark, we count it as an exclamatory sentence. Exclamatory sentences end with exclamation marks, and imperative sentences end with periods.

Look at the following sentences from *Black Beauty*. Name each sentence type, then change it to another type.

> Ginger stamped her foot as if the very thought of him made her angry.

> "Stand back," said the master.

> "Didn't you know that Farmer Grey's old Duchess was the mother of them both?"

Angels in the Early Morning
By Emily Dickinson

Angels in the early morning
May be seen the dews among,
Stooping, plucking, smiling, flying:
Do the buds to them belong?
Angels when the sun is hottest
May be seen the sands among,
Stooping, plucking, sighing, flying;
Parched the flowers they bear along.

Writing: Oral Narration

Read your new model story below, and then give your instructor an oral narration of it.

Why We See Ants Carrying Bundles as Big as Themselves

From *West African Folk-Tales* by William H. Barker

    Kweku Anansi and Kweku Tsin—his son—were both very clever farmers. Generally they succeeded in getting fine harvests from each of their farms. One year, however, they were very unfortunate. They had sown their seeds as usual, but no rain had fallen for more than a month after and it looked as if the seeds would be unable to sprout.
    Kweku Tsin was walking sadly through his fields one day looking at the bare, dry ground, and wondering what he and his family would do for food, if they were unable to get any harvest. To his surprise he saw a tiny dwarf seated by the roadside. The little hunchback asked the reason for his sadness, and Kweku Tsin told him. The dwarf promised to help him by bringing rain on the farm. He bade Kweku fetch two small sticks and tap him lightly on the hump, while he sang:
    "O water, go up! O water, go up, And let rain fall, and let rain fall!"
    To Kweku's great joy rain immediately began to fall, and continued till the ground was thoroughly well soaked. In the days following the seeds germinated, and the crops began to promise well.
    Anansi soon heard how well Kweku's crops were growing—whilst his own were still bare and hard. He went straightway to his son and demanded to know the reason. Kweku Tsin, being an honest fellow, at once told him what had happened.
    Anansi quickly made up his mind to get his farm watered in the same way, and accordingly set out toward it. As he went, he cut two big, strong sticks, thinking,

"My son made the dwarf work with little sticks. I will make him do twice as much with my big ones." He carefully hid, the big sticks, however, when he saw the dwarf coming toward him. As before, the hunchback asked what the trouble was, and Anansi told him. "Take two small sticks, and beat me lightly on the hump," said the dwarf. "I will get rain for you."

But Anansi took his big sticks and beat so hard that the dwarf fell down dead. The greedy fellow was now thoroughly frightened, for he knew that the dwarf was jester to the King of the country, and a very great favorite of his. He wondered how he could fix the blame on some one else. He picked up the dwarf's dead body and carried it to a kola-tree. There he laid it on one of the top branches and sat down under the tree to watch.

By and by Kweku Tsin came along to see if his father had succeeded in getting rain for his crops. "Did you not see the dwarf, father?" he asked, as he saw the old man sitting alone. "Oh, yes!" replied Anansi; "but he has climbed this tree to pick kola. I am now waiting for him." "I will go up and fetch him," said the young man—and immediately began to climb. As soon as his head touched the body the latter, of course, fell to the ground. "Oh! What have you done, you wicked fellow?" cried his father. "You have killed the King's jester!" "That is all right," quietly replied the son (who saw that this was one of Anansi's tricks). "The King is very angry with him, and has promised a bag of money to any one who would kill him. I will now go and get the reward." "No! No! No!" shouted Anansi. "The reward is mine. I killed him with two big sticks. I will take him to the King." "Very well," was the son's reply. "As you killed him, you may take him."

Off set Anansi, quite pleased with the prospect of getting a reward. He reached the King's court, only to find the King very angry at the death of his favorite. The body of the jester was shut up in a great box and Anansi was condemned—as a punishment—to carry it on his head for ever. The King enchanted the box so that it could never be set down on the ground. The only way in which Anansi could ever get rid of it was by getting some other man to put it on his head. This, of course, no one was willing to do.

At last, one day, when Anansi was almost worn out with his heavy burden, he met the Ant. "Will you hold this box for me while I go to market and buy some things I need badly?" said Anansi to Mr. Ant. "I know your tricks, Anansi," replied Ant. "You want to be rid of it." "Oh, no, indeed, Mr. Ant," protested Anansi. "Indeed I will come back for it, I promise."

Mr. Ant, who was an honest fellow, and always kept his own promises, believed him. He took the box on his head, and Anansi hurried off. Needless to say, the sly fellow had not the least intention of keeping his word. Mr. Ant waited in vain for his return—and was obliged to wander all the rest of his life with the box in his head. That is the reason we so often see ants carrying great bundles as they hurry along.

Exercise

Review memory work. Copy each sentence below. Double underline the predicate, and underline the subject. Label the part of speech of each word. Noun, N; Proper Noun, PN; Pronoun, PRO; Verb, V; Adjective, ADJ; Article, ART. Diagram each sentence.

Strong, tall, bold Samson boasted.

The kindly old master helped.

Steady, thoughtful Job trained.

Commonplace Book

With your instructor's approval, add the passage below to your commonplace book, or choose your own passage from a work of fiction. This can be from either school reading or free reading.

> "He looked closely at it, shook his head, and told the man to fetch a good bran mash and put some meal into it. How good that mash was! And so soft and healing to my mouth. He stood by all the time I was eating, stroking me and talking to the man."

Dictation

> "He was a very fine old gentleman with quite white hair, but his voice was what I should know him by among a thousand. It was not high, nor yet low, but full, and clear, and kind, and when he gave orders it was so steady and decided that every one knew, both horses and men, that he expected to be obeyed."

14. Linking Verbs; Predicate Nominatives

- Black Beauty, Chapters 8-9

The linking verbs are: am, are, is, was, were, be, being, been, become, seem.

The linking verb list is almost identical to the list of state of being verbs. While the state of being verbs just state that something exists, the linking verbs link the subject of the sentence together with interesting information about the subject.

When a noun or pronoun follows a linking verb, we call it a **predicate nominative**. It renames the subject of the sentence.

Black Beauty is a horse.

As for Merrylegs, he and I soon became great friends.

The predicate nominative answers the question **who** or **what** after a linking verb. Notice that the noun which follows the linking verb may have modifiers. Black Beauty is what? A **horse**. He and I became what? Great **friends**.

We mark linking verbs LV. We diagram a predicate nominative by placing a diagonal line after the linking verb, and placing the predicate nominative after it.

```
    ——pn——  lv art  n
Black Beauty is  a   horse.
```

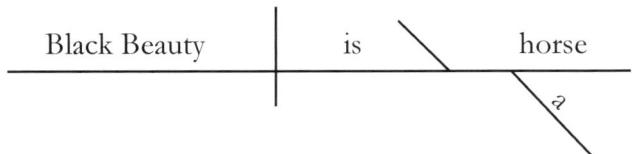

Jack Frost

By Hannah Flagg Gould

The Frost looked forth, one still, clear night,
And whispered, "Now I shall be out of sight;
So through the valley and over the height,
  In silence I'll take my way:
I will not go on with that blustering train,
The wind and the snow, the hail and the rain,
Who make so much bustle and noise in vain,
  But I'll be as busy as they."

Then he flew to the mountain and powdered its crest;
He lit on the trees, and their boughs he dressed
In diamond beads—and over the breast
  Of the quivering lake he spread
A coat of mail, that it need not fear
The downward point of many a spear
That hung on its margin far and near,
  Where a rock could rear its head.

He went to the windows of those who slept,
And over each pane, like a fairy, crept;
Wherever he breathed, wherever he slept,
  By the light of the moon were seen
Most beautiful things—there were flowers and trees;
There were bevies of birds and swarms of bees;
There were cities with temples and towers, and these
  All pictured in silver sheen!

But he did one thing that was hardly fair;
He peeped in the cupboard, and finding there
That all had forgotten for him to prepare—
  "Now just to set them a-thinking,
I'll bite this basket of fruit," said he,
  "This costly pitcher I'll burst in three,
And the glass of water they've left for me
  Shall 'tchich!' to tell them I'm drinking."

Adzanumee and Her Mother

From *West African Folk-Tales* by William H. Barker

    There once lived a woman who had one great desire. She longed to have a daughter—but alas! She was childless. She could never feel happy, because of this unfulfilled wish. Even in the midst of a feast the thought would be in her mind—"Ah! If only I had a daughter to share this with me!"
    One day she was gathering yams in the field, and it chanced that she pulled out one which was very straight and well shaped. "Ah!" she thought to herself, "if only this fine yam were a daughter, how happy I should be!" To her astonishment the yam

answered, "If I were to become your daughter, would you promise never to reproach me with having been a yam?" She eagerly gave her promise, and at once the yam changed into a beautiful, well-made girl. The woman was overjoyed and was very kind to the girl. She named her Adzanumee. The latter was exceedingly useful to her mother. She would make the bread, gather the yams, and sell them at the market-place.

She had been detained, one day, longer than usual. Her mother became impatient at her non-appearance and angrily said, "Where can Adzanumee be? She does not deserve that beautiful name. She is only a yam."

A bird singing near by heard the mother's words and immediately flew off to the tree under which Adzanumee sat. There he began to sing:

"Adzanumee! Adzanumee!

Your mother is unkind—she says you are only a yam,

You do not deserve your name!

Adzanumee! Adzanumee!"

The girl heard him and returned home weeping. When the woman saw her she said, "My daughter, my daughter! What is the matter?" Adzanumee replied:

"O my mother! My mother!

You have reproached me with being a yam.

You said I did not deserve my name.

O my mother! My mother!"

With these words she made her way toward the yam-field. Her mother, filled with fear, followed her, wailing:

"Nay, Adzanumee! Adzanumee!

Do not believe it—do not believe it.

You are my daughter, my dear daughter

Adzanumee!"

But she was too late. Her daughter, still singing her sad little song, quickly changed back into a yam. When the woman arrived at the field there lay the yam on the ground, and nothing she could do or say would give her back the daughter she had desired so earnestly and treated so inconsiderately.

Writing: Copia, Playing with Words

Take each of the following words from your model story and look them up in the thesaurus. Give two or three different ways to say each word.

condemn, punishment, reward, favorite, quiet

Exercise

Review memory work. Copy each sentence below. Double underline the predicate, and underline the subject. Label the part of speech of each word. Noun, N; Proper Noun, PN; Pronoun, PRO; Verb, V; Linking Verb, LV; Adjective, ADJ; Article, ART. Diagram each sentence.

"I am the best riding-master."

"We were colts."

"He was a good master."

Commonplace Book

With your instructor's approval, add the poem below to your commonplace book, or choose your own poem.

> The Frost looked forth, one still, clear night,
> And whispered, "Now I shall be out of sight;
> So through the valley and over the height,
>   In silence I'll take my way:
> I will not go on with that blustering train,
> The wind and the snow, the hail and the rain,
> Who make so much bustle and noise in vain,
>   But I'll be as busy as they."

Dictation

Psalm 1:2

But his delight is in the law of the Lord,
And in His law he meditates day and night.

Children on the Beach by Mary Cassatt

Picture Study

1. Read the title and the name of the artist. Study the picture for several minutes, then put the picture away.

2. Describe the picture.

3. Look at the picture again. Do you notice any details that you missed before? What do you like or dislike about this painting? Does it remind you of anything?

15. Literary Analysis

- Black Beauty, Chapter 10

Writing: Literary Analysis

This should be an oral exercise.

With your instructor's approval, choose *Black Beauty*, or one of the other books you're currently reading, and answer the following questions.

What is the book about? Give a brief summary, just a few sentences. Do you have sympathy for any of the characters? Why or why not?

The Jackal and the Wolf

From *South-African Folk-Tales* by James A. Honey

Once on a time Jackal, who lived on the borders of the colony, saw a wagon returning from the seaside laden with fish; he tried to get into the wagon from behind, but he could not; he then ran on before and lay in the road as if dead. The wagon came up to him, and the leader cried to the driver, "Here is a fine kaross for your wife!"

"Throw it into the wagon," said the driver, and Jackal was thrown in.

The wagon traveled on, through a moonlight night, and all the while Jackal was throwing out the fish into the road; he then jumped out himself and secured a great prize. But stupid old Wolf (hyena), coming by, ate more than his share, for which Jackal owed him a grudge, and he said to him, "You can get plenty of fish, too, if you lie in the way of a wagon as I did, and keep quite still whatever happens."

"So!" mumbled Wolf.

Accordingly, when the next wagon came from the sea, Wolf stretched himself out in the road. "What ugly thing is this?" cried the leader, and kicked Wolf. He then took a stick and thrashed him within an inch of his life. Wolf, according to the directions of Jackal, lay quiet as long as he could; he then got up and hobbled off to tell his misfortune to Jackal, who pretended to comfort him.

"What a pity," said Wolf, "I have not got such a handsome skin as you have!"

Exercise

Review memory work. Copy each sentence below. Double underline the predicate, and underline the subject. Label the part of speech of each word. Noun, N; Proper Noun, PN; Pronoun, PRO; Verb, V; Linking Verb, LV; Adjective, ADJ; Article, ART. Diagram each sentence.

"They were a valuable kind."

"Men are blockheads."

"Blinkers are dangerous things."

Commonplace Book

With your instructor's approval, add the passage below to your commonplace book, or choose your own passage from a work of non-fiction. This can be from the Bible, a biography, or one of your history or science books.

> Oh! If people knew what a comfort to horses a light hand is, and how it keeps a good mouth and a good temper, they surely would not chuck, and drag, and pull at the rein as they often do. Our mouths are so tender that where they have not been spoiled or hardened with bad or ignorant treatment, they feel the slightest movement of the driver's hand, and we know in an instant what is required of us.

16. Adjectives That Tell Which One and Whose

- Black Beauty, Chapters 11-12

Adjectives tell what kind, how many, which one, and whose.

You've learned about adjectives that tell **what kind** and **how many**. Adjectives that tell **what kind** are descriptive in nature. Adjectives that tell **how many** can either be specific numbers, or they can give a general idea like **plenty** or **several**.

Adjectives also tell **which one** and **whose**. Adjectives that tell **which one** modify nouns and pronouns by pointing towards them. **This, that, these,** and **those** are adjectives that tell **which one**. Ordinal numbers—first, second, third—are also adjectives that tell **which one**. Which boy? **That** boy. Which girl? The **third** girl. Other adjectives that tell **which one** are words like **first** and **last**.

Oh, what a good supper he gave me <u>that</u> night.

But the moment my feet touched the <u>first</u> part of the bridge, I felt sure there was something wrong.

Adjectives that tell **whose** modify nouns and pronouns by telling to whom they belong; they show ownership or relationship. You don't own your mother, but she still belongs to you. Possessive nouns and pronouns are adjectives that tell **whose**. To make a noun possessive, we add an apostrophe and an *s* (**'s**). Pronouns take a different form to show possession. The possessive pronouns are:

First person: my, mine, our, ours
Second person: your, yours
Third person: his, her, hers, its, their, theirs

Since possessive nouns and pronouns tell **whose**, they are adjectives. Label them adjectives when you do your exercises.

          adj
John went with his master.

   adj
The master's business engaged him a long time.

The Owl

By Alfred Tennyson

When cats run home and light is come,
  And dew is cold upon the ground,
And the far-off stream is dumb,
  And the whirring sail goes round,
  And the whirring sail goes round;
Alone and warming his five wits,
The white owl in the belfry sits.

When merry milkmaids click the latch,
  And rarely smells the new-mown hay,
And the cock hath sung beneath the thatch
  Twice or thrice his roundelay,
  Twice or thrice his roundelay;
Alone and warming his five wits,
The white owl in the belfry sits.

"Morning Sunrise"

From *West African Folk-Tales* by William H. Barker

    A man in one of the villages had a very beautiful daughter. She was so lovely that people called her "Morning Sunrise:" Every young man who saw her wanted to marry her. Three, in particular, were very anxious to have her for their wife. Her father found it difficult to decide among them. He determined to find out by a trick which of the three was most worthy of her.
    He bade her lie down on her bed as if she were dead. He then sent the report of her death to each of the three lovers, asking them to come and help him with her funeral.
    The messenger came first to "Wise Man." When he heard the message, he exclaimed, "What can this man mean? The girl is not my wife. I certainly will not pay any money for her funeral."
    The messenger came next to the second man. His name was "Wit." The latter at once said, "Oh dear, no! I shall not pay any money for her funeral expenses. Her father did not even let me know she was ill." So he refused to go.
    "Thinker," the third young man—when he received the message—at once got ready to start. "Certainly I must go and mourn for Morning Sunrise," said he. "Had she lived, surely she would have been my wife." So he took money with him and set out for her home.
    When he reached it her father called out, "Morning Sunrise, Morning Sunrise. Come here. This is your true husband."
    That very day the betrothal took place, and soon after the wedding followed. "Thinker" and his beautiful wife lived very happily together.

Writing: Copia

Take the following sentence and play with it. Remember that the point is not necessarily to make the sentence better. The point is to play with the sentence and make it different. Make a new sentence with a change from each of the following categories.

He reached the King's court, only to find the King very angry at the death of his favorite.

1. Change the grammar.
   - Change the nouns from common to proper and vice versa.
   - Change the nouns from singular to plural and vice versa.
   - Change the sentence type.
   - Change the adjectives from articles to descriptive to possessive, etc.

2. Condense the sentence.
   - Remove details.
   - Remove modifiers.

3. Use synonyms and antonyms.
   - Substitute synonyms.
   - Say the opposite thing using antonyms.

Exercise

Review memory work. Copy each sentence below. Double underline the predicate, and underline the subject. Label the part of speech of each word. Noun, N; Proper Noun, PN; Pronoun, PRO; Verb, V; Linking Verb, LV; Adjective, ADJ; Article, ART. Diagram each sentence.

"They are a handsome pair."

"You are a military man."

My master rode.

Commonplace Book

With your instructor's approval, add the passage below to your commonplace book, or choose your own passage from a work of fiction. This can be from either school reading or free reading.

"Well, sir, we can't drive over that tree, nor yet get round it; there will be nothing for it, but to go back to the four crossways, and that will be a good six miles before we get round to the wooden bridge again; it will make us late, but the horse is fresh."

Dictation

The squire and Farmer Grey had worked together, as they said, for more than twenty years to get check-reins on the cart-horses done away with, and in our parts you seldom saw them; and sometimes, if mistress met a heavily laden horse with his head strained up, she would stop the carriage and get out, and reason with the driver in her sweet serious voice, and try to show him how foolish and cruel it was.

17. Predicate Adjectives

• Black Beauty, Chapter 13

The linking verbs are: am, are, is, was, were, be, being, been, become, seem.

When a noun or pronoun follows a linking verb, we call it a **predicate nominative**. It renames the subject of the sentence.

When an adjective follows a linking verb, we call it a **predicate adjective**. It modifies the subject of the sentence.

> They were kind.

> The river banks were high.

Predicate nominatives and predicate adjectives are both **subject complements**. A subject complement completes the subject. Notice the spelling of the word **complement**. There are two words which are so similar in spelling that people often confuse them.

> compl<u>i</u>ment
> compl<u>e</u>ment

A compl<u>e</u>ment compl<u>e</u>tes something. A compl<u>i</u>ment is what <u>I</u> give to praise you.

Remember to mark linking verbs LV. This will help you recognize subject complements because they always follow linking verbs.

We diagram a predicate adjective the same way we diagram a predicate nominative, by placing a diagonal line after the linking verb, and placing the predicate adjective after it.

```
            lv
The river banks were high.
```

```
   banks    |  were  \  high
      \The \river
```

Robert of Lincoln

By William Cullen Bryant

Merrily swinging on brier and weed,
  Near to the nest of his little dame,
Over the mountain-side or mead,
  Robert of Lincoln is telling his name.
  Bob-o'-link, bob-o'-link,
    Spink, spank, spink,
Snug and safe is this nest of ours,
Hidden among the summer flowers.
  Chee, chee, chee.

Robert of Lincoln is gayly dressed,
  Wearing a bright, black wedding-coat;
White are his shoulders, and white his crest,
  Hear him call in his merry note,
  Bob-o'-link, bob-o'-link,
    Spink, spank, spink,
Look what a nice, new coat is mine;
Sure there was never a bird so fine.
  Chee, chee, chee.

Robert of Lincoln's Quaker wife,
  Pretty and quiet, with plain brown wings,
Passing at home a patient life,
  Broods in the grass while her husband sings,
  Bob-o'-link, bob-o'-link,
    Spink, spank, spink,
Brood, kind creature, you need not fear
Thieves and robbers while I am here.
  Chee, chee, chee.

Modest and shy as a nun is she;
  One weak chirp is her only note;
Braggart, and prince of braggarts is he,
  Pouring boasts from his little throat,
  Bob-o'-link, bob-o'-link,
    Spink, spank, spink,
Never was I afraid of man,
Catch me, cowardly knaves, if you can.
  Chee, chee, chee.

Six white eggs on a bed of hay,
  Flecked with purple, a pretty sight:
There as the mother sits all day,
  Robert is singing with all his might,
  Bob-o'-link, bob-o'-link,
    Spink, spank, spink,

Nice good wife that never goes out,
Keeping house while I frolic about.
  Chee, chee, chee.

Soon as the little ones chip the shell,
  Six wide mouths are open for food;
Robert of Lincoln bestirs him well,
  Gathering seeds for the hungry brood:
  Bob-o'-link, bob-o'-link,
  Spink, spank, spink,
This new life is likely to be
Hard for a gay young fellow like me.
  Chee, chee, chee.

Robert of Lincoln at length is made
  Sober with work, and silent with care,
Off is his holiday garment laid,
  Half forgotten that merry air,
  Bob-o'-link, bob-o'-link,
  Spink, spank, spink,
Nobody knows but my mate and I,
Where our nest and our nestlings lie.
  Chee, chee, chee.

Summer wanes; the children are grown;
  Fun and frolic no more he knows;
Robert of Lincoln's a hum-drum drone;
  Off he flies, and we sing as he goes,
  Bob-o'-link, bob-o'-link,
  Spink, spank, spink,
When you can pipe that merry old strain,
Robert of Lincoln, come back again.
  Chee, chee, chee.

Why the Sea-Turtle When Caught Beats Its Breast with Its Forelegs

From *West African Folk-Tales* by William H. Barker

Many centuries ago, the people of this earth were much troubled by floods. The sea used at times to overflow its usual boundaries and sweep across the low, sandy stretches of land which bordered it. Time and again this happened, many lives being lost at each flood. Mankind was very troubled to find an escape from this oft-repeated disaster. He could think of no way of avoiding it.

Fortunately for him the wise turtle came to his help. "Take my advice," said she, "and plant rows of palms along the sea-coast. They will bind the sand together and keep it from being washed so easily away." He did so, with great success. The roots of the palms kept the sand firmly in its place. When the time came again for the sea to overflow, it washed just to the line of trees and came no farther. Thus many lives were saved annually by the kind forethought of the turtle.

In return—one would think—mankind would protect and cherish this poor animal. But no! Each time a turtle comes to the seashore to lay her eggs among the sand, she is caught and killed for the sake of her flesh. It is the thought of the ingratitude of mankind to her, which makes her beat her breast with her forelegs when she is caught. She seems to be saying, "Ah! This is all the return I get for my kindness to you."

Exercise

Review memory work. Copy each sentence below. Double underline the predicate, and underline the subject. Label the part of speech of each word. Noun, N; Proper Noun, PN; Pronoun, PRO; Verb, V; Linking Verb, LV; Adjective, ADJ; Article, ART. Diagram each sentence.

"The horse is fresh."

"The bridge is broken."

"That young fellow is a liar."

Writing: Commonplace Book

Add the passage below from your model story to your commonplace book.

Mr. Ant, who was an honest fellow, and always kept his own promises, believed him. He took the box on his head, and Anansi hurried off. Needless to say, the sly fellow had not the least intention of keeping his word. Mr. Ant waited in vain for his return, and was obliged to wander all the rest of his life with the box in his head.

Dictation

Use part of today's poem for dictation.

18. Condensed Narrative: Why We See Ants Carrying Bundles

- Black Beauty, Chapters 14-15

Write "Why We See Ants Carrying Bundles" as a condensed narrative, or summary. Remember, just include the main content of the story and leave out unnecessary details. What is the beginning, the middle, and the end of the story?

Berries

By Walter De La Mare

There was an old woman
Went blackberry picking
Along the hedges
From Weep to Wicking.
Half a pottle—
No more she had got,
When out steps a Fairy
From her green grot;
And says, "Well, Jill,
Would 'ee pick 'ee mo?"
And Jill, she curtseys,
And looks just so.
"Be off," says the Fairy,
"As quick as you can,
Over the meadows
To the little green lane,
That dips to the hayfields
Of Farmer Grimes:
I've berried those hedges
A score of times;
Bushel on bushel
I'll promise 'ee, Jill,
This side of supper
If 'ee pick with a will."
She glints very bright,
And speaks her fair;

Then lo, and behold!
She has faded in air.
Be sure old Goodie
She trots betimes
Over the meadows
To Farmer Grimes.
And never was queen
With jewelry rich
As those same hedges
From twig to ditch;
Like Dutchmen's coffers,
Fruit, thorn, and flower—
They shone like William
And Mary's bower.
And be sure Old Goodie
Went back to Weep,
So tired with her basket
She scarce could creep.
When she comes in the dusk
To her cottage door,
There's Towser wagging
As never before,
To see his Missus

So glad to be
Come from her fruit-picking
Back to he.
As soon as next morning
Dawn was grey,
The pot on the hob
Was simmering away;
And all in a stew
And a hugger-mugger
Towser and Jill
A-boiling of sugar,
And the dark clear fruit
That from Faërie came,
For syrup and jelly
And blackberry jam.
Twelve jolly gallipots
Jill put by;
And one little teeny one,
One inch high;
And that she's hidden
A good thumb deep,
Half way over
From Wicking to Weep.

Editing

- Did you meet the goal of this writing exercise?

- Look at your word choice. Is there a good mixture of nouns and pronouns? Is the antecedent of each pronoun clear?

19. Helping Verbs

• Black Beauty, Chapter 16

The helping verbs are:
am, are, is,	was, were,	be, being, been,
do, does, did,	have, has, had,	may, might, must,
can, could,	shall, should,	will, would

Helping verbs come before the main verb in the sentence. They "help" by providing more specific information. Consider this sentence from *Black Beauty*.

I <u>heard</u> Ginger coughing.

In the above sentence, we have a simple verb with no helpers. Look at how the meaning of the sentence changes when we add helping verbs.

I <u>had heard</u> Ginger coughing.

I <u>have heard</u> Ginger coughing.

I <u>should have heard</u> Ginger coughing.

I <u>must have heard</u> Ginger coughing.

Each of these sentences means something slightly different than what the verb can say without helping verbs.

Sometimes, helping verbs are separated from the main verb by other words, and you have to play Verb Roundup. The word **not** especially loves to sit in this position.

The first horse <u>would</u> not <u>go</u> with him.

He <u>could</u> not yet <u>speak</u>.

When you label sentences for your exercises, make arms to spread over the main verb and all of its helpers. If the parts of the verb are separated, just underline the helping verbs and mark the main verb, or label the helping verbs HV.

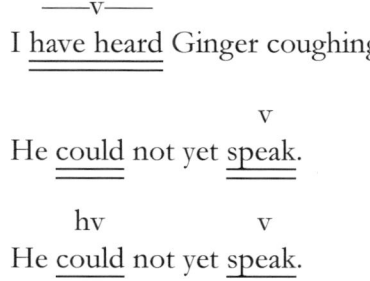

I have heard Ginger coughing.

He could not yet speak.

He could not yet speak.

Like action verbs, linking verbs can have helping verbs. They are still linking verbs, linking the subject to its subject complement.

"You have been my best friend."

Helping verbs are part of the verb. They are diagrammed with the main verb, even when they are separated in the sentence.

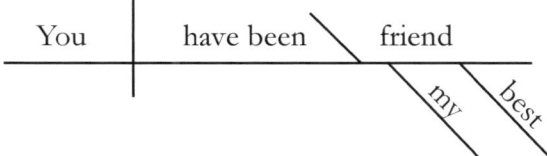

The Butterfly and the Bee
By William Lisle Bowles

Methought I heard a butterfly
  Say to a laboring bee:
    "Thou hast no colors of the sky
  On painted wings like me."

  "Poor child of vanity! Those dyes,
  And colors bright and rare,"
With mild reproof, the bee replies,
  "Are all beneath my care.

  "Content I toil from morn to eve,
  And scorning idleness,
To tribes of gaudy sloth I leave
  The vanity of dress."

Writing: Oral Narration

Read your new model story below, and then give your instructor an oral narration of it.

The Fox and the Grapes
An Aesop's Fable

    A Fox one day spied a beautiful bunch of ripe grapes hanging from a vine trained along the branches of a tree. The grapes seemed ready to burst with juice, and the

Fox's mouth watered as he gazed longingly at them.

The bunch hung from a high branch, and the Fox had to jump for it. The first time he jumped he missed it by a long way. So he walked off a short distance and took a running leap at it, only to fall short once more. Again and again he tried, but in vain.

Now he sat down and looked at the grapes in disgust.

"What a fool I am," he said. "Here I am wearing myself out to get a bunch of sour grapes that are not worth gaping for."

And off he walked very, very scornfully.

There are many who pretend to despise and belittle that which is beyond their reach.

Exercise

Review memory work. Copy each sentence below. Double underline the predicate, and underline the subject. Label the part of speech of each word. Noun, N; Proper Noun, PN; Pronoun, PRO; Verb, V; Linking Verb, LV; Adjective, ADJ; Article, ART. Diagram each sentence.

"He is a brave lad."

A fine horse had died.

Our mistress had been alarmed.

Commonplace Book

With your instructor's approval, add the passage below to your commonplace book, or choose your own passage from a work of fiction. This can be from either school reading or free reading.

"And now," said master, "when you have got your breath, James, we'll get out of this place as quickly as we can," and we were moving toward the entry, when from the market-place there came a sound of galloping feet and loud rumbling wheels.

Dictation

We got out as fast as we could into the broad quiet market-place; the stars were shining, and except the noise behind us, all was still. Master led the way to a large hotel on the other side, and as soon as the hostler came, he said, "James, I must now hasten to your mistress. I trust the horses entirely to you; order whatever you think is needed," and with that he was gone. The master did not run, but I never saw mortal man walk so fast as he did that night.

20. Plurals with -f and -fe

- Black Beauty, Chapters 17-18

Today's lesson is on forming plurals with words that end in *f* or *fe*. First, though, let's review forming other plurals.

In most cases, forming the plural of a noun is simple and straightforward: just add an *s*: **boys**, **girls**.

If the word hisses at the end (ends with *ch*, *sh*, *s*, *x*, or *z*), add *es*: **branches**, **foxes**.

Sometimes, *ch* says /k/. When it does, it doesn't hiss, so just add *s*: **epochs**.

If the word ends in a vowel plus *y* (*ay*, *ey*, *oy*), add an *s*. If the word ends in *y* acting alone as a vowel, change the *y* to *i* and add *es*. We have **plays**, **monkeys**, and **toys**, but **spies** and **collies**.

Of course, there are also a few irregular words which either change completely, or don't change at all, when forming plurals. **Mouse** becomes **mice**, but **deer** remains **deer**. In most of cases, however, there's a straightforward rule that tells you what to do when a word ends in a certain sound or combination of letters.

Words which end in *f* or *fe* also have rules to determine how they form plurals. When the word ends in two vowels plus *f*, just add an *s*

　　Two vowels + *f*: chiefs, spoofs

When the word ends in *ff*, just add *s*.

　　cliffs, tiffs

However, when a word ends in a consonant plus *f*, or a single vowel plus *fe*, change the *f* or *fe* to *ves*.

　　Consonant + *f*: wolf→wolves

　　Single vowel + *fe*: knife→knives

Listen closely, and you can hear when *f* should change to *v*. The sound changes, not just the spelling.

When in doubt about forming a plural, always check the dictionary.

Old Grimes

By Albert Gorton Greene

Old Grimes is dead; that good old man,
  We ne'er shall see him more;
He used to wear a long, black coat,
  All buttoned down before.

His heart was open as the day,
  His feelings all were true;
His hair was some inclined to gray,
  He wore it in a queue.

He lived at peace with all mankind,
  In friendship he was true;
His coat had pocket-holes behind,
  His pantaloons were blue.

He modest merit sought to find,
  And pay it its desert;
He had no malice in his mind,
  No ruffles on his shirt.

His neighbors he did not abuse,
  Was sociable and gay;
He wore large buckles on his shoes,
  And changed them every day.

His knowledge, hid from public gaze,
  He did not bring to view,
Nor make a noise town-meeting days,
  As many people do.

His worldly goods he never threw
  In trust to fortune's chances,
But lived (as all his brothers do)
  In easy circumstances.

Thus undisturbed by anxious cares
  His peaceful moments ran;
And everybody said he was
  A fine old gentleman.

How Beasts and Serpents First Came into the World

From *West African Folk-Tales* by William H. Barker

The famine had lasted nearly three years. Kweku Tsin, being very hungry, looked daily in the forest in the hope of finding food. One day he was fortunate enough to discover three palm-kernels lying on the ground. He picked up two stones with which to crack them. The first nut, however, slipped when he hit it, and fell into a hole behind him. The same thing happened to the second and to the third. Very much annoyed at his loss, Kweku determined to go down the hole to see if he could find his lost nuts.

To his surprise, however, he discovered that this hole was really the entrance to a town, of which he had never before even heard. When he reached it he found absolute silence everywhere. He called out, "Is there nobody in this town?" and presently heard a voice in answer. He went in its direction and found an old woman sitting in one of the houses. She demanded the reason of his appearance—which he readily gave.

The old woman was very kind and sympathetic, and promised to help him. "You must do exactly as I tell you," said she. "Go into the garden and listen attentively. You will hear the yams speak. Pass by any yam that says, 'Dig me out, dig me out!' But take the one that says, 'Do not dig me out!' Then bring it to me."

When he brought it, she directed him to remove the peel from the yam and throw the latter away. He was then to boil the rind, and while boiling, it would become yam. It did actually do so, and they sat down to eat some of it. Before beginning their meal the old woman requested Kweku not to look at her while she ate. Being very polite and obedient, he did exactly as he was told.

In the evening the old woman sent him into the garden to choose one of the drums which stood there. She warned him: "If you come to a drum which says 'Ding-ding' on being touched—take it. But be very careful not to take one which sounds 'Dong-dong.'" He obeyed her direction in every detail. When he showed her the drum, she looked pleased and told him, to his great delight, that he had only to beat it if at any time he were hungry. That would bring him food in plenty. He thanked the old woman heartily and went home.

As soon as he reached his own hut, he gathered his household together, and then beat the drum. Immediately, food of every description appeared before them, and they all ate as much as they wished.

The following day Kweku Tsin gathered all the people of the village together in the Assembly Place, and then beat the drum once more. In this way every family got sufficient food for their wants, and all thanked Kweku very much for thus providing for them.

Kweku's father, however, was not at all pleased to see his son thus able to feed the whole village. Anansi thought he, too, ought to have a drum. Then the people would be grateful to him instead of to Kweku Tsin. Accordingly, he asked the young man where the wonderful drum had come from. His son was most unwilling to tell him, but Anansi gave him no peace until he had heard the whole story. He then wasted no time, but set off at once toward the entrance hole. He had taken the precaution to carry with him an old nut which he pretended to crack. Then throwing it into the hole, he jumped in after it and hurried along to the silent village. Arrived at the first house, he shouted, "Is there no one in this town?" The old woman answered as before, and Anansi entered her house.

He did not trouble to be polite to her, but addressed her most rudely, saying,

"Hurry up, old woman, and get me something to eat." The woman quietly directed him to go into the garden and choose the yam which should say, "Do not dig me out." Anansi laughed in her face and said, "You surely take me for a fool. If the yam does not want me to dig it out I will certainly not do so. I will take the one which wants to be gathered." This he did.

When he brought it to the old woman she told him, as she told his son, to throw away the inside and boil the rind. Again he refused to obey. "Who ever heard of such a silly thing as throwing away the yam? I will do nothing of the sort. I will throw away the peel and boil the inside." He did so, and the yam turned into stones. He was then obliged to do as she first suggested, and boil the rind. The latter while boiling turned into yam. Anansi turned angrily to the old woman and said, "You are a witch." She took no notice of his remark, but went on setting the table. She placed his dinner on a small table, lower than her own, saying. "You must not look at me while I eat." He rudely replied, "Indeed, I will look at you if I choose. And I will have my dinner at your table, not at that small one." Again she said nothing—but she left her dinner untouched. Anansi ate his own, then took hers and ate it also.

When he had finished she said, "Now go into the garden and choose a drum. Do not take one which sounds 'Dong-dong'; only take one which says 'Ding-ding.'" Anansi retorted, "Do you think I will take your advice, you witch? No, I will choose the drum which says 'Dong-dong.' You are just trying to play a trick on me."

He did as he wished. Having secured the drum he marched off without so much as a Thank you to the old woman.

No sooner had he reached home, than he longed to show off his new power to the villagers. He called all to the Assembly Place, telling them to bring dishes and trays, as he was going to provide them with food. The people in great delight hurried to the spot. Anansi, proudly taking his position in the midst of them, began to beat his drum. To his horror and dismay, instead of the multitude of food-stuffs which Kweku had summoned, Anansi saw, rushing toward him, beasts and serpents of all kinds. Such creatures had never been seen on the earth before.

The people fled in every direction—all except Anansi, who was too terrified to move. He speedily received fitting punishment for his disobedience. Fortunately, Kweku, with his mother and sisters, had been at the outer edge of the crowd, so easily escaped into shelter. The animals presently scattered in every direction, and ever since they have roamed wild in the great forests.

Writing: Copia, Playing with Words

Take each of the following words from your model story and look them up in the thesaurus. Give two or three different ways to say each word.

leap, disgust, fox, ripe, burst

Exercise

Review memory work. Make the following words plural.

kerchief, reef, bluff, scarf

Review memory work. Copy each sentence below. Double underline the predicate, and underline the subject. Label the part of speech of each word. Noun, N; Proper Noun, PN; Pronoun, PRO; Verb, V; Linking Verb, LV; Adjective, ADJ; Article, ART. Diagram each sentence.

"I will be ready."

"Black Beauty will go."

We had left.

Commonplace Book

With your instructor's approval, add the poem below to your commonplace book, or choose your own poem.

His heart was open as the day,
  His feelings all were true;
His hair was some inclined to gray,
  He wore it in a queue.

He lived at peace with all mankind,
  In friendship he was true;
His coat had pocket-holes behind,
  His pantaloons were blue.

Dictation

Ephesians 2:8-9

For by grace you have been saved through faith; and that not of yourselves, it is the gift of God; not as a result of works, so that no one may boast.

Summertime by Mary Cassatt

Picture Study

1. Read the title and the name of the artist. Study the picture for several minutes, then put the picture away.

2. Describe the picture.

3. Look at the picture again. Do you notice any details that you missed before? What do you like or dislike about this painting? Does it remind you of anything?

21. Descriptive Writing

• Black Beauty, Chapter 19

Writing: Descriptive Writing

The purpose of descriptive writing is to describe a person, place, thing, or event so well that an image forms in the mind of the reader.

In today's chapter of *Black Beauty*, Ginger explains the reasons for her bad temper. Read that passage below, paying close attention to the details that make a vivid picture in your mind, and then write a narration of it. How does she describe her old master? Look at the descriptive words she uses to describe his voice when he speaks to her, and again when he speaks to Samson. Does the tone of his voice change? How does the author let us know?

Add details if you wish. Remember, the point of this exercise is to write as descriptively as possible, not just to narrate the passage exactly.

Black Beauty

"At last, just as the sun went down, I saw the old master come out with a sieve in his hand. He was a very fine old gentleman with quite white hair, but his voice was what I should know him by among a thousand. It was not high, nor yet low, but full, and clear, and kind, and when he gave orders it was so steady and decided that every one knew, both horses and men, that he expected to be obeyed. He came quietly along, now and then shaking the oats about that he had in the sieve, and speaking cheerfully and gently to me: 'Come along, lassie, come along, lassie; come along, come along.' I stood still and let him come up; he held the oats to me, and I began to eat without fear; his voice took all my fear away. He stood by, patting and stroking me while I was eating, and seeing the clots of blood on my side he seemed very vexed. 'Poor lassie! It was a bad business, a bad business;' then he quietly took the rein and led me to the stable; just at the door stood Samson. I laid my ears back and snapped at him. 'Stand back,' said the master, 'and keep out of her way; you've done a bad day's work for this filly.' He growled out something about a vicious brute. 'Hark ye,' said the father, 'a bad-tempered man will never make a good-tempered horse. You've not learned your trade yet, Samson.' Then he led me into my box, took off the saddle and bridle with his own hands, and tied me up; then he called for a pail of warm water and a sponge, took off his coat, and while the stable-man held the pail, he sponged my sides a good while, so tenderly that I was sure he knew how sore and bruised they were. 'Whoa! My pretty one,' he said, 'stand still, stand still.' His very voice did me good, and the bathing was very comfortable. The skin was so broken at the corners of my mouth that I could not eat the hay, the stalks hurt me. He looked closely at it, shook his head, and told the man to fetch a good bran mash and put some meal into it. How good that mash was! And so soft and healing to my mouth. He stood by all the time I was eating, stroking me and talking to the man. 'If a high-mettled creature like this,' said he, 'can't be broken by fair means, she will never be good for anything.'

"After that he often came to see me, and when my mouth was healed the other breaker, Job, they called him, went on training me; he was steady and thoughtful, and I soon learned what he wanted."

The Mocking Fairy

By Walter De La Mare

"Won't you look out of your window, Mrs. Gill?"
Quoth the Fairy, nidding, nodding in the garden;
"Can't you look out of your window, Mrs. Gill?"
Quoth the Fairy, laughing softly in the garden;
But the air was still, the cherry boughs were still,
And the ivy-tod 'neath the empty sill,
And never from her window looked out Mrs. Gill
On the Fairy shrilly mocking in the garden.
"What have they done with you, you poor Mrs. Gill?"
Quoth the Fairy, brightly glancing in the garden;
"Where have they hidden you, you poor old Mrs. Gill?"
Quoth the Fairy dancing lightly in the garden;
But night's faint veil now wrapped the hill,
Stark 'neath the stars stood the dead-still Mill,
And out of her cold cottage never answered Mrs. Gill
The Fairy mimbling mambling in the garden.

Honorable Minu

From *West African Folk-Tales* by William H. Barker

It happened one day that a poor Akim-man had to travel from his own little village to Accra—one of the big towns on the coast. This man could only speak the language of his own village—which was not understood by the men of the town. As he approached Accra he met a great herd of cows. He was surprised at the number of them, and wondered to whom they could belong. Seeing a man with them he asked him, "To whom do these cows belong?" The man did not know the language of the Akim-man, so he replied, "Minu" (I do not understand). The traveler, however, thought that Minu was the name of the owner of the cows and exclaimed, "Mr. Minu must be very rich."

He then entered the town. Very soon he saw a fine large building, and wondered to whom it might belong. The man he asked could not understand his question, so he also answered, "Minu." "Dear me! What a rich fellow Mr. Minu must be!" cried the Akim-man.

Coming to a still finer building with beautiful gardens round it, he again asked the owner's name. Again came the answer, "Minu." "How wealthy Mr. Minu is!" said our wondering traveler.

Next he came to the beach. There he saw a magnificent steamer being loaded in the harbour. He was surprised at the great cargo which was being put on board and inquired of a bystander, "To whom does this fine vessel belong?"

"Minu," replied the man. "To the Honorable Minu also! He is the richest man I ever heard of!" cried the Akim-man.

Having finished his business, the Akim-man set out for home. As he passed down one of the streets of the town he met men carrying a coffin, and followed by a long procession, all dressed in black. He asked the name of the dead person, and received the usual reply, "Minu." "Poor Mr. Minu!" cried the Akim-man. "So he has had to leave all his wealth and beautiful houses and die just as a poor person would do! Well, well—in future I will be content with my tiny house and little money." And the Akim-man went home quite pleased to his own hut.

Exercise

Review memory work. Make the following words plural.

life, cliff, roof, dwarf

Review memory work. Copy each sentence below. Double underline the predicate, and underline the subject. Label the part of speech of each word. Noun, N; Proper Noun, PN; Pronoun, PRO; Verb, V; Linking Verb, LV; Adjective, ADJ; Article, ART. Diagram each sentence.

"The boy is broken-hearted."

"It was only ignorance."

He was feeling better.

Commonplace Book

With your instructor's approval, add the passage below to your commonplace book, or choose your own passage from a work of non-fiction. This can be from the Bible, a biography, or one of your history or science books.

> Ginger and Merrylegs had been moved into the other stable, so that I might be quiet, for the fever made me very quick of hearing; any little noise seemed quite loud, and I could tell every one's footstep going to and from the house. I knew all that was going on. One night John had to give me a draught; Thomas Green came in to help him.

22. Direct Objects

• Black Beauty, Chapters 20-21

Definition: A direct object is the noun or pronoun that receives the action of the verb.

When a noun or pronoun follows a linking verb, it is a predicate nominative. A predicate nominative renames the subject, telling us **who** or **what** the subject is.

Nouns and pronouns can also follow action verbs. They receive the action of the verb, answering the question **whom** or **what**. Look at these sentences from *Black Beauty*.

Master gave the address.

They hugged poor Merrylegs.

The master gave what? The **address**. **Address** is the direct object because it receives the action of the verb; it is what the master gave. The girls hugged whom? Poor **Merrylegs**. **Merrylegs** is the direct object because he receives the action of the verb; he is whom the girls hugged.

Follow this procedure for analyzing sentences.

What is the predicate? The main verb is often easier to find than its subject, so find it first. Double underline it.

Is the verb an action verb or a linking verb? Label it.

What is the subject? Underline it once.

For action verbs, is there a direct object?

For linking verbs, is there a subject complement—a predicate nominative or a predicate adjective?

The direct object is diagrammed in a similar way to the predicate nominative. Instead of following a linking verb and a diagonal line, it follows an action verb and a straight line. As always, place the modifiers on diagonal lines under the words they modify.

Master gave the address.

They hugged poor Merrylegs.

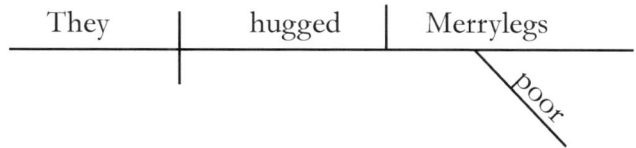

Song of Life

By Charles Mackay

A traveler on a dusty road
  Strewed acorns on the lea;
And one took root and sprouted up,
  And grew into a tree.
Love sought its shade at evening-time,
  To breathe its early vows;
And Age was pleased, in heights of noon,
  To bask beneath its boughs.
The dormouse loved its dangling twigs,
  The birds sweet music bore—
It stood a glory in its place,
  A blessing evermore.

A little spring had lost its way
  Amid the grass and fern;
A passing stranger scooped a well
  Where weary men might turn.
He walled it in, and hung with care
  A ladle on the brink;
He thought not of the deed he did,
  But judged that Toil might drink.
He passed again; and lo! The well,
  By summer never dried,
Had cooled ten thousand parched tongues,
  And saved a life beside.

A nameless man, amid the crowd
  That thronged the daily mart,
Let fall a word of hope and love,
  Unstudied from the heart,
A whisper on the tumult thrown,

> A transitory breath,
> It raised a brother from the dust,
> It saved a soul from death.
> O germ! O fount! O word of love!
> O thought at random cast!
> Ye were but little at the first,
> But mighty at the last.

Why the Moon and the Stars Receive their Light from the Sun

From *West African Folk-Tales* by William H. Barker

Once upon a time there was great scarcity of food in the land. Father Anansi and his son, Kweku Tsin, being very hungry, set out one morning to hunt in the forest. In a short time Kweku Tsin was fortunate enough to kill a fine deer—which he carried to his father at their resting-place. Anansi was very glad to see such a supply of food, and requested his son to remain there on guard, while he went for a large basket in which to carry it home. An hour or so passed without his return, and Kweku Tsin became anxious. Fearing lest his father had lost his way, he called out loudly, "Father, father!" to guide him to the spot. To his joy he heard a voice reply, "Yes, my son," and immediately he shouted again, thinking it was Anansi. Instead of the latter, however, a terrible dragon appeared. This monster breathed fire from his great nostrils, and was altogether a dreadful sight to behold. Kweku Tsin was terrified at his approach and speedily hid himself in a cave near by.

The dragon arrived at the resting-place, and was much annoyed to find only the deer's body. He vented his anger in blows upon the latter and went away. Soon after, Father Anansi made his appearance. He was greatly interested in his son's tale, and wished to see the dragon for himself. He soon had his desire, for the monster, smelling human flesh, hastily returned to the spot and seized them both. They were carried off by him to his castle, where they found many other unfortunate creatures also awaiting their fate. All were left in charge of the dragon's servant—a fine, white rooster—which always crowed to summon his master, if anything unusual happened in the latter's absence. The dragon then went off in search of more prey.

Kweku Tsin now summoned all his fellow-prisoners together, to arrange a way of escape. All feared to run away—because of the wonderful powers of the monster. His eyesight was so keen that he could detect a fly moving miles away. Not only that, but he could move over the ground so swiftly that none could outdistance him. Kweku Tsin, however, being exceedingly clever, soon thought of a plan.

Knowing that the white rooster would not crow as long as he has grains of rice to pick up, Kweku scattered on the ground the contents of forty bags of grain which were stored in the great hall. While the rooster was thus busily engaged, Kweku Tsin ordered the spinners to spin fine hempen ropes, to make a strong rope ladder. One end of this he intended to throw up to heaven, trusting that the gods would catch it and hold it fast, while he and his fellow-prisoners mounted.

While the ladder was being made, the men killed and ate all the cattle they needed—reserving all the bones for Kweku Tsin at his express desire. When all was ready the young man gathered the bones into a great sack. He also procured the dragon's fiddle and placed it by his side.

Everything was now ready. Kweku Tsin threw one end of the ladder up to the sky. It was caught and held. The dragon's victims began to mount, one after the other, Kweku remaining at the bottom.

By this time, however, the monster's powerful eyesight showed him that something unusual was happening at his abode. He hastened his return. On seeing his approach, Kweku Tsin also mounted the ladder—with the bag of bones on his back, and the fiddle under his arm. The dragon began to climb after him. Each time the monster came too near the young man threw him a bone, with which, being very hungry, he was obliged to descend to the ground to eat.

Kweku Tsin repeated this performance till all the bones were gone, by which time the people were safely up in the heavens. Then he mounted himself, as rapidly as possible, stopping every now and then to play a tune on the wonderful fiddle. Each time he did this, the dragon had to return to earth, to dance—as he could not resist the magic music. When Kweku was quite close to the top, the dragon had very nearly reached him again. The brave youth bent down and cut the ladder away below his own feet. The dragon was dashed to the ground but Kweku was pulled up into safety by the gods.

The latter were so pleased with his wisdom and bravery in giving freedom to his fellowmen, that they made him the sun the source of all light and heat to the world. His father, Anansi, became the moon, and his friends the stars. Thereafter, it was Kweku Tsin's privilege to supply all these with light, each being dull and powerless without him.

Writing: Copia

Take the following sentence and play with it. Remember that the point is not necessarily to make the sentence better. The point is to play with the sentence and make it different. Make a new sentence with a change from each of the following categories.

> The grapes seemed ready to burst with juice, and the Fox's mouth watered as he gazed longingly at them.

1. Change the grammar.
   - Change the nouns from common to proper and vice versa.
   - Change the nouns from singular to plural and vice versa.
   - Change the sentence type.
   - Change the adjectives from articles to descriptive to possessive, etc.

2. Condense the sentence.
   - Remove details.
   - Remove modifiers.

3. Use synonyms and antonyms.
   - Substitute synonyms.
   - Say the opposite thing using antonyms.

Exercise

Review memory work. Copy each sentence below. Double underline the predicate, and underline the subject. Label the part of speech of each word. Noun, N; Proper Noun, PN; Pronoun, PRO; Verb, V; Linking Verb, LV; Adjective, ADJ; Article, ART. Diagram each sentence.

> The master gave some directions.

> "You understand horses."

> The last sad day had come.

Commonplace Book

With your instructor's approval, add the passage below to your commonplace book, or choose your own passage from a work of fiction. This can be from either school reading or free reading.

> It was wonderful what a change had come over Joe. John laughed and said he had grown an inch taller in that week, and I believe he had. He was just as kind and gentle as before, but there was more purpose and determination in all that he did, as if he had jumped at once from a boy into a man.

Dictation

> Joe Green went on very well; he learned quickly, and was so attentive and careful that John began to trust him in many things; but as I have said, he was small of his age, and it was seldom that he was allowed to exercise either Ginger or me; but it so happened one morning that John was out with Justice in the luggage cart, and the master wanted a note to be taken immediately to a gentleman's house, about three miles distant.

23. Plurals with -o

- Black Beauty, Chapter 22

When a word ends in *o*, we form the plural by adding either **s** or **es**.

As with words ending in *f*, the way we form plurals for words ending in *o* often depends on what letter comes before the *o*. We use **s** when the word ends in a vowel plus *o*.

   Vowel + *o*: radio→radios

When a consonant comes before the *o*, add *es*.

   Consonant + *o*: potato→potatoes

However, there are some words which break these rules. **Piano** is actually short for **pianoforte**. When this happens, the plural is formed by adding **s**.

   Abbreviated word: piano→pianos

And for some words, both endings are correct!

   zeros, zeroes; halos, haloes; banjos, banjoes

When in doubt, always check the dictionary for information on forming plurals.

Fairy Song

By John Keats

Shed no tear! O shed no tear!
The flower will bloom another year.
Weep no more! O, weep no more!
Young buds sleep in the root's white core.
Dry your eyes! Oh! Dry your eyes!
For I was taught in Paradise
To ease my breast of melodies—
Shed no tear.

Overhead! Look overhead!
  'Mong the blossoms white and red—
Look up, look up. I flutter now
On this flush pomegranate bough.
See me! 'tis this silvery bell
Ever cures the good man's ill.
Shed no tear! O, shed no tear!
The flowers will bloom another year.
Adieu, adieu—I fly, adieu,
I vanish in the heaven's blue—
Adieu, adieu!

Quarcoo Bah-Boni (The Bad Boy)

From *West African Folk-Tales* by William H. Barker

    Once upon a time in a certain village lived a man and his wife who were childless. One day, however, when the husband was away hunting, the woman had a baby son. She was greatly troubled at her husband's absence, because she was unable to let him know of the child's arrival. In that country it is the custom for the father to give the baby its name when it is a week old. As the time approached for the naming, the woman wondered to herself what name she could give the child if her husband did not return in time. To her amazement, the child himself answered, "My name is Quarcoo Bah-boni." As he was only a week old she was astonished to hear him talk. The next day she got a greater surprise. She had been grumbling because her husband was not there to go to the farm for her and fetch food. The baby announced, "I will go to the farm"—which he did.

    When he was a few weeks old, she was one day very busy. She laid him down on the bed while she went on with her task. In a few minutes several boys came up to her in great anger. "Your son has been beating us and ill-treating us in the street," said they. "My son!" she cried. "Why, my son is only a tiny baby. He is lying asleep on my bed." To convince them she went indoors to show them the baby. Imagine her surprise when he was nowhere to be seen! She had to apologize to the boys and beg them to forgive the child. Shortly after, he came in and put himself to bed.

    He continued these mischievous tricks till his mother could no longer endure them. So she turned him out of the house and forbade him to return. He departed in great glee.

    After walking a few miles, he came to a building where a goat, wolf, tiger, lion, and elephant lived very happily together. These animals were all sitting round their fire when he approached. After many polite speeches, he begged their permission to stay and be their servant, as he was motherless. The animals, after a little discussion, agreed to this, thinking that he would be able to help them in many ways. He was given a seat and some food, which he ate with great relish.

    These five animals usually took it in turns to go out to their farm—a few miles away every morning, to bring home food for the day. It being Goat's turn, he asked Quarcoo to come with him to carry back the load.

    The basket was accordingly handed to the little boy and he set off meekly after the goat. When they reached the farm, Quarcoo set down the basket and ran off to play. He paid no heed at all to the goat's calls for assistance, but went on quietly playing. At last the goat was so annoyed that he came up to Quarcoo and boxed his ears. To his great astonishment, the boy gave him such a blow that he fell to the ground. Quarcoo then proceeded to beat him till he cried for mercy. Nor would he stop his blows till the goat had promised to finish the work, carry home the load, and tell no one what had happened. Having promised this, the goat was allowed to go free. By this time the poor animal's face was bruised and swollen.

When the time came to go home the goat had to pack up the load and put it on his head. Then they set out.

As soon as they came in sight of their cottage, Quarcoo took the basket from the goat and he himself carried it into the cottage.

The other animals all exclaimed in wonder when they saw the goat's face, and asked him how it had happened. "I was unfortunate enough to get into a swarm of bees when I was working. They stung me," answered the poor goat.

Next day it was the wolf's turn to go to the farm. He also returned, much bruised and swollen. Goat (guessing what had happened) listened with a smile to the excuses made by Wolf to the others.

Goat and Wolf afterward talked the matter over and wondered much at the strength of the little boy.

Each day another animal took his turn at the farm, and each day he returned in the same condition as his friends had done. At last all the animals had been, and all now came together to discuss how best they might get rid of Quarcoo Bah-boni.

They made up their minds that, early the following morning, they would start off together and leave the boy in possession of the house. They prepared a big basket of food and set it ready.

Unfortunately for them, Quarcoo had heard their discussion and decided that he also would go with them. He quietly got himself a large leaf, rolled it round him (for he was very tiny) and laid himself down in the basket of food.

At dawn the animals got up very quietly. Goat, being the youngest, was given the basket to carry. They started, feeling very thankful to get away from the tiresome boy—never dreaming that they were carrying him along with them.

When they had gone a fair distance Goat, feeling very hot and tired, sat down to rest for a little while. As soon as the others had gone out of sight, he opened the basket, meaning to have some food unknown to his friends. His greed was rewarded, however, by a terrible blow on the face. He then heard the words, "Shut the basket at once, and say nothing to the others." He obeyed and hurried after the others in fear of this terrible boy.

As soon as he reached them he called out, "Wolf, Wolf, it is your turn now to take the basket. I am very tired." Wolf took the load at once.

They had not gone far when Wolf began to think of all the nice things in the basket and he also said he was going to rest a little while in the shade. Having got rid of the others in this way, he hastily opened the basket. He was greeted by Quarcoo in the same way as Goat had been, and speedily closed the basket and followed the others. In this way each animal got his turn of carrying the basket, and each was punished for his greed.

Finally, Elephant's turn came. When he rejoined the others and asked some one to relieve him of his load they cried out, "If you do not want to carry it any farther, throw it away." He did so, and they all took to their heels. They ran for several miles and only stopped when they came to a huge tree, in whose shade they sat down to rest, being quite breathless.

Quarcoo, however, had got there before them. He had quietly stepped out of the basket, taken a short cut across country and arrived at the tree some time before them. He guessed that they would probably rest there—so he climbed up into the branches. There he remained, hidden among the leaves, while the animals sat on the ground below.

    There they discussed Quarcoo and all the trouble he had caused them. They blamed Goat for having been the one to persuade them to take the boy as a servant. Goat being the youngest of the company had the domestic work to do and he had welcomed the idea of help. Goat indignantly denied being the cause of all their troubles, saying: "If I am really to blame for the admission of Quarcoo—let him appear before us." Quarcoo promptly jumped down from the tree and stood in front of them. They were so alarmed at his appearance they scattered in all directions. The wolf ran to the woods—the tiger into the heart of the forest, the elephant to Nigeria, the lion to the desert, and the goat to the abode of human beings. That is the reason why they live now in these various places instead of all together as they did previously.

Exercise

Review memory work. Make the following words plural. Use the dictionary if necessary!

> wife, staff, stereo, tomato, photo

Copy each sentence below. Double underline the predicate, and underline the subject. Label the part of speech of each word. Noun, N; Proper Noun, PN; Pronoun, PRO; Verb, V; Linking Verb, LV; Adjective, ADJ; Article, ART. Diagram each sentence.

> He took the reins.

> He mounted the box.

> His voice was sad.

Writing: Commonplace Book

Add the passage below from your model story to your commonplace book.

> The bunch hung from a high branch, and the Fox had to jump for it. The first time he jumped he missed it by a long way. So he walked off a short distance and took a running leap at it, only to fall short once more. Again and again he tried, but in vain.

Dictation

Use the first stanza of today's poem for dictation.

24. Amplified Narrative: The Fox and the Grapes

• Black Beauty, Chapters 23-24

So far, your narrations have been **condensed**, which means that you shortened the stories. Your next three narrations will be the opposite. You will **amplify** the stories, which means that you will expand the stories and make them longer.

Today, write "The Fox and the Grapes" as an amplified narrative. For this narration, amplify the narrative by adding descriptive detail. Be careful to actually add descriptive detail. Do not just throw in a couple of adjectives! Add the kind of details that will paint a picture in the reader's mind.

You can choose which types of details to add. What was the fox like, both in appearance and character? What time of day was it? What was the landscape like? What did the grapes look like? How did the fox try to get the grapes? What was his appearance and attitude as he walked away?

The Enchanted Hill

By Walter De La Mare

From height of noon, remote and still,
The sun shines on the empty hill.
No mist, no wind, above, below;
No living thing strays to and fro.
No bird replies to bird on high,
Cleaving the skies with echoing cry.
Like dreaming water, green and wan,
Glassing the snow of mantling swan,
Like a clear jewel encharactered
With secret symbol of line and word,
Asheen, unruffled, slumbrous, still,
The sunlight streams on the empty hill.
But soon as Night's dark shadows ride
Across its shrouded Eastern side,
When at her kindling, clear and full,
Star beyond star stands visible;
Then course pale phantoms, fleet-foot deer

Lap of its waters icy-clear;
Mounts the large moon, and pours her beams
On bright-fish-flashing, singing streams;
Voices re-echo; coursing by,
Horsemen, like clouds, wheel silently.
Glide then from out their pitch-black lair
Beneath the dark's ensilvered arch,
Witches becowled into the air;
And iron pine and emerald larch,
Tents of delight for ravished bird,
Are by loud music thrilled and stirred.
Winging the light, with silver feet,
Beneath their bowers of fragrance met,
In dells of rose and meadowsweet,
In mazed dance the fairies flit;
While drives his share the Ploughman high
Athwart the daisy-powdered sky:
Till far away, in thickening dew,
Piercing the Eastern shadows through
Rilling in crystal clear and still,
Light 'gins to tremble on the hill.
And like a mist on faint winds borne,
Silent, forlorn, wells up the morn.
Then the broad sun with burning beams
Steeps slope and peak and gilded streams.
Then no foot stirs; the brake shakes not;
Soundless and wet in its green grot
As if asleep, the leaf hangs limp;
The white dews drip untrembling down,
From bough to bough, orblike, unblown;
And in strange quiet, shimmering and still,
Morning enshrines the empty hill.

Editing

• Did you meet the goal of this writing exercise?

• Look at your word choice. Is there a good mixture of nouns and pronouns? Is the antecedent of each pronoun clear?

25. Nouns as Adjectives

- Black Beauty, Chapter 25

You've already learned that the possessive form of nouns and pronouns act as adjectives. Other nouns can also act as adjectives.

When nouns act as adjectives, they usually answer the question **what kind** for another noun. What kind of chair? A **wicker** chair. What kind of ball? A **soccer** ball. What kind of cake? A **birthday** cake.

Look at the following sentence from *Black Beauty*.

His poor wife and little children had to turn out of the pretty cottage by the <u>park</u> gate and go where they could.

Here, the word **park** is an adjective that tells which gate. The property has multiple gates, and each gate may be identified based on something that it is near, like the park.

Just as some nouns can be proper, some adjectives can be as well. A possessive proper noun, such as **Farmer Grey's**, is a proper adjective, and so are words made from proper nouns, such as **American**.

Even though these words are normally nouns, they are adjectives when they modify other nouns. Label such a word ADJ, and diagram it on a diagonal line under the noun it modifies like other adjectives.

Beauty remembered Farmer Grey's pleasant meadow.

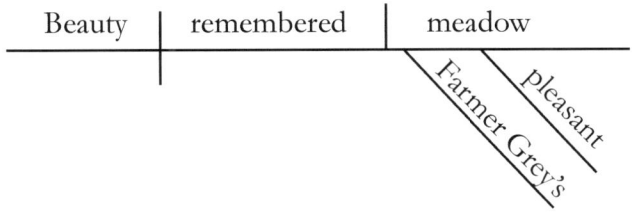

A word's part of speech is determined by the job it is performing.

The Mountain

By Emily Dickinson

The mountain sat upon the plain
In his eternal chair,
His observation omnifold,
His inquest everywhere.
The seasons prayed around his knees,
Like children round a sire:
Grandfather of the days is he,
Of dawn the ancestor.

Writing: Oral Narration

Read your new model story below, and then give your instructor an oral narration of it.

The Bundle of Sticks

An Aesop's Fable

    A certain Father had a family of Sons, who were forever quarreling among themselves. No words he could say did the least good, so he cast about in his mind for some very striking example that should make them see that discord would lead them to misfortune.

    One day when the quarreling had been much more violent than usual and each of the Sons was moping in a surly manner, he asked one of them to bring him a bundle of sticks. Then handing the bundle to each of his Sons in turn he told them to try to break it. But although each one tried his best, none was able to do so.

    The Father then untied the bundle and gave the sticks to his Sons to break one by one. This they did very easily.

    "My Sons," said the Father, "do you not see how certain it is that if you agree with each other and help each other, it will be impossible for your enemies to injure you? But if you are divided among yourselves, you will be no stronger than a single stick in that bundle."

    In unity is strength.

Exercise

Review memory work. Make the following words plural. Use the dictionary if necessary!

video, mango, studio, echo, hero

Copy each sentence below. Double underline the predicate, and underline the subject. Label the part of speech of each word. Noun, N; Proper Noun, PN; Pronoun, PRO; Verb, V; Linking Verb, LV; Adjective, ADJ; Article, ART. Diagram each sentence.

The roads were stony.

He was a handsome man.

He had pleasant manners.

Commonplace Book

With your instructor's approval, add the passage below to your commonplace book, or choose your own passage from a work of fiction. This can be from either school reading or free reading.

At the station the colonel put some money into Smith's hand and bid him good-by, saying, "Take care of your young mistress, Reuben, and don't let Black Auster be hacked about by any random young prig that wants to ride him; keep him for the lady."

Dictation

We left the carriage at the maker's, and Smith rode me to the White Lion, and ordered the hostler to feed me well, and have me ready for him at four o'clock. A nail in one of my front shoes had started as I came along, but the hostler did not notice it till just about four o'clock. Smith did not come into the yard till five, and then he said he should not leave till six, as he had met with some old friends. The man then told him of the nail, and asked if he should have the shoe looked to.

26. Diagramming Interrogative Sentences

• Black Beauty, Chapters 26-27

Interrogative sentences, or questions, are a type of **inverted** sentence. **Inverted** just means that the normal word order is reversed. Normally, the subject of the sentence comes before the verb, but in a question, a helping verb often comes before the subject. Look at the following interrogative sentences from *Black Beauty*, and notice the inversion of the subject and verb.

"Can you ride?"

Which way had she turned?

To diagram a question, first put the sentence back into normal word order. The subject and predicate then become obvious.

You can ride.

you	Can ride

She had turned which way.

she	had turned

Interrogative sentences can have subject complements (predicate nominatives and predicate adjectives) and direct objects just as other sentences can. These parts of the sentence are also easier to see when the words of the sentence are in their normal order.

Remember that a subject complement renames (predicate nominative) or modifies (predicate adjective) the subject of the sentence. The linking verb is like an equal sign in math.

"Are you tired?"

<u>You</u> <u>are</u> <u>tired</u>.

You = tired

```
  you  |  Are  \  tired
       |
```

The direct object, on the other hand, is what the verb acts upon. It receives the action of the verb, whether it is a ball being kicked or a letter being given.

<u>Would</u> <u>they</u> <u>ask</u> this question?

<u>They</u> <u>would</u> <u>ask</u> this question.

```
  they  |  Would ask  |  question
        |             \this
```

A Boy's Song

By James Hogg

Where the pools are bright and deep,
Where the gray trout lies asleep,
Up the river and o'er the lea,
That's the way for Billy and me.

Where the blackbird sings the latest,
Where the hawthorn blooms the sweetest,
Where the nestlings chirp and flee,
That's the way for Billy and me.

Where the mowers mow the cleanest,
Where the hay lies thick and greenest,
There to trace the homeward bee,
That's the way for Billy and me.

Where the hazel bank is steepest,
Where the shadow falls the deepest,
Where the clustering nuts fall free.
That's the way for Billy and me.

Why the boys should drive away,
Little sweet maidens from the play,
Or love to banter and fight so well,
That's the thing I never could tell.

But this I know, I love to play,
Through the meadow, among the hay;
Up the water and o'er the lea,
That's the way for Billy and me.

How the Tortoise Got Its Shell

From *West African Folk-Tales* by William H. Barker

A few hundred years ago, the chief Mauri (God) determined to have a splendid yam festival. He therefore sent his messengers to invite all his chiefs and people to the gathering, which was to take place on Fida (Friday).

On the morning of that day he sent some of his servants to the neighboring towns and villages to buy goats, sheep, and cows for the great feast. Mr. Klo (the tortoise), who was a tall and handsome fellow was sent to buy palm wine. He was directed to the palm-fields of Koklovi (the chicken).

At that time Klo was a very powerful traveler and speedily reached his destination although it was many miles distant from Mauri's palace.

When he arrived Koklovi was taking his breakfast. When they had exchanged polite salutations Koklovi asked the reason of Klo's visit. He replied, "I was sent by His Majesty Mauri, the ruler of the world, to buy him palm wine." "Whether he's ruler of the world or not," answered Koklovi, "no one can buy my wine with money. If you want it you must fight for it. If you win you can have it all and the palm trees too."

This answer delighted Klo as he was a very strong fighter. Koklovi was the same, so that the fighting continued for several hours before Klo was able to overcome Koklovi. He was at last successful, however, and securely bound Koklovi before he left him.

Then, taking his great pot, he filled it with wine. Finding that there was more wine than the pot would hold, Klo foolishly drank all the rest. He then piled the palm trees on his back and set out for the palace with the pot of wine. The amount which he had drunk, however, made him feel so sleepy and tired that he could not walk fast with his load. Added to this, a terrible rain began to fall, which made the ground very slippery and still more difficult to travel over.

By the time, Klo succeeded in reaching his master's palace the gates were shut and locked. Mauri, finding it so late, had concluded that every one was inside.

There were many people packed into the great hall, and all were singing and dancing. The noise of the concert was so great that no one heard Klo's knocking at the gate, and there he had to stay with his great load of wine and palm trees.

The rain continued for nearly two months and was so terrible that the people all remained in the palace till it had finished. By that time Klo had died, under the weight of his load—which he had been unable to get off his back. There he lay, before the gate, with the pile of palm trees on top of him.

When the rain ceased and the gates were opened the people were amazed to see this great mound in front of the gate, where before there had been nothing. They fetched spades and began to shovel it away.

When they came to the bottom of the pile there lay Klo. His earthenware pot and the dust had caked together and formed quite a hard cover on his back.

He was taken into the palace—and by the use of many wonderful medicines he was restored to life. But since that date he has never been able to stand upright. He has been a creeping creature, with a great shell on his back.

Writing: Copia, Playing with Words

Take each of the following words from your model story and look them up in the thesaurus. Give two or three different ways to say each word.

>quarrel, discord, misfortune, surly, unity

Exercise

Review memory work. Copy each sentence below. Double underline the predicate, and underline the subject. Label the part of speech of each word. Noun, N; Proper Noun, PN; Pronoun, PRO; Verb, V; Linking Verb, LV; Adjective, ADJ; Article, ART. Diagram each sentence.

>Did Beauty enjoy the sweet grass?

>Had they become fast friends?

>Was Beauty lonely?

Commonplace Book

With your instructor's approval, add the poem below to your commonplace book, or choose your own poem.

>Where the pools are bright and deep,
>Where the gray trout lies asleep,
>Up the river and o'er the lea,
>That's the way for Billy and me.
>
>Where the blackbird sings the latest,
>Where the hawthorn blooms the sweetest,
>Where the nestlings chirp and flee,
>That's the way for Billy and me.

Dictation

>Psalm 27:1-3
>
>The Lord is my light and my salvation;
>Whom shall I fear?
>The Lord is the defense of my life;
>Whom shall I dread?
>When evildoers came upon me to devour my flesh,
>My adversaries and my enemies, they stumbled and fell.
>Though a host encamp against me,
>My heart will not fear;
>Though war arise against me,
>In spite of this I shall be confident.

The Boating Party by Mary Cassatt

Picture Study

1. Read the title and the name of the artist. Study the picture for several minutes, then put the picture away.

2. Describe the picture.

3. Look at the picture again. Do you notice any details that you missed before? What do you like or dislike about this painting? Does it remind you of anything?

27. Literary Analysis

- Black Beauty, Chapter 28

Writing: Literary Analysis

This should be an oral exercise.

With your instructor's approval, choose *Black Beauty*, or one of the other books you're currently reading, and answer the following questions.

What is the book about? Give a brief summary, just a few sentences. Who is your favorite character? Why?

The Rainbow

By Thomas Campbell

Triumphal arch, that fills the sky
  When storms prepare to part,
I ask not proud Philosophy
  To teach me what thou art.

Still seem, as to my childhood's sight,
  A midway station given,
For happy spirits to alight,
  Betwixt the earth and heaven.

The Hunter and the Tortoise

From *West African Folk-Tales* by William H. Barker

    A village hunter had one day gone farther afield than usual. Coming to a part of the forest with which he was unacquainted, he was astonished to hear a voice singing. He listened; this was the song:
    "It is man who forces himself on things,
      Not things which force themselves on him."
    The singing was accompanied by sweet music—which entirely charmed the hunter's heart.

When the little song was finished, the hunter peeped through the branches to see who the singer could be. Imagine his amazement when he found it was none other than a tortoise, with a tiny harp slung in front of her. Never had he seen such a marvellous thing.

Time after time he returned to the same place in order to listen to this wonderful creature. At last he persuaded her to let him carry her back to his hut, that he might enjoy her singing daily in comfort. This she permitted, only on the understanding that she sang to him alone.

The hunter did not rest long content with this arrangement, however. Soon he began to wish that he could show off this wonderful tortoise to all the world, and thereby thought he would gain great honor. He told the secret, first to one, then to another, until finally it reached the ears of the chief himself. The hunter was commanded to come and tell his tale before the Assembly. When, however, he described the tortoise who sang and played on, the harp, the people shouted in scorn. They refused to believe him.

At last he said, "If I do not speak truth, I give you leave to kill me. Tomorrow I will bring the tortoise to this place and you may all hear her. If she cannot do as I say, I am willing to die." "Good," replied the people, "and if the tortoise can do as you say, we give you leave to punish us in any way you choose."

The matter being then settled, the hunter returned home, well pleased with the prospect. As soon as the morrow dawned, he carried tortoise and harp down to the Assembly Place—where a table had been placed ready for her. Every one gathered round to listen. But no song came. The people were very patient, and quite willing to give both tortoise and hunter a chance. Hours went by, and, to the hunter's dismay and shame, the tortoise remained mute. He tried every means in his power to coax her to sing, but in vain. The people at first whispered, then spoke outright, in scorn of the boaster and his claims.

Night came on and brought with it the hunter's doom. As the last ray of the setting sun faded, he was beheaded. The instant this had happened the tortoise spoke. The people looked at one another in troubled wonder: "Our brother spoke truth, then, and we have killed him." The tortoise, however, went on to explain. "He brought his punishment on himself. I led a happy life in the forest, singing my little song. He was not content to come and listen to me. He had to tell my secret (which did not at all concern him) to all the world. Had he not tried to make a show of me this would never have happened."

"It is man who forces himself on things,
Not things which force themselves on him."

Exercise

Review memory work. Copy each sentence below. Double underline the predicate, and underline the subject. Label the part of speech of each word. Noun, N; Proper Noun, PN; Pronoun, PRO; Verb, V; Linking Verb, LV; Adjective, ADJ; Article, ART. Diagram each sentence.

These drivers are careless.

He lifted his hat.

Did he have a stone?

Commonplace Book

With your instructor's approval, add the passage below to your commonplace book, or choose your own passage from a work of non-fiction. This can be from the Bible, a biography, or one of your history or science books.

> Besides, a slovenly way of driving gets a horse into bad and often lazy habits, and when he changes hands, he has to be whipped out of them with more or less pain and trouble. Squire Gordon always kept us to our best paces and our best manners. He said that spoiling a horse and letting him get into bad habits was just as cruel as spoiling a child, and both had to suffer for it afterward.

28. Compound Subjects and Predicates

• Black Beauty, Chapters 29-30

Sometimes, a sentence can have more than one subject or predicate. This is called a compound subject or a compound predicate. Look at these sentences from *Black Beauty*.

    Mr. Gordon or John would have seen.

    His wife bred and fattened poultry and rabbits.

In the first sentence, the simple predicate is **would have seen**. Who would have seen? Mr. Gordon or John. This is a compound subject joined by the word **or**.

In the second sentence, the simple subject is **wife**. What did his wife do? She **bred** and **fattened** poultry and rabbits. This is a compound predicate joined by the word **and**.

To diagram sentences with compound structures, we have to add extra lines to the diagram.

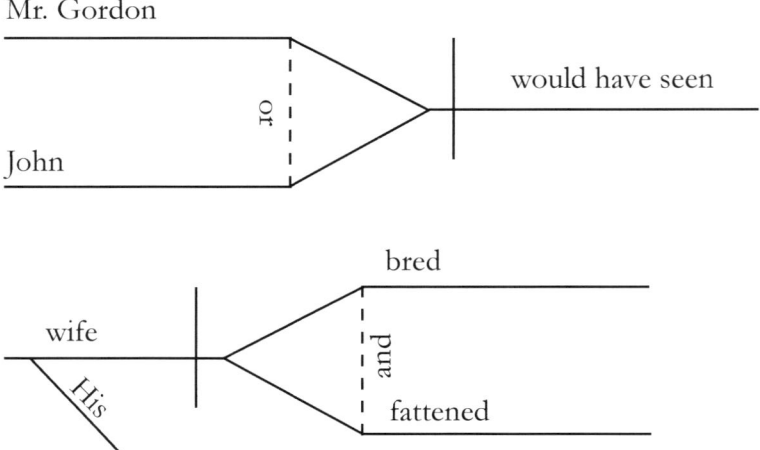

The sentence with the compound predicate has a direct object. The way we diagram a compound predicate with a direct object (or a subject complement) depends on a couple of factors. First, does the compound predicate share the direct object? In this case, the two verbs do share the direct object. She bred poultry, and she fattened poultry. The diagram shows it like this:

His wife <u><u>bred</u></u> and <u><u>fattened</u></u> poultry.

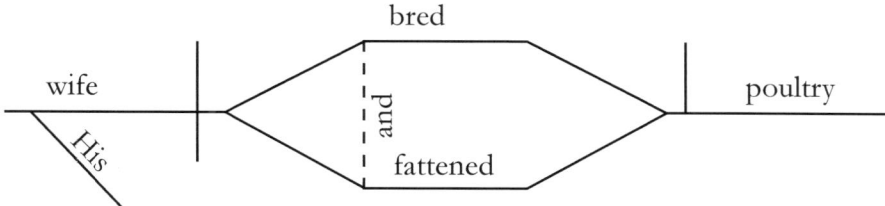

But wait a minute. She didn't just breed and fatten poultry, did she? She bred and fattened poultry **and** rabbits. This is a compound direct object joined by the word **and**.

His wife <u><u>bred</u></u> and <u><u>fattened</u></u> poultry and rabbits.

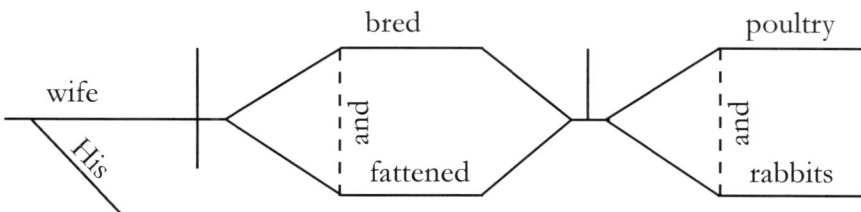

The direct object, or direct objects, will not always be shared by the verbs. Consider this sentence.

His wife <u><u>bred</u></u> poultry and <u><u>fattened</u></u> rabbits.

Now the direct objects are not shared. Each part of the compound predicate has its own direct object. We diagram it like this:

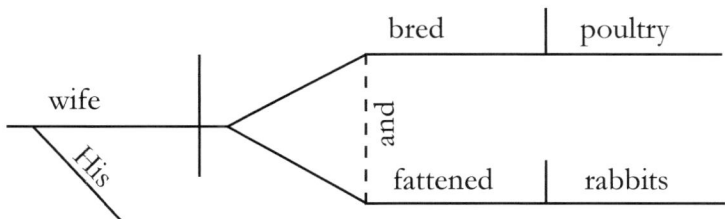

The differences in how to diagram all depend on whether or not there is a direct object or subject complement, and if there is one, whether or not it is shared.

And here's one more, just for fun. A sentence can have multiple compound structures. This sentence has a compound subject, a compound predicate, and a compound direct object.

<u>He</u> and his <u>wife</u> <u><u>bred</u></u> and <u><u>fattened</u></u> poultry and rabbits.

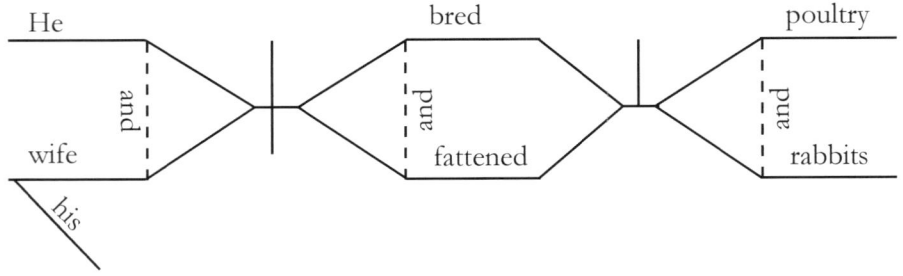

And and **or** are conjunctions, which we'll discuss in another lesson. Label them CJ in your exercises.

Old Ironsides

By Oliver Wendell Holmes

Ay, tear her tattered ensign down!
  Long has it waved on high,
And many an eye has danced to see
  That banner in the sky;
Beneath it rung the battle shout,
  And burst the cannon's roar;—
The meteor of the ocean air
  Shall sweep the clouds no more.

Her deck, once red with heroes' blood,
  Where knelt the vanquished foe,
When winds were hurrying o'er the flood
  And waves were white below.
No more shall feel the victor's tread,
  Or know the conquered knee;
The harpies of the shore shall pluck
  The eagle of the sea!

O, better that her shattered hulk
  Should sink beneath the wave;
Her thunders shook the mighty deep,
  And there should be her grave;
Nail to the mast her holy flag,
  Set every threadbare sail,
And give her to the god of storms,
  The lightning and the gale!

Kwofi and the Gods

From *West African Folk-Tales* by William H. Barker

    Kwofi was the eldest son of a farmer who had two wives. Kwofi's mother had no other children.
    When the boy was three years old his mother died. Kwofi was given to his step-

mother to mind. After this she had many children. Kwofi, of course, was the eldest of all.

When he was about ten years old his father also died. Kwofi had now no relative but his stepmother, for whom he had to work.

As he grew older, she saw how much more clever and handsome he was than her own children, and grew very jealous of him. He was such a good hunter that day after day he came home laden with meat or with fish.

Every day she treated him in the same way. She cooked the meat, then portioned it out. She gave to each a large helping, but when it came to Kwofi's turn she would say, "Oh, my son Kwofi, there is none left for you! You must go to the field and get some ripe paw-paw." Kwofi never complained. Never once did he taste any of the meat he had hunted. At every meal the others were served, but there was never enough for him.

One evening, when the usual thing had happened, Kwofi was preparing to go to the field to fetch some paw-paw for his supper. All at once one of the gods appeared in the village, carrying a great bag over his shoulder. He summoned all the villagers together with these words: "Oh, my villagers, I come with a bag of death for you!"

Thereupon he began to distribute the contents of his bag among them. When he came to Kwofi he said: "Oh, my son Kwofi, there was never sufficient meat for you, neither is there any death."

As he said these words every one in the village died except Kwofi. He was left to reign there in peace, which he did very happily.

Writing: Copia

Take the following sentence and play with it. Remember that the point is not necessarily to make the sentence better. The point is to play with the sentence and make it different. Make a new sentence with a change from each of the following categories.

> The Father then untied the bundle and gave the sticks to his Sons to break one by one.

1. Change the grammar.
    - Change the nouns from common to proper and vice versa.
    - Change the nouns from singular to plural and vice versa.
    - Change the sentence type.
    - Change the adjectives from articles to descriptive to possessive, etc.
    - Change a quotation from direct to indirect and vice versa.

2. Condense the sentence.
    - Remove details.
    - Remove modifiers.

3. Amplify the sentence.
    - Add details.
    - Add modifiers.

4. Use synonyms and antonyms.
    - Substitute synonyms.
    - Say the opposite thing using antonyms.

Exercise

Review memory work. Copy each sentence below. Double underline the predicate, and underline the subject. Label the part of speech of each word. Noun, N; Proper Noun, PN; Pronoun, PRO; Verb, V; Linking Verb, LV; Adjective, ADJ; Article, ART; Conjunction, CJ. Diagram each sentence.

"Has he been well?"

The farmer dismounted and held his rein.

Beauty and Peggy pulled the carriage.

Commonplace Book

With your instructor's approval, add the passage below to your commonplace book, or choose your own passage from a work of fiction. This can be from either school reading or free reading.

> "He is as warm and damp as a horse just come up from grass. I advise you to look into your stable a little more. I hate to be suspicious, and, thank heaven, I have no cause to be, for I can trust my men, present or absent; but there are mean scoundrels, wicked enough to rob a dumb beast of his food. You must look into it."

Dictation

> My new master was an unmarried man. He lived at Bath, and was much engaged in business. His doctor advised him to take horse exercise, and for this purpose he bought me. He hired a stable a short distance from his lodgings, and engaged a man named Filcher as groom. My master knew very little about horses, but he treated me well, and I should have had a good and easy place but for circumstances of which he was ignorant.

29. Quotations

- Black Beauty, Chapter 31

Look at these two sentences from *Black Beauty*.

> One day his master came in and said, "Alfred, the stable smells rather strong."
>
> He said that spoiling a horse and letting him get into bad habits was just as cruel as spoiling a child.

Both sentences report what someone has said. The first sentence is a direct quotation which reports the exact words that someone used. The second sentence is an indirect quotation which reports what someone has said, but without using his exact words.

Direct quotations need quotation marks, but indirect quotations do not. Indirect quotations often use the word **that** to indicate an indirect quotation.

Sentences can be changed from direct to indirect and vice versa. Look again at the sentences above. How would you change them?

Here's one way that you could change each of them:

> One day his master came in and said **that** the stable smelled rather strong.
>
> He said**,** **"**Spoiling a horse and letting him get into bad habits is just as cruel as spoiling a child.**"**

The Mermaids

By Walter De La Mare

Sand, sand; hills of sand;
And the wind where nothing is
Green and sweet of the land;
No grass, no trees,
No bird, no butterfly,
But hills, hills of sand,
And a burning sky.
Sea, sea, mounds of the sea,

Hollow, and dark, and blue,
Flashing incessantly
The whole sea through;
No flower, no jutting root,
Only the floor of the sea,
With foam afloat.
Blow, blow, winding shells;
And the watery fish,
Deaf to the hidden bells,
In the water splash;
No streaming gold, no eyes,
Watching along the waves,
But far-blown shells, faint bells,
From the darkling caves.

The Lion and the Wolf

From *West African Folk-Tales* by William H. Barker

A certain old lady had a very fine flock of sheep. She had fed and cared for them so well that they became famous for their fatness. In time a wicked wolf heard of them and determined to eat them.

Night after night he stole up to the old dame's cottage and killed a sheep. The poor woman tried her best to save her animals from harm—but failed.

At last there was only one sheep left of all the flock. Their owner was very sad. She feared that it, too, would be taken away from her, in spite of all she could do. While she was grieving over the thought of this a lion came to her village.

Seeing her sad face, he asked the reason of it. She soon told him all about it. He thereupon offered to do his best to punish the wicked wolf. He himself went to the place where the sheep was generally kept—while the latter was removed to another place.

In the meantime the wolf was on his way to the cottage. As he came he met a fox. The fox was somewhat afraid of him and prepared to run away. The wolf, however, told him where he was going, and invited him to go too. The fox agreed and the two set off together. They arrived at the cottage and went straight to the place where the sheep generally slept. The wolf at once rushed upon the animal, while Fox waited a little behind. Just as Fox was deciding to enter and help Wolf there came a bright flash of lightning. By the light of it the fox could see that the wolf was attacking—not a sheep—but a lion. He hastily ran away, shouting as he went: "Look at his face! Look at his face!"

During the flash Wolf did look at the pretended sheep. To his dismay he found he had made a great mistake. At once he began to make humble apologies—but all in vain. Lion refused to listen to any of his explanations, and speedily put him to death.

Exercise

Review memory work. Copy each sentence below. Double underline the predicate, and underline the subject. Label the part of speech of each word. Noun, N; Proper Noun, PN; Pronoun, PRO; Verb, V; Linking Verb, LV; Adjective, ADJ; Article, ART; Conjunction, CJ. Diagram each sentence.

"I will attend the hoof and direct your man."

He was ignorant and conceited.

The bricklayer came and pulled many bricks.

Writing: Commonplace Book

Add the passage below from your model story to your commonplace book.

"My Sons," said the Father, "do you not see how certain it is that if you agree with each other and help each other, it will be impossible for your enemies to injure you? But if you are divided among yourselves, you will be no stronger than a single stick in that bundle."

Dictation

Use part of today's poem for dictation.

30. Amplified Narrative: The Bundle of Sticks

- Black Beauty, Chapters 32-33

Today, write "The Bundle of Sticks" as an amplified narrative. For this narration, amplify the narrative by adding **dialogue**, which is conversation between the characters. What do you think the father said to his sons? How would the sons have responded to their father, and what might they have said to one another?

The Gnomies

By Walter De La Mare

As I lay awake in the white moonlight,
I heard a sweet singing in the wood—
'Out of bed,
Sleepyhead,
Put your white foot now,
Here are we,
'Neath the tree,
Singing round the root now!'
I looked out of window in the white moonlight,
The trees were like snow in the wood—
'Come away
Child and play,
Light wi' the gnomies;
In a mound,
Green and round,
That's where their home is!
'Honey sweet,
Curds to eat,
Cream and frumenty,
Shells and beads,
Poppy seeds,
You shall have plenty.'
But soon as I stooped in the dim moonlight

To put on my stocking and my shoe,
The sweet, sweet singing died sadly away,
And the light of the morning peep'd through:
Then instead of the gnomies there came a red robin
To sing of the buttercups and dew.

Editing

• Did you meet the goal of this writing exercise?

• Look at your word choice. Is there a good mixture of nouns and pronouns? Is the antecedent of each pronoun clear?

31. Diagramming Imperative Sentences

- Black Beauty, Chapter 34

An imperative sentence gives a command or makes a request. Look at the following sentences from *Black Beauty*.

"Send for the bricklayer and have it seen to," said his master.

"Say twenty-five, and you shall have him."

Can you find the subject in those sentences? When we give a command or make a request, the subject is always the person to whom we are speaking. Do you remember what pronoun we use for the person to whom we are speaking?

You! The word **you** is always the subject of an imperative sentence. Sometimes it is stated, but sometimes, it is understood to be the subject even though it's not actually in the sentence.

When we diagram an imperative sentence, we put the understood **you** in parentheses to show that it wasn't actually in the sentence.

Say twenty-five.

(you)	Say	twenty-five

Sometimes, **you** is stated in the sentence. In that case, the parentheses on the diagram are not necessary.

You say twenty-five.

You	say	twenty-five

The Wind

By Emily Dickinson

Of all the sounds despatched abroad,
There's not a charge to me
Like that old measure in the boughs,
That phraseless melody
The wind does, working like a hand
Whose fingers brush the sky,
Then quiver down, with tufts of tune
Permitted gods and me.
When winds go round and round in bands,
And thrum upon the door,
And birds take places overhead,
To bear them orchestra,
I crave him grace, of summer boughs,
If such an outcast be,
He never heard that fleshless chant
Rise solemn in the tree,
As if some caravan of sound
On deserts, in the sky,
Had broken rank,
Then knit, and passed
In seamless company.

Writing: Oral Narration

Read your new model story below, and then give your instructor an oral narration of it.

The Leap at Rhodes

An Aesop's Fable

    A certain man who visited foreign lands could talk of little when he returned to his home except the wonderful adventures he had met with and the great deeds he had done abroad.

    One of the feats he told about was a leap he had made in a city called Rhodes. That leap was so great, he said, that no other man could leap anywhere near the distance. A great many persons in Rhodes had seen him do it and would prove that what he told was true.

    "No need of witnesses," said one of the hearers. "Suppose this city is Rhodes. Now show us how far you can jump."

    Deeds count, not boasting words.

Exercise

Review memory work. Copy each sentence below. Double underline the predicate, and underline the subject. Label the part of speech of each word. Noun, N; Proper Noun, PN; Pronoun, PRO; Verb, V; Linking Verb, LV; Adjective, ADJ; Article, ART; Conjunction, CJ. Diagram each sentence.

He was a good-humored, sensible man.

My master and I understood each other. [Hint: **each other** is a two-word pronoun.]

"Open the gates."

Commonplace Book

With your instructor's approval, add the passage below to your commonplace book, or choose your own passage from a work of fiction. This can be from either school reading or free reading.

> "Fearful as it was, no one stopped, no one turned back. Every moment the ranks were thinned, but as our comrades fell, we closed in to keep them together; and instead of being shaken or staggered in our pace, our gallop became faster and faster as we neared the cannon."

Dictation

> "It was one autumn morning, and as usual, an hour before daybreak our cavalry had turned out, ready caparisoned for the day's work, whether it might be fighting or waiting. The men stood by their horses waiting, ready for orders. As the light increased there seemed to be some excitement among the officers; and before the day was well begun we heard the firing of the enemy's guns."

32. Parts of Speech: Adverbs

- Black Beauty, Chapters 35-36

Definition: An adverb is a word that modifies a verb, an adjective, or another adverb. Adverbs tell how, when, where, how often, and to what extent.

Nouns and pronouns have adjectives to tell more about them. Verbs and adjectives have adverbs. Adverbs modify verbs, adjectives, and other adverbs by telling **how, when, where, how often,** and **to what extent**. We'll be looking at each type of adverb in other lessons.

Look at the following sentences from *Black Beauty*.

I never knew a better man.

In this sentence, the adverb **never** modifies the verb **knew**; it tells **when**.

He was so good-tempered.

In this sentence, the adverb **so** modifies the adjective **good-tempered**; it tells **to what extent**.

She spoke very slowly.

In this sentence, the adverb **very** modifies the adverb **slowly**; it tells **to what extent**. The adverb **slowly** modifies the verb **spoke**, telling **how**.

Many adverbs are formed by adding *ly* to adjectives, like **slowly** above. Can you think of some other *ly* words, or any other adverbs? Be careful, though. Adjectives sometimes end in *ly*, too.

The boy ran **quickly**, but he did **poorly** on a test. The sun shone **brightly**. All of these adverbs are formed by adding *ly* to an adjective.

From the lesson on helping verbs, do you remember that sometimes other words come between a verb and its helpers? These words are adverbs. **Not** is a common adverb which likes to sit between the verb and its helpers, but other adverbs will sit in that position as well. **Not** is always an adverb, and it always modifies the verb.

He <u>could</u> not <u>bear</u> any careless loitering.

Like an adjective, an adverb is diagrammed by placing it on a diagonal line underneath the word it modifies.

I <u>never</u> knew a better man.

He was <u>so</u> good-tempered.

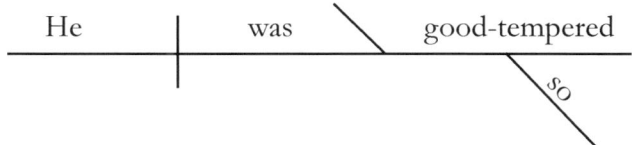

Adjectives and adverbs are often already on diagonal lines, so to modify those words, we add a diagonal line to the diagonal line.

She spoke <u>very</u> <u>slowly</u>.

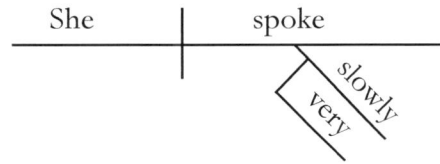

The Wind and the Moon

George MacDonald

Said the Wind to the Moon, "I will blow you out,
    You stare
    In the air
    Like a ghost in a chair,
Always looking what I am about—
I hate to be watched; I'll blow you out."

The Wind blew hard, and out went the Moon.
    So, deep
    On a heap
    Of clouds to sleep,
Down lay the Wind, and slumbered soon,
Muttering low, "I've done for that Moon."

He turned in his bed; she was there again!
    On high
    In the sky,
    With her one ghost eye,

The Moon shone white and alive and plain.
Said the Wind, "I will blow you out again."

The Wind blew hard, and the Moon grew dim.
      "With my sledge,
    And my wedge,
    I have knocked off her edge!
If only I blow right fierce and grim,
The creature will soon be dimmer than dim."

He blew and he blew, and she thinned to a thread.
      "One puff
    More's enough
    To blow her to snuff!
One good puff more where the last was bred,
And glimmer, glimmer, glum will go the thread."

He blew a great blast, and the thread was gone
    In the air
    Nowhere
    Was a moonbeam bare;
Far off and harmless the shy stars shone—
Sure and certain the Moon was gone!

The Wind he took to his revels once more;
    On down,
    In town,
    Like a merry-mad clown,
He leaped and hallooed with whistle and roar—
  "What's that?" The glimmering thread once more!

He flew in a rage—he danced and blew;
    But in vain
    Was the pain
    Of his bursting brain;
For still the broader the Moon-scrap grew,
The broader he swelled his big cheeks and blew.

Slowly she grew—till she filled the night,
    And shone
    On her throne
    In the sky alone,
A matchless, wonderful silvery light,
Radiant and lovely, the queen of the night.

Said the Wind: "What a marvel of power am I
    With my breath,
    Good faith!
    I blew her to death—
First blew her away right out of the sky—
Then blew her in; what strength have I!"

But the Moon she knew nothing about the affair;
>For high
>In the sky,
>With her one white eye,
Motionless, miles above the air,
She had never heard the great Wind blare.

Maku Mawu and Maku Fia

From *West African Folk-Tales* by William H. Barker

Once upon a time there were two men who were such great friends that they were almost always together. If one was seen the other was sure to be near. They had given one another special names, which were to be used only by themselves. One name, Maku Mawu, meant, "I will die God's death," and the other, Maku Fia, "I will die the King's death."

By and by, however, the other villagers heard these names and gradually every one got into the habit of calling the two friends by the nicknames in preference to the real ones. Finally, the King of the country heard of them and wished to see the men who had chosen such strange titles. He sent for them to Court, and they came together. He was much pleased with the one who had chosen the name of "Maku Fia," but he was annoyed at the other man's choice and sought a chance of punishing him.

When he had talked to them a little while, he invited both to a great feast which he was to give in three days' time. As they went away he gave a fine large yam to Maku Mawu and only a small round stone to his own favorite. The latter felt somewhat aggrieved at getting only a stone, while his friend got such a fine yam. Very soon he said, "Oh, dear! I do not think it is any use carrying this stone home. How I wish it were a yam! Then I could cook it for dinner." Maku Mawu being very generous—immediately replied, "Then change with me, for I am quite tired of carrying my great yam." They exchanged, and each went off to his own home. Maku Fia cut up his yam and cooked it. Maku Mawu broke his stone in half and found inside some beautiful ornaments which the King had hidden there. He thought that he would play a trick on the King, so told nobody what had been in the stone.

On the third day they dressed to go to the King's feast. Maku Mawu put on all the beautiful ornaments out of the stone. Maku Fia dressed himself just as usual.

When they reached the palace the King was amazed to see the wrong man wearing his ornaments, and determined to punish him more effectually next time. He asked Maku Fia what he had done with the stone, and the man told him he had exchanged it for his friend's yam.

At first the King could not think of any way to punish Maku Mawu, as, of course, the latter had not done anything wrong. He soon had an idea, however. He pretended to be very pleased with the poor man and presented him with a beautiful ring from his own finger. He then made him promise to come back in seven days and show the ring to the King again, to let the latter see that it was not lost. If by any chance he could not produce the ring—he would lose his head. This the King did, meaning to get hold of the ring in some way, and so get the young man killed.

Maku Mawu saw what the King's design was, so determined to hide the ring. He made a small hole in the wall of his room, put the ring in it, and carefully plastered over the place again. No one could see that the wall had been touched.

After two days the King sent for the wife of Maku Mawu and asked her to find the ring. He promised her a large sum of money for it not telling her, of course, what would happen to her husband if the ring were lost. The woman went home and searched diligently but found nothing. Next day she tried again with no better success. Then she asked her husband what he had done with it. He innocently told her it was in the wall. Next day, when he was absent, she searched so carefully that at last she found it.

Delighted, she ran off to the King's palace and gave the ring to him. She got the promised money and returned home, never dreaming that she had really sold her husband's life.

On the sixth day the King sent a message to Maku Mawu, telling him to prepare for the next day. The poor man bethought himself of the ring and went to look if it were still safe. To his despair the hole was empty. He asked his wife and his neighbours. All denied having seen it. He made up his mind that he must die.

In the meantime the King had laid the ring in one of the dishes in his palace and promptly forgot about it. When the seventh morning had arrived he sent messengers far and wide, to summon the people to come and see a man punished for disobeying the King's orders. Then he commanded his servants to set the palace in order, and to take the dishes out of his room and wash them.

The careless servants—never looking to see if the dishes were empty or not took them all to a pool near by. Among them was the dish containing the ring. Of course, when the dish was being washed, out fell the ring into the water—without being noticed by the servants.

The palace being all in readiness, the King went to fetch the ring. It was nowhere to be found and he was obliged to go to the Assembly without it.

When every one was ready the poor man, Maku Mawu, was called to come forward and show the ring. He walked boldly up to the King and knelt down before him, saying. "The ring is lost and I am prepared to die. Only grant me a few hours to put my house in order." At first the king was unwilling to grant even that small favor, but finally he said, "Very well, you may have four hours. Then you must return here and be beheaded before the people." The innocent man returned to his home and put everything in order. Then, feeling hungry, he thought, "I may as well have some food before I die. I will go and catch a fish in the pool."

He accordingly took his fish-net and bait, and started off to the very pool where the King's dishes had been washed. Very soon he caught a fine large fish. Cutting it open, to clean it, his delight may be imagined at finding the lost ring inside it.

At once he ran off to the palace crying: "I have found the ring! I have found the ring!" When the people heard him, they all shouted in joy: "He named himself rightly 'Maku Mawu,' for see—the death God has chosen for him, that only will he die." So the King had no excuse to harm him, and he went free.

Writing: Copia, Playing with Words

Take each of the following words from your model story and look them up in the thesaurus. Give two or three different ways to say each word.

foreign, adventures, deeds, abroad, witness

Exercise

Review memory work. Copy each sentence below. Double underline the predicate, and underline the subject. Label the part of speech of each word. Noun, N; Proper Noun, PN; Pronoun, PRO; Verb, V; Linking Verb, LV; Adjective, ADJ; Article, ART; Conjunction, CJ. Diagram each sentence.

I never knew a better man.

"They are not religious."

"I do not believe."

Commonplace Book

With your instructor's approval, add the poem below to your commonplace book, or choose your own poem.

> Said the Wind to the Moon, "I will blow you out,
>   You stare
>   In the air
>   Like a ghost in a chair,
> Always looking what I am about—
> I hate to be watched; I'll blow you out."
>
> The Wind blew hard, and out went the Moon.
>   So, deep
>   On a heap
>   Of clouds to sleep,
> Down lay the Wind, and slumbered soon,
> Muttering low, "I've done for that Moon."

Dictation

Exodus 15:11

Who is like You among the gods, O Lord?
Who is like You, majestic in holiness,
Awesome in praises, working wonders?

Young Mother by Mary Cassatt

Picture Study

1. Read the title and the name of the artist. Study the picture for several minutes, then put the picture away.

2. Describe the picture.

3. Look at the picture again. Do you notice any details that you missed before? What do you like or dislike about this painting? Does it remind you of anything?

33. Descriptive Writing

- Black Beauty, Chapter 37

Writing: Descriptive Writing

Remember that the purpose of descriptive writing is to describe a person, place, thing, or event so well that an image forms in the mind of the reader.

Your last six picture studies have been on paintings by Mary Cassatt. Today, choose one of her paintings, either one from this book or one from another source, and write a description of it. Imagine that you're describing the picture to someone who has never seen it before. Get creative if you wish. Write a description for a museum catalog, or as part of a police report describing stolen merchandise. Or get really creative. Imagine that the painting is a window to another dimension, and you've just been pulled in. Describe the environment in which you find yourself. Or, write a story about the picture, or about your experiences within it. Be as creative as you want. Just don't forget to describe the picture.

Ingratitude

By William Shakespeare

Blow, blow, thou winter wind,
Thou are not so unkind
  As man's ingratitude;
Thy tooth is not so keen
Because thou are not seen,
  Although thy breath be rude.

Freeze, freeze, thou bitter sky,
Thou dost not bite so nigh
  As benefits forgot;
Though thou the waters warp,
Thy sting is not so sharp
  As friend remembered not.

The Robber and the Old Man

From *West African Folk-Tales* by William H. Barker

In a big town lived a very rich gentleman. The fame of his wealth soon spread. A clever thief heard of it and determined to have some for himself.

He managed to hide himself in a dark corner of the gentleman's room—while the latter was counting his bags of money. As soon as the old gentleman left the room to fetch something, the thief caught up two of the bags and escaped.

The owner was astonished, on his return a few minutes later, to find two bags short. He could find no trace of the thief.

Next morning, however, he chanced to meet the robber just outside the house. The dishonest man looked so confused that the rich man at once suspected he was the thief. He could not, however, prove it, so took the case before the judge.

The thief was much alarmed when he heard this. He sought a man in the village and asked his advice. The wise man undertook to help him—if he would promise to pay him half the money when he got off. This the robber at once said he would do.

The old man then advised him to go home and dress in rags. He must ruffle his hair and beard and behave as if he were mad. If any one asked a question he must answer, "Moo."

The thief did so. To every question asked by the judge he said, "Moo, moo." The judge at last grew angry and dismissed the court. The thief went home in great glee.

Next day, the wise man came to him for his half of the stolen money. But he could get no answer but "Moo" from the thief, and at last, in despair, he had to go home without a penny. The ungrateful robber kept everything for himself. The wise man regretted very much that he had saved the thief from his just punishment but it was now too late.

Exercise

Review memory work. Copy each sentence below. Double underline the predicate, and underline the subject. Label the part of speech of each word. Noun, N; Proper Noun, PN; Pronoun, PRO; Verb, V; Linking Verb, LV; Adjective, ADJ; Article, ART; Conjunction, CJ. Diagram each sentence.

"Her mother is dangerously ill."

"She must go directly."

"It would be a rare treat."

Commonplace Book

With your instructor's approval, add the passage below to your commonplace book, or choose your own passage from a work of non-fiction. This can be from the Bible, a biography, or one of your history or science books.

> When my harness was taken off, I did not know what I should do first—whether to eat the grass, or roll over on my back, or lie down and rest, or have a gallop across the meadow out of sheer spirits at being free; and I did all by turns. Jerry seemed to be quite as happy as I was; he sat down by a bank under a shady tree and listened to the birds, then he sang himself, and read out of the little brown book he is so fond of.

34. Adverbs That Tell How and When

- Black Beauty, Chapters 38-39

Adverbs tell how, when, where, how often, and to what extent.

Just as there are different types of adjectives, there are also different types of adverbs. Adverbs tell **how, when, where, how often,** and **to what extent**. If you memorize this list, and understand what each one means, adverbs will be easy to find in sentences.

First, adverbs tell **how**. Adverbs that tell **how** tell us how something is done. These adverbs are the most descriptive of the adverbs. Adverbs which are formed by adding *ly* to adjectives are usually adverbs that tell **how**. Look at the following sentence from *Black Beauty*.

    Jerry thanked him <u>kindly</u>.

Jerry thanked who? **Him; him** is the direct object because it receives the action of the verb. He thanked him **how**? **Kindly; kindly** is the adverb that modifies **thanked**. It tells **how** he thanked him.

Adverbs that tell **how** do not have to end in *ly*. **Well** and **hard** are also adverbs which tell how. He worked hard; she did well.

Adverbs that tell **how** tell **how something was done**, so they modify the verb of the sentence.

Adverbs also tell **when**. Adverbs that tell **when** tell us when something is done. Words like **sometimes, never,** and **always** are adverbs that tell **when**.

    <u>Now</u> we know.

Some adverbs which modify the verb can move around the sentence without changing the meaning of the sentence. Consider these changes to the sentence above. The word order is different, but the meaning is the same.

    We <u>now</u> know.

    We know <u>now</u>.

Adverbs that tell **when** tell **when something was done**, so they modify the verb of the sentence.

Some other adverbs that tell when are: after, afterwards, already, before, ever, finally, later, now, soon, still, then, today, tomorrow, when, and yesterday.

This is not a complete list, but you should understand now how adverbs can tell **when**. Pick three of the words from the list above and make sentences with them. Tell what word your adverb that tells **when** modified.

The Ivy Green

By Charles Dickens

O, a dainty plant is the ivy green,
  That creepeth o'er ruins old!
Of right choice food are his meals, I ween,
  In his cell so lone and cold.
The walls must be crumbled, the stones decayed.
  To pleasure his dainty whim;
And the moldering dust that years have made
  Is a merry meal for him.
Creeping where no life is seen,
A rare old plant is the ivy green.

Fast he stealeth on, though he wears no wings,
  And a staunch old heart has he!
How closely he twineth, how tight he clings
  To his friend, the huge oak tree!
And slyly he traileth along the ground,
  And his leaves he gently waves,
And he joyously twines and hugs around
  The rich mould of dead men's graves.
Creeping where no life is seen,
A rare old plant is the ivy green.

Whole ages have fled, and their works decayed,
  And nations have scattered been;
But the stout old ivy shall never fade
  From its hale and hearty green.
The brave old plant in its lonely days
  Shall fatten upon the past;
For the stateliest building man can raise
  Is the ivy's food at last.
Creeping where no life is seen,
A rare old plant is the ivy green.

The Leopard and the Ram

From *West African Folk-Tales* by William H. Barker

A Ram once decided to make a clearing in the woods and build himself a house. A leopard who lived near also made up his mind to do the very same thing.

Unknown to each other they both chose the same site. Ram came one day and worked at the clearing. Leopard arrived after Ram had gone and was much surprised to find some of his work already done. However, he continued what Ram had begun. Each was daily surprised at the progress made in his absence, but concluded that the fairies had been helping him. He gave them thanks and continued with his task.

Thus the matter went on—the two working alternately at the building and never seeing one another. At last the house was finished to the satisfaction of both.

The two prepared to take up their abode in the new home. To their great astonishment they met. Each told his tale, and after some friendly discussion, they decided to live together.

Both Leopard and Ram had sons. These two young animals played together while their parents hunted. The leopard was very much surprised to find that every evening his friend Ram brought home just as much meat or venison from the hunt as he himself did. He did not dare, however, to ask the other how he obtained it.

One day, before setting out to hunt, Leopard requested his son to find out, if possible, from young Ram, how his father managed to kill the animals. Accordingly while they were at play, little Leopard inquired how Father Ram, having neither claws nor sharp teeth, succeeded in catching and killing the beasts. Ram refused to tell unless young Leopard would promise to show his father's way also. The latter agreed. Accordingly they took two large pieces of plantain stem and set out into the woods.

Young Leopard then took one piece and placed it in position. Then, going first to the right, then to the left—bowing and standing on his hind legs and peeping at the stem just as his father did—he took aim, sprang toward the stem and tore it.

Young Ram then took the other piece and placed it in position. Wasting no time he went backward a little way, took aim, then ran swiftly forward-pushing his head against the stem and tearing it to pieces. When they had finished they swept the place clean and went home.

In the evening the leopard obtained all the information about the hunt from his son. The latter warned him that he must always be careful when he saw the ram go backward. He kept this in mind, and from that day watched the ram very closely.

Some time afterward it rained, making the floor of the house very slippery. The leopard called the ram, as usual, to dine with him. As he was coming, the ram slipped backward on the wet floor. The leopard, seeing this, thought the other was about to kill him. Calling to his son to follow, he sprang with all his might over the wall of the house and fled to the woods. The ram called him back, but he did not listen. From that time leopards have made their abode in the woods while rams have remained at home.

Writing: Copia

Take the following sentence and play with it. Remember that the point is not necessarily to make the sentence better. The point is to play with the sentence and make it different. Make a new sentence with a change from each of the following categories.

One of the feats he told about was a leap he had made in a city called Rhodes.

1. Change the grammar.
   - Change the nouns from common to proper and vice versa.
   - Change the nouns from singular to plural and vice versa.
   - Change the sentence type.
   - Change the adjectives from articles to descriptive to possessive, etc.
   - Change a quotation from direct to indirect and vice versa.

2. Condense the sentence.
   - Remove details.
   - Remove modifiers.

3. Amplify the sentence.
   - Add details.
   - Add dialogue.
   - Add modifiers.

4. Use synonyms and antonyms.
   - Substitute synonyms.
   - Say the opposite thing using antonyms.

Exercise

Review memory work. Copy each sentence below. Double underline the predicate, and underline the subject. Label the part of speech of each word. Noun, N; Proper Noun, PN; Pronoun, PRO; Verb, V; Linking Verb, LV; Adjective, ADJ; Article, ART; Conjunction, CJ. Diagram each sentence.

Winter came early.

The high-wheeled gig ran easily.

Dinah's family lived there.

Commonplace Book

With your instructor's approval, add the passage below to your commonplace book, or choose your own passage from a work of fiction. This can be from either school reading or free reading.

> "You that have your own horses and cabs, or drive for good masters, have a chance of getting on and a chance of doing right; I haven't. We can't charge more than sixpence a mile after the first, within the four-mile radius. This very morning I had to go a clear six miles and only took three shillings."

Dictation

> "If the police have any business with the matter, it ought to be with the masters who charge us so much, or with the fares that are fixed so low. If a man has to pay eighteen shillings a day for the use of a cab and two horses, as many of us have to do in the season, and must make that up before we earn a penny for ourselves, I say 'tis more than hard work; nine shillings a day to get out of each horse before you begin to get your own living."

35. Adverbs That Tell Where and How Often

• Black Beauty, Chapter 40

Adverbs tell how, when, where, how often, and to what extent.

Today, we'll be discussing adverbs that tell **where** and **how often**.

Adverbs tell us **where** something is done. Words like **here**, **there**, and **outside** are all adverbs that tell **where**. Look at the following sentences from *Black Beauty*.

"His wife sent a boy this morning to say his father was in a high fever and could not get out, so I'm here instead."

There were bags and boxes enough to have brought in a good many twopences if they had been put outside.

The adverb **here** tells **where** the speaker is. The adverb **outside** tells **where** the bags and boxes should have been put.

Adverbs that tell **where** tell **where something was done**, so they modify the verb of the sentence.

Some other adverbs that tell where are: abroad, anywhere, downstairs, everywhere, here, in, inside, nowhere, out, somewhere, there, underground, and upstairs.

Pick three of the words from the list above and make sentences with them, and tell what word your adverb that tells **where** modified.

Adverbs also tell **how often** an event occurs. Words such as **daily, frequently,** and **occasionally** are adverbs that tell **how often**.

Ginger coughed frequently.

"I often feel like an old man."

Adverbs that tell **how often** tell **how often something was done**, so they modify the verb of the sentence.

Some other adverbs that tell how often are: constantly, generally, infrequently, often, normally, once, periodically, rarely, regularly, seldom, sometimes, twice, usually, weekly, and yearly.

Pick three of the words from the list above and make sentences with them, and tell what word your adverb that tells **how often** modified.

Adverbs that tell **where** and **how often** are diagrammed like other adverbs, on diagonal lines under the words they modify.

In this first sentence, notice that to diagram the contraction, we un-contract it. I like to label contractions with the abbreviation for the first part of speech, an apostrophe, then the abbreviation for the second part of speech, like this:

pro'hv v
"I'm here."

Ginger coughed frequently.

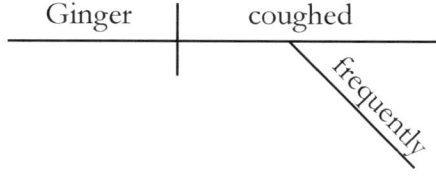

Tartary

By Walter De La Mare

If I were Lord of Tartary,
Myself and me alone,
My bed should be of ivory,
Of beaten gold my throne;
And in my court should peacocks flaunt,
And in my forests tigers haunt,
And in my pools great fishes slant
Their fins athwart the sun.
If I were Lord of Tartary,
Trumpeters every day
To all my meals should summon me,
And in my courtyards bray;
And in the evenings lamps should shine,
Yellow as honey, red as wine,
While harp, and flute, and mandoline,
Made music sweet and gay.
If I were Lord of Tartary,
I'd wear a robe of beads,

White, and gold, and green they'd be—
And small, and thick as seeds;
And ere should wane the morning-star,
I'd don my robe and scimitar,
And zebras seven should draw my car
Through Tartary's dark glades.
Lord of the fruits of Tartary,
Her rivers silver-pale!
Lord of the hills of Tartary,
Glen, thicket, wood, and dale!
Her flashing stars, her scented breeze,
Her trembling lakes, like foamless seas,
Her bird-delighting citron-trees
In every purple vale!

Why the Leopard Can Only Catch Prey on Its Left Side

From *West African Folk-Tales* by William H. Barker

At one time leopards did not know how to catch animals for food. Knowing that the cat was very skilful in this way, Leopard one day went to Cat and asked very politely if she would teach him the art. Cat readily consented.

The first thing Leopard had to learn was to hide himself among the bushes by the roadside, so that he would not be seen by any animal passing by. Next, he must learn how to move noiselessly through the woods. He must never allow the animal he chased to know that he was following it. The third great principle was how to use his left paws and side in springing upon his prey.

Having taught him these three things, Cat requested him to go and practice them well. When he had learnt them thoroughly he could return to her and she would give him more lessons in hunting.

Leopard obeyed. At first he was very successful and obtained all the food he wanted. One day, however, he was unable to catch anything at all.

Being very hungry, he bethought himself what he could have for dinner. Suddenly he remembered that the cat had quite a large family. He went straight to her home and found her absent.

Never thinking of her kindness to him—Leopard only remembered that he was hungry—he ate all her kittens. Puss, on discovering this dreadful fact, was so angry that she refused to have anything more to do with the great creature.

Consequently the leopard has never been able to learn how to catch animals that pass him on the right side.

Exercise

Review memory work. Copy each sentence below. Double underline the predicate, and underline the subject. Label the part of speech of each word. Noun, N; Proper Noun, PN; Pronoun, PRO; Verb, V; Linking Verb, LV; Adjective, ADJ; Article, ART; Conjunction, CJ. Diagram each sentence.

"Yesterday he was raving."

Now he took his handkerchief out.

They often lost a fare.

Writing: Commonplace Book

Add the passage below from your model story to your commonplace book.

One of the feats he told about was a leap he had made in a city called Rhodes. That leap was so great, he said, that no other man could leap anywhere near the distance. A great many persons in Rhodes had seen him do it and would prove that what he told was true.

Dictation

Use part of today's poem for dictation.

36. Amplified Narrative: The Leap at Rhodes

- Black Beauty, Chapters 41-42

Today, write "The Leap at Rhodes" as an amplified narrative. For this narration, amplify the narrative by adding both dialogue and descriptive detail. Remember, add details, not just adjectives!

In the story, a man describes a leap he made at Rhodes. Imagine the conversation that took place. You can describe the people and the setting where this conversation takes place. You can also have the man, in his dialogue, describe the scene at Rhodes.

The Flying Squirrel

Mary E. Burt

Of all the woodland creatures,
  The quaintest little sprite
Is the dainty flying squirrel
  In vest of shining white,
In coat of silver gray,
  And vest of shining white.

His furry Quaker jacket
  Is trimmed with stripe of black;
A furry plume to match it
  Is curling o'er his back;
New curved with every motion,
  His plume curls o'er his back.

No little new-born baby
  Has pinker feet than he;
Each tiny toe is cushioned
  With velvet cushions three;
Three wee, pink, velvet cushions
  Almost too small to see.

Who said, "The foot of baby
  Might tempt an angel's kiss"?
I know a score of school-boys
  Who put their lips to this,—
This wee foot of the squirrel,
  And left a loving kiss.

The tiny thief has hidden
  My candy and my plum;
Ah, there he comes unbidden
  To gently nip my thumb,—
Down in his home (my pocket)
  He gently nips my thumb.

How strange the food he covets,
  The restless, restless wight;—
Fred's old stuffed armadillo
  He found a tempting bite,
Fred's old stuffed armadillo,
  With ears a perfect fright.

The Lady Ruth's great bureau,
  Each foot a dragon's paw!
The midget ate the nails from
  His famous antique claw.
Oh, what a cruel beastie
  To hurt a dragon's claw!

To autographic copies
  Upon my choicest shelf,—
To every dainty volume
  The rogue has helped himself.
My books! Oh dear! No matter!
  The rogue has helped himself.

And yet, my little squirrel,
  Your taste is not so bad;
You've swallowed Caird completely
  And psychologic Ladd.
Rosmini you've digested,
  And Kant in rags you've clad.

Gnaw on, my elfish rodent!
  Lay all the sages low!
My pretty lace and ribbons,
  They're yours for weal or woe!
My pocket-book's in tatters
  Because you like it so.

Editing

• Did you meet the goal of this writing exercise?

• Look at your word choice. Is there a good mixture of nouns and pronouns? Is the antecedent of each pronoun clear?

37. Adverbs That Tell to What Extent

- Black Beauty, Chapter 43

Adverbs tell how, when, where, how often, and to what extent.

The final kind of adverbs tell **to what extent**. While the other kinds of adverbs only modify verbs, adverbs that tell **to what extent** can modify verbs, adjectives, and other adverbs. They tell us to what degree something was done. He had **just** finished. She had **barely** started.

When adverbs that tell **to what extent** modify adjectives and other adverbs, they strengthen or weaken the other modifiers. Time passed **so** slowly. They ran **very** fast.

Look at the following sentences from *Black Beauty*.

> He had <u>scarcely</u> begun when a gentleman held up his umbrella.

> It was a <u>very</u> rare thing for any one to notice the horse that had been working for him.

Some other adverbs that tell to what extent are: almost, barely, entirely, extremely, not, quite, so, rather, terribly, too, and very.

Pick three of the words from the list above and make sentences with them, and tell what word your adverb that tells **to what extent** modified.

Christmas Carol

by Sara Teasdale

The kings they came from out the south,
All dressed in ermine fine,
They bore Him gold and chrysoprase,
And gifts of precious wine.

The shepherds came from out the north,
Their coats were brown and old,
They brought Him little new-born lambs—
They had not any gold.

The wise-men came from out the east,
And they were wrapped in white;
The star that led them all the way
Did glorify the night.

The angels came from heaven high,
And they were clad with wings;
And lo, they brought a joyful song
The host of heaven sings.

The kings they knocked upon the door,
The wise-men entered in,
The shepherds followed after them
To hear the song begin.

And Mary held the little child
And sat upon the ground;
She looked up, she looked down,
She looked all around.

The angels sang thro' all the night
Until the rising sun,
But little Jesus fell asleep
Before the song was done.

Writing: Oral Narration

Read your new model story below, and then give your instructor an oral narration of it.

This is a story about a group of young people who find a humble bee's nest, what we call a bumble bee now. There are two parts to the story. The first part is the narrative portion. It tells about the events—the people who found the nest, what they did, what they said. The second part is the scientific discovery portion. It tells about the observations made about the life cycle of the bumble bee.

The Humble Bee's Nest

From *Wild Life in Woods and Fields* by Arabella B. Buckley

Last March, when the days began to be warm, we saw a big Humble Bee, or Bumble Bee, as the little ones call it, buzzing along across the field.

"Look out, Peter," said Peggy; "that is a mother humble bee, who has been asleep all the winter. She must be making a nest." So Peter followed her. She flew to a bank, and went in among some tufts of grass. Peter put a large stick there and we went to see her every day.

We used to find her dragging in little pieces of moss. But we did not look in, for fear she should go away. After a fortnight Paul said we might look, and, hidden in the grass, we found a small round patch of moss lined with bees-wax. It was like a tiny saucer turned upside down. We lifted it up and found under it a few round flat pockets, some as big as a halfpenny, some not larger than a farthing. (1) They were made of brown, sticky wax, and when we opened one we found inside seven tiny eggs, as small as poppy seeds, and some little brown balls. The balls, Paul said, were made of honey, and of the yellow dust from flowers. In another pocket we found grubs which had already been hatched from eggs. These were feeding on the brown balls near them.

The mother bee was very uneasy while we were looking at her nest. She sat down quite near. We could see how big and stout she was. She was so handsome. Her brown body was covered with soft yellow hairs, with stripes of black hairs between. Her wings were broad, and shone so brightly in the sun. She did not sting us. Paul says that humble bees are very gentle. But she was afraid we would hurt the grubs, which were going to grow up into working bees. We put the cover back and waited two months. Then it was June. We were afraid the horses might tread on the nest when the hay was cut. So we went to look at it.

(2) Oh! How big it was now. There was a large round moss roof. It was lined with wax, and was so strong that we had to cut it with a knife. The only way for the bees to get into it was by a long tunnel just under the ground. (3) Under the roof were a number of dirty yellow silk cocoons. In these were the grubs, growing into humble bees. The cocoons were stuck together with wax. Some of them were open, for the young bees had come out. These had honey in them.

(4) There were a great many humble bees going in and out. These had all come from eggs laid by the mother bee in two months. They were very busy bringing in honey and bee-bread for the grubs to eat. But Paul says they do not store honey, like our hive-bees. For when the cold damp weather comes, they all die, except a few mothers. These creep into holes in the trees or into a warm haystack, and sleep till the spring comes again.

About Christmas time we went to look at the nest. The roof was broken, and the cells all crushed. There was not one humble bee to be found.

Exercise

Review memory work. Copy each sentence below. Double underline the predicate, and underline the subject. Label the part of speech of each word. Noun, N; Proper Noun, PN; Pronoun, PRO; Verb, V; Linking Verb, LV; Adjective, ADJ; Article, ART; Conjunction, CJ. Diagram each sentence.

Jerry and I had not eaten many mouthfuls.

Presently she approached Jerry.

Had she been Polly's mistress?

Commonplace Book

With your instructor's approval, add the passage below to your commonplace book, or choose your own passage from a work of fiction. This can be from either school reading or free reading.

"No, sir, no; I can't do that, thank you, I have only just money enough to get back with. Please tell me the way."

"Look you here, missis," said Jerry, "I've got a wife and dear children at home, and I know a father's feelings; now get you into that cab, and I'll take you there for nothing. I'd be ashamed of myself to let a woman and a sick child run a risk like that."

Dictation

And they soon were gone, for when they understood Jerry's dodge, they got out, calling him all sorts of bad names and blustering about his number and getting a summons. After this little stoppage, we were soon on our way to the hospital, going as much as possible through by-streets. Jerry rung the great bell and helped the young woman out.

"Thank you a thousand times," she said. "I could never have got here alone."

38. Writing an Outline

- Black Beauty, Chapters 44-45

An outline is a special way to write down details. You can write an outline of a story to list the main details, or you can write an outline of something you want to write to help you remember all the points you want to include.

In this lesson, we're going to outline a portion of "The Dragon-Fly and His Companions." Then, you'll outline part of "The Humble Bee's Nest," your new model story from the last lesson. From now on, you'll be outlining each new model story.

Like a summary, a one-level outline includes only the main content from a narrative. For this lesson, we're going to focus only on the changes that the dragon-fly goes through. First, read the story below.

The Dragon-Fly and His Companions

From *By Pond and River* by Arabella B. Buckley

If you go often in April to a pond where dragon-flies are, you may perhaps see one begin its life in the air. This is how it happens.

(1) Under the water a large insect crawls up the stem of a plant. He has a body as big as a dragon-fly and has six legs. But he has a curious dull look in his face, and where his wings should be there are only two short stumps.

He crawls very slowly up the stem, till he comes out of the water into the air. Then a strange thing happens. (2) The skin of his back cracks, and out creeps a real dragon-fly.

(3) First his head, then his body with its six legs and four soft, crumpled wings, and lastly his tail. He cannot fly yet. (4) He stands by his old empty skin, and slowly stretches out his wings to the sun. In a few hours they are long and strong and hard. (5) Then he is ready to fly over the pond and feed.

This is how the dragon-fly comes up to the air. You will not find him so easily under the water, but we will try next week with our net. We have seen so much at the top of the pond today that we have not had time to dredge in the mud below.

Outlines have a very specific form. For the first level, which is also the only level in a one-level outline, we number each main point with a capital Roman numeral as follows.

In the story, the main changes for the dragon-fly are numbered 1-5. These are our main points.

I. A six-legged insect crawls up the stem of a plant.

II. The skin of his back cracks.

III. The dragon-fly creeps out, body, legs, wings, then tail.

IV. He stretches his wings to dry in the sun.

V. After a few hours, he is ready to fly.

Now you can write an outline detailing the life cycle of the humble bee from the last lesson. See the instructions on the next page.

The Father's Vineyard

Anonymous

As round their dying father's bed
His sons attend, the peasant said:
"Children, deep hid from prying eyes,
A treasure in my vineyard lies;
When you have laid me in the grave,
Dig, search-and your reward you'll have."

"Father," cries one, "but where's the spot?"
He sighs! He sinks! He answers not.

The tedious burial service over,
Home go his sons, and straight explore
Each corner of the vineyard round,
Dig up, beat, break, and sift the ground;
Yet though to search so well inclined,
Nor gold, nor treasure could they find;
But when the autumn next drew near,
A double vintage crowned the year.

"Now," quoth the peasant's wisest son,
"Our father's legacy is known,
In yon rich purple grapes 'tis seen,
Which, but for digging, never had been.
Then let us all reflect with pleasure.
That labor is the source of treasure."

Writing: Outline

Your new model story from the last lesson, "The Humble Bee's Nest," tells about the life cycle of the humble bee. Each stage is numbered, 1-4, within the story. Write an outline about this transformation. Make sure you write about each stage in your own words.

Exercise

Review memory work. Copy each sentence below. Double underline the predicate, and underline the subject. Label the part of speech of each word. Noun, N; Proper Noun, PN; Pronoun, PRO; Verb, V; Linking Verb, LV; Adjective, ADJ; Article, ART; Conjunction, CJ. Diagram each sentence.

The wind had been very changeable.

Sometimes driver and horse must wait.

"Can't I do something?" [Hint: **something** is a pronoun.]

Commonplace Book

With your instructor's approval, add the poem below to your commonplace book, or choose your own poem.

As round their dying father's bed
His sons attend, the peasant said:
"Children, deep hid from prying eyes,
A treasure in my vineyard lies;
When you have laid me in the grave,
Dig, search-and your reward you'll have."

"Father," cries one, "but where's the spot?"
He sighs! He sinks! He answers not.

Dictation

2 Peter 3:9

The Lord is not slow about His promise, as some count slowness, but is patient toward you, not wishing for any to perish but for all to come to repentance.

Women on a Cafe Terrace in the Evening by Claude Monet

Picture Study

1. Read the title and the name of the artist. Study the picture for several minutes, then put the picture away.

2. Describe the picture.

3. Look at the picture again. Do you notice any details that you missed before? What do you like or dislike about this painting? Does it remind you of anything?

39. Literary Analysis

- Black Beauty, Chapter 46

Writing: Literary Analysis

Today you have another literary analysis assignment. Now that you've had some practice, this should be a written assignment, though it can be helpful to discuss your ideas before writing.

With your instructor's approval, choose *Black Beauty*, or one of the other books you're currently reading, and answer the following questions. If you've already used *Black Beauty* twice for literary analysis, choose one of your other books.

What is the book about? Give a brief summary, just a few sentences. Do any of the characters change in the story? What caused them to change?

The Song in Camp

By Bayard Taylor

  "Give us a song!" the soldiers cried,
    The outer trenches guarding,
When the heated guns of the camps allied
    Grew weary of bombarding.

The dark Redan, in silent scoff,
    Lay, grim and threatening, under;
And the tawny mound of the Malakoff
    No longer belched its thunder.

There was a pause. A guardsman said,
    "We storm the forts tomorrow;
Sing while we may, another day
    Will bring enough of sorrow."

They lay along the battery's side,
  Below the smoking cannon:
Brave hearts, from Severn and from Clyde,
  And from the banks of Shannon.

They sang of love, and not of fame;
  Forgot was Britain's glory:
Each heart recalled a different name,
  But all sang "Annie Laurie."

Voice after voice caught up the song,
  Until its tender passion
Rose like an anthem, rich and strong,—
  Their battle-eve confession.

Dear girl, her name he dared not speak,
  But, as the song grew louder,
Something upon the soldier's cheek
  Washed off the stains of powder.

Beyond the darkening ocean burned
  The bloody sunset's embers,
While the Crimean valleys learned
  How English love remembers.

And once again a fire of hell
  Rained on the Russian quarters,
With scream of shot, and burst of shell,
  And bellowing of the mortars!

And Irish Nora's eyes are dim
  For a singer, dumb and gory;
And English Mary mourns for him
  Who sang of "Annie Laurie."

Sleep, soldiers! Still in honored rest
  Your truth and valour wearing:
The bravest are the tenderest,—
  The loving are the daring.

To Lose an Elephant for the Sake of a Wren Is a Very Foolish Thing To Do

From *West African Folk-Tales* by William H. Barker

In the olden times there stood in the King's town a very great tree. This tree was so huge that it began to overshadow the neighboring fields. The King decided to have it cut down. He caused his servants to proclaim throughout the country that any one who succeeded in cutting down the tree with a wooden axe should have an elephant in payment.

People thought it would be impossible to cut down such a great tree with an axe of wood. Spider, however, decided to try by cunning to gain the elephant. He accordingly presented himself before the King and expressed his readiness to get rid of the tree.

A servant was sent with him to keep watch and to see that he only used the wooden axe given him. Spider, however, had taken care to have another, made of steel, hidden in his bag.

He now began to fell the tree. In a very few minutes, he said to the servant, "See, yonder is a fine antelope. If you are quick, you will be able to hit it with a stone. Run!" The lad did as he was bid, and ran a long way—but could see no sign of the antelope. In his absence, Spider seized the sharp axe and hastened to cut as much of the tree as he could, carefully hiding the axe in his bag before the servant's return.

This trick he repeated several times, till finally the tree was cut down. Spider went to the King to get the elephant, and took the servant to prove that he had used only the wooden axe. He got his promised reward, and started for home in great glee. On the way, however, he began to think over the matter. "Shall I take this animal home?" thought he. "That would be foolish, for then I would be obliged to share it with my family. No! I will hide it in the forest, and eat it at my leisure. In that way I can have the whole of it for myself. Now what can I take home for the children's dinner?"

Thereupon he looked around and a little distance away saw a tiny wren sitting on a tree. "Exactly what I want," he said to himself. "That will be quite sufficient for them. I will tie my elephant to this tree while I catch the bird."

This he did, but when he tried to seize the latter, it flew off. He chased it for some time, without success. "Well! Well!" said he. "My family will just have to go without dinner. I will now go back and get my elephant." He returned to the spot where he had left the animal, but to his dismay the latter had escaped. Spider was obliged to go home empty-handed, and he, as well as his family, went dinnerless that day.

Exercise

Review memory work. Copy each sentence below. Double underline the predicate, and underline the subject. Label the part of speech of each word. Noun, N; Proper Noun, PN; Pronoun, PRO; Verb, V; Linking Verb, LV; Adjective, ADJ; Article, ART; Conjunction, CJ. Diagram each sentence.

Dolly was crying and kissed me too.

"Is it a heavy load?"

He was raising the whip again.

Commonplace Book

With your instructor's approval, add the passage below to your commonplace book, or choose your own passage from a work of non-fiction. This can be from the Bible, a biography, or one of your history or science books.

The lady had walked along the footpath, and now came across into the road. She stroked and patted my neck, as I had not been patted for many a long day.
"You see, he was quite willing when you gave him the chance; I am sure he is a fine-tempered creature, and I dare say has known better days. You won't put that rein on again, will you?" for he was just going to hitch it up on the old plan.

Editing

• Did you meet the goal of this writing exercise?

• Look at your word choice. Is there a good mixture of nouns and pronouns? Is the antecedent of each pronoun clear?

40. The Paragraph

• Black Beauty, Chapters 47-48

Definition: A paragraph is a group of sentences on a single topic.

A paragraph must have a **topic**. The **topic** is what the paragraph is about. I like turtles. Every sentence should be related to this topic and to one another. Otherwise, the paragraph becomes confusing.

Did you catch the turtle sentence in the above paragraph? That was not on topic. Did it confuse you? Usually, an off-topic sentence won't be that obvious. What if I'd started talking about punctuation instead? Then, I'd still be talking about writing. But my topic was the paragraph and how it needs a topic, so it would have been just as out of place as the mention of turtles, which are very cool.

A topic can be **broad** or **narrow**. A **broad topic** is one which is very general. For example, a paragraph about the solar system would not be very detailed. You could mention what's in the solar system, but not much else. You could not tell about the atmosphere, terrain, temperature, and moons of all the planets, plus other features of the solar system, all in one paragraph. You'd need more paragraphs to do that.

Perhaps you'd decide to have a paragraph for a single planet instead. Now, your topic is much more **narrow**. You could make the topic even more narrow by writing about only the special features of the planet. Do you want to make the topic more narrow still? Then you could write about what you can find in a corner of your own backyard.

After you read today's story, "The Ungrateful Man," look back at each paragraph and decide what the topic of the paragraph is.

The Sandpiper

By Celia Thaxter

Across the lonely beach we flit,
  One little sandpiper and I,
And fast I gather, bit by bit,
  The scattered driftwood, bleached and dry.
The wild waves reach their hands for it,

The wild wind raves, the tide runs high,
As up and down the beach we flit,
  One little sandpiper and I.

Above our heads the sullen clouds
  Scud, black and swift, across the sky;
Like silent ghosts in misty shrouds
  Stand out the white lighthouses high.
Almost as far as eye can reach
  I see the close-reefed vessels fly,
As fast we flit along the beach,
  One little sandpiper and I.

I watch him as he skims along,
  Uttering his sweet and mournful cry;
He starts not at my fitful song,
  Nor flash of fluttering drapery.
He has no thought of any wrong,
  He scans me with a fearless eye;
Stanch friends are we, well tried and strong,
  The little sandpiper and I.

Comrade, where wilt thou be to-night,
  When the loosed storm breaks furiously?
My driftwood fire will burn so bright!
  To what warm shelter canst thou fly?
I do not fear for thee, though wroth
  The tempest rushes through the sky;
For are we not God's children both,
  Thou, little sandpiper, and I?

The Ungrateful Man

From *West African Folk-Tales* by William H. Barker

    A hunter, who was terribly poor, was one day walking through the forest in search of food. Coming to a deep hole, he found there a leopard, a serpent, a rat, and a man. These had all fallen into the trap and were unable to get out again. Seeing the hunter, they begged him to help them out of the hole.
    At first he did not wish to release any but the man. The leopard, he said, had often stolen his cattle and eaten them. The serpent very frequently bit men and caused their death. The rat did no good to any one. He saw no use in setting them free.
    However, these animals pleaded so hard for life that at last he helped them out of the pit. Each, in turn, promised to reward him for his kindness—except the man. He, saying he was very poor, was taken home by the kind-hearted hunter and allowed to stay with him.
    A short time after, Serpent came to the hunter and gave him a very powerful antidote for snake-poison. "Keep it carefully," said Serpent. "You will find it very useful one day. When you are using it, be sure to ask for the blood of a traitor to mix with it." The hunter, having thanked Serpent very much, took great care of the

powder and always carried it about with him.

The leopard also showed his gratitude by killing animals for the hunter and supplying him with food for many weeks.

Then, one day, the rat came to him and gave him a large bundle. "These," said he, "are some native cloths, gold dust, and ivory. They will make you rich." The hunter thanked the rat very heartily and took the bundle into his cottage.

After this the hunter was able to live in great comfort. He built himself a fine new house and supplied it with everything needful. The man whom he had taken out of the pit still lived with him.

This man, however, was of a very envious disposition. He was not at all pleased at his host's good fortune, and only waited an opportunity to do him some harm. He very soon had a chance.

A proclamation was sounded throughout the country to say that some robbers had broken into the King's palace and stolen his jewels and many other valuables. The ungrateful man instantly hurried to the King and asked what the reward would be if he pointed out the thief. The King promised to give him half of the things which had been stolen. The wicked fellow thereupon falsely accused his host of the theft, although he knew quite well that he was innocent.

The honest hunter was immediately thrown into prison. He was then brought into Court and requested to show how he had become so rich. He told them, faithfully, the source of his income, but no one believed him. He was condemned to die the following day at noon.

Next morning, while preparations were being made for his execution, word was brought to the prison that the King's eldest son had been bitten by a serpent and was dying. Any one who could cure him was begged to come and do so.

The hunter immediately thought of the powder which his serpent friend had given him, and asked to be allowed to use it. At first they were unwilling to let him try, but finally he received permission. The King asked him if there were anything he needed for it and he replied, "A traitor's blood to mix it with." His Majesty immediately pointed out the wicked fellow who had accused the hunter and said: "There stands the worst traitor for he gave up the kind host who had saved his life." The man was at once beheaded and the powder was mixed as the serpent had commanded. As soon as it was applied to the prince's wound the young man was cured. In great delight, the King loaded the hunter with honors and sent him happily home.

Writing: Copia

Take the following sentence and play with it. Remember that the point is not necessarily to make the sentence better. The point is to play with the sentence and make it different. Make a new sentence with a change from each of the following categories.

The mother bee was very uneasy while we were looking at her nest.

1. Change the grammar.
    - Change the nouns from common to proper and vice versa.
    - Change the nouns from singular to plural and vice versa.
    - Change the sentence type.
    - Change the adjectives from articles to descriptive to possessive, etc.
    - Change a quotation from direct to indirect and vice versa.

2. Condense the sentence.
   - Remove details.
   - Remove modifiers.

3. Amplify the sentence.
   - Add details.
   - Add dialogue.
   - Add modifiers.

4. Use synonyms and antonyms.
   - Substitute synonyms.
   - Say the opposite thing using antonyms.

Exercise

Review memory work. Copy each sentence below. Double underline the predicate, and underline the subject. Label the part of speech of each word. Noun, N; Proper Noun, PN; Pronoun, PRO; Verb, V; Linking Verb, LV; Adjective, ADJ; Article, ART; Conjunction, CJ. Diagram each sentence.

He had black eyes and a hooked nose.

"Can your horse do it?"

"Do take a second cab."

Commonplace Book

With your instructor's approval, add the passage below to your commonplace book, or choose your own passage from a work of fiction. This can be from either school reading or free reading.

> My gentle friend had to obey, and box after box was dragged up and lodged on the top of the cab or settled by the side of the driver. At last all was ready, and with his usual jerk at the rein and slash of the whip, he drove out of the station.

Dictation

> The boy was proud of his charge, and undertook it in all seriousness. There was not a day when he did not pay me a visit, sometimes picking me out from among the other horses and giving me a bit of carrot or something good, or sometimes standing by me while I ate my oats. He always came with kind words and caresses, and of course I grew very fond of him. He called me Old Crony, as I used to come to him in the field and follow him about.

41. 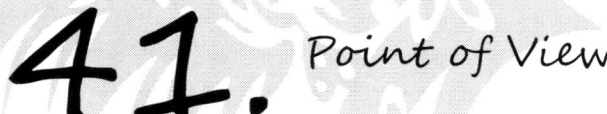 Point of View

- Black Beauty, Chapter 49

Definition: Point of view is the perspective from which a writer tells a story or presents information.

You've learned, and hopefully memorized, the personal pronouns. We use first person pronouns when we speak of ourselves.

The first person pronouns are: I, me, my, mine, we, us, our, ours.

We use second person pronouns to refer to the person to whom we are speaking. Singular and plural pronouns are the same in the second person.

The second person pronouns are: you, your, yours.

We use third person pronouns to refer to people and things which we are discussing.

The third person pronouns are: he, him, his, she, her, hers, it, its, they, them, their, theirs.

Writers must choose from which point of view to write. We describe different points of view based on which pronouns we would use. In your model story, "The Humble Bee's Nest," the author writes from the point of view of one of the group of children making observations. She is no mere spectator, observing the actions of the children. Instead, she is one of them. We know this because of the use of the first person pronouns.

<u>We</u> used to find her dragging in little pieces of moss. But <u>we</u> did not look in, for fear she should go away. After a fortnight Paul said <u>we</u> might look, and, hidden in the grass, <u>we</u> found a small round patch of moss lined with bees-wax.

She could have chosen to write the story from the third person point of view.

<u>They</u> used to find her dragging in little pieces of moss. But <u>they</u> did not look in, for fear she should go away. After a fortnight Paul said <u>they</u> might look, and, hidden in the grass, <u>they</u> found a small round patch of moss lined with bees-wax.

The first person point of view makes the story feel more personal, and the third person makes the story feel more objective. Both points of view have merit, but they serve different purposes.

There was another first person point of view the author could have chosen: that of the bee!

> "Look out, Peter," said one child; "that is a mother humble bee, who has been asleep all the winter. She must be making a nest." So the one called Peter followed me. I flew to a bank, and went in among some tufts of grass. Peter put a large stick there and they came to see me every day.
>
> They used to find me dragging in little pieces of moss. But they did not look in, for fear I would go away. After a fortnight Paul said they might look, and, hidden in the grass, they found my small round patch of moss lined with bees-wax.

Each change in point of view gives the story a slightly different feel. It will also change some details. The children and the bee, for instance, experienced different events within the same narrative. Just as the bee had experiences that the children did not observe, the children had experiences about which the bee would know nothing.

Read today's story. From what point of view is the story written? Look back at each paragraph and decide what the topic of the paragraph is.

The Three Bells of Glasgow

By John Greenleaf Whittier

Beneath the low-hung night cloud
  That raked her splintering mast
The good ship settled slowly,
  The cruel leak gained fast.

Over the awful ocean
  Her signal guns pealed out.
Dear God! Was that Thy answer
  From the horror round about?

A voice came down the wild wind,
  "Ho! Ship ahoy!" its cry:
    "Our stout *Three Bells* of Glasgow
  Shall stand till daylight by!"

Hour after hour crept slowly,
  Yet on the heaving swells
Tossed up and down the ship-lights,
  The lights of the *Three Bells*!

And ship to ship made signals,
  Man answered back to man,
While oft, to cheer and hearten,
  The *Three Bells* nearer ran:

And the captain from her taffrail
  Sent down his hopeful cry.
    "Take heart! Hold on!" he shouted,
"The *Three Bells* shall stand by!"

All night across the waters
  The tossing lights shone clear;
All night from reeling taffrail
  The *Three Bells* sent her cheer.

And when the dreary watches
  Of storm and darkness passed,
Just as the wreck lurched under,
  All souls were saved at last.

Sail on, *Three Bells*, forever,
  In grateful memory sail!
Ring on, *Three Bells* of rescue,
  Above the wave and gale!

Type of the Love eternal,
  Repeat the Master's cry,
As tossing through our darkness
  The lights of God draw nigh!

Why Tigers Never Attack Men Unless they Are Provoked

From *West African Folk-Tales* by William H. Barker

    A man, hunting one day in the forest, met a tiger. At first each was afraid of the other; but after some talking they became quite friendly. They agreed to live together for a little time. First the man would live with the tiger in his forest home for two weeks. Then the tiger would come and live in the man's home.

    The tiger behaved so well to the man during his visit that the man felt he had never been so well treated in all his life. Then came the time for the tiger to return home with the man. As they were going the tiger was somewhat afraid. He asked the man if he really thought he would be safe. "What if your friends do not like my face and kill me?" he asked. "You need fear nothing," said his host; "no one will touch you while I am there." The tiger therefore came to the man's house and stayed with him three weeks. He had brought his male cub with him, and the young tiger became very friendly with the man's son.

    Some months later the man's father died. When Tiger heard of his friend's great loss, he and his cub set out at once to see and condole with him. They brought a large sum of money to help the man.

    As Tiger was going home again two of the man's friends lay in hiding for him and shot him. Fortunately he was not killed, but he was very much grieved lest these men had shot him at his friend's wish. He determined to find out if the man had known anything at all about the shot.

    Accordingly he went to the place in the forest where he had first met his friend. There he lay down as if he were dead, after telling his cub to watch and see what would happen.

By and by the man came along. When he saw the tiger lying, as he thought, dead, he was terribly troubled. He began to cry and mourn for his friend, and sat there all night long with Tiger's cub, to watch that no harm should befall the body.

When morning came and Tiger was quite assured that his friend had had nothing at all to do with the shot, he was very glad. He got up, then, to the man's great astonishment, and explained why he had pretended to be dead.

"Go home," said Tiger, "and remember me always. In future for your sake I will never touch a man unless he first meddles with me."

Exercise

Review memory work. Copy each sentence below. Double underline the predicate, and underline the subject. Label the part of speech of each word. Noun, N; Proper Noun, PN; Pronoun, PRO; Verb, V; Linking Verb, LV; Adjective, ADJ; Article, ART; Conjunction, CJ. Diagram each sentence.

The boy could hardly control his delight.

The groom cleaned and dressed me.

"Check his mouth."

Writing: Commonplace Book

Add the passage below from your model story to your commonplace book.

The mother bee was very uneasy while we were looking at her nest. She sat down quite near. We could see how big and stout she was. She was so handsome. Her brown body was covered with soft yellow hairs, with stripes of black hairs between. Her wings were broad, and shone so brightly in the sun. She did not sting us. Paul says that humble bees are very gentle. But she was afraid we would hurt the grubs, which were going to grow up into working bees.

Dictation

Use part of today's poem for dictation.

42. Point of View Narration: The Humble Bee's Nest

- Ozma of Oz, Chapter 1

Today, write your narration on "The Humble Bee's Nest." Choose a point of view from which to write your narration. Are you the bee, one of the children, or an objective observer of the events? Use your outline to keep the life cycle of the bumble bee in the proper order. Pay attention to your pronouns as you write!

Lady Clare

By Alfred Tennyson

It was the time when lilies blow
  And clouds are highest up in air;
Lord Ronald brought a lily-white doe
  To give his cousin, Lady Clare.

I trow they did not part in scorn:
  Lovers long-betroth'd were they:
They too will wed the morrow morn:
  God's blessing on the day!

  "He does not love me for my birth,
    Nor for my lands so broad and fair;
He loves me for my own true worth,
    And that is well," said Lady Clare.

In there came old Alice the nurse;
  Said: "Who was this that went from thee?"
  "It was my cousin," said Lady Clare;
"Tomorrow he weds with me."

  "O God be thank'd!" said Alice the nurse,
"That all comes round so just and fair:
Lord Ronald is heir of all your lands,
  And you are not the Lady Clare."

"Are ye out of your mind, my nurse, my nurse,"
   Said Lady Clare, "that ye speak so wild?"
"As God's above," said Alice the nurse,
"I speak the truth: you are my child.

"The old Earl's daughter died at my breast;
   I speak the truth, as I live by bread!
I buried her like my own sweet child,
   And put my child in her stead."

"Falsely, falsely have ye done,
   O mother," she said, "if this be true,
To keep the best man under the sun
   So many years from his due."

"Nay now, my child," said Alice the nurse,
   "But keep the secret for your life,
And all you have will be Lord Ronald's
   When you are man and wife."

"If I'm a beggar born," she said,
   "I will speak out, for I dare not lie.
Pull off, pull off the brooch of gold,
   And fling the diamond necklace by."

"Nay now, my child," said Alice the nurse,
   "But keep the secret all ye can."
She said: "Not so: but I will know
   If there be any faith in man."

"Nay now, what faith?" said Alice the nurse,
   "The man will cleave unto his right,"
"And he shall have it," the lady replied,
   "Tho' I should die to-night."

"Yet give one kiss to your mother dear!
   Alas! My child, I sinn'd for thee."
"O mother, mother, mother," she said,
"So strange it seems to me.

"Yet here's a kiss for my mother dear,
   My mother dear, if this be so,
And lay your hand upon my head,
   And bless me, mother, ere I go."

She clad herself in a russet gown,
   She was no longer Lady Clare:
She went by dale, and she went by down,
   With a single rose in her hair.

The lily-white doe Lord Ronald had brought
  Leapt up from where she lay,
Dropt her head in the maiden's hand,
  And follow'd her all the way.

Down stept Lord Ronald from his tower:
  "O Lady Clare, you shame your worth!
Why come you drest like a village maid,
  That are the flower of the earth?"

"If I come drest like a village maid,
  I am but as my fortunes are:
I am a beggar born," she said,
  "And not the Lady Clare."

"Play me no tricks," said Lord Ronald,
"For I am yours in word and in deed.
Play me no tricks," said Lord Ronald,
  "Your riddle is hard to read."

O and proudly stood she up!
  Her heart within her did not fail:
She look'd into Lord Ronald's eyes,
  And told him all her nurse's tale.

He laugh'd a laugh of merry scorn:
  He turn'd and kiss'd her where she stood:
  "If you are not the heiress born?
And I," said he, "the next in blood—

"If you are not the heiress born,
  And I," said he, "the lawful heir,
We two will wed tomorrow morn,
  And you shall still be Lady Clare."

Editing

• Did you meet the goal of this writing exercise?

• Look at your word choice. Is there a good mixture of nouns and pronouns? Is the antecedent of each pronoun clear?

• Look at your paragraphs. Are all the sentences related? Does each paragraph focus on a single topic?

43. Phrases and Clauses

• Ozma of Oz, Chapter 2

> Definition: A phrase is a group of related words which does not include a subject-predicate pair.

> Definition: A clause is a group of words which contains a subject-predicate pair.

You probably noticed that the two definitions above are almost identical. The defining characteristic of both phrases and clauses is whether or not they have a subject-predicate pair. A subject-predicate pair is simply a verb with its subject.

Phrases can be short or long. Some phrases have specific names based on the main word or usage of the phrase. A noun phrase consists of a noun and its modifiers. A verb phrase consists of the helping verbs, main verb, and any ending the main verb needs. Look at the following sentences from *Ozma of Oz*. The first has a noun phrase and the second has a verb phrase, both of which are underlined.

> <u>The little girl</u> was quite an experienced traveler.

> He <u>had been working</u> hard on his Kansas farm.

Unlike a phrase, a clause must have a subject and a predicate. Look at these clauses. The predicate is double underlined, and the subject is underlined, in each clause.

> when the <u>wind</u> <u><u>began</u></u> blowing

> while <u>he</u> <u><u>traveled</u></u> far away to Australia

> <u>Dorothy</u> <u><u>had</u></u> almost <u><u>fallen</u></u> asleep

Notice that some clauses express a complete thought. That makes them sentences. But some of the clauses do not express a complete thought. Why do you think that is? Which of the clauses above could be a sentence? What's different about it?

The last clause could be a complete sentence on its own. The other clauses begin with certain words that tell us that there is more to the thought. When a clause begins with a word like **when, while,** or **before**, it leaves us wondering, "And then what?" We need the rest of the information to have a complete thought expressed. Look at those clauses again, this time with that beginning word removed.

The <u>wind</u> <u>began</u> blowing.

He <u>traveled</u> far away to Australia.

When I took away that beginning word, I also took away the expectation for the rest of the story. Now these clauses can stand alone as complete sentences.

John Barleycorn

By Robert Burns

There were three kings into the East,
  Three kings both great and high;
And they ha'e sworn a solemn oath
  John Barleycorn should die.

They took a plow and plowed him down,
  Put clods upon his head;
And they ha'e sworn a solemn oath
  John Barleycorn was dead.

But the cheerful spring came kindly on,
  And showers began to fall;
John Barleycorn got up again,
  And sore surprised them all.

The sultry suns of summer came,
  And he grew thick and strong;
His head well arm'd wi' pointed spears,
  That no one should him wrong.

The sober autumn entered mild,
  And he grew wan and pale;
His bending joints and drooping head
  Showed he began to fail.

His color sickened more and more,
  He faded into age;
And then his enemies began
  To show their deadly rage.

They took a weapon long and sharp,
  And cut him by the knee,
Then tied him fast upon a cart,
  Like a rogue for forgery.

They laid him down upon his back,
  And cudgelled him full sore;
They hung him up before the storm,
  And turn'd him o'er and o'er.

They filled up then a darksome pit
  With water to the brim,
And heaved in poor John Barleycorn,
  To let him sink or swim.

They laid him out upon the floor,
  To work him further woe;
And still as signs of life appeared,
  They tossed him to and fro.

They wasted o'er a scorching flame
  The marrow of his bones;
But a miller used him worst of all—
  He crushed him 'tween two stones.

And they have taken his very heart's blood,
  And drunk it round and round;
And still the more and more they drank,
  Their joy did more abound.

Writing: Oral Narration

Read your new model story below, and then give your instructor an oral narration of it.

A Frog's Life

From By Pond and River by Arabella Buckley

Croak, croak, croak, we hear the frogs in the month of March. They make a great deal of noise in this month, because they are just awake from their winter's sleep, at the bottom of the pond.

(1) The mother frogs are laying their tiny dark eggs in the water. Each egg is not bigger than a grain of sand. But it has a coat of jelly, and this jelly swells and swells in the water, till it is as large as a pea, with a little black dot in the middle. The jelly lumps all cling together. You may see them in almost any pond, driven up to the side by the wind.

Soon the dark speck lengthens. A head grows at one end, and a tail at the other. The head has a mouth but no eyes as yet. The tail has a fin all round it, and the tadpole wriggles about in its slimy bed.

In about a week it wriggles out of the jelly, and hangs by its mouth to the weeds (2). Then two curious tufts grow on each side of its head. It uses these tufts to breathe, by taking air out of the water. You can see them if you dip a glass into the pond and catch a few tadpoles.

By this time the tadpole has let go of the weed and is swimming about. A sharp beak has grown on to his mouth. He uses it to tear off pieces of weed to eat. Now he grows eyes, nose-holes and flat ears. His tufts shrivel up, and a cover grows over them (3), so that you cannot see them. They are now like the gills of a fish. He gulps water in at his mouth and sends it out through the cover. As it passes, the gills take the air out of it, and so the tadpole breathes.

Soon two small lumps appear on each side of his body, behind the cover, just where it joins his tail. They grow larger and larger, till at last two hind legs come out.

These legs grow very long and strong, and he uses them to swim. Two front legs are growing as well, but you cannot see them, because they are under the cover. In a few days these peep out (4), but they are short and stumpy.

Our tadpole has now four legs and a tail. He has four toes on the front feet, and five toes on the hind feet, with a skin between the toes. So his hind legs are web-footed, and this helps him to swim.

He comes to the top of the water much more often than before, and sends a bubble of air out of his mouth. What do you think has happened? The gills under his cover have closed up, and a small air-bag has grown inside him. So he comes up to breathe in the air through his mouth, instead of taking it out of the water through his gills.

Now he likes to jump on a piece of weed and sit in the shade. He does not want his tail any longer, for he can swim quite well with his legs. So his tail is slowly sucked in to feed his body.

There you have your little frog (5). If you look through the web of his foot at the sun, you will see that he has red blood now. But it is not warm blood like ours. He is always cold and clammy because his blood moves slowly.

He has a number of teeth in the top of his mouth, and such a curious tongue. It is tied down to the front of his mouth, and the tip, which is very sticky, lies back down his throat. He does not eat weed now. He feeds on insects and slugs. He catches them by throwing out his tongue and drawing it back very quickly.

He lives chiefly on land during the summer if he is not eaten by ducks, rats, or snakes. Then he drops to the bottom of the pond to sleep in the mud all winter.

Exercise

Review memory work. Identify each group of words below as either a phrase or a clause. If it is a clause, double underline the predicate and underline the subject.

in his little sleeping-berth

the wind blew hard and joggled the water of the ocean

she sat down in a corner of the coop

Copy each sentence below. Double underline the predicate, and underline the subject. Label the part of speech of each word. Noun, N; Proper Noun, PN; Pronoun, PRO; Verb, V; Linking Verb, LV; Adjective, ADJ; Article, ART; Conjunction, CJ. Diagram each sentence.

"Have you been here, too?"

"Do I speak quite properly?"

"You may have my egg."

Commonplace Book

With your instructor's approval, add the passage below to your commonplace book, or choose your own passage from a work of fiction. This can be from either school reading or free reading.

> "Very well, Billina. My name is Dorothy Gale—just Dorothy to my friends and Miss Gale to strangers. You may call me Dorothy, if you like. We're getting very near the shore. Do you suppose it is too deep for me to wade the rest of the way?"

Dictation

> "Why, as for that," answered the yellow hen thoughtfully, "I've clucked and cackled all my life, and never spoken a word before this morning, that I can remember. But when you asked a question, a minute ago, it seemed the most natural thing in the world to answer you. So I spoke, and I seem to keep on speaking, just as you and other human beings do. Strange, isn't it?"

44. Parts of Speech: Conjunctions

- Ozma of Oz, Chapter 3

> Definition: A conjunction is a word that joins words and groups of words together. There are three types of conjunctions: coordinating, subordinating, and correlative.

Conjunctions join words and groups of words together. The most common conjunctions are the seven coordinating conjunctions.

> The seven coordinating conjunctions are For, And, Nor, But, Or, Yet, and So. (FANBOYS)

The seven coordinating conjunctions can be easily remembered with the mnemonic FANBOYS: For, And, Nor, But, Or, Yet, and So.

And and **or** are two of the most common of the FANBOYS. They often join words to create compound subjects, predicates, and other compound structures. Look at these sentences from *Ozma of Oz*.

> "Of course we'll have to stay in the cabin," she said to Uncle Henry <u>and</u> the other passengers.

> "I do not know what I have said <u>or</u> done that leads you to insult me!"

In the first sentence, **and** joins the proper noun **Uncle Henry** to the noun phrase **the other passengers**. In the second sentence, **or** joins the verbs **have said** and **done**.

The other FANBOYS are frequently seen joining clauses.

> "When the coop blew away from the ship I clung fast to this corner, with claws and beak, <u>for</u> I knew if I fell into the water I'd surely be drowned."

> He had sailed his ship through them in safety, <u>but</u> he knew that his passengers would be in danger if they tried to stay on deck.

> But there were no houses to be seen, <u>nor</u> any sign of people who might inhabit this unknown land.

> As soon as she got there the wind struck her so fiercely that it almost tore away

the skirts of her dress, <u>yet</u> Dorothy felt a sort of joyous excitement in defying the storm.

Uncle Henry thought she would be good company and help cheer him up, <u>so</u> he decided to take her along.

The FANBOYS do *not* keep clauses from expressing a complete thought! Any of the above sentences could become two sentences quite easily by separating the two clauses with a period.

As soon as she got there the wind struck her so fiercely that it almost tore away the skirts of her dress**. Yet** Dorothy felt a sort of joyous excitement in defying the storm.

Remember that the part of speech of a word is determined by the job it is performing in a sentence. **Soccer** is a noun when we're talking about the sport. **Soccer** is an adjective when we're describing the type of ball. In the same way, **so** is a conjunction when it's joining words or groups of words together. **So** is an adverb when it shows to what extent.

A Life on the Ocean Wave

By Epes Sargent

A life on the ocean wave,
  A home on the rolling deep,
Where the scattered waters rave,
  And the winds their revels keep!
Like an eagle caged, I pine
  On this dull, unchanging shore:
Oh! Give me the flashing brine,
  The spray and the tempest's roar!

Once more on the deck I stand
  Of my own swift-gliding craft:
Set sail! Farewell to the land!
  The gale follows fair abaft.
We shoot through the sparkling foam
  Like an ocean-bird set free;—
Like the ocean-bird, our home
  We'll find far out on the sea.

The land is no longer in view,
  The clouds have begun to frown;
But with a stout vessel and crew,
  We'll say, Let the storm come down!
And the song of our hearts shall be,
  While the winds and the waters rave,
A home on the rolling sea!
  A life on the ocean wave!

The Omanhene Who Liked Riddles

From *West African Folk-Tales* by William H. Barker

The Omanhene is the chief of a village. A certain Omanhene had three sons, who were very anxious to see the world. They went to their father and asked permission to travel. This permission he readily gave.

It was the turn of the eldest to go first. He was provided with a servant and with all he could possibly require for the journey.

After traveling for some time he came to a town where lived an Omanhene who loved riddles. Being a stranger the traveler was, according to custom, brought by the people before the chief.

The latter explained to him that they had certain laws in their village. One law was that every stranger must best the Omanhene in answering riddles or he would be beheaded. He must be prepared to begin the contest the following morning.

Next day he came to the Assembly Place, and found the Omanhene there with all his attendants. The Omanhene asked many riddles. As the young man was unable to answer any of them, he was judged to have failed and was beheaded.

After some time the second son of the Omanhene started on his travels. By a strange chance he arrived at the same town where his brother had died. He also was asked many riddles, and failed to answer them. Accordingly he too was put to death.

By and by the third brother announced his intention of traveling. His mother did all in her power to persuade him to stay at home. It was quite in vain.

She was sure that if he also reached the town where his brothers had died, the same thing would happen to him. Rather than allow this, she thought she would prefer him to die on the way.

She prepared for him a food called cankey—which she filled with poison. Having packed it away in his bag, he set off. Very soon he began to feel hungry. Knowing, however, that his mother had not wished him to leave home, and therefore might have put some poison in the food, he thought he would test it before eating it himself. Seeing a vulture near by, he threw it half the cake.

The bird ate the cankey, and immediately fell dead by the roadside. Three panthers came along and began to eat the vulture. They also fell dead.

The young man cut off some of the flesh of the panthers and roasted it. He then packed it carefully away in his bundle.

A little farther on he was attacked by seven highway robbers. They wanted to kill him at once. He told them that he had some good roast meat in his bundle and invited them to eat with him first. They agreed and divided up the food into eight parts.

While they were eating the young man carefully hid his portion. Soon all the seven robbers fell ill and died. The young man then went on his way.

At last he reached the town where his brothers had died. Like them, he was summoned to the Assembly Place to answer the riddles of the Omanhene. For two days the contest proved equal. At the end of that time, the young man said, "I have only one riddle left. If you are able to answer that, you may put me to death." He then gave this riddle to the Omanhene:

Half kills one—
One kills three—
Three kills seven.

The ruler failed to answer it that evening, so it was postponed till the next day.

During the night the Omanhene disguised himself and went to the house where the stranger was staying. There he found the young man asleep in the hall.

Imagining that the man before him was the stranger's servant, and never dreaming-that it was the stranger himself, he roused the sleeper and promised him a large reward if he would give him the solution to the riddle.

The young man replied that he would tell the answer if the Omanhene would bring him the costume which he always wore at the Assembly.

The ruler was only too pleased to go and fetch it for him. When the young man had the garments quite safely, he explained the riddle fully to the crafty Omanhene. He said that as they were leaving home, the mother of his master made him cankey. In order to find out if the cankey were good, they gave half to a vulture. The latter died. Three panthers which tasted the vulture also died. A little of the panther's roasted flesh killed seven robbers.

The Omanhene was delighted to have found out the answer. He warned the supposed servant not to tell his master what had happened.

In the morning all the villagers assembled together again. The Omanhene proudly gave the answer to the riddle as if he himself had found it out. But the young man asked him to produce his ceremonial dress, which he ought to be wearing in Assembly. This, of course, he was unable to do, as the young man had hidden it carefully away.

The stranger then told what had happened in the night, and how the ruler had got the answer to the riddle by cheating.

The Assembly declared that the Omanhene had failed to find out the riddle and must die. Accordingly he was beheaded—and the young man was appointed Omanhene in his place.

Writing: Outline

Your new model story from the last lesson, "A Frog's Life," tells of the transformation of a tadpole into a frog. Each stage is numbered, 1-5, within the story. Read the story today and write an outline about this transformation. Make sure you write about each stage in your own words.

Exercise

Review memory work. Identify each group of words below as either a phrase or a clause. If it is a clause, double underline the predicate and underline the subject.

while she was speaking

when Billina suddenly cried

upon all fours

Copy each sentence below. Double underline the predicate, and underline the subject. Label the part of speech of each word. Noun, N; Proper Noun, PN; Pronoun, PRO; Verb, V; Linking Verb, LV; Adjective, ADJ; Article, ART; Conjunction, CJ. Diagram each sentence.

"Can I tell metal?"

"Run!"

The Wheeler gave a sharp, wild cry and chased her.

Commonplace Book

With your instructor's approval, add the poem below to your commonplace book, or choose your own poem.

> A life on the ocean wave,
>   A home on the rolling deep,
> Where the scattered waters rave,
>   And the winds their revels keep!
> Like an eagle caged, I pine
>   On this dull, unchanging shore:
> Oh! Give me the flashing brine,
>   The spray and the tempest's roar!

Dictation

Lamentations 3:22-23

The Lord's lovingkindnesses indeed never cease,
For His compassions never fail.
They are new every morning;
Great is Your faithfulness.

A Woman Seated Beside a Vase of Flowers by Edgar Degas

Picture Study

1. Read the title and the name of the artist. Study the picture for several minutes, then put the picture away.

2. Describe the picture.

3. Look at the picture again. Do you notice any details that you missed before? What do you like or dislike about this painting? Does it remind you of anything?

45. Descriptive Writing

- Ozma of Oz, Chapter 4

Writing: Descriptive Writing

In the last chapter of *Ozma of Oz*, Dorothy and Billina encounter the Wheelers. Read that passage below, paying close attention to the details that make a vivid picture in your mind, and then write a narration of it. Add details if you wish. Remember, the point of this exercise is to write as descriptively as possible, not just to narrate the passage exactly.

Ozma of Oz

Dorothy turned quickly around, and saw coming out of a path that led from between the trees the most peculiar person her eyes had ever beheld.

It had the form of a man, except that it walked, or rather rolled, upon all fours, and its legs were the same length as its arms, giving them the appearance of the four legs of a beast. Yet it was no beast that Dorothy had discovered, for the person was clothed most gorgeously in embroidered garments of many colors, and wore a straw hat perched jauntily upon the side of its head. But it differed from human beings in this respect, that instead of hands and feet there grew at the end of its arms and legs round wheels, and by means of these wheels it rolled very swiftly over the level ground. Afterward Dorothy found that these odd wheels were of the same hard substance that our finger-nails and toe-nails are composed of, and she also learned that creatures of this strange race were born in this queer fashion. But when our little girl first caught sight of the first individual of a race that was destined to cause her a lot of trouble, she had an idea that the brilliantly-clothed personage was on roller-skates, which were attached to his hands as well as to his feet.

"Run!" screamed the yellow hen, fluttering away in great fright. "It's a Wheeler!"

The Silver Penny

By Walter De La Mare

'Sailorman, I'll give to you'
My bright silver penny,'
If out to sea you'll sail me'

And my dear sister Jenny.'
'Get in, young sir, I'll sail ye'
And your dear sister Jenny,'
But pay she shall her golden locks'
Instead of your penny.'
They sail away, they sail away,'
O fierce the winds blew!'
The foam flew in clouds,'
And dark the night grew!
And all the wild sea-water'
Climbed steep into the boat;'
Back to the shore again'
Sail they will not.
Drowned is the sailorman,'
Drowned is sweet Jenny,'
And drowned in the deep sea'
A bright silver penny.

The Hunt of Lion and Jackal

From *South-African Folk-Tales* by James A. Honey

Lion and Jackal, it is said, were one day lying in wait for Eland. Lion shot (with a bow) and missed, but Jackal hit and sang out, "Hah! Hah!"

Lion said, "No, you did not shoot anything. It was I who hit."

Jackal answered, "Yea, my father, thou hast hit."

Then they went home in order to return when the eland was dead, and cut it up. Jackal, however, turned back, unknown to Lion, hit his nose so that the blood ran on the spoor of the eland, and followed their track thus, in order to cheat Lion. When he had gone some distance, he returned by another way to the dead eland, and creeping into its carcass, cut out all the fat.

Meanwhile Lion followed the blood-stained spoor of Jackal, thinking that it was eland blood, and only when he had gone some distance did he find out that he had been deceived. He then returned on Jackal's spoor, and reached the dead eland, where, finding Jackal in its carcass, he seized him by his tail and drew him out with a swing.

Lion upbraided Jackal with these words: "Why do you cheat me?"

Jackal answered: "No, my father, I do not cheat you; you may know it, I think. I prepared this fat for you, father."

Lion said: "Then take the fat and carry it to your mother" (the lioness); and he gave him the lungs to take to his own wife and children.

When Jackal arrived, he did not give the fat to Lion's wife, but to his own wife and children; he gave, however, the lungs to Lion's wife, and he pelted Lion's little children with the lungs, saying:

"You children of the big-pawed one!

You big-pawed ones!"

He said to Lioness, "I go to help my father" (the lion); but he went far away with his wife and children.

Exercise

Review memory work. Identify each group of words below as either a phrase or a clause. If it is a clause, double underline the predicate and underline the subject.

  that crack in the rock

  so I think

  don't be frightened

Copy each sentence below. Double underline the predicate, and underline the subject. Label the part of speech of each word. Noun, N; Proper Noun, PN; Pronoun, PRO; Verb, V; Linking Verb, LV; Adjective, ADJ; Article, ART; Conjunction, CJ. Diagram each sentence.

  "We could unlock it."

  "Try it and see."

  "Don't be frightened."

Commonplace Book

With your instructor's approval, add the passage below to your commonplace book, or choose your own passage from a work of non-fiction. This can be from the Bible, a biography, or one of your history or science books.

> Dorothy stepped inside the little room to get a back view of the copper man, and in this way discovered a printed card that hung between his shoulders, it being suspended from a small copper peg at the back of his neck. She unfastened this card and returned to the path, where the light was better, and sat herself down upon a slab of rock to read the printing.

46. Parts of Speech: Interjections; Nouns of Direct Address

- Ozma of Oz, Chapter 5

Definition: An interjection is a word or group of words that shows sudden or strong feeling.

There is no set list of words that can be used as interjections. Although the word **why** usually begins a question, it is also often used as an interjection at the beginning of a sentence, as are **yes**, **no**, and **indeed**. **Hello** is an interjection when it is used as a greeting or to express surprise. Look at the examples below from *Ozma of Oz*.

"<u>Dear me</u>!" said Dorothy, in a frightened tone. "What can the matter be?"

"<u>Oh</u>, I'm sure it was ripe," declared Dorothy.

"<u>No</u>, that can't be," answered the little girl.

Interjections can be one word or more than one word, and they are set apart from the rest of the sentence by commas or exclamation marks.

Definition: A noun of direct address is the name or other reference directly to the person being addressed.

We use nouns of direct address to refer directly to the person or persons to whom we are speaking. This can be the person's name, but it can also be another word or phrase, such as **my friends**, **boys and girls**, or a title like **sir**. The second sentence has both an interjection and a noun of direct address.

"So I don't believe there can be any automobiles, <u>Billina</u>."

"<u>Now</u>, <u>Tiktok</u>," said Dorothy, "the first thing to be done is to find a way for us to escape from these rocks."

What do interjections and nouns of direct address have in common that made me put them both in the same lesson?

Neither has any grammatical relationship to the rest of the sentence! In other words, we can take them out of a sentence without changing the meaning of the sentence at all.

Interjections and nouns of direct address are also both diagrammed and punctuated exactly the same way. Both should be set apart from the rest of the sentence, usually with commas, but both are sometimes set apart with exclamation marks as well.

Because nouns of direct address have no grammatical relationship to the rest of the sentence, they will never be the subject of the sentence.

That last sentence is important. Nouns of direct address will never be the subject of the sentence. They also will not fill any other role, but they often look like the subject, especially when the real subject is the understood you.

"Dorothy, run!"

In the sentence above, **Dorothy** is the noun of direct address. The subject is the understood you. Does this sound like nonsense? Try removing the direct address from the sentence.

"Run!"

The sentence still makes sense. It still expresses a complete thought. The subject is an essential part of the sentence, even when it's the unstated, understood you. The direct address is never an essential part of the sentence, not in a grammatical sense.

Interjections and nouns of direct address are both diagrammed on a floating line above the rest of the diagram.

"Now, Tiktok, we should escape."

```
 Now      Tiktok
_____   _____


  we  |  should escape
_____
      |
```

Brookland Road

By Rudyard Kipling

I was very well pleased with what I knowed,
I reckoned myself no fool—
Till I met with a maid on the Brookland Road
That turned me back to school.

Low down—low down!
Where the liddle green lanterns shine—
Oh! maids, I've done with 'ee all but one,
And she can never be mine!
'Twas right in the middest of a hot June night,
With thunder duntin' round,
And I seed her face by the fairy light
That beats from off the ground.

She only smiled and she never spoke,
She smiled and went away;
But when she'd gone my heart was broke,
And my wits was clean astray.

Oh! Stop your ringing and let me be—
Let be, O Brookland bells!
You'll ring Old Goodman * out of the sea,
Before I wed one else!

Old Goodman's farm is rank sea sand,
And was this thousand year;
But it shall turn to rich plough land
Before I change my dear!

Oh! Fairfield Church is water-bound
From Autumn to the Spring;
But it shall turn to high hill ground
Before my bells do ring!

Oh! leave me walk on the Brookland Road,
In the thunder and warm rain—
Oh! leave me look where my love goed
And p'raps I'll see her again!
Low down—low down!
Where the liddle green lanterns shine—
Oh! maids, I've done with 'ee all but one,
And she can never be mine!

Farmer Mybrow and the Fairies

From *West African Folk-Tales* by William H. Barker

Farmer Mybrow was one day looking about for a suitable piece of land to convert into a field. He wished to grow corn and yams. He discovered a fine spot, close to a great forest—which latter was the home of some fairies. He set to work at once to prepare the field.

Having sharpened his great knife, he began to cut down the bushes. No sooner had he touched one than he heard a voice say, "Who is there, cutting down the bushes?" Mybrow was too much astonished to answer. The question was repeated. This time the farmer realized that it must be one of the fairies, and so replied, "I am Mybrow, come to prepare a field." Fortunately for him the fairies were in great good humour. He heard one say, "Let us all help Farmer Mybrow to cut down the bushes." The rest agreed. To Mybrow's great delight, the bushes were all rapidly cut down with very little trouble on his part. He returned home, exceedingly well pleased with his day's work, having resolved to keep the field a secret even from his wife.

Early in January, when it was time to burn the dry bush, he set off to his field, one afternoon, with the means of making a fire. Hoping to have the fairies' assistance once more, he intentionally struck the trunk of a tree as he passed. Immediately came the question, "Who is there, striking the stumps?" He promptly replied, "I am Mybrow, come to burn down the bush." Accordingly, the dried bushes were all burned down, and the field left clear in less time that it takes to tell it.

Next day the same thing happened. Mybrow came to chop up the stumps for firewood and clear the field for digging. In a very short time his faggots and firewood were piled ready, while the field was bare.

So it went on. The field was divided into two parts—one for maize and one for yams. In all the preparations—digging, sowing, planting—the fairies gave great assistance. Still, the farmer had managed to keep the whereabouts of his field a secret from his wife and neighbors.

The soil having been so carefully prepared, the crops promised exceedingly well. Mybrow visited them from time to time, and congratulated himself on the splendid harvest he would have.

One day, while maize and yams were still in their green and milky state, Mybrow's wife came to him. She wished to know where his field lay, that she might go and fetch some of the firewood from it. At first he refused to tell her. Being very persistent, however, she finally succeeded in obtaining the information—but on one condition. She must not answer any question that should be asked her. This she readily promised, and set off for the field.

When she arrived there she was utterly amazed at the wealth of the corn and yam. She had never seen such magnificent crops. The maize looked most tempting—being still in the milky state—so she plucked an ear. While doing so she heard a voice say, "Who is there, breaking the corn?" "Who dares ask me such a question?" she replied angrily—quite forgetting her husband's command. Going to the field of yams she plucked one of them also. "Who is there, picking the yams?" came the question again. "It is I, Mybrow's wife. This is my husband's field and I have a right to pick." Out came the fairies. "Let us all help Mybrow's wife to pluck her corn and yams," said they. Before the frightened woman could say a word, the fairies had all set to work with a will, and the corn and yams lay useless on the ground. Being all green and unripe, the harvest was now utterly spoiled. The farmer's wife wept bitterly, but to no purpose. She returned slowly home, not knowing what to say to her husband about such a terrible catastrophe. She decided to keep silence about the matter.

Accordingly, next day the poor man set off gleefully to his field to see how his fine crops were going on. His anger and dismay may be imagined when he saw his field a complete ruin. All his work and foresight had been absolutely ruined through his wife's forgetfulness of her promise.

Writing: Copia

Take the following sentence and play with it. Remember that the point is not necessarily to make the sentence better. The point is to play with the sentence and make it different. Make a new sentence with a change from each of the following categories.

> He comes to the top of the water much more often than before, and sends a bubble of air out of his mouth.

1. Change the grammar.
    - Change the nouns from common to proper and vice versa.
    - Change the nouns from singular to plural and vice versa.
    - Change the sentence type.
    - Change the adjectives from articles to descriptive to possessive, etc.
    - Change a quotation from direct to indirect and vice versa.

2. Condense the sentence.
   - Remove details.
   - Remove modifiers.
   - Remove phrases or clauses.

3. Amplify the sentence.
   - Add details.
   - Add dialogue.
   - Add modifiers.
   - Add phrases or clauses.

4. Use synonyms and antonyms.
   - Substitute synonyms.
   - Say the opposite thing using antonyms.

5. Point of view.
   - Change the point of view.

Exercise

Review memory work. Identify each group of words below as either a phrase or a clause. If it is a clause, double underline the predicate and underline the subject.

until suddenly he became motionless

that low bow to you

she ran around the copper man

Copy each sentence below. Double underline the predicate, and underline the subject. Label the part of speech of each word. Noun, N; Proper Noun, PN; Pronoun, PRO; Verb, V; Linking Verb, LV; Adjective, ADJ; Article, ART; Conjunction, CJ; Interjection, INJ. Diagram each sentence.

"Haven't you a club?"

"He must have been a great loss." [Hint: **loss** has an article modifier. What part of speech does that make it?]

"The best thinker was a scarecrow."

Commonplace Book

With your instructor's approval, add the passage below to your commonplace book, or choose your own passage from a work of fiction. This can be from either school reading or free reading.

> He gave a sort of gurgle and stopped short, waving his hands frantically until suddenly he became motionless, with one arm in the air and the other held stiffly before him with all the copper fingers of the hand spread out like a fan.

Dictation

At once she wound up Tiktok's voice, taking care to give the key as many turns as it would go around. She found this quite a task, as you may imagine if you have ever tried to wind a clock, but the machine man's first words were to assure Dorothy that he would now run for at least twenty-four hours.

"You did not wind me much, at first," he calmly said, "and I told you that long story about King Evoldo; so it is no wonder that I ran down."

47. Appositives

• Ozma of Oz, Chapter 6

Definition: An appositive is a noun, noun phrase, or series of nouns placed next to another noun to identify or rename it.

An appositive is very like a predicate nominative in that it identifies or renames another noun. However, it doesn't need a linking verb. Instead, it sits beside the noun it identifies or renames. In fact, **apposition** means to be side by side. In *Ozma of Oz*, so far you've met:

Dorothy, the little **girl** from Kansas,
Billina the yellow **hen**, and
Tiktok the machine **man**.

The appositive is the noun which renames the noun it sits beside. Each appositive above also has modifiers. The appositive of **Dorothy** is **girl**. The appositive of **Billina** is **hen**, and the appositive of **Tiktok** is **man**.

Look at the following sentence from *Ozma of Oz*. It has two appositives. Can you find them?

"I was purchased from Smith & Tinker, my manufacturers, by a cruel King of Ev, Evoldo, who used to beat all his servants until they died."

In the above sentence, **Smith & Tinker** has the appositive **manufacturers**. **King of Ev** has the appositive **Evoldo**.

The appositive identifies or renames the noun it sits beside. We diagram an appositive by placing it beside the noun it identifies or renames and placing it in parentheses **( )**. When the appositive has a modifier, it goes on a diagonal line under the appositive, just as always.

Tiktok the machine man spoke.

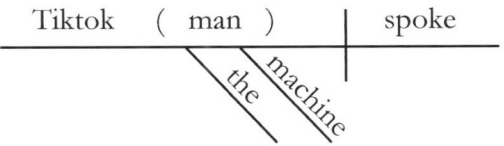

Evoldo, the cruel king, purchased Tiktok.

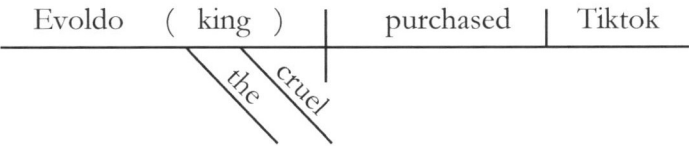

The Grinding-Stone That Ground Flour by Itself

From *West African Folk-Tales* by William H. Barker

There had been another great famine throughout the land. The villagers looked thin and pale for lack of food. Only one family appeared healthy and well. This was the household of Anansi's cousin.

Anansi was unable to understand this, and felt sure his cousin was getting food in some way. The greedy fellow determined to find out the secret.

What had happened was this: Spider's cousin, while hunting one morning, had discovered a wonderful stone. The stone lay on the grass in the forest and ground flour of its own accord. Near by ran a stream of honey. Kofi was delighted. He sat down and had a good meal. Not being a greedy man, he took away with him only enough for his family's needs.

Each morning he returned to the stone and got sufficient food for that day. In this manner he and his family kept well and plump, while the surrounding villagers were starved and miserable-looking.

Anansi gave him no peace till he promised to show him the stone. This he was most unwilling to do—knowing his cousin's wicked ways. He felt sure that when Anansi saw the stone he would not be content to take only what he needed. However, Anansi troubled him so much with questions that at last he promised. He told Anansi that they would start next morning, as soon as the women set about their work. Anansi was too impatient to wait. In the middle of the night he bade his children get up and make a noise with the pots as if they were the women at work. Spider at once ran and wakened his cousin, saying, "Quick! It is time to start." His cousin, however, saw he had been tricked, and went back to bed again, saying he would not start till the women were sweeping. No sooner was he asleep again than Spider made his children take brooms and begin to sweep very noisily. He roused Kofi once more, saying, "It is time we had started." Once more his cousin refused to set off—saying it was only another trick of Spider's. He again returned to bed and to sleep. This time Spider slipped into his cousin's room and cut a hole in the bottom of his bag, which he then filled with ashes. After that he went off and left Kofi in peace.

When morning came the cousin awoke. Seeing no sign of Spider he very gladly set off alone to the forest, thinking he had got rid of the tiresome fellow. He was no sooner seated by the stone, however, than Anansi appeared, having followed him by the trail of ashes.

"Aha!" cried he. "Here is plenty of food for all. No more need to starve."
"Hush," said his cousin. "You must not shout here. The place is too wonderful. Sit down quietly and eat."

They had a good meal, and Kofi prepared to return home with enough for his family. "No, no!" cried Anansi. "I am going to take the stone." In vain did his friend try to overcome his greed. Anansi insisted on putting the stone on his head, and setting out for the village.

"Spider, Spider, put me down, said the stone.
The pig came and drank and went away,
The antelope came and fed and went away:
Spider, Spider, put me down."

Spider, however, refused to listen. He carried the stone from village to village selling flour, until his bag was full of money. He then set out for home.

Having reached his hut and feeling very tired he prepared to put the stone down. But the stone refused to be moved from his head. It stuck fast there, and no efforts could displace it. The weight of it very soon grew too much for Anansi, and ground him down into small pieces, which were completely covered over by the stone. That is why we often find tiny spiders gathered together under large stones.

Exercise

Review memory work. Identify each group of words below as either a phrase or a clause. If it is a clause, double underline the predicate and underline the subject.

from those ugly creatures

and the copper fingers closed firmly over the stout handle

the yellow hen gave a cackle of delight

Copy each sentence below. Double underline the predicate, and underline the subject. Label the part of speech of each word. Noun, N; Proper Noun, PN; Pronoun, PRO; Verb, V; Linking Verb, LV; Adjective, ADJ; Article, ART; Conjunction, CJ; Interjection, INJ. Diagram each sentence.

"Will you exchange heads?"

"Wind me up, quick."

"You have company, Your Highness."

Writing: Commonplace Book

Add the passage below from your model story to your commonplace book.

> He comes to the top of the water much more often than before, and sends a bubble of air out of his mouth. What do you think has happened? The gills under his cover have closed up, and a small air-bag has grown inside him. So he comes up to breathe in the air through his mouth, instead of taking it out of the water through his gills.

Dictation

Use part of today's poem for dictation.

48. Point of View Narration: A Frog's Life

- Ozma of Oz, Chapter 7

Today, write your narration on "A Frog's Life." Choose a point of view from which to write your narration. Are you the frog, one of the children, or an objective observer of the events? Use your outline to keep the life cycle of the frog in the proper order. Pay attention to your pronouns as you write!

The Death of the Old Year

By Alfred Tennyson

Full knee-deep lies the winter snow,
And the winter winds are wearily sighing:
Toll ye the church-bell sad and slow,
And tread softly and speak low,
For the old year lies a-dying.
Old year, you must not die;
You came to us so readily,
You lived with us so steadily,
Old year, you shall not die.

He lieth still: he doth not move:
He will not see the dawn of day.
He hath no other life above.
He gave me a friend, and a true true-love,
And the New-year will take 'em away.
Old year, you must not go;
So long as you have been with us,
Such joy as you have seen with us,
Old year, you shall not go.

He froth'd his bumpers to the brim;
A jollier year we shall not see.
But tho' his eyes are waxing dim,
And tho' his foes speak ill of him,
He was a friend to me.

Old year, you shall not die;
We did so laugh and cry with you,
I've half a mind to die with you,
Old year, if you must die.

He was full of joke and jest,
But all his merry quips are o'er.
To see him die, across the waste
His son and heir doth ride post-haste,
But he'll be dead before.
Every one for his own.
The night is starry and cold, my friend,
And the New-year blithe and bold, my friend,
Comes up to take his own.

How hard he breathes! Over the snow
I heard just now the crowing cock.
The shadows flicker to and fro:
The cricket chirps: the light burns low:
   'Tis nearly twelve o'clock.
Shake hands, before you die.
Old year, we'll dearly rue for you:
What is it we can do for you?
Speak out before you die.

His face is growing sharp and thin.
Alack! Our friend is gone.
Close up his eyes: tie up his chin:
Step from the corpse, and let him in
That standeth there alone,
And waiteth at the door.
There's a new foot on the floor, my friend,
And a new face at the door, my friend,
A new face at the door.

Editing

• Did you meet the goal of this writing exercise?

• Look at your word choice. Is there a good mixture of nouns and pronouns? Is the antecedent of each pronoun clear?

• Look at your paragraphs. Are all the sentences related? Does each paragraph focus on a single topic?

49. Commas in a Series

• Ozma of Oz, Chapter 8

When we are joining only two words, we only need a coordinating conjunction to do so.

"He is holding the Queen <u>and</u> her children prisoners."

"But you are wrong to think yourself terrible <u>or</u> fierce."

However, when we have more than two words, we can use commas to separate items in a series instead of using the word **and** every time.

Dorothy and the Tin Woodman and the Scarecrow were reunited.
Dorothy**,** the Tin Woodman**,** and the Scarecrow were reunited.

The little servant bowed <u>and</u> withdrew <u>and</u> went through several passages.
The little servant bowed**,** withdrew**,** and went through several passages.

Dorothy Gale <u>and</u> Billina <u>and</u> Tiktok saw the princess.
Dorothy Gale**,** Billina**,** and Tiktok saw the princess.

Note that each word in our list except for the last one is followed by a comma instead of the conjunction **and**. We only use the conjunction **and** before the last word in our list.

Abou Ben Adhem

By Leigh Hunt

Abou Ben Adhem (may his tribe increase!)
Awoke one night from a deep dream of peace,
And saw within the moonlight in his room,
Making it rich and like a lily in bloom,
An angel writing in a book of gold.

Exceeding peace had made Ben Adhem bold;
And to the presence in the room he said,

"What writest thou?" The vision raised its head,
And, with a look made of all sweet accord,
Answered, "The names of those who love the Lord."

"And is mine one?" said Abou. "Nay, not so,"
Replied the angel. Abou spoke more low,
But cheerly still; and said, "I pray thee, then,
Write me as one that loves his fellow-men."

The angel wrote, and vanished. The next night
It came again, with a great wakening light,
And showed the names whom love of God had blessed;
And, lo! Ben Adhem's name led all the rest.

Writing: Oral Narration

Read your new model story below, and then give your instructor an oral narration of it.

The Greedy Stranger

From *Wild Life in Woods and Fields* by Arabella B. Buckley

It was the middle of April this year when we first heard the cuckoo. We love to hear it, for it tells us that spring has come. This year we were very lucky. We saw a young cuckoo grow up in his nest.

This was how it happened.

We had heard the cuckoo for some time, cuck-oo, cuck-oo, and it seemed as if many cuckoos were singing. One day we heard such a funny noise, like kik-kik-kik. "Ah!" said Peggy, "father says that is the cry of the mother cuckoo which lays the eggs. That is why there are so many cuckoos about. They are singing to her."

"Well then," said Peter, "if she stops here, perhaps we may find one of her eggs. I do so want to see a young cuckoo."

About a week after this Peter found a titlark's nest. It was in a tuft of grass, on the bank near the wood. Two small dull-grey eggs, spotted with brown, were lying in the nest. The next day, as we went to school, there were three eggs. The next morning there were four. But as we came back from school that afternoon there were five eggs.

"The titlark cannot have laid two eggs in one day," said Peter. "I wonder if the cuckoo has brought one of her eggs here."

For we know that the cuckoo lays her eggs on the ground, and brings it in her wide beak to the nest of some other bird. We looked every day for a fortnight. The little titlark was so used to our coming, she did not even fly off the nest. She was a pretty little bird, with brown spotted wings and a yellow throat and chin.

At the end of a fortnight two little titlarks came out of their shells, and the next day two more. They opened their beaks for food, and the father titlark flew out to the field, and brought flies and caterpillars to feed them. But the mother still sat on the fifth egg.

Two day later the fifth bird came out. It had a curved beak, and bent toes with short, sharp claws. Its toes were two in front and two at the back. Titlarks have straight beaks and flat toes, three in front and one at the back.

So we knew our young cuckoo by his beak and toes.

We came next day to look. The little titlarks had quills on their wings where the feathers were growing, and their eyes were open. The cuckoo was naked and blind. But he had pushed two of the titlarks out of the nest, and they lay on the bank quite dead.

The cuckoo had grown bigger even in one day, and the old titlarks kept feeding him with insects as he sat with his beak wide open. While we were looking at him the cuckoo pushed about in the nest and shoved another little titlark over the edge, on to the bank. We put it back in the nest and then we had to go on to school. When we came back the cuckoo sat in the nest alone. All the four little titlarks were dead on the bank. He had pushed them all out.

The old birds did not seem to see their dead children. They were so busy feeding the big hungry stranger. They fed him for five or six weeks, even after he could come out of the nest.

It was so funny to see! The cuckoo was larger than a thrush and the titlarks not bigger than a sparrow. Yet the big bird sat on a branch with his beak open, and let these little birds carry all his food.

At last he flew away. We heard a cuckoo singing in August, when we knew the old birds were all gone. We wondered if it was our young "greedy stranger."

Exercise

Review memory work. Punctuate the following sentence.

> Dorothy was guided to the chicken house by a loud cackling crowing and distracting hubbub of sounds

Identify each group of words below as either a phrase or a clause. If it is a clause, double underline the predicate and underline the subject.

> as cowardly as ever

> but suddenly the bunch of feathers stopped whirling

> which Dorothy unlatched

Copy each sentence below. Double underline the predicate, and underline the subject. Label the part of speech of each word. Noun, N; Proper Noun, PN; Pronoun, PRO; Verb, V; Linking Verb, LV; Adjective, ADJ; Article, ART; Conjunction, CJ; Interjection, INJ. Diagram each sentence.

> "Why, Billina! Have you been fighting?"

> The Cowardly Lion introduced his friend the Hungry Tiger.

> "Don't worry."

Commonplace Book

With your instructor's approval, add the passage below to your commonplace book, or choose your own passage from a work of fiction. This can be from either school reading or free reading.

> Then Dorothy carried her pet into the drawing-room of the palace, where Tiktok, being invited to do so by Ozma, had seated himself between the Scarecrow and the Tin Woodman. Opposite to them sat Ozma herself and the Princess Langwidere, and beside them there was a vacant chair for Dorothy.

Dictation

> "They are, all except one," answered the Tin Woodman. "I have in my Army eight Generals, six Colonels, seven Majors and five Captains, besides one private for them to command. I'd like to promote the private, for I believe no private should ever be in public life; and I've also noticed that officers usually fight better and are more reliable than common soldiers. Besides, the officers are more important looking, and lend dignity to our army."

50. Writing an Outline

• Ozma of Oz, Chapter 9

So far, you've created outlines from just a small portion of your model story. Today, you'll learn how to write an outline of the whole model story.

When you learned how to write a summary, you learned to include only the most important parts of the story. You learned to identify the beginning, the middle, and the end of the story.

To write an outline of the whole story, you do the same thing. The first Roman numeral will have the story's beginning. The last Roman numeral will have the story's ending. And then you will include a Roman numeral, or perhaps more than one, to list the events in the middle of the story.

Read the following story.

King Chameleon and the Animals

From *West African Folk-Tales* by William H. Barker

In the olden days all the animals of the world lived together in friendship. They had no one to rule over them and judge them. In consequence, many very wicked deeds were constantly being done, as no one needed to fear any punishment.

At last they all met together to discuss this bad state of affairs, and, as a result, they decided to choose a king. The great difficulty was how to choose him.

Lion was the first animal suggested. But all opposed him because, they said, he was too fierce. Wolf was next named—but the sheep and goats refused to have him because he was their foe. They knew they would have bad treatment if he were chosen.

As it was impossible to please every one by choice, they decided in another way. Two miles away was a great stool, placed under a very ancient tree which they believed to be the abode of some of their gods. They would have a great race. The animal which reached and sat down first on the stool should be chosen king.

The day of the race arrived. All animals, great and small, prepared to take part in it. The signal being given, they started off. The hare—being a very fine runner—speedily outdistanced the others. He reached the stool quite five hundred yards ahead of the next animal. You may judge of his annoyance when, just as he was going to sit down, a voice came from the stool saying, "Take care, Mr. Hare, take care. I was here first." This was the chameleon. He, being able to change his colour to suit his surroundings, had seized Mr. Hare's tail just as the race began. Having made his color match the hare's, no one had noticed him. He had held on very tightly, and when the hare turned round to take his seat Chameleon dropped off and landed on the stool.

The hare saw how he had been tricked and was very angry. The other animals, however, arrived before he could harm the chameleon. According to the agreement they had made, they had no choice but to make Chameleon king.

But none of the animals were satisfied with the choice. So as soon as the meeting was over, all scattered in every direction and left Chameleon quite alone.

He was so ashamed that he went and made his home at the top of a very high tree on a mountain. In the dead of night you may hear him calling his attendants to come and stay with him. But he is left quite alone. "A king without subjects is no king."

Remember that outlines have a very specific form. What are the main points in the story?

I. The animals have no ruler, so the wicked were never punished.

II. The animals decided to have a race to choose a king.

III. The Chameleon cheated and became the king, but the animals were unhappy about this and left him alone.

IV. The ashamed Chameleon made his home at the top of a high tree on a mountain, and sometimes at night he calls for his attendants.

The one-level outline just includes the most important parts of the story, just like the summary. The main difference between a summary and an outline is the form that the outline takes.

Today, you'll write an outline of your new model story which you read in the last lesson.

Lochinvar

By Sir Walter Scott

Oh, young Lochinvar is come out of the west.
Through all the wide Border his steed was the best,
And save his good broadsword he weapons had none;
He rode all unarmed, and he rode all alone.
So faithful in love, and so dauntless in war,
There never was knight like the young Lochinvar.

He stayed not for brake, and he stopped not for stone,
He swam the Eske River where ford there was none;

But ere he alighted at Netherby gate
The bride had consented, the gallant came late:
For a laggard in love, and a dastard in war
Was to wed the fair Ellen of brave Lochinvar.

So boldly he entered the Netherby Hall,
Among bridesmen and kinsmen and brothers and all:
Then spoke the bride's father, his hand on his sword
(For the poor craven bridegroom said never a word),
  "Oh, come ye in peace here, or come ye in war,
Or to dance at our bridal, young Lord Lochinvar?"

  "I long woo'd your daughter, my suit you denied;—
Love swells like the Solway, but ebbs like its tide—
And now am I come, with this lost love of mine,
To lead but one measure, drink one cup of wine.
There are maidens in Scotland more lovely by far,
That would gladly be bride to the young Lochinvar."

The bride kissed the goblet; the knight took it up;
He quaffed of the wine, and he threw down the cup.
She looked down to blush, and she looked up to sigh,
With a smile on her lips and a tear in her eye.
He took her soft hand ere her mother could bar,—
  "Now tread we a measure!" said young Lochinvar.

So stately his form, and so lovely her face,
That never a hall such a galliard did grace;
While her mother did fret, and her father did fume,
And the bridegroom stood dangling his bonnet and plume,
And the bridemaidens whispered, "'Twere better by far
To have matched our fair cousin with young Lochinvar."

One touch to her hand, and one word in her ear,
When they reached the hall door, and the charger stood near;
So light to the croupe the fair lady he swung,
So light to the saddle before her he sprung!
  "She is won! We are gone, over bank, bush, and scaur;
They'll have fleet steeds that follow," quoth young Lochinvar.

There was mounting 'mong Græmes of the Netherby clan;
Forsters, Fenwicks, and Musgraves, they rode and they ran:
There was racing and chasing, on Cannobie Lee,
But the lost bride of Netherby ne'er did they see.
So daring in love, and so dauntless in war,
Have ye e'er heard of gallant like young Lochinvar?

Writing: Outline

Write or type an outline of the new model story which you read in the last lesson.

Exercise

Review memory work. Punctuate the following sentence.

> Please to get me about thirty pounds of tenderloin steak a peck of boiled potatoes and five gallons of ice-cream for dessert

Identify each group of words below as either a phrase or a clause. If it is a clause, double underline the predicate and underline the subject.

> a queen mother and her ten children

> for the sake of the poor prisoners

> I will now retire to my cabinet

Copy each sentence below. Double underline the predicate, and underline the subject. Label the part of speech of each word. Noun, N; Proper Noun, PN; Pronoun, PRO; Verb, V; Linking Verb, LV; Adjective, ADJ; Article, ART; Conjunction, CJ; Interjection, INJ. Diagram each sentence.

> "Are you so very hungry?"

> He bowed politely and blinked his eyes.

> "My uncle, Evoldo, was a very wicked man."

Commonplace Book

With your instructor's approval, add the poem below to your commonplace book, or choose your own poem.

> Oh, young Lochinvar is come out of the west.
> Through all the wide Border his steed was the best,
> And save his good broadsword he weapons had none;
> He rode all unarmed, and he rode all alone.
> So faithful in love, and so dauntless in war,
> There never was knight like the young Lochinvar.
>
> He stayed not for brake, and he stopped not for stone,
> He swam the Eske River where ford there was none;
> But ere he alighted at Netherby gate
> The bride had consented, the gallant came late:
> For a laggard in love, and a dastard in war
> Was to wed the fair Ellen of brave Lochinvar.

Dictation

> Psalm 19:14
>
> Let the words of my mouth and the meditation of my heart
> Be acceptable in Your sight,
> O Lord, my rock and my Redeemer.

Ballet Class: The Dance Hall by Edgar Degas

Picture Study

1. Read the title and the name of the artist. Study the picture for several minutes, then put the picture away.

2. Describe the picture.

3. Look at the picture again. Do you notice any details that you missed before? What do you like or dislike about this painting? Does it remind you of anything?

51. Literary Analysis

- Ozma of Oz, Chapter 10

Writing: Literary Analysis

Today you have another literary analysis assignment. Now that you've had some practice, this should be a written assignment, though it can be helpful to discuss your ideas before writing.

With your instructor's approval, choose *Ozma of Oz,* or one of the other books you're currently reading, and answer the following questions.

What is the book about? Give a brief summary, just a few sentences. Has any part of the book made you laugh so far? Has any part of the book made you sad? Has any part of the book made you bored?

To a Mouse

By Robert Burns

Wee, sleekit, cow'rin', tim'rous beastie,
Oh, what a panic's in thy breastie!
Thou needna start awa' sae hasty,
  Wi' bickering brattle!
I wad be laith to rin and chase thee,
  Wi' murd'ring pattle!

I'm truly sorry man's dominion
Has broken Nature's social union,
And justifies that ill opinion,
  Which makes thee startle
At me, thy poor earth-born companion
  And fellow-mortal!

I doubtna, whiles, but thou may thieve;
What then? poor beastie, thou maun live!
A daimen icker in a thrave
 'S a sma' request:
I'll get a blessin' wi' the lave,
  And never miss 't!

Thy wee bit housie, too, in ruin!
Its silly wa's the win's are strewin'!
And naething now to big a new ane
 O' foggage green,
And bleak December's winds ensuin',
  Baith snell and keen!

Thou saw the fields laid bare and waste,
And weary winter comin' fast,
And cozie here, beneath the blast,
  Thou thought to dwell,
Till, crash! The cruel coulter passed
  Out through thy cell.

That wee bit heap o' leaves and stibble
Has cost thee monie a weary nibble!
Now thou's turned out for a' thy trouble,
  But house or hald,
To thole the winter's sleety dribble,
  And cranreuch cauld!

But, Mousie, thou art no thy lane,
In proving foresight may be vain:
The best-laid schemes o' mice and men
  Gang aft a-gley,
And lea'e us naught but grief and pain,
  For promised joy.

Still thou art blest, compared wi' me!
The present only toucheth thee:
But, och! I backward cast my e'e
  On prospects drear!
And forward, though I canna see,
  I guess and fear.

The Lioness and the Ostrich

From *South-African Folk-Tales* by James A. Honey

It is said, once a lioness roared, and the ostrich also roared. The lioness went toward the place where the ostrich was. They met. The lioness said to the ostrich, "Please to roar." The ostrich roared. Then the lioness roared. The voices were equal. The lioness said to the ostrich, "You are my match."

Then the lioness said to the ostrich, "Let us hunt game together." They saw eland and made toward it. The lioness caught only one; the ostrich killed a great many by striking them with the claw which was on his leg; but the lioness killed only one. When they had met after the hunting they went to the game, and the lioness saw that the ostrich had killed a great deal.

Now, the lioness also had young cubs. They went to the shade to rest themselves. The lioness said to the ostrich, "Get up and rip open; let us eat." Said the ostrich, "Go and rip open; I shall eat the blood." The lioness stood up and ripped open, and ate with the cubs. And when she had eaten, the ostrich got up and ate the blood. They went to sleep.

The cubs played about. While they were playing, they went to the ostrich, who was asleep. When he went to sleep he also opened his mouth. The young lions saw that the ostrich had no teeth. They went to their mother and said, "This fellow, who says he is your equal, has no teeth; he is insulting you." Then the lioness went to wake the ostrich, and said, "Get up, let us fight"; and they fought. And the ostrich said, "Go to that side of the ant-hill, and I will go to this side of it." The ostrich struck the ant-hill, and sent it toward the lioness. But the second time he struck the lioness in a vulnerable spot, near the liver, and killed her.

Exercise

Review memory work. Identify each group of words below as either a phrase or a clause. If it is a clause, double underline the predicate and underline the subject.

she lays one every morning

about this time

although all were restless and anxious [Hint: **all** is a pronoun.]

Copy each sentence below. Double underline the predicate, and underline the subject. Label the part of speech of each word. Noun, N; Proper Noun, PN; Pronoun, PRO; Verb, V; Linking Verb, LV; Adjective, ADJ; Article, ART; Conjunction, CJ; Interjection, INJ. Diagram each sentence.

"Why, Billina is laying her egg."

"Billina won't be long." [Hint: **long** tells when.]

The Cowardly Lion was dreadfully nervous.

Commonplace Book

With your instructor's approval, add the passage below to your commonplace book, or choose your own passage from a work of non-fiction. This can be from the Bible, a biography, or one of your history or science books.

"I'll get it," said the Scarecrow; and at his command the Sawhorse pranced into the bushes. The straw man soon found the egg, which he placed in his jacket pocket. The cavalcade, having moved rapidly on, was even then far in advance; but it did not take the Sawhorse long to catch up with it, and presently the Scarecrow was riding in his accustomed place behind Ozma's chariot.

52. Homonyms

- Ozma of Oz, Chapter 11

Definitions:

Homophones are words that sound the same but have different meanings and may have different spellings.

Homographs are words that have the same spelling but have different meanings and may have different pronunciations.

The prefix **homo** is from the Greek language. It means **the same**.

Phono means **sound**, so **homophone** means **same sound**. You can remember this by thinking of words like tele<u>phone</u>; we use telephones to transfer sound. **Homophones** sound the same, but they do not mean the same thing, and they may be spelled differently. Some examples include: dear and deer; to, two, and too; blew and blue.

Graph means **drawn** or **written**. So **homograph** means **same writing**. You can remember this by thinking of photo<u>graphs</u>; photographs are light drawings. **Homographs** look the same, but they do not mean the same thing, and they may sound different. Since homographs look the same, we can only tell which word a homograph is by looking at the **context**—the other words in the sentence. Some examples include: I **live**, and once I saw a **live** bear. I **read** a book once about children who **read** books. The **wind**-up toy blew about in the **wind**.

The word **homonyms** is a word which means a homophone or a homograph. Look at the following sentences from *Ozma of Oz*. The homonyms are underlined. Are they **homophones**, same sound, or **homographs**, same writing?

<u>There</u> were <u>no</u> birds.

They were now <u>close</u> to the Nome King's dominions.

There is a homophone. **There** is an adverb, **their** is a possessive pronoun, and **they're** is a contraction for **they are**.

No is a homophone. It expresses a negative, while **know** is the verb which means to understand or to have information.

Close is a homograph. Here, it means near. **Close** can also be the verb which means to shut.

To a Mountain Daisy

By Robert Burns

Wee, modest, crimson-tipped flower,
Thou's met me in an evil hour;
For I maun crush amang the stoure
  Thy slender stem:
To spare thee now is past my power,
  Thou bonny gem.

Alas! It's no thy neebor sweet,
The bonny lark, companion meet,
Bending thee 'mang the dewy weet,
  Wi' speckled breast,
When upward-springing, blithe, to greet
  The purpling east!

Cauld blew the bitter biting north
Upon thy early, humble birth;
Yet cheerfully thou glinted forth
  Amid the storm,
Scarce reared above the parent earth
  Thy tender form.

The flaunting flowers our gardens yield,
High sheltering woods and wa's maun shield,
But thou, beneath the random bield
  O' clod or stane,
Adorns the histie stibble-field,
  Unseen, alane.

There, in thy scanty mantle clad,
Thy snawie bosom sunward spread,
Thou lifts thy unassuming head
  In humble guise;
But now the share uptears thy bed,
  And low thou lies!

Such is the fate of artless maid,
Sweet floweret of the rural shade!
By love's simplicity betrayed,
  And guileless trust,
Till she, like thee, all soiled, is laid
  Low i' the dust.

Such is the fate of simple bard,
On life's rough ocean luckless starr'd!
Unskilful he to note the card
  Of prudent lore,
Till billows rage, and gales blow hard,
  And whelm him o'er!

Such fate to suffering worth is given,
Who long with wants and woes has striven,
By human pride or cunning driven
  To misery's brink,
Till wrenched of every stay but Heaven,
  He, ruined, sink!

Even thou who mourn'st the Daisy's fate,
That fate is thine—no distant date;
Stern Ruin's plowshare drives, elate,
  Full on thy bloom,
Till crushed beneath the furrow's weight
  Shall be thy doom.

The Lost Message

From *South-African Folk-Tales* by James A. Honey

    The ant has had from time immemorial many enemies, and because he is small and destructive, there have been a great many slaughters among them. Not only were most of the birds their enemies, but Anteater lived almost wholly from them, and Centipede beset them every time and at all places when he had the chance.

    So now there were a few among them who thought it would be well to hold council together and see if they could not come to some arrangement whereby they could retreat to some place of safety when attacked by robber birds and animals.

    But at the gathering their opinions were most discordant, and they could come to no decision.

    There was Red-ant, Rice-ant, Black-ant, Wagtail-ant, Gray-ant, Shining-ant, and many other varieties. The discussion was a true babel of diversity, which continued for a long time and came to nothing.

    A part desired that they should all go into a small hole in the ground, and live there; another part wanted to have a large and strong dwelling built on the ground, where nobody could enter but an ant; still another wanted to dwell in trees, so as to get rid of Anteater, forgetting entirely that there they would be the prey of birds; another part seemed inclined to have wings and fly.

    And, as has already been said, this deliberation amounted to nothing, and each party resolved to go to work in its own way, and on its own responsibility.

    Greater unity than that which existed in each separate faction could be seen nowhere in the world; each had his appointed task, each did his work regularly and well. And all worked together in the same way. From among them they chose a king—that is to say some of the groups did—and they divided the labor so that all went as smoothly as it possibly could.

    But each group did it in its own way, and not one of them thought of protecting themselves against the onslaught of birds or Anteater.

The Red-ants built their house on the ground and lived under it, but Anteater leveled to the ground in a minute what had cost them many days of precious labor. The Rice-ants lived under the ground, and with them it went no better. For whenever they came out, Anteater visited them and took them out sack and pack. The Wagtail-ants fled to the trees, but there on many occasions sat Centipede waiting for them, or the birds gobbled them up. The Gray-ants had intended to save themselves from extermination by taking to flight, but this also availed them nothing, because the Lizard, the Hunting-spider, and the birds went a great deal faster than they.

When the Insect-king heard that they could come to no agreement he sent them the secret of unity, and the message of Work-together. But unfortunately he chose for his messenger the Beetle, and he has never yet arrived at the Ants, so that they are still today the embodiment of discord and consequently the prey of enemies.

Writing: Copia

Take the following sentence and play with it. Remember that the point is not necessarily to make the sentence better. The point is to play with the sentence and make it different. Make a new sentence with a change from each of the following categories.

"I wonder if the cuckoo has brought one of her eggs here."

1. Change the grammar.
   - Change the nouns from common to proper and vice versa.
   - Change the nouns from singular to plural and vice versa.
   - Change the sentence type.
   - Change the adjectives from articles to descriptive to possessive, etc.
   - Change a quotation from direct to indirect and vice versa.

2. Condense the sentence.
   - Remove details.
   - Remove modifiers.
   - Remove phrases or clauses.

3. Amplify the sentence.
   - Add details.
   - Add dialogue.
   - Add modifiers.
   - Add phrases or clauses.

4. Use synonyms and antonyms.
   - Substitute synonyms.
   - Say the opposite thing using antonyms.

5. Point of view.
   - Change the point of view.

Exercise

Review memory work. In the following sentences, label homographs GR and homophones PH.

Ozma and Dorothy were a little awed by the silence.

We will dig him out of his hole, like a fox.

Copy each sentence below. Double underline the predicate, and underline the subject. Label the part of speech of each word. Noun, N; Proper Noun, PN; Pronoun, PRO; Verb, V; Linking Verb, LV; Adjective, ADJ; Article, ART; Conjunction, CJ; Interjection, INJ. Diagram each sentence.

"PLEASE Mr. Nome King, come here and see us."

"Isn't it a trick?"

The Nome King, the underground monarch, answered.

Commonplace Book

With your instructor's approval, add the passage below to your commonplace book, or choose your own passage from a work of fiction. This can be from either school reading or free reading.

> So Ozma led the way, hand in hand with Dorothy, and they passed through the arched doorway of rock and entered a long passage which was lighted by jewels set in the walls and having lamps behind them. There was no one to escort them, or to show them the way, but all the party pressed through the passage until they came to a round, domed cavern that was grandly furnished.

Dictation

> This important monarch of the Underground World was a little fat man clothed in gray-brown garments that were the exact color of the rock throne in which he was seated. His bushy hair and flowing beard were also colored like the rocks, and so was his face. He wore no crown of any sort, and his only ornament was a broad, jewel-studded belt that encircled his fat little body.

53. Parts of Speech: Prepositions

- Ozma of Oz, Chapter 12

Definition: A preposition is a word that shows the relationship between a noun or a pronoun and another word in the sentence.

Some of the most common prepositions are:

aboard, about, above, across, after, against, along, among, around, at, before, behind, below, beneath, beside, between, beyond, by, down, during, except, for, from, in, inside, into, like, near, of, off, on, onto, outside, over, past, round, since, through, throughout, till, to, toward, under, underneath, until, up, upon, with, within, without.

Look at the following sentences from *Ozma of Oz*.

Ozma went <u>into</u> the royal palace.

The Nome King had left her <u>at</u> the entrance.

The King climbed down <u>with</u> some difficulty.

The sentences above all show the relationship between a noun or pronoun and another word in the sentence. In the first sentence, **into** shows the relationship between **palace** and **went**; it tells where Ozma went. In the second sentence, **at** shows the relationship between **entrance** and **left**; it tells where he left Ozma. In the third sentence, **with** shows the relationship between **difficulty** and **climbed**. It tells how he climbed.

One clue for finding prepositions is to remember pre**POSITION**. Prepositions often tell the position of nouns and pronouns. Prepositions can show the position in space—the physical world—as well as the position in time. Look at the following sentence.

<u>After</u> her acceptance, Ozma went <u>into</u> the palace.

Her position in space was **into the palace**. Her position in time was **after her acceptance**.

Another way to find prepositions is to think of **anywhere a rabbit can hop**. You can use this sentence as a test: The rabbit hopped _____ the hat(s).

The rabbit hopped **over** the hat. The rabbit hopped **past** the hat. The rabbit hopped **between** the hats. The rabbit hopped **with** the hat. The rabbit hopped **through** the hat.

Not all prepositions will fit into that sentence, though we can still use our rabbit theme. A rabbit hops **according to** his nature, **since** the beginning, **during** his lifetime, and **until** bedtime. The rabbit hopped high **like** his father, high **as** a bird. Each preposition shows the relationship between its **object** and another word in the sentence. A preposition needs an object to be complete. We'll discuss the object of the preposition in another lesson.

The Fairies Dancing

By Walter De La Mare

I heard along the early hills,
Ere yet the lark was risen up,
Ere yet the dawn with firelight fills
The night-dew of the bramble-cup,—
I heard the fairies in a ring
Sing as they tripped a lilting round
Soft as the moon on wavering wing.
The starlight shook as if with sound,
As if with echoing, and the stars
Prankt their bright eyes with trembling gleams;
While red with war the gusty Mars
Rained upon earth his ruddy beams.
He shone alone, adown the West,
While I, behind a hawthorn-bush,
Watched on the fairies flaxen-tressed
The fires of the morning flush.
Till, as a mist, their beauty died,
Their singing shrill and fainter grew;
And daylight tremulous and wide
Flooded the moorland through and through;
Till Urdon's copper weathercock
Was reared in golden flame afar,
And dim from moonlit dreams awoke
The towers and groves of Arroar.

The Monkey's Fiddle

From *South-African Folk-Tales* by James A. Honey

    Hunger and want forced Monkey one day to forsake his land and to seek elsewhere among strangers for much-needed work. Bulbs, earth beans, scorpions, insects, and such things were completely exhausted in his own land. But fortunately he received, for the time being, shelter with a great uncle of his, Orang Outang, who lived in another part of the country.

When he had worked for quite a while he wanted to return home, and as recompense his great uncle gave him a fiddle and a bow and arrow and told him that with the bow and arrow he could hit and kill anything he desired, and with the fiddle he could force anything to dance.

The first he met upon his return to his own land was Brer Wolf. This old fellow told him all the news and also that he had since early morning been attempting to stalk a deer, but all in vain.

Then Monkey laid before him all the wonders of the bow and arrow that he carried on his back and assured him if he could but see the deer he would bring it down for him. When Wolf showed him the deer, Monkey was ready and down fell the deer.

They made a good meal together, but instead of Wolf being thankful, jealousy overmastered him and he begged for the bow and arrow. When Monkey refused to give it to him, he thereupon began to threaten him with his greater strength, and so when Jackal passed by, Wolf told him that Monkey had stolen his bow and arrow. After Jackal had heard both of them, he declared himself unqualified to settle the case alone, and he proposed that they bring the matter to the court of Lion, Tiger, and the other animals. In the meantime he declared he would take possession of what had been the cause of their quarrel, so that it would be safe, as he said. But he immediately brought to earth all that was eatable, so there was a long time of slaughter before Monkey and Wolf agreed to have the affair in court.

Monkey's evidence was weak, and to make it worse, Jackal's testimony was against him. Jackal thought that in this way it would be easier to obtain the bow and arrow from Wolf for himself.

And so fell the sentence against Monkey. Theft was looked upon as a great wrong; he must hang.

The fiddle was still at his side, and he received as a last favor from the court the right to play a tune on it.

He was a master player of his time, and in addition to this came the wonderful power of his charmed fiddle. Thus, when he struck the first note of "Cockcrow" upon it, the court began at once to show an unusual and spontaneous liveliness, and before he came to the first waltzing turn of the old tune the whole court was dancing like a whirlwind.

Over and over, quicker and quicker, sounded the tune of "Cockcrow" on the charmed fiddle, until some of the dancers, exhausted, fell down, although still keeping their feet in motion. But Monkey, musician as he was, heard and saw nothing of what had happened around him. With his head placed lovingly against the instrument, and his eyes half closed, he played on, keeping time ever with his foot.

Wolf was the first to cry out in pleading tones breathlessly, "Please stop, Cousin Monkey! For love's sake, please stop!"

But Monkey did not even hear him. Over and over sounded the resistless waltz of "Cockcrow."

After a while Lion showed signs of fatigue, and when he had gone the round once more with his young lion wife, he growled as he passed Monkey, "My whole kingdom is yours, ape, if you just stop playing."

"I do not want it," answered Monkey, "but withdraw the sentence and give me my bow and arrow, and you, Wolf, acknowledge that you stole it from me."

"I acknowledge, I acknowledge!" cried Wolf, while Lion cried, at the same instant, that he withdrew the sentence.

Monkey gave them just a few more turns of the "Cockcrow," gathered up his bow and arrow, and seated himself high up in the nearest camel thorn tree.

The court and other animals were so afraid that he might begin again that they hastily disbanded to new parts of the world.

Exercise

Review memory work. Punctuate the following sentence.

> Dorothy the Scarecrow and the Tin Woodman each gave a start of dismay and stared into one another's eyes.

In the following sentences, label homographs GR and homophones PH.

> "Surely I ought to guess one object in eleven correctly."

> "It would be weak and cowardly in us to abandon the adventure."

Copy each sentence below. Double underline the predicate, and underline the subject. Label the part of speech of each word. Noun, N; Proper Noun, PN; Pronoun, PRO; Verb, V; Linking Verb, LV; Adjective, ADJ; Article, ART; Conjunction, CJ; Interjection, INJ. Diagram each sentence.

> Ozma the pretty grasshopper was an emerald.

> "Has she failed?"

> The Nome King suddenly looked up and smiled.

Writing: Commonplace Book

Add the passage below from your model story to your commonplace book.

> For we know that the cuckoo lays her eggs on the ground, and brings it in her wide beak to the nest of some other bird. We looked every day for a fortnight. The little titlark was so used to our coming, she did not even fly off the nest. She was a pretty little bird, with brown spotted wings and a yellow throat and chin.

Dictation

Use part of today's poem for dictation.

54. Point of View Narration: The Greedy Stranger

• Ozma of Oz, Chapter 13

Today, use your outline to write your narration on "The Greedy Stranger." Choose a point of view from which to write your narration. Are you the cuckoo, one of the children, or an objective observer of the events? Pay attention to your pronouns as you write!

Barbara Frietchie

By John Greenleaf Whittier

Up from the meadows rich with corn,
Clear in the cool September morn,

The clustered spires of Frederick stand
Green-walled by the hills of Maryland.

Roundabout them orchards sweep,
Apple and peach tree fruited deep,

Fair as the garden of the Lord
To the eyes of the famished rebel horde,

On that pleasant morn of the early fall
When Lee marched over the mountain-wall,

Over the mountains winding down,
Horse and foot, into Frederick town.

Forty flags with their silver stars,
Forty flags with their crimson bars,

Flapped in the morning wind: the sun
Of noon looked down, and saw not one.

Up rose old Barbara Frietchie then,
Bowed with her fourscore years and ten,

Bravest of all in Frederick town,
She took up the flag the men hauled down.

In her attic window the staff she set,
To show that one heart was loyal yet.

Up the street came the rebel tread,
Stonewall Jackson riding ahead.

Under his slouched hat left and right
He glanced: the old flag met his sight.

  "Halt!"—the dust-brown ranks stood fast.
  "Fire!"—out blazed the rifle-blast.

It shivered the window, pane and sash;
It rent the banner with seam and gash.

Quick, as it fell, from the broken staff
Dame Barbara snatched the silken scarf.

She leaned far out on the window-sill,
And shook it forth with a royal will.

  "Shoot, if you must, this old gray head,
But spare your country's flag," she said.

A shade of sadness, a blush of shame,
Over the face of the leader came;

The nobler nature within him stirred
To life at that woman's deed and word:

  "Who touches a hair of yon gray head
Dies like a dog! March on!" he said.

All day long through Frederick street
Sounded the tread of marching feet:

All day long that free flag tost
Over the heads of the rebel host.

Even its torn folds rose and fell
On the loyal winds that loved it well;

And through the hill-gaps sunset light
Shone over it with a warm good-night.

Barbara Frietchie's work is o'er,
And the rebel rides on his raids no more.

Honor to her! And let a tear
Fall, for her sake, on Stonewall's bier.

Over Barbara Frietchie's grave,
Flag of Freedom and Union, wave!

Peace and order and beauty draw
Round thy symbol of light and law;

And ever the stars above look down
On thy stars below in Frederick town!

Editing

• Did you meet the goal of this writing exercise?

• Look at your word choice. Is there a good mixture of nouns and pronouns? Is the antecedent of each pronoun clear?

• Look at your paragraphs. Are all the sentences related? Does each paragraph focus on a single topic?

55. Object of the Preposition

• Ozma of Oz, Chapter 14

Definition: The object of the preposition is a noun or pronoun which teams up with the preposition and completes its meaning.

Some of the most common prepositions are:

aboard, about, above, across, after, against, along, among, around, at, before, behind, below, beneath, beside, between, beyond, by, down, during, except, for, from, in, inside, into, like, near, of, off, on, onto, outside, over, past, round, since, through, throughout, till, to, toward, under, underneath, until, up, upon, with, within, without.

A preposition shows the relationship between a **noun or a pronoun** and another word in the sentence. We call that noun or pronoun the **object of the preposition**. A preposition needs an object in order to make sense. The object of the preposition answers the question **what** or **whom**. We call the preposition, its object, and any modifiers of the object the **prepositional phrase**.

Look at the following sentence from *Ozma of Oz*. The prepositional phrase is in brackets, which is how you'll mark them in your exercises.

Meantime the Chief Steward had returned [to the throne room].

Above, the word **room** is the object of the preposition. It completes the meaning of the preposition. The prepositional phrase is **to the throne room**. Without the object of the preposition, the sentence reads:

Meantime the Chief Steward had returned to.

To **what**? The preposition no longer makes sense. It must have its object to complete its meaning.

"But there are no other purple ornaments [in the palace]."

Above, the word **palace** is the object of the preposition. It completes the meaning of the preposition. The prepositional phrase is **in the palace**. Without the object of the preposition, the sentence reads:

"But there are no other purple ornaments in."

In **what**? The preposition no longer makes sense. It must have its object to complete its meaning.

"So we do not care much what becomes [of us] ."

Above, the word **us** is the object of the preposition. It completes the meaning of the preposition. The prepositional phrase is **of us**. Without the object of the preposition, the sentence reads:

"So we do not care much what becomes of."

Of **whom**? The preposition no longer makes sense. It must have its object to complete its meaning.

Be careful not to depend upon a list to determine the part of speech of any word. While the above words all can be prepositions, some of them are not always prepositions. For instance, **but** and **for** are on the list. You've learned another list—coordinating conjunctions—that included both words.

But and **for** are conjunctions when they join words or groups of words together. When **for** is a conjunction, it means **because.**

"I shall have nothing to do but admire my new ornaments."

Now follow me to my chamber, for I am going to bed.

But and **for** are prepositions when one shows a relationship between its object and another word in the sentence. When **but** is a preposition, it shows an exception, meaning **other than**.

None knew the secret but Billina.

"It serves to keep me amused for a long time."

When you understand the functions of the different parts of speech, you can more easily tell the difference in sentences.

The Tournament

By Sidney Lanier

I.
Bright shone the lists, blue bent the skies,
  And the knights still hurried amain
To the tournament under the ladies' eyes,
  Where the jousters were Heart and Brain.

II.
Flourished the trumpets, entered Heart,
  A youth in crimson and gold;

    Flourished again; Brain stood apart,
      Steel-armored, dark and cold.

III.
Heart's palfrey caracoled gaily round,
  Heart tra-li-ra'd merrily;
But Brain sat still, with never a sound,
  So cynical-calm was he.

IV.
Heart's helmet-crest bore favours three
  From his lady's white hand caught;
While Brain wore a plumeless casque; not he
  Or favour gave or sought.

V.
The trumpet blew; Heart shot a glance
  To catch his lady's eye.
But Brain gazed straight ahead, his lance
  To aim more faithfully.

VI.
They charged, they struck; both fell, both bled;
  Brain rose again, ungloved;
Heart, dying, smiled and faintly said,
  "My love to my beloved."

Writing: Oral Narration

Read your new model story below, and then give your instructor an oral narration of it.

The Ants and the Grasshopper

An Aesop's Fable

One bright day in late autumn a family of Ants were bustling about in the warm sunshine, drying out the grain they had stored up during the summer, when a starving Grasshopper, his fiddle under his arm, came up and humbly begged for a bite to eat.

"What!" cried the Ants in surprise, "haven't you stored anything away for the winter? What in the world were you doing all last summer?"

"I didn't have time to store up any food," whined the Grasshopper. "I was so busy making music that before I knew it the summer was gone."

The Ants shrugged their shoulders in disgust.

"Making music, were you?" they cried. "Very well; now dance!" And they turned their backs on the Grasshopper and went on with their work.

There's a time for work and a time for play.

Exercise

Review memory work. Punctuate the following sentence.

Dorothy the Lion and Tiger were given their breakfast in their rooms

Identify each group of words below as either a phrase or a clause. If it is a clause, double underline the predicate and underline the subject.

where he said to the King

in so enraged a voice

squatting under the throne

Copy each sentence below. Double underline the predicate, and underline the subject. Put brackets around any prepositional phrases. Label the part of speech of each word. Noun, N; Proper Noun, PN; Pronoun, PRO; Verb, V; Linking Verb, LV; Adjective, ADJ; Article, ART; Conjunction, CJ; Preposition, Prep; Interjection, INJ. Diagram each sentence.

Had Billina listened carefully?

"Your Majesty, you are a fool."

"Oh, cease your tiresome chatter!"

Commonplace Book

With your instructor's approval, add the passage below to your commonplace book, or choose your own passage from a work of fiction. This can be from either school reading or free reading.

> So Dorothy, trying to be brave in spite of her fears, passed through the doorway into the gorgeous rooms of the palace. The stillness of the place awed her, at first, and the child drew short breaths, and pressed her hand to her heart, and looked all around with wondering eyes.

Dictation

> Dorothy begged to be allowed to go first into the palace, but Tiktok firmly maintained that the slave should face danger before the mistress. The Scarecrow agreed with him in that, so the Nome King opened the door for the machine man, who tramped into the palace to meet his fate. Then his Majesty returned to his throne and puffed his pipe so contentedly that a small cloud of smoke formed above his head.

56. Diagramming Prepositions

• Ozma of Oz, Chapter 15

Prepositional phrases are modifiers. Sometimes, they are **adjective phrases** and modify nouns or pronouns. Other times, they are **adverb phrases** and modify verbs. Like other modifiers, several prepositional phrases can modify the same word. Adjective prepositional phrases can even modify the object of another preposition.

Occasionally, it can be difficult to determine which word a prepositional phrase modifies. **Remember**: Just like adjectives, an adjective prepositional phrase will stay with the noun or pronoun which it modifies. Adjectives normally come before the noun or pronoun, while adjective prepositional phrases come after.

    She touched a <u>bowl</u> [of alabaster].

What kind of bowl? An alabaster bowl. **Of alabaster** modifies **bowl**.

And just like adverbs which modify the verb, an adverb prepositional phrase can often be moved around in the sentence without changing the meaning.

    Billina laid her egg [under the Nome King's throne].
    Under the Nome King's throne, Billina laid her egg.
    Billina, under the Nome King's throne, laid her egg.

Notice that while some of those sentences above sound better than others, they all make sense. This is because the prepositional phrase modifies the verb. Try doing that with the adjective prepositional phrase in the first sentence above. Can you move it and have it still make sense?

Remember that **adjectives** tell what kind, how many, which one, and whose; **adverbs** tell how, when, where, how often, and to what extent. This information will tell you whether the prepositional phrase is an adjective or an adverb, which will in turn point towards the word it modifies. Knowing this information is imperative. If you do not know the difference between what adjectives tell and what adverbs tell, you will struggle with knowing which word a prepositional phrase modifies. Use these words as questions when evaluating a prepositional phrase: Does it tell which one? Where? How many?

Like other modifiers, prepositional phrases are diagrammed on a diagonal line under the word the prepositional phrase modifies. The entire prepositional phrase is diagrammed like this:

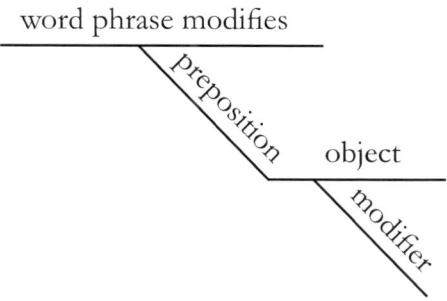

Follow this procedure for analyzing sentences.

Put brackets around prepositional phrases.

What is the predicate? The main verb is often easier to find than its subject, so find it first. Double underline it. Is it an action verb or a linking verb?

What is the subject? Underline it once.

For action verbs, is there a direct object which receives the action of the verb by answering the question **whom** or **what**?

For linking verbs, is there a subject complement—a predicate nominative or a predicate adjective—which renames or modifies the subject?

The object of a prepositional phrase will never be the subject of a sentence, a predicate nominative, or a direct object, so marking them from the beginning simplifies the process.

His little <u>friend</u> <u><u>would suffer</u></u> the fate [of Ozma] .

Whose fate? Ozma's fate. A prepositional phrase which tells **whose** can often be replaced with the possessive form of the object of the preposition.

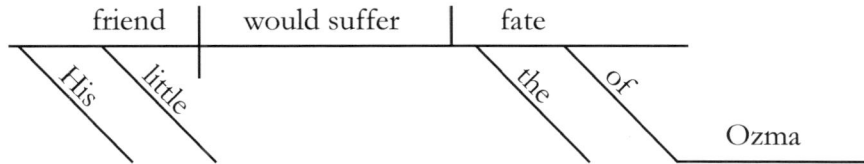

<u>He</u> <u><u>placed</u></u> the egg [in another pocket] [of his jacket] .

He placed the egg **where**? In another pocket. **What kind** of pocket? The pocket of his jacket.

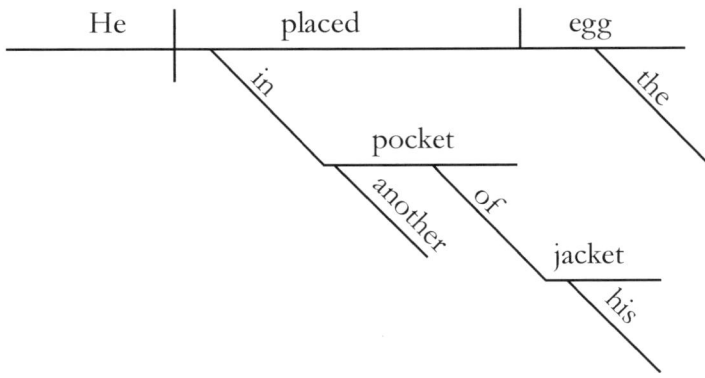

If you think a prepositional phrase modifies a word other than the verb, remove that word from the sentence. Does the prepositional phrase still make since? If it does, then it's not modifying the word you removed. Consider the sentence from the beginning of the lesson.

She touched a bowl [of alabaster].

Imagine that you couldn't decide whether **of alabaster** modified the verb or the noun **bowl**. Try taking the word **bowl** out of the sentence. Does the sentence still make sense?

The two sat [in moody silence] [for several minutes].

Notice that in the next sentence, the word **two** acts as a pronoun, meaning the two individuals. They sat how? In moody silence. They sat **when**? For several minutes. Both of these prepositional phrases are adverbs which modify the verb **sat**.

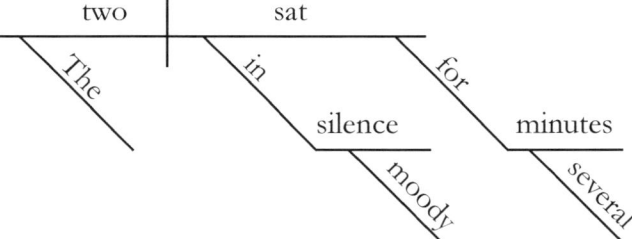

Does the prepositional phrase tell what kind, how many, which one, or whose? Does it tell how, when, where, how often, or to what extent? Sometimes, these descriptions fit in a way that feels rather odd. However, only one will work, and that will tell you whether the prepositional phrase is an adjective or an adverb.

Jesus the Carpenter

By Catherine C. Liddell

"Isn't this Joseph's son?"—ay, it is He;
Joseph the carpenter—same trade as me—
I thought as I'd find it—I knew it was here—
But my sight's getting queer.

I don't know right where as His shed must ha' stood—
But often, as I've been a-planing my wood,

I've took off my hat, just with thinking of He
At the same work as me.

He warn't that set up that He couldn't stoop down
And work in the country for folks in the town;
And I'll warrant He felt a bit pride, like I've done,
At a good job begun.

The parson he knows that I'll not make too free,
But on Sunday I feels as pleased as can be,
When I wears my clean smock, and sits in a pew,
And has taught a few.

I think of as how not the parson hissen,
As is teacher and father and shepherd o' men,
Not he knows as much of the Lord in that shed,
Where He earned His own bread.

And when I goes home to my missus, says she,
  "Are ye wanting your key?"
For she knows my queer ways, and my love for the shed
(We've been forty years wed).

So I comes right away by mysen, with the book,
And I turns the old pages and has a good look
For the text as I've found, as tells me as He
Were the same trade as me.

Why don't I mark it? Ah, many say so,
But I think I'd as lief, with your leaves, let it go:
It do seem that nice when I fall on it sudden—
Unexpected, you know!

The Tiger, the Ram, and the Jackal

From South-African Folk-Tales by James A. Honey

Tiger (leopard) was returning home from hunting on one occasion, when he lighted on the kraal of Ram. Now, Tiger had never seen Ram before, and accordingly, approaching submissively, he said, "Good day, friend! What may your name be?"

The other in his gruff voice, and striking his breast with his forefoot, said, "I am Ram. Who are you?"

"Tiger," answered the other, more dead than alive, and then, taking leave of Ram, he ran home as fast as he could.

Jackal lived at the same place as Tiger did, and the latter going to him, said, "Friend Jackal, I am quite out of breath, and am half dead with fright, for I have just seen a terrible looking fellow, with a large and thick head, and on my asking him what his name was, he answered, 'I am Ram.'"

"What a foolish fellow you are," cried Jackal, "to let such a nice piece of flesh stand! Why did you do so? But we shall go tomorrow and eat it together."

Next day the two set off for the kraal of Ram, and as they appeared over a hill, Ram, who had turned out to look about him, and was calculating where he should that day crop a tender salad, saw them, and he immediately went to his wife and said, "I fear this is our last day, for Jackal and Tiger are both coming against us. What shall we do?"

"Don't be afraid," said the wife, "but take up the child in your arms, go out with it, and pinch it to make it cry as if it were hungry." Ram did so as the confederates came on.

No sooner did Tiger cast his eyes on Ram than fear again took possession of him, and he wished to turn back. Jackal had provided against this, and made Tiger fast to himself with a leathern thong, and said, "Come on," when Ram cried in a loud voice, and pinching his child at the same time, "You have done well, Friend Jackal, to have brought us Tiger to eat, for you hear how my child is crying for food."

On these dreadful words Tiger, notwithstanding the entreaties of Jackal to let him go, to let him loose, set off in the greatest alarm, dragged Jackal after him over hill and valley, through bushes and over rocks, and never stopped to look behind him till he brought back himself and half-dead Jackal to his place again. And so Ram escaped.

Writing: Outline

Write or type an outline of the new model story which you read in the last lesson.

Exercise

Review memory work. Punctuate the following sentences.

> The Scarecrow Billina and the Nome King were in the throne room

> Why it's Billina

In the following sentences, label homographs GR and homophones PH.

> "I've got a right to cackle, I guess."

> "Well, you'll have to bear this one around."

Copy each sentence below. Double underline the predicate, and underline the subject. Put brackets around any prepositional phrases. Label the part of speech of each word. Noun, N; Proper Noun, PN; Pronoun, PRO; Verb, V; Linking Verb, LV; Adjective, ADJ; Article, ART; Conjunction, CJ; Preposition, Prep; Interjection, INJ. Diagram each sentence.

> "Take it away at once!" [Hint: **once** is usually an adverb, but it is a noun in this sentence.]

> "Will she now return to us in safety?"

> Dorothy led the little Prince Evring by the hand.

Commonplace Book

With your instructor's approval, add the poem below to your commonplace book, or choose your own poem.

> "Isn't this Joseph's son?"—ay, it is He;
> Joseph the carpenter—same trade as me—
> I thought as I'd find it—I knew it was here—
> But my sight's getting queer.
>
> I don't know right where as His shed must ha' stood—
> But often, as I've been a-planing my wood,
> I've took off my hat, just with thinking of He
> At the same work as me.

Dictation

Matthew 11:28-30

"Come to Me, all who are weary and heavy-laden, and I will give you rest. Take My yoke upon you and learn from Me, for I am gentle and humble in heart, and you will find rest for your souls. For My yoke is easy and My burden is light."

Ballet School by Edgar Degas

Picture Study

1. Read the title and the name of the artist. Study the picture for several minutes, then put the picture away.

2. Describe the picture.

3. Look at the picture again. Do you notice any details that you missed before? What do you like or dislike about this painting? Does it remind you of anything?

57. Descriptive Writing

- Ozma of Oz, Chapter 16

Writing: Descriptive Writing

In the last chapter of *Ozma of Oz*, Billina and the Nome King had a discussion on the propriety of laying eggs in the throne room. Read that passage below, paying close attention to the details that make a vivid picture in your mind, and then write a narration of it. Both Billina and the Nome King get rather emotional during this discussion. How does the L. Frank Baum let us know what they're feeling, and how they're expressing these emotions?

Add details if you wish. Remember, the point of this exercise is to write as descriptively as possible, not just to narrate the passage exactly.

Ozma of Oz

"I've got a right to cackle, I guess," replied Billina. "I've just laid my egg."

"What! Laid an egg! In my throne room! How dare you do such a thing?" asked the King, in a voice of fury.

"I lay eggs wherever I happen to be," said the hen, ruffling her feathers and then shaking them into place.

"But—thunderation! Don't you know that eggs are poison?" roared the King, while his rock-colored eyes stuck out in great terror.

"Poison! Well, I declare," said Billina, indignantly. "I'll have you know all my eggs are warranted strictly fresh and up to date. Poison, indeed!"

"You don't understand," retorted the little monarch, nervously. "Eggs belong only to the outside world—to the world on the earth's surface, where you came from. Here, in my underground kingdom, they are rank poison, as I said, and we Nomes can't bear them around."

"Well, you'll have to bear this one around," declared Billina; "for I've laid it."

"Where?" asked the King.

"Under your throne," said the hen.

The King jumped three feet into the air, so anxious was he to get away from the throne.

"Take it away! Take it away at once!" he shouted.

A Dream

By William Blake

Once a dream did wave a shade
O'er my angel-guarded bed,
That an emmet lost its way
When on grass methought I lay.

Troubled, 'wildered, and forlorn,
Dark, benighted, travel-worn,
Over many a tangled spray,
All heart-broke, I heard her say:

"Oh, my children! Do they cry?
Do they hear their father sigh?
Now they look abroad to see.
Now return and weep for me."

Pitying, I dropped a tear;
But I saw a glow-worm near,
Who replied, "What wailing wight
Calls the watchman of the night?

"I am set to light the ground
While the beetle goes his round.
Follow now the beetle's hum—
Little wanderer, hie thee home!"

Jackal's Bride

From *South-African Folk-Tales* by James A. Honey

Jackal, it is said, married Hyena, and carried off a cow belonging to the ants, to slaughter her for the wedding; and when he had slaughtered her, he put the cowskin over his bride; and when he had fixed a pole (on which to hang the flesh), he placed on the top of the pole (which was forked) the hearth for the cooking, in order to cook upon it all sorts of delicious food. There came also Lion, and wished to go up. Jackal, therefore, asked his little daughter for a thong with which he could pull Lion up; and he began to pull him up; and when his face came near to the cooking-pot, he cut the thong in two, so that Lion tumbled down. Then Jackal upbraided his little daughter with these words: "Why do you give me such an old thong?" And he added, "Give me a fresh thong." She gave him a new thong, and he pulled Lion up again, and when his face came near the pot, which stood on the fire, he said, "Open your mouth." Then he put into his mouth a hot piece of quartz which had been boiled together with the fat, and the stone went down, burning his throat. Thus died Lion.

There came also the ants running after the cow, and when Jackal saw them he fled. Then they beat the bride in her brookaross dress. Hyena, believing that it was Jackal, said:

"You tawny rogue! Have you not played at beating long enough? Have you no more loving game than this?"

But when she had bitten a hole through the cowskin, she saw that they were other people; then she fled, falling here and there, yet made her escape.

Exercise

Review memory work. Identify each group of words below as either a phrase or a clause. If it is a clause, double underline the predicate and underline the subject.

with an air of vast importance

then I thank you for the gracious favor

don't worry

Copy each sentence below. Double underline the predicate, and underline the subject. Put brackets around any prepositional phrases. Label the part of speech of each word. Noun, N; Proper Noun, PN; Pronoun, PRO; Verb, V; Linking Verb, LV; Adjective, ADJ; Article, ART; Conjunction, CJ; Preposition, Prep; Interjection, INJ. Diagram each sentence.

"Why, my name is Bill, by rights."

"Am I a good guesser, Mr. Nome King?"

Evanna, a sweet-faced girl, stood beside them.

Commonplace Book

With your instructor's approval, add the passage below to your commonplace book, or choose your own passage from a work of non-fiction. This can be from the Bible, a biography, or one of your history or science books.

> Then she disenchanted another girl, whom the Queen addressed as Evrose, and afterwards a boy named Evardo, who was older than his brother Evring. Indeed, the yellow hen kept the good Queen exclaiming and embracing for some time, until five Princesses and four Princes, all looking very much alike except for the difference in size, stood in a row beside their happy mother.

58. Prepositions and Adverbs

• Ozma of Oz, Chapter 17

Some of the most common prepositions are:

aboard, about, above, across, after, against, along, among, around, at, before, behind, below, beneath, beside, between, beyond, by, down, during, except, for, from, in, inside, into, like, near, of, off, on, onto, outside, over, past, round, since, through, throughout, till, to, toward, under, underneath, until, up, upon, with, within, without.

An important thing to remember about this list is that some of the words on it are not always prepositions. Many of these words can also be adverbs. How can you tell the difference?

A preposition must have an object. An adverb never has an object. Look at these sentences closely. Does the prep-adverb have an object?

The boy wants to color <u>outside</u> with his siblings.

The boy wants to color <u>outside</u> the lines.

To determine whether the prep-adverb has an object, we can ask the question **what** or **whom**. In the first sentence, the boy wants to color outside **what**? Well, just **outside**. There's not another answer to that. There is no object.

In the second sentence, the boy wants to color outside **what**? The lines;

he wants to color **outside the lines**. The object of the preposition outside is **lines**, and the prepositional phrase is **outside the lines**.

In the first sentence, **outside** is an adverb. It does not have an object. In the second sentence, **outside** is a preposition with **lines** as the object.

Look at the sentences below from *Ozma of Oz*. Which underlined words are adverbs, and which are prepositions?

"Ah, I'd forgotten that," said the King, getting <u>up</u>.

The ten men in the first row fell <u>over</u> like so many toy soldiers.

The warriors fairly tumbled <u>over</u> one another.

In the first sentence, **up** is an adverb. It has no object. In the second sentence, **over** is an adverb. It has no object. In the third sentence, however, **over** is a preposition. They tumbled over **what**? One another. **Another** is the object of the prepositional phrase **over one another**.

The direct object can never be the object of a preposition. If you have a phrase which follows a prep-adverb, you have to decide if it's part of a prepositional phrase, or if it's receiving the action of the verb by answering the question **whom** or **what**, as in the sentences at the beginning of this lesson.

Heaven Is Not Reached at a Single Bound (A Fragment)

J. G. Holland

Heaven is not reached at a single bound,
  But we build the ladder by which we rise
    From the lowly earth to the vaulted skies,
And we mount to its summit round by round.

I count this thing to be grandly true:
  That a noble deed is a step toward God,—
    Lifting the soul from the common clod
To a purer air and a broader view.

The Lion, the Jackal, and the Man

From *South-African Folk-Tales* by James A. Honey

    It so happened one day that Lion and Jackal came together to converse on affairs of land and state. Jackal, let me say, was the most important adviser to the king of the forest, and after they had spoken about these matters for quite a while, the conversation took a more personal turn.
    Lion began to boast and talk big about his strength. Jackal had, perhaps, given him cause for it, because by nature he was a flatterer. But now that Lion began to assume so many airs, said he, "See here, Lion, I will show you an animal that is still more powerful than you are."
    They walked along, Jackal leading the way, and met first a little boy.
    "Is this the strong man?" asked Lion.
    "No," answered Jackal, "he must still become a man, O king."
    After a while they found an old man walking with bowed head and supporting his bent figure with a stick.
    "Is this the wonderful strong man?" asked Lion.
    "Not yet, O king," was Jackal's answer, "he has been a man."
    Continuing their walk a short distance farther, they came across a young hunter, in the prime of youth, and accompanied by some of his dogs.
    "There you have him now, O king," said Jackal. "Pit your strength against his, and if you win, then truly you are the strength of the earth."
    Then Jackal made tracks to one side toward a little rocky kopje from which he

would be able to see the meeting.

Growling, growling, Lion strode forward to meet the man, but when he came close the dogs beset him. He, however, paid but little attention to the dogs, pushed and separated them on all sides with a few sweeps of his front paws. They howled aloud, beating a hasty retreat toward the man.

Thereupon the man fired a charge of shot, hitting him behind the shoulder, but even to this Lion paid but little attention. Thereupon the hunter pulled out his steel knife, and gave him a few good jabs. Lion retreated, followed by the flying bullets of the hunter.

"Well, are you strongest now?" was Jackal's first question when Lion arrived at his side.

"No, Jackal," answered Lion, "let that fellow there keep the name and welcome. Such as he I have never before seen. In the first place he had about ten of his bodyguard storm me. I really did not bother myself much about them, but when I attempted to turn him to chaff, he spat and blew fire at me, mostly into my face, that burned just a little but not very badly. And when I again endeavored to pull him to the ground he jerked out from his body one of his ribs with which he gave me some very ugly wounds, so bad that I had to make chips fly, and as a parting he sent some warm bullets after me. No, Jackal, give him the name."

Writing: Copia

Take the following sentence and play with it. Remember that the point is not necessarily to make the sentence better. The point is to play with the sentence and make it different. Make a new sentence with a change from each of the following categories.

"I was so busy making music that before I knew it the summer was gone."

1. Change the grammar.
   - Change the nouns from common to proper and vice versa.
   - Change the nouns from singular to plural and vice versa.
   - Change the sentence type.
   - Change the adjectives from articles to descriptive to possessive, etc.
   - Change a quotation from direct to indirect and vice versa.

2. Condense the sentence.
   - Remove details.
   - Remove modifiers.
   - Remove phrases or clauses.

3. Amplify the sentence.
   - Add details.
   - Add dialogue.
   - Add modifiers.
   - Add phrases or clauses.

4. Use synonyms and antonyms.
   - Substitute synonyms.
   - Say the opposite thing using antonyms.

5. Point of view.
   • Change the point of view.

Exercise

Review memory work. Punctuate the following sentence.

> The generals the colonels the majors and the captains all commanded Forward, march

In the following sentences, label homographs GR and homophones PH.

> "The creature is made of wood."

> At once the army filed out in great numbers, led by their captain.

Copy each sentence below. Double underline the predicate, and underline the subject. Put brackets around any prepositional phrases. Label the part of speech of each word. Noun, N; Proper Noun, PN; Pronoun, PRO; Verb, V; Linking Verb, LV; Adjective, ADJ; Article, ART; Conjunction, CJ; Preposition, Prep; Interjection, INJ. Diagram each sentence.

> "The creature is made of wood."

> "Don't mind them!"

> "Do you surrender?"

Commonplace Book

With your instructor's approval, add the passage below to your commonplace book, or choose your own passage from a work of fiction. This can be from either school reading or free reading.

> But in spite of the magic the Sawhorse moved; and he moved so quickly toward the King, that the fat little man could not get out of his way. Thump—BANG! Came the wooden heels, right against his round body, and the King flew into the air and fell upon the head of his captain, who let him drop flat upon the ground.

Dictation

> The captain of the Nomes was so surprised by this sudden onslaught that he forgot to command his warriors to fight, so that the ten men in the first row, who stood in front of the private's spear, fell over like so many toy soldiers. The spear could not go through their steel armor, however, so the warriors scrambled to their feet again, and by that time the private had knocked over another row of them.

59. Slant Narratives

- Ozma of Oz, Chapter 18

Many stories are told in the third person. That means that we don't always know what the characters are thinking. The person telling the tale is different from the characters experiencing the tale.

Often, the story would read much differently if one of the people involved in the story were to tell the tale. Have you ever had to tell your side of a story when you've been in an argument with someone, or have you heard another tell his side of a story? What does it mean for a story to have "sides"? Your side of the story is your version, the way you remember it. Even if you don't mean to, the story you tell will usually favor yourself over the other person. We call this a **slant**. When something is slanted, it's tipped to one side.

Read "The Cat and the Birds" below. And then read the same story, first from the Cat's point of view, and then from the Birds'.

The Cat and the Birds

An Aesop's Fable

A Cat was growing very thin. As you have guessed, he did not get enough to eat. One day he heard that some Birds in the neighborhood were ailing and needed a doctor. So he put on a pair of spectacles, and with a leather box in his hand, knocked at the door of the Bird's home.

The Birds peeped out, and Dr. Cat, with much solicitude, asked how they were. He would be very happy to give them some medicine.

"Tweet, tweet," laughed the Birds. "Very smart, aren't you? We are very well, thank you, and more so, if you only keep away from here."

Be wise and shun the quack.

The Cat's Point of View

Once, during a sad time in my life, I was growing thin from lack of food. I was in desperate need of work, so when I heard that some Birds needed a doctor, I put on my spectacles, grabbed my leather box, and went to their home to offer my services.

When they answered, I asked how they were. I offered both my services and my medicines.

The Birds laughed at me! They said that they would stay very well indeed, if only I would keep away.

The Birds' Point of View

Some of us birds were ailing once and needed a doctor. One day during this time, a knock sounded at the door. We opened the door to find a skinny cat standing there, wearing spectacles and carrying a leather box! He asked how we were and offered us medicine.

How we laughed! We told him that we'd stay very well indeed, as long as he should stay away. As if we didn't know that his only medicine was in his belly.

Crossing the Bar

By Alfred Tennyson

Sunset and evening star,
  And one clear call for me!
And may there be no moaning of the bar,
  When I put out to sea,

But such a tide as moving seems asleep,
  Too full for sound and foam,
When that which drew from out the boundless deep
  Turns again home.

Twilight and evening bell,
  And after that the dark!
And may there be no sadness of farewell,
  When I embark;

For tho' from out our bourne of Time and Place
  The flood may bear me far,
I hope to see my Pilot face to face
  When I have cross'd the bar.

The World's Reward

From *South-African Folk-Tales* by James A. Honey

Once there was a man that had an old dog, so old that the man desired to put him aside. The dog had served him very faithfully when he was still young, but ingratitude is the world's reward, and the man now wanted to dispose of him. The old dumb creature, however, ferreted out the plan of his master, and so at once resolved to go away of his own accord.

After he had walked quite a way he met an old bull in the veldt.

"Don't you want to go with me?" asked the dog.

"Where?" was the reply.

"To the land of the aged," said the dog, "where troubles don't disturb you and thanklessness does not deface the deeds of man."

"Good," said the bull, "I am your companion."

The two now walked on and found a ram.

The dog laid the plan before him, and all moved off together, until they afterwards came successively upon a donkey, a cat, a rooster, and a goose.

These joined their company, and the seven set out on their journey.

Late one night they came to a house and through the open door they saw a table spread with all kinds of nice food, of which some robbers were having their fill. It would help nothing to ask for admittance, and seeing that they were hungry, they must think of something else.

Therefore the donkey climbed up on the bull, the ram on the donkey, the dog on the ram, the cat on the dog, the goose on the cat, and the rooster on the goose, and with one accord they all let out terrible (threatening) noises (cryings).

The bull began to bellow, the donkey to bray, the dog to bark, the ram to bleat, the cat to mew, the goose to giggle gaggle, and the rooster to crow, all without cessation.

The people in the house were frightened perfectly limp; they glanced out through the front door, and there they stared on the strange sight. Some of them took to the ropes over the back lower door, some disappeared through the window, and in a few counts the house was empty.

Then the seven old animals climbed down from one another, stepped into the house, and satisfied themselves with the delicious food.

But when they had finished, there still remained a great deal of food, too much to take with them on their remaining journey, and so together they contrived a plan to hold their position until the next day after breakfast.

The dog said, "See here, I am accustomed to watch at the front door of my master's house," and thereupon flopped himself down to sleep; the bull said, "I go behind the door," and there he took his position; the ram said, "I will go up on to the loft"; the donkey, "I at the middle door"; the cat, "I in the fireplace"; the goose, "I in the back door"; and the rooster said, "I am going to sleep on the bed."

The captain of the robbers after a while sent one of his men back to see if these creatures had yet left the house.

The man came very cautiously into the neighborhood, listened and listened, but he heard nothing; he peeped through the window, and saw in the grate just two coals still glimmering, and thereupon started to walk through the front door.

There the old dog seized him by the leg. He jumped into the house, but the bull was ready, swept him up with his horns, and tossed him on to the loft. Here the ram received him and pushed him off the loft again. Reaching ground, he made for the middle door, but the donkey set up a terrible braying and at the same time gave him a kick that landed him in the fireplace, where the cat flew at him and scratched him nearly to pieces. He then jumped out through the back door, and here the goose got him by the trousers. When he was some distance away the rooster crowed. He thereupon ran so that you could hear the stones rattle in the dark.

Purple and crimson and out of breath, he came back to his companions.

"Frightful, frightful!" was all that they could get from him at first, but after a while he told them.

"When I looked through the window I saw in the fireplace two bright coals shining, and when I wanted to go through the front door to go and look, I stepped into an iron trap. I jumped into the house, and there some one seized me with a fork and pitched me up on to the loft, there again some one was ready, and threw me down on all fours. I wanted to fly through the middle door, but there some one blew on a trumpet, and smote me with a sledge hammer so that I did not know where I landed; but coming to very quickly, I found I was in the fireplace, and there another flew at me and scratched the eyes almost out of my head. I thereupon fled out of the back door, and lastly I was attacked on the leg by the sixth with a pair of fire tongs, and when I was still running away, some one shouted out of the house, 'Stop him, stop h—i—m!'"

Exercise

Review memory work. Identify each group of words below as either a phrase or a clause. If it is a clause, double underline the predicate and underline the subject.

   although I wonder why

   so the King stopped and looked at them in surprise

   where the king jeered at Dorothy

Copy each sentence below. Double underline the predicate, and underline the subject. Put brackets around any prepositional phrases. Label the part of speech of each word. Noun, N; Proper Noun, PN; Pronoun, PRO; Verb, V; Linking Verb, LV; Adjective, ADJ; Article, ART; Conjunction, CJ; Preposition, Prep; Interjection, INJ. Diagram each sentence.

   "Why, you are not wearing your magic belt."

   Dorothy welcomed back Ozma and the Queen of Ev.
   [Hint: **what kind** of queen.]

   The others went with Dorothy.

Writing: Commonplace Book

Add the passage below from your model story to your commonplace book.

   One bright day in late autumn a family of Ants were bustling about in the warm sunshine, drying out the grain they had stored up during the summer, when a starving Grasshopper, his fiddle under his arm, came up and humbly begged for a bite to eat.
   "What!" cried the Ants in surprise, "haven't you stored anything away for the winter? What in the world were you doing all last summer?"

Dictation

Use part of today's poem for dictation.

60. Slant Narrative: The Ants and the Grasshopper

• Ozma of Oz, Chapter 19

Today, use your outline to write "The Ants and the Grasshopper" as a slant narrative. Write it in the first person. Who are you—the grasshopper or one of the ants? Remember to watch your pronouns. And don't be objective! Cast blame, make accusations, and show how **you** were not at fault!

The Chambered Nautilus

By Oliver Wendell Holmes

This is the ship of pearl, which, poets feign,
  Sailed the unshadowed main,—
  The venturous bark that flings
On the sweet summer wind its purpled wings
In gulfs enchanted, where the Siren sings,
  And coral reefs lie bare,
Where the cold sea-maids rise to sun their streaming hair.

Its webs of living gauze no more unfurl;
  Wrecked is the ship of pearl!
  And every chambered cell,
Where its dim dreaming life was wont to dwell,
As the frail tenant shaped his growing shell,
  Before thee lies revealed,—
Its irised ceiling rent, its sunless crypt unsealed!

Year after year beheld the silent toil
  That spread his lustrous coil;
  Still, as the spiral grew,
He left the past year's dwelling for the new,
Stole with soft step its shining archway through,
  Built up its idle door,
Stretched in his last-found home, and knew the old no more.

Thanks for the heavenly message brought by thee,
  Child of the wandering sea,
  Cast from her lap, forlorn!
From thy dead lips a clearer note is born
Than ever Triton blew from wreathed horn!
  While on mine ear it rings,
Through the deep caves of thought I hear a voice that sings:—

Build thee more stately mansions, O my soul,
  As the swift seasons roll!
  Leave thy low-vaulted past!
Let each new temple, nobler than the last,
Shut thee from heaven with a dome more vast,
  Till thou at length art free,
Leaving thine outgrown shell by life's unresting sea!

Editing

- Did you meet the goal of this writing exercise?

- Look at your word choice. Is there a good mixture of nouns and pronouns? Is the antecedent of each pronoun clear?

- Look at your paragraphs. Are all the sentences related? Does each paragraph focus on a single topic?

61. Noun and Pronouns Cases

• Ozma of Oz, Chapter 20

Definition: Cases are changes in form based on a noun or pronoun's job in the sentence.

	Subjective/ Nominative	Objective	Possessive
1st Person Singular	I	me	my, mine
1st Person Plural	we	us	our, ours
2nd Person	you	you	your, yours
3rd Person Singular	he, she, it	him, her, it	his, her, hers, its
3rd Person Plural	they	them	their, theirs

There are twenty-six personal pronouns—the first person, second person, and third person pronouns which you've learned. We need so many because we use different pronouns for different jobs. You would not say, "My going to my room." Babies often talk like that while they're learning, but as you learned to speak proper English, you learned to say, "I'm going to my room."

The word **cases** is just a way to talk about the different jobs that nouns and pronouns perform. In English, the cases are **subjective, objective,** and **possessive**. Although pronouns have different forms for all three cases, English nouns only change for possessive case.

Subjective case is also called **nominative case**. We use subjective/nominative case for the subject of a verb and for predicate nominatives. Subject does not have to mean the main subject of the sentence. In this case, it simply means the subject of a verb.

Look at the following sentences from *Ozma of Oz*.

"<u>He</u> will know better next time, <u>I</u> am sure."

Afterward <u>they</u> sat down to a splendid feast.

Objective case is used for objects. That can mean a direct object, an indirect object, or the object of a preposition.

"I promote <u>you</u> to be Captain General."

The army caught sight of <u>him</u> and set up a cheer.

Possessive case is also called **genitive case**. Possessive case shows that someone or something belongs to someone or something. Possessive case nouns and pronouns always acts as adjectives.

"Where is <u>your</u> husband?"

"I am happy and contented and willing to lead a quiet life and mind <u>my</u> own business."

The Night-Swans

By Walter De La Mare

'Tis silence on the enchanted lake,
And silence in the air serene,
Save for the beating of her heart,
The lovely-eyed Evangeline.
She sings across the waters clear
And dark with trees and stars between,
The notes her fairy godmother
Taught her, the child Evangeline.
As might the unrippled pool reply,
Faltering an answer far and sweet,
Three swans as white as mountain snow
Swim mantling to her feet.
And still upon the lake they stay,
Their eyes black stars in all their snow,
And softly, in the glassy pool,
Their feet beat darkly to and fro.
She rides upon her little boat,
Her swans swim through the starry sheen,
Rowing her into Fairyland—
The lovely-eyed Evangeline.
'Tis silence on the enchanted lake,
And silence in the air serene;
Voices shall call in vain again
On earth the child Evangeline.
'Evangeline! Evangeline!'

Upstairs, downstairs, all in vain.
Her room is dim; her flowers faded;
She answers not again.

Writing: Oral Narration

Read your new model story below, and then give your instructor an oral narration of it.

The Town Mouse and the Country Mouse

An Aesop's Fable

A Town Mouse once visited a relative who lived in the country. For lunch the Country Mouse served wheat stalks, roots, and acorns, with a dash of cold water for drink. The Town Mouse ate very sparingly, nibbling a little of this and a little of that, and by her manner making it very plain that she ate the simple food only to be polite.

After the meal the friends had a long talk, or rather the Town Mouse talked about her life in the city while the Country Mouse listened. They then went to bed in a cozy nest in the hedgerow and slept in quiet and comfort until morning. In her sleep the Country Mouse dreamed she was a Town Mouse with all the luxuries and delights of city life that her friend had described for her. So the next day when the Town Mouse asked the Country Mouse to go home with her to the city, she gladly said yes.

When they reached the mansion in which the Town Mouse lived, they found on the table in the dining room the leavings of a very fine banquet. There were sweetmeats and jellies, pastries, delicious cheeses, indeed, the most tempting foods that a Mouse can imagine. But just as the Country Mouse was about to nibble a dainty bit of pastry, she heard a Cat mew loudly and scratch at the door. In great fear the Mice scurried to a hiding place, where they lay quite still for a long time, hardly daring to breathe. When at last they ventured back to the feast, the door opened suddenly and in came the servants to clear the table, followed by the House Dog.

The Country Mouse stopped in the Town Mouse's den only long enough to pick up her carpet bag and umbrella.

"You may have luxuries and dainties that I have not," she said as she hurried away, "but I prefer my plain food and simple life in the country with the peace and security that go with it."

Poverty with security is better than plenty in the midst of fear and uncertainty.

Exercise

Review memory work. Punctuate the following sentence.

> For Ozma of Oz ruled the King of the Munchkins the King of the Winkies the King of the Quadlings and the King of the Gillikins

In the following sentences, label homographs GR and homophones PH.

> She lives in the Emerald City, which is in the exact center of the four kingdoms of the Land of Oz.

"Now I am happy and contented and willing to lead a quiet life and mind my own business."

Copy each sentence below. Double underline the predicate, and underline the subject. Put brackets around any prepositional phrases. Label the part of speech of each word. Noun, N; Proper Noun, PN; Pronoun, PRO; Verb, V; Linking Verb, LV; Adjective, ADJ; Article, ART; Conjunction, CJ; Preposition, Prep; Interjection, INJ. Diagram each sentence.

"Have we any other privates in the armies?"

"Omby Amby, I promote you."

Ozma, the Ruler of Oz, returned to the Emerald City.

Commonplace Book

With your instructor's approval, add the passage below to your commonplace book, or choose your own passage from a work of fiction. This can be from either school reading or free reading.

That evening there was a grand reception in the royal palace, attended by the most important persons of Oz, and Jack Pumpkinhead, who was a little overripe but still active, read an address congratulating Ozma of Oz upon the success of her generous mission to rescue the royal family of a neighboring kingdom.

Dictation

Then magnificent gold medals set with precious stones were presented to each of the twenty-six officers; and the Tin Woodman was given a new axe studded with diamonds; and the Scarecrow received a silver jar of complexion powder. Dorothy was presented with a pretty coronet and made a Princess of Oz, and Tiktok received two bracelets set with eight rows of very clear and sparkling emeralds.

62. Pronoun Cases: Correct Usage

• Ozma of Oz, Chapter 21

When you use a noun and a pronoun together, it can be difficult to determine whether to use the subjective/nominative case or objective case pronoun. It is sometimes helpful to think of it as two sentences instead of one.

>The King said good-bye. She said good-bye.
>The King and she said good-bye.

>The feast was for Ozma. The feast was for them.
>The feast was for Ozma and them.

>You read the chapter. I read the chapter.
>You and I read the chapter.

You can do the same thing, of course, by determining what part of the sentence the pronoun is and which case that part needs. However, this can be quicker, especially when speaking.

The first column of sentences below has linking verbs and predicate nominatives. A predicate nominative is always in the subjective/nominative case. Nowadays, it is common to hear these sentences spoken incorrectly.

>It is I.
>This is he.
>This is she.
>It is we.
>It was I.
>It was not I; it was she.
>I think it was he.
>I am sure it is she.
>It was we.
>It might have been they.
>It was he and I.
>It was they.
>No, it is not she.
>Yes, it is he.

>Did you call her?
>Did you call me?
>Did you call him and me?
>Mother bought a ball for you.
>Mother bought a ball for me.
>Mother bought a ball for you and me.
>Between you and me, I wanted a dinosaur.

The Overland-Mail

By Rudyard Kipling

In the name of the Empress of India, make way,
O Lords of the Jungle wherever you roam,
The woods are astir at the close of the day—
We exiles are waiting for letters from Home—
Let the robber retreat; let the tiger turn tail,
In the name of the Empress the Overland-Mail!

With a jingle of bells as the dusk gathers in,
He turns to the foot-path that leads up the hill—
The bags on his back, and a cloth round his chin,
And, tucked in his belt, the Post-Office bill;—
  "Despatched on this date, as received by the rail,
Per runner, two bags of the Overland-Mail."

Is the torrent in spate? He must ford it or swim.
Has the rain wrecked the road? He must climb by the cliff.
Does the tempest cry "Halt"? What are tempests to him?
The service admits not a "but" or an "if";
While the breath's in his mouth, he must bear without fail,
In the name of the Empress the Overland-Mail.

From aloe to rose-oak, from rose-oak to fir,
From level to upland, from upland to crest,
From rice-field to rock-ridge, from rock-ridge to spur,
Fly the soft-sandaled feet, strains the brawny brown chest.
From rail to ravine—to the peak from the vale—
Up, up through the night goes the Overland-Mail.

There's a speck on the hillside, a dot on the road—
A jingle of bells on the foot-path below—
There's a scuffle above in the monkeys' abode—
The world is awake, and the clouds are aglow—
For the great Sun himself must attend to the hail;—
In the name of the Empress the Overland-Mail.

Tink-Tinkje

From *South-African Folk-Tales* by James A. Honey

   The birds wanted a king. Men have a king, so have animals, and why shouldn't they? All had assembled.
   "The Ostrich, because he is the largest," one called out.
   "No, he can't fly."
   "Eagle, on account of his strength."
   "Not he, he is too ugly."
   "Vulture, because he can fly the highest."
   "No, Vulture is too dirty, his odor is terrible."

"Peacock, he is so beautiful."

"His feet are too ugly, and also his voice."

"Owl, because he can see well."

"Not Owl, he is ashamed of the light."

And so they got no further. Then one shouted aloud, "He who can fly the highest will be king." "Yes, yes," they all screamed, and at a given signal they all ascended straight up into the sky.

Vulture flew for three whole days without stopping, straight toward the sun. Then he cried aloud, "I am the highest, I am king."

"T-sie, t-sie, t-sie," he heard above him. There Tink-tinkje was flying. He had held fast to one of the great wing feathers of Vulture, and had never been felt, he was so light. "T-sie, t-sie, t-sie, I am the highest, I am king," piped Tink-tinkje.

Vulture flew for another day still ascending. "I am highest, I am king."

"T-sie, t-sie, t-sie, I am the highest, I am king," Tink-tinkje mocked. There he was again, having crept out from under the wing of Vulture.

Vulture flew on the fifth day straight up in the air. "I am the highest, I am king," he called.

"T-sie, t-sie, t-sie," piped the little fellow above him. "I am the highest, I am king."

Vulture was tired and now flew direct to earth. The other birds were mad through and through. Tink-tinkje must die because he had taken advantage of Vulture's feathers and there hidden himself. All flew after him and he had to take refuge in a mouse hole. But how were they to get him out? Some one must stand guard to seize him the moment he put out his head.

"Owl must keep guard; he has the largest eyes; he can see well," they exclaimed.

Owl went and took up his position before the hole. The sun was warm and soon Owl became sleepy and presently he was fast asleep.

Tink-tinkje peeped, saw that Owl was asleep, and z-zip away he went. Shortly afterwards the other birds came to see if Tink-tinkje were still in the hole. "T-sie, t-sie," they heard in a tree; and there the little vagabond was sitting.

White-crow, perfectly disgusted, turned around and exclaimed, "Now I won't say a single word more." And from that day to this White-crow has never spoken. Even though you strike him, he makes no sound, he utters no cry.

Writing: Outline

Write or type an outline of the new model story which you read in the last lesson.

Exercise

Review memory work. Punctuate the following sentence.

The belt has magical powers only while it is in some fairy country my little friend

Copy each sentence below. Double underline the predicate, and underline the subject. Put brackets around any prepositional phrases. Label the part of speech of each word. Noun, N; Proper Noun, PN; Pronoun, PRO; Verb, V; Linking Verb, LV; Adjective, ADJ; Article, ART; Conjunction, CJ; Preposition, Prep; Interjection, INJ. Diagram each sentence.

Uncle Henry was seated in an easy chair.

Instantly the farmhouse appeared in the picture.

Dorothy, the little Kansas girl, might visit.

Commonplace Book

With your instructor's approval, add the poem below to your commonplace book, or choose your own poem.

> In the name of the Empress of India, make way,
> O Lords of the Jungle wherever you roam,
> The woods are astir at the close of the day—
> We exiles are waiting for letters from Home—
> Let the robber retreat; let the tiger turn tail,
> In the name of the Empress the Overland-Mail!
>
> With a jingle of bells as the dusk gathers in,
> He turns to the foot-path that leads up the hill—
> The bags on his back, and a cloth round his chin,
> And, tucked in his belt, the Post-Office bill;—
>   "Despatched on this date, as received by the rail,
> Per runner, two bags of the Overland-Mail."

Dictation

James 2:8-9

If, however, you are fulfilling the royal law according to the Scripture, "You shall love your neighbor as yourself," you are doing well. But if you show partiality, you are committing sin and are convicted by the law as transgressors.

Racehorses at Longchamp by Edgar Degas

Picture Study

1. Read the title and the name of the artist. Study the picture for several minutes, then put the picture away.

2. Describe the picture.

3. Look at the picture again. Do you notice any details that you missed before? What do you like or dislike about this painting? Does it remind you of anything?

63. Literary Analysis

- The Reluctant Dragon, approximately 10 pages (1/5 of the story)

Writing: Literary Analysis

Today you have another literary analysis assignment. Now that you've had some practice, this should be a written assignment, though it can be helpful to discuss your ideas before writing.

With your instructor's approval, choose *Ozma of Oz*, or one of the other books you've finished reading, and answer the following questions.

What is the book about? Give a brief summary, just a few sentences. Did you hope the book would end another way? If so, how? If not, what did you like about the ending?

The Battle of Blenheim

By Robert Southey

It was a summer's evening,
  Old Kaspar's work was done,
And he before his cottage door
  Was sitting in the sun;
And by him sported on the green
His little grandchild Wilhelmine.

She saw her brother Peterkin
  Roll something large and round,
Which he, beside the rivulet,
  In playing there, had found.
He came to ask what he had found,
That was so large, and smooth, and round.

Old Kaspar took it from the boy,
  Who stood expectant by;
And then the old man shook his head,
  And, with a natural sigh,
   "'Tis some poor fellow's skull," said he,
  "Who fell in the great victory!

"I find them in the garden,
  For there's many hereabout;
And often when I go to plow,
  The plowshare turns them out;
For many thousand men," said he,
  "Were slain in that great victory!"

"Now tell us what 'twas all about,"
  Young Peterkin he cries;
And little Wilhelmine looks up
  With wonder-waiting eyes;
  "Now tell us all about the war,
And what they killed each other for."

"It was the English," Kaspar cried,
  "Who put the French to rout;
But what they killed each other for
  I could not well make out.
But everybody said," quoth he,
  "That 'twas a famous victory!

"My father lived at Blenheim then,
  Yon little stream hard by:
They burned his dwelling to the ground
  And he was forced to fly;
So with his wife and child he fled,
Nor had he where to rest his head.

"With fire and sword the country round
  Was wasted far and wide;
And many a childing mother then
  And new-born baby died.
But things like that, you know, must be
At every famous victory.

"They say it was a shocking sight
  After the field was won;
For many thousand bodies here
  Lay rotting in the sun.
But things like that, you know, must be
After a famous victory.

"Great praise the Duke of Marlborough won,
  And our good Prince Eugene."
  "Why, 'twas a very wicked thing!"
Said little Wilhelmine.
  "Nay, nay, my little girl," quoth he,
  "It was a famous victory!

"And everybody praised the Duke
Who this great fight did win."
"But what good came of it at last?"
Quoth little Peterkin.
"Why, that I cannot tell," said he,
"But 'twas a famous victory."

Cloud-Eating

From *South-African Folk-Tales* by James A. Honey

Jackal and Hyena were together, it is said, when a white cloud rose. Jackal descended upon it, and ate of the cloud as if it were fat.

When he wanted to come down, he said to Hyena, "My sister, as I am going to divide with thee, catch me well." So she caught him, and broke his fall. Then she also went up and ate there, high up on the top of the cloud.

When she was satisfied, she said, "My greyish brother, now catch me well." The greyish rogue said to his friend, "My sister, I shall catch thee well. Come therefore down."

He held up his hands, and she came down from the cloud, and when she was near, Jackal cried out (painfully jumping to one side), "My sister, do not take it ill. Oh me! Oh me! A thorn has pricked me and sticks in me." Thus she fell down from above, and was sadly hurt.

Since that day, it is said that Hyena's hind feet have been shorter and smaller than the front ones.

Exercise

Review memory work. Copy each sentence below. Double underline the predicate, and underline the subject. Put brackets around any prepositional phrases. Label the part of speech of each word. Noun, N; Proper Noun, PN; Pronoun, PRO; Verb, V; Linking Verb, LV; Adjective, ADJ; Article, ART; Conjunction, CJ; Preposition, Prep; Interjection, INJ. Diagram each sentence.

"Oh, yes, he was a peaceable sort of beast."

"Tell us about it first." [Hint: **first** tells when in this sentence.]

His parents were very fond of him.

Commonplace Book

With your instructor's approval, add the passage below to your commonplace book, or choose your own passage from a work of non-fiction. This can be from the Bible, a biography, or one of your history or science books.

> Long ago—might have been hundreds of years ago—in a cottage half-way between this village and yonder shoulder of the Downs up there, a shepherd lived with his wife and their little son. Now the shepherd spent his days—and at certain times of the year his nights too—up on the wide ocean-bosom of the Downs, with only the sun and the stars and the sheep for company, and the friendly chattering world of men and women far out of sight and hearing.

64. Interrogative Adverbs

- **The Reluctant Dragon**, approximately 10 pages (1/5 of the story)

The interrogative adverbs are when, where, why, and how.

Interrogative adverbs introduce questions. They do not always introduce questions, though, and not all questions need them. They are only called interrogative adverbs when they are performing the task of introducing a question.

You already know that some adverbs answer the questions **how**, **when**, and **where**.

"Going to make a long stay here?" he asked, politely.

How? Politely. When? Now. Where? Here, at the dragon's cave.

The words **how**, **when**, and **where** are adverbs themselves, and so is **why**. They are diagrammed just like other adverbs when they introduce questions.

How are you?   Where are we?

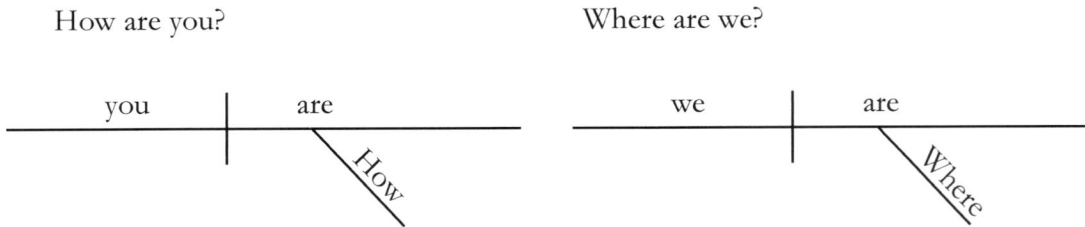

Notice that when we diagram interrogative adverbs, which introduce questions, we have to turn the sentence around, just as we have to do with other questions.

Where are we?   →   We are where?

An adverb cannot be the subject of the sentence. When we rearrange the sentence, we can more clearly see the subject. Adverbs that tell **how**, **when**, **where**, and **how often** modify verbs, so these interrogative adverbs modify the verb.

Look at this sentence from "The Reluctant Dragon." What is **why** in this sentence?

"Why, St. George, of course," replied his friend.

In the above sentence, **why** is not an interrogative adverb. It is an interjection! You are learning many lists of words, but don't let those lists take the place of your brain. Compare the following two diagrams:

Why, is he St. George?

```
____Why____

____he____|____is_____St. George____
          |
```

Why is St. George coming?

```
____St. George____|____is coming____
                  \
                   \Why
```

How Sleep the Brave

By William Collins

How sleep the brave, who sink to rest
By all their country's wishes blest!
When Spring, with dewy fingers cold,
Returns to deck their hallow'd mould,
She there shall dress a sweeter sod
Than Fancy's feet have ever trod.

By fairy hands their knell is rung,
By forms unseen their dirge is sung:
There Honor comes, a pilgrim gray,
To bless the turf that wraps their clay;
And Freedom shall a while repair
To dwell a weeping hermit there!

The Lion and Jackal

From *South-African Folk-Tales* by James A. Honey

Lion had now caught a large eland which lay dead on the top of a high bank. Lion was thirsty and wanted to go and drink water. "Jackal, look after my eland, I am going to get a drink. Don't you eat any."

"Very well, Uncle Lion."

Lion went to the river and Jackal quietly removed a stone on which Lion had to step to reach the bank on his return. After that Jackal and his wife ate heartily of the eland. Lion returned, but could not scale the bank. "Jackal, help me," he shouted.

"Yes, Uncle Lion, I will let down a rope and then you can climb up."

Jackal whispered to his wife, "Give me one of the old, thin hide ropes." And then aloud he added, "Wife, give me one of the strong, buffalo ropes, so Uncle Lion won't fall."

His wife gave him an old rotten rope. Jackal and his wife first ate ravenously of the meat, then gradually let the rope down. Lion seized it and struggled up. When he neared the brink Jackal gave the rope a jerk. It broke and down Lion began to roll—rolled the whole way down, and finally lay at the foot near the river.

Jackal began to beat a dry hide that lay there as he howled, cried, and shouted: "Wife, why did you give me such a bad rope that caused Uncle Lion to fall?"

Lion heard the row and roared, "Jackal, stop beating your wife. I will hurt you if you don't cease. Help me to climb up."

"Uncle Lion, I will give you a rope." Whispering again to his wife, "Give me one of the old, thin hide ropes," and shouting aloud again, "Give me a strong, buffalo rope, wife, that will not break again with Lion."

Jackal gave out the rope, and when Lion had nearly reached the top, he cut the rope through. Snap! And Lion began to roll to the bottom. Jackal again beat on the hide and shouted, "Wife, why did you give me such a rotten rope? Didn't I tell you to give me a strong one?" Lion roared, "Jackal, stop beating your wife at once. Help me instantly or you will be sorry."

"Wife," Jackal said aloud, "give me now the strongest rope you have," and aside to her, "Give me the worst rope of the lot."

Jackal again let down a rope, but just as Lion reached the top, Jackal gave a strong tug and broke the rope. Poor old Lion rolled down the side of the hill and lay there roaring from pain. He had been fatally hurt.

Jackal inquired, "Uncle Lion, have you hurt yourself? Have you much pain? Wait a while, I am coming directly to help you." Jackal and his wife slowly walked away.

Writing: Copia

Take the following sentence and play with it. Remember that the point is not necessarily to make the sentence better. The point is to play with the sentence and make it different. Make a new sentence with a change from each of the following categories.

"I prefer my plain food and simple life in the country with the peace and security that go with it."

1. Change the grammar.
   - Change the nouns from common to proper and vice versa.
   - Change the nouns from singular to plural and vice versa.
   - Change the sentence type.
   - Change the adjectives from articles to descriptive to possessive, etc.
   - Change a quotation from direct to indirect and vice versa.

2. Condense the sentence.
   - Remove details.
   - Remove modifiers.
   - Remove phrases or clauses.

3. Amplify the sentence.
   - Add details.
   - Add dialogue.

- Add modifiers.
- Add phrases or clauses.

4. Use synonyms and antonyms.
   - Substitute synonyms.
   - Say the opposite thing using antonyms.

5. Point of view.
   - Change the point of view.
   - Slant the sentence.

Exercise

Review memory work. Copy each sentence below. Double underline the predicate, and underline the subject. Put brackets around any prepositional phrases. Label the part of speech of each word. Noun, N; Proper Noun, PN; Pronoun, PRO; Verb, V; Linking Verb, LV; Adjective, ADJ; Article, ART; Conjunction, CJ; Preposition, Prep; Interjection, INJ. Diagram each sentence.

"Now don't hit me."

Where did he see the dragon?

A cool breeze played over the surface of the grass.

Commonplace Book

With your instructor's approval, add the passage below to your commonplace book, or choose your own passage from a work of fiction. This can be from either school reading or free reading.

> "Hullo, dragon!" said the Boy, quietly, when he had got up to him.
> The dragon, on hearing the approaching footsteps, made the beginning of a courteous effort to rise. But when he saw it was a Boy, he set his eyebrows severely.
> "Now don't you hit me," he said; "or bung stones, or squirt water, or anything. I won't have it, I tell you!"

Dictation

> "It's the sad truth," the dragon went on, settling down between his paws and evidently delighted to have found a listener at last: "and I fancy that's really how I came to be here. You see all the other fellows were so active and earnest and all that sort of thing—always rampaging, and skirmishing, and scouring the desert sands, and pacing the margin of the sea, and chasing knights all over the place, and devouring damsels, and going on generally—whereas I liked to get my meals regular and then to prop my back against a bit of rock and snooze a bit, and wake up and think of things going on and how they kept going on just the same, you know!"

65. The Principal Parts of the Verb

- The Reluctant Dragon, approximately 10 pages (1/5 of the story)

The five principal parts of the verb are the infinitive, the present tense, the present participle, the past tense, and the past participle.

Verbs have five principal parts. You've used all of these parts before, and even diagrammed most of them.

The first part is the **infinitive**. The infinitive is formed by using the word **to** in front of the simplest form of the verb. **To walk** is the infinitive form of **walk**.

The second part is the **present tense**, simplest form of the verb. **Tense** means time, so the present tense tells us that the action is happening in the present rather than in the past or in the future.

The third part is called the **present participle**. It is formed by using a adding the ending **ing** to the base form. If the verb ends in silent final **e**, drop the **e** before adding **ing**. To use the present participle as a verb, it needs a helping verb.

The fourth part is called the **past tense** form. Regular verbs form the past tense by adding the ending **ed**.

The fifth part is called the **past participle**. For regular verbs, it is the same as the past tense form. To use the past participle as a verb, it needs a helping verb.

So we have:

> To bake, I bake, I am baking, I baked, I have baked.
> To cry, I cry, I am crying, I cried, I have cried.
> To play, I play, I am playing, I played, I have played.

Infinitive	Simple Present	Present Participle	Simple Past	Past Participle
to bake	bake	baking	baked	baked
to cry	cry	crying	cried	cried
to try	try	trying	tried	tried
to play	play	playing	played	played
to obey	obey	obeying	obeyed	obeyed
to crack	crack	cracking	cracked	cracked

The Flag Goes By

By Henry Holcomb Bennett

Hats off!
Along the street there comes
A blare of bugles, a ruffle of drums,
A flash of color beneath the sky:
Hats off!
The flag is passing by!

Blue and crimson and white it shines
Over the steel-tipped, ordered lines.
Hats off!
The colors before us fly;
But more than the flag is passing by.

Sea-fights and land-fights, grim and great,
Fought to make and to save the State:
Weary marches and sinking ships;
Cheers of victory on dying lips;

Days of plenty and years of peace;
March of a strong land's swift increase;
Equal justice, right, and law,
Stately honor and reverend awe;

Sign of a nation, great and strong
Toward her people from foreign wrong:
Pride and glory and honor,—all
Live in the colors to stand or fall.

Hats off!
Along the street there comes
A blare of bugles, a ruffle of drums;
And loyal hearts are beating high:
Hats off!
The flag is passing by!

Lion and Jackal

From *South-African Folk-Tales* by James A. Honey

The Lion and the Jackal agreed to hunt on shares, for the purpose of laying in a stock of meat for the winter months for their families.

As the Lion was by far the more expert hunter of the two, the Jackal suggested that he (himself) should be employed in transporting the game to their dens, and that Mrs. Jackal and the little Jackals should prepare and dry the meat, adding that they would take care that Mrs. Lion and her family should not want.

This was agreed to by the Lion, and the hunt commenced.

After a very successful hunt, which lasted for some time, the Lion returned to see his family, and also to enjoy, as he thought, a plentiful supply of his spoil; when, to his utter surprise, he found Mrs. Lion and all the young Lions on the point of death from sheer hunger, and in a mangy state. The Jackal, it appeared, had only given them a few entrails of the game, and in such limited quantities as barely to keep them alive; always telling them that they (i. e., the Lion and himself) had been most unsuccessful in their hunting; while his own family was reveling in abundance, and each member of it was sleek and fat.

This was too much for the Lion to bear. He immediately started off in a terrible fury, vowing certain death to the Jackal and all his family, wherever he should meet them. The Jackal was more or less prepared for a storm, and had taken the precaution to remove all his belongings to the top of a krantz (i. e., a cliff), accessible only by a most difficult and circuitous path, which he alone knew.

When the Lion saw him on the krantz, the Jackal immediately greeted him by calling out, "Good morning, Uncle Lion."

"How dare you call me uncle, you impudent scoundrel," roared out the Lion, in a voice of thunder, "after the way in which you have behaved to my family?"

"Oh, Uncle! How shall I explain matters? That beast of a wife of mine!" Whack, whack was heard, as he beat with a stick on dry hide, which was a mere pretence for Mrs. Jackal's back; while that lady was preinstructed to scream whenever he operated on the hide, which she did with a vengeance, joined by the little Jackals, who set up a most doleful chorus. "That wretch!" said the Jackal. "It is all her doing. I shall kill her straight off," and away he again belabored the hide, while his wife and children uttered such a dismal howl that the Lion begged of him to leave off flogging his wife. After cooling down a little, he invited Uncle Lion to come up and have something to eat. The Lion, after several ineffectual attempts to scale the precipice, had to give it up.

The Jackal, always ready for emergencies, suggested that a reim should be lowered to haul up his uncle. This was agreed to, and when the Lion was drawn about halfway up by the whole family of Jackals, the reim was cleverly cut, and down went the Lion with a tremendous crash which hurt him very much. Upon this, the Jackal again performed upon the hide with tremendous force, for their daring to give him such a rotten reim, and Mrs. Jackal and the little ones responded with some fearful screams and yells. He then called loudly out to his wife for a strong buffalo reim which would support any weight. This again was lowered and fastened to the Lion, when all hands pulled away at their uncle; and, just when he had reached so far that he could look over the precipice into the pots to see all the fat meat cooking, and all the biltongs hanging out to dry, the reim was again cut, and the poor Lion fell with such force that he was fairly stunned for some time. After the Lion had recovered his senses, the Jackal, in a most sympathizing tone, suggested that he was afraid that it was of no use to attempt to haul him up onto the precipice, and recommended, instead, that a nice fat piece of eland's breast be roasted and dropped into the Lion's mouth. The Lion, half famished with hunger, and much bruised, readily accepted the offer, and sat eagerly awaiting the fat morsel. In the mean time, the Jackal had a round stone made red-hot, and wrapped a quantity of inside fat, or suet, round it, to make it appear like a ball of fat. When the Lion saw it held out, he opened his capacious mouth to the utmost extent, and the wily Jackal cleverly dropped the hot ball right into it, which ran through the poor old beast, killing him on the spot.

It need hardly be told that there was great rejoicing on the precipice that night.

Exercise

Review memory work. Name the parts of the verb underlined in the following sentences.

> I hear so much of it, and it's monotonous, and makes me tired.
>
> I began to think it would be fun to work my way upstairs.

Copy each sentence below. Double underline the predicate, and underline the subject. Put brackets around any prepositional phrases. Label the part of speech of each word. Noun, N; Proper Noun, PN; Pronoun, PRO; Verb, V; Linking Verb, LV; Adjective, ADJ; Article, ART; Conjunction, CJ; Preposition, Prep; Interjection, INJ. Diagram each sentence.

> Where is St. George?
>
> "My dear little man, just understand."
>
> The Boy jumped round in sheer delight.

Writing: Commonplace Book

Add the passage below from your model story to your commonplace book.

> A Town Mouse once visited a relative who lived in the country. For lunch the Country Mouse served wheat stalks, roots, and acorns, with a dash of cold water for drink. The Town Mouse ate very sparingly, nibbling a little of this and a little of that, and by her manner making it very plain that she ate the simple food only to be polite.

Dictation

Use part of today's poem for dictation.

66. Slant Narrative: The Town Mouse and the Country Mouse

- The Reluctant Dragon, approximately 10 pages (1/5 of the story)

Today, use your outline to write "The Town Mouse and the Country Mouse" as a slant narrative. Write it in the first person. Who are you—the town mouse or the country mouse? Remember to watch your pronouns. And don't be objective! Cast blame, make accusations, and show how *you* were not at fault!

Fidelity

By William Wordsworth

A barking sound the Shepherd hears,
A cry as of a dog or fox;
He halts—and searches with his eyes
Among the scattered rocks;
And now at distance can discern
A stirring in a brake of fern;
And instantly a Dog is seen,
Glancing through that covert green.

The Dog is not of mountain breed;
Its motions, too, are wild and shy;
With something, as the Shepherd thinks,
Unusual in its cry:
Nor is there any one in sight
All round, in hollow or on height;
Nor shout, nor whistle strikes his ear;
What is the Creature doing here?

It was a cove, a huge recess,
That keeps, till June, December's snow.
A lofty precipice in front,
A silent tarn below!
Far in the bosom of Helvellyn,
Remote from public road or dwelling,
Pathway, or cultivated land;
From trace of human foot or hand.

There sometimes doth a leaping fish
Send through the tarn a lonely cheer;
The crags repeat the raven's croak,
In symphony austere;
Thither the rainbow comes—the cloud—
And mists that spread the flying shroud;
And sunbeams; and the sounding blast,
That, if it could, would hurry past,
But that enormous barrier binds it fast.

Not free from boding thoughts, a while
The Shepherd stood: then makes his way
Toward the Dog, o'er rocks and stones,
As quickly as he may;
Nor far had gone, before he found
A human skeleton on the ground;
The appalled discoverer with a sigh
Looks round, to learn the history.

From those abrupt and perilous rocks
The Man had fallen, that place of fear!
At length upon the Shepherd's mind
It breaks, and all is clear:
He instantly recalled the name,
And who he was, and whence he came;
Remembered, too, the very day
On which the traveler passed this way.

But hear a wonder, for whose sake
This lamentable tale I tell!
A lasting monument of words
This wonder merits well.
The Dog, which still was hovering nigh,
Repeating the same timid cry,
This Dog had been through three months space
A dweller in that savage place.

Yes, proof was plain that, since the day
When this ill-fated traveler died,
The Dog had watched about the spot,
Or by his master's side:
How nourished here through such long time
He knows, who gave that love sublime;
And gave that strength of feeling, great
Above all human estimate.

Editing

- Did you meet the goal of this writing exercise?

- Look at your word choice. Is there a good mixture of nouns and pronouns? Is the antecedent of each pronoun clear?

- Look at your paragraphs. Are all the sentences related? Does each paragraph focus on a single topic?

67. The Infinitive; Verb Properties: Person

- The Reluctant Dragon, approximately 10 pages (1/5 of the story)

The five properties of verbs are: person, number, tense, voice, mood.

To use the infinitive **to walk** as a verb, we need to conjugate it. We conjugate a verb by changing its form depending on who is or who is doing the action (person), how many are or are doing the action (number), and when they are or are doing the action (tense). These are called properties of the verb.

to walk	Singular	Plural
1st Person	I walk	we walk
2nd Person	you walk	you walk
3rd Person	he, she, or it walks	they walk

Verbs have five properties. We'll be learning about three of them in this book. The first one is that verbs have **person**. Does that sound familiar? (Hint: Look at the chart above.) Person tells us the identity of the subject—first person, second person, or third person. Look at the following sentences from "The Reluctant Dragon." Notice how the verb changes depending on the property of **person**.

"I take a cast round by the cave, quietly."

He takes to the road like any tame civilized tax-payer.

They take his word without a murmur.

Reverie

By Walter De La Mare

When slim Sophia mounts her horse
And paces down the avenue,
It seems an inward melody
She paces to.
Each narrow hoof is lifted high
Beneath the dark enclust'ring pines,
A silver ray within his bit
And bridle shines.
His eye burns deep, his tail is arched,
And streams upon the shadowy air,
The daylight sleeks his jetty flanks,
His mistress' hair.
Her habit flows in darkness down,
Upon the stirrup rests her foot,
Her brow is lifted, as if earth
She heeded not.
'Tis silent in the avenue,
The sombre pines are mute of song,
The blue is dark, there moves no breeze
The boughs among.
When slim Sophia mounts her horse
And paces down the avenue,
It seems an inward melody
She paces to.

Writing: Oral Narration

Read your new model story below, and then give your instructor an oral narration of it.

The Hare and the Tortoise

An Aesop's Fable

   A Hare was making fun of the Tortoise one day for being so slow.
   "Do you ever get anywhere?" he asked with a mocking laugh.
   "Yes," replied the Tortoise, "and I get there sooner than you think. I'll run you a race and prove it.
   The Hare was much amused at the idea of running a race with the Tortoise, but for the fun of the thing he agreed. So the Fox, who had consented to act as judge, marked the distance and started the runners off.
   The Hare was soon far out of sight, and to make the Tortoise feel very deeply how ridiculous it was for him to try a race with a Hare, he lay down beside the course to take a nap until the Tortoise should catch up.
   The Tortoise meanwhile kept going slowly but steadily, and, after a time, passed the place where the Hare was sleeping. But the Hare slept on very peacefully; and

when at last he did wake up, the Tortoise was near the goal. The Hare now ran his swiftest, but he could not overtake the Tortoise in time.

The race is not always to the swift.

Exercise

Review memory work. Name the part of the verb underlined in the following sentences.

"Are you going to make a long stay here?"

"I am going off home."

Copy each sentence below. Double underline the predicate, and underline the subject. Put brackets around any prepositional phrases. Label the part of speech of each word. Noun, N; Proper Noun, PN; Pronoun, PRO; Verb, V; Linking Verb, LV; Adjective, ADJ; Article, ART; Conjunction, CJ; Preposition, Prep; Interjection, INJ. Diagram each sentence.

The Boy had secured a good front place.

"Boy, can't you arrange a Princess?"

When did St. George the dragon slayer arrive?

Commonplace Book

With your instructor's approval, add the passage below to your commonplace book, or choose your own passage from a work of fiction. This can be from either school reading or free reading.

> It all seemed so genuine that the Boy ran in breathlessly, hoping the dear old dragon wasn't really hurt. As he approached, the dragon lifted one large eyelid, winked solemnly, and collapsed again. He was held fast to earth by the neck, but the Saint had hit him in the spare place agreed upon, and it didn't even seem to tickle.

Dictation

"Oh, it's this great lumbering pig of a dragon!" sobbed the Boy. "First he makes me promise to see him home, and then he says I'd better do it, and goes to sleep! Might as well try to see a haystack home! And I'm so tired, and mother's—" here he broke down again.

"Now don't take on," said St. George. "I'll stand by you, and we'll both see him home. Wake up, dragon!" he said sharply, shaking the beast by the elbow.

68. Verb Properties: Number

• Heidi, Chapter 1

The second property of verbs that we're discussing is **number**. Verbs have number. That means that verbs change form depending on how many are or are doing. Look at the chart again. One column is singular, and the other is plural.

to walk	Singular	Plural
1st Person	I walk	we walk
2nd Person	you walk	you walk
3rd Person	he, she, or it walks	they walk

Most verbs are **regular**. That means that they all change the same way. Notice that all of the verb forms above are the same except the third person singular, which has an **ending**. Its ending is *s*. Now conjugate **to move**. Look at the chart above to remember the order if necessary.

Did you notice that **to move** is exactly the same? Only the third person singular has an ending, and that ending is *s*. Most verbs are regular. The exact same thing happens when you conjugate **bake**, **ask**, **joke**, or **squeeze**.

Look at the following sentences from *Heidi*. Notice how the verb changes depending on the property of **number**.

> She climbs up the mountain.
>
> They climb up the mountain.
>
> Heidi is tired.
>
> They are tired.

The Death of Napoleon

By Isaac McClellan

Wild was the night, yet a wilder night
  Hung round the soldier's pillow;
In his bosom there waged a fiercer fight
  Than the fight on the wrathful billow.

A few fond mourners were kneeling by,
  The few that his stern heart cherished;
They knew, by his glazed and unearthly eye,
  That life had nearly perished.

They knew by his awful and kingly look,
  By the order hastily spoken,
That he dreamed of days when the nations shook,
  And the nations' hosts were broken.

He dreamed that the Frenchman's sword still slew,
  And triumphed the Frenchman's eagle,
And the struggling Austrian fled anew,
  Like the hare before the beagle.

The bearded Russian he scourged again,
  The Prussian's camp was routed,
And again on the hills of haughty Spain
  His mighty armies shouted.

Over Egypt's sands, over Alpine snows,
  At the pyramids, at the mountain,
Where the wave of the lordly Danube flows,
  And by the Italian fountain,

On the snowy cliffs where mountain streams
  Dash by the Switzer's dwelling,
He led again, in his dying dreams,
  His hosts, the proud earth quelling.

Again Marengo's field was won,
  And Jena's bloody battle;
Again the world was overrun,
  Made pale at his cannon's rattle.

He died at the close of that darksome day,
  A day that shall live in story;
In the rocky land they placed his clay,
  "And left him alone with his glory."

Story of Lion and Little Jackal

From *South-African Folk-Tales* by James A. Honey

Little Jackal one day went out hunting, when he met Lion. Lion proposed that they should hunt together, on condition that if a small antelope was killed it was to be Little Jackal's, and if a large one was killed it was to be Lion's. Little Jackal agreed to this.

The first animal killed was a large eland. Lion was very glad, and said to Little Jackal: "I will continue hunting while you go to my house and call my children to carry the meat home."

Little Jackal replied: "Yes, I agree to that."

Lion went away to hunt. When he had gone, Little Jackal went to his own house and called his own children to carry away the meat. He said: "Lion takes me for a fool if he thinks I will call his children while my own are dying with hunger."

So Little Jackal's children carried the meat to their home on the top of a high rock, where the only way to get to their house was by means of a rope.

Lion caught nothing more, and after a time he went home and asked his wife where the meat was. She told him there was no meat. He said: "Did not Little Jackal bring a message to my children to carry meat?"

His wife replied: "No, he was not here. We are still dying with hunger."

Lion then went to Little Jackal's house, but he could not get up the rock to it. So he sat down by the water, waiting. After a time Little Jackal went to get some water. He was close to the water when he saw Lion. He at once ran away, and Lion ran after him. He ran into a hole under a tree, but Lion caught his tail before he got far in. He said to him: "That is not my tail you have hold of; it is a root of the tree. If you do not believe me, take a stone and strike it, and see if any blood comes."

Lion let go the tail, and went for a stone to prove what it was. While he was gone for the stone, Little Jackal went far into the hole. When Lion returned he could not be found. Lion lay down by the hole and waited. After a long time Little Jackal wanted to come out. He went to the entrance and looked round, but he could not see Lion. To make sure, he said: "Ho, I see you, my master, although you are in hiding."

Lion did not move from the place where he lay concealed. Then Little Jackal went out, and Lion pursued him, but he got away.

Lion watched for him, and one day, when Little Jackal was out hunting, he came upon him in a place where he could not escape. Lion was just about to spring upon him, when Little Jackal said softly: "Be still, do you not see that bushbuck on the other side of the rock? I am glad you have come to help me. Just remain here while I run round and drive him toward you."

Lion did so, and Little Jackal made his escape.

At another time there was a meeting of the animals, and Lion was the chief at the meeting. Little Jackal wanted to attend, but there was a law made that no one should be present unless he had horns. So Little Jackal took wax out of a nest of bees, and made horns for himself with it. He fastened the horns on his head, and went to the meeting. Lion did not know him on account of the horns. But he sat near the fire and went to sleep, when the horns melted.

Lion looked at him and saw who it was. He immediately tried to catch him, but Little Jackal was quick in springing away. He ran under an overhanging rock and sang out: "Help! Help! This rock is falling upon me!"

Lion went for a pole to prop up the rock that he might get at Little Jackal. While he was away, Little Jackal escaped.

After that they became companions again, and went hunting another time. They killed an ox. Lion said: "I will watch it while you carry the pieces away."

Lion gave him the breast, and said: "Take this to my wife."

Little Jackal took it to his own wife. When he returned, Lion gave him a shin, and said: "Take this to your wife."

Little Jackal took the shin to Lion's house. Lion's wife said: "I cannot take this because it should not come here."

Little Jackal thereupon struck Lion's wife in the face, and went back to the place where the ox was killed. Lion gave him a large piece of meat and said: "Take this to my wife."

Little Jackal took it to his own wife. This continued till the ox was finished. Then they both went home. When Lion arrived at his house he found there was weeping in his family.

His wife said: "Is it you who sent Little Jackal to beat me and my children, and is it you who sent this shin? Did I ever eat a shin?"

When Lion heard this he was very angry and at once went to Little Jackal's house. When he reached the rock, Little Jackal looked down and said: "Who are you, and what is your name, and whose son are you, and where are you from, and where are you going to, and whom do you want, and what do you want him for?"

Lion replied: "I have merely come to see you. I wish you to let down the rope."

Little Jackal let down a rope made of mouse skins, and when Lion climbed a little way up, the rope broke, and he fell and was hurt. He then went home.

Writing: Outline

Write or type an outline of the new model story which you read in the last lesson.

Exercise

Review memory work. Name the part of the verb underlined in the following sentences.

Then she <u>looked</u> around <u>to see</u> that the child was not close.

"I <u>have</u> often <u>noticed</u> that and I am glad for her."

Copy each sentence below. Double underline the predicate, and underline the subject. Put brackets around any prepositional phrases. Label the part of speech of each word. Noun, N; Proper Noun, PN; Pronoun, PRO; Verb, V; Linking Verb, LV; Adjective, ADJ; Article, ART; Conjunction, CJ; Preposition, Prep; Interjection, INJ. Diagram each sentence.

"Where are you taking the child, Deta?"

"Why are his eyes so fierce?"

"She is climbing up with the goatherd Peter."

Commonplace Book

With your instructor's approval, add the poem below to your commonplace book, or choose your own poem.

> Wild was the night, yet a wilder night
>   Hung round the soldier's pillow;
> In his bosom there waged a fiercer fight
>   Than the fight on the wrathful billow.
>
> A few fond mourners were kneeling by,
>   The few that his stern heart cherished;
> They knew, by his glazed and unearthly eye,
>   That life had nearly perished.

Dictation

Philippians 4:11-13

Not that I speak from want, for I have learned to be content in whatever circumstances I am. I know how to get along with humble means, and I also know how to live in prosperity; in any and every circumstance I have learned the secret of being filled and going hungry, both of having abundance and suffering need. I can do all things through Him who strengthens me.

The Dance Class by Edgar Degas

Picture Study

1. Read the title and the name of the artist. Study the picture for several minutes, then put the picture away.

2. Describe the picture.

3. Look at the picture again. Do you notice any details that you missed before? What do you like or dislike about this painting? Does it remind you of anything?

69. Descriptive Writing

- Heidi, Chapter 2

Writing: Descriptive Writing

Remember that the purpose of descriptive writing is to describe a person, place, thing, or event so well that an image forms in the mind of the reader.

Your last six picture studies have been on paintings by Edgar Degas. Today, choose one of his paintings, either one from this book or one from another source, and write a description of it. Imagine that you're describing the picture to someone who has never seen it before. Get creative if you wish. Write a description for a museum catalog, or as part of a police report describing stolen merchandise. Or get really creative. Imagine that the painting is a window to another dimension, and you've just been pulled in. Describe the environment in which you find yourself. Or, write a story about the picture, or about your experiences within it. Be as creative as you want. Just don't forget to describe the picture.

Old Folks at Home

By Stephen Collins Foster

Way down upon de Swanee Ribber,
  Far, far away,
Dere's wha my heart is turning ebber,
  Dere's wha de old folks stay.
All up and down de whole creation
  Sadly I roam,
Still longing for de old plantation,
  And for de old folks at home.

All de world am sad and dreary,
  Eberywhere I roam;
Oh, darkeys, how my heart grows weary,
  Far from de old folks at home!

All round de little farm I wandered
  When I was young,
Den many happy days I squandered,
  Many de songs I sung.
When I was playing wid my brudder
  Happy was I;
Oh, take me to my kind old mudder!
  Dere let me live and die.

One little hut among de bushes,
  One dat I love,
Still sadly to my memory rushes,
  No matter where I rove.
When will I see de bees a-humming
  All round de comb?
When will I hear de banjo tumming,
  Down in my good old home?

All de world am sad and dreary,
  Eberywhere I roam;
Oh, darkeys, how my heart grows weary,
  Far from de old folks at home!

Lion's Illness

From *South-African Folk-Tales* by James A. Honey

Lion, it is said, was ill, and they all went to see him in his suffering. But Jackal did not go, because the traces of the people who went to see him did not turn back. Thereupon, he was accused by Hyena, who said, "Though I go to look, yet Jackal does not want to come and look at the man's sufferings."

Then Lion let Hyena go, in order that she might catch Jackal; and she did so, and brought him.

Lion asked Jackal: "Why did you not come here to see me?"

Jackal said, "Oh, no! When I heard that my uncle was so very ill, I went to the witch (doctor) to consult him, whether and what medicine would be good for my uncle against the pain. The doctor said to me, 'Go and tell your uncle to take hold of Hyena and draw off her skin, and put it on while it is still warm. Then he will recover.' Hyena is one who does not care for my uncle's sufferings."

Lion followed his advice, got hold of Hyena, drew the skin over her ears, whilst she howled with all her might, and put it on.

Exercise

Review memory work. Identify each group of words below as either a phrase or a clause. If it is a clause, double underline the predicate and underline the subject.

    after looking around attentively in the room

    Heidi followed him into a fairly spacious room

    when he opened it

Copy each sentence below. Double underline the predicate, and underline the subject. Put brackets around any prepositional phrases. Label the part of speech of each word. Noun, N; Proper Noun, PN; Pronoun, PRO; Verb, V; Linking Verb, LV; Adjective, ADJ; Article, ART; Conjunction, CJ; Preposition, Prep; Interjection, INJ. Diagram each sentence.

"Why don't you need them?"

"Come then."

Beside the old man's bed she saw a ladder.

Commonplace Book

With your instructor's approval, add the passage below to your commonplace book, or choose your own passage from a work of non-fiction. This can be from the Bible, a biography, or one of your history or science books.

"All right, you can; but fetch the things and we'll put them in the cupboard." The child obeyed the command. The old man now opened the door, and Heidi followed him into a fairly spacious room, which took in the entire expanse of the hut. In one corner stood a table and a chair, and in another the grandfather's bed.

70. Verb Properties: Tense

• Heidi, Chapter 3

The third property of verbs that we're discussing is **tense**. Tense means time. Today we'll be discussing the simple forms of the three basic tenses: past, present, and future. The first chart shows just the first person singular so that you can see the forms of all three tenses.

Infinitive	Past Simple	Present Simple	Future Simple
to ask	I asked	I ask	I will/shall ask
to move	I moved	I move	I will move
to bake	I baked	I bake	I will bake
to hurry	I hurried	I hurry	I will hurry

Notice that the past tense has an **ending**, *ed*. Regular verbs form the past tense by adding *ed*.

Notice the helping verb **will** in the future tense. Verbs form the future tense by using the helping verb **will**. In the first person, we can use **shall** or **will**.

The next two charts show the conjugation of the past tense and the future tense. Notice that the verb does not change.

Past Tense

to walk	Singular	Plural
1st Person	I walked	we walked
2nd Person	you walked	you walked
3rd Person	he, she, or it walked	they walked

Future Tense

to walk	Singular	Plural
1st Person	I will/shall walk	we will/shall walk
2nd Person	you will walk	you will walk
3rd Person	he, she, or it will walk	they will walk

Look at the following sentences from *Heidi*. Notice how the tense changes.

"Yes," <u>cried</u> Heidi.

"The sun <u>will laugh</u> at you if he <u>sees</u> how dirty you are."

You may notice that you've seen other ways to speak about the past, present, and future which are not listed on these charts. That's because there are actually nine tenses in English. Today, you only learned the simple forms.

Robert Bruce's Address to His Army

By Robert Burns

Scots, wha hae wi' Wallace bled,
Scots, wham Bruce has aften led;
Welcome to your gory bed,
  Or to victorie.

Now's the day, and now's the hour;
See the front o' battle lower;

See approach proud Edward's power—
  Chains and slaverie!

Wha will be a traitor knave?
Wha can fill a coward's grave?
Wha sae base as be a slave?
  Let him turn and flee!

Wha for Scotland's King and law
Freedom's sword will strongly draw,
Freeman stand, or freeman fa'?
  Let him follow me!

By oppression's woes and pains!
By your sons in servile chains!
We will drain our dearest veins,
  But they shall be free!

Lay the proud usurpers low!
Tyrants fall in every foe!
Liberty's in every blow!
  Let us do, or die!

The Story of a Dam

From *South-African Folk-Tales* by James A. Honey

There was a great drought in the land; and Lion called together a number of animals so that they might devise a plan for retaining water when the rains fell.

The animals which attended at Lion's summons were Baboon, Leopard, Hyena, Jackal, Hare, and Mountain Tortoise.

It was agreed that they should scratch a large hole in some suitable place to hold water; and the next day they all began to work, with the exception of Jackal, who continually hovered about in that locality, and was overheard to mutter that he was not going to scratch his nails off in making water holes.

When the dam was finished the rains fell, and it was soon filled with water, to the great delight of those who had worked so hard at it. The first one, however, to come and drink there, was Jackal, who not only drank, but filled his clay pot with water, and then proceeded to swim in the rest of the water, making it as muddy and dirty as he could.

This was brought to the knowledge of Lion, who was very angry and ordered Baboon to guard the water the next day, armed with a huge knobkirrie. Baboon was concealed in a bush close to the water; but Jackal soon became aware of his presence there, and guessed its cause. Knowing the fondness of baboons for honey, Jackal at once hit upon a plan, and marching to and fro, every now and then dipped his fingers into his clay pot, and licked them with an expression of intense relish, saying, in a low voice to himself, "I don't want any of their dirty water when I have a pot full of delicious honey." This was too much for poor Baboon, whose mouth began to water. He soon began to beg Jackal to give him a little honey, as he had been watching for several hours, and was very hungry and tired.

After taking no notice of Baboon at first, Jackal looked round, and said, in a patronizing manner, that he pitied such an unfortunate creature, and would give him some honey on certain conditions, viz., that Baboon should give up his knobkirrie and allow himself to be bound by Jackal. He foolishly agreed; and was soon tied in such a manner that he could not move hand or foot.

Jackal now proceeded to drink of the water, to fill his pot, and to swim in the sight of Baboon, from time to time telling him what a foolish fellow he had been to be so easily duped, and that he (Jackal) had no honey or anything else to give him, excepting a good blow on the head every now and then with his own knobkirrie.

The animals soon appeared and found poor Baboon in this sorry plight, looking the picture of misery. Lion was so exasperated that he caused Baboon to be severely punished, and to be denounced as a fool.

Tortoise hereupon stepped forward, and offered his services for the capture of Jackal. It was at first thought that he was merely joking; but when he explained in what manner he proposed to catch him, his plan was considered so feasible that his offer was accepted. He proposed that a thick coating of "bijenwerk" (a kind of sticky black substance found on beehives) should be spread all over him, and that he should then go and stand at the entrance of the dam, on the water level, so that Jackal might tread upon him and stick fast. This was accordingly done and Tortoise posted there.

The next day, when Jackal came, he approached the water very cautiously, and wondered to find no one there. He then ventured to the entrance of the water, and remarked how kind they had been in placing there a large black stepping-stone for him. As soon, however, as he trod upon the supposed stone, he stuck fast, and saw that he had been tricked; for Tortoise now put his head out and began to move. Jackal's hind feet being still free he threatened to smash Tortoise with them if he did not let him go. Tortoise merely answered, "Do as you like." Jackal thereupon made a violent jump, and found, with horror, that his hind feet were now also fast. "Tortoise," said he, "I have still my mouth and teeth left, and will eat you alive if you do not let me go." "Do as you like," Tortoise again replied. Jackal, in his endeavors to free himself, at last made a desperate bite at Tortoise, and found himself fixed, both head and feet. Tortoise, feeling proud of his successful capture, now marched quietly up to the top of the bank with Jackal on his back, so that he could easily be seen by the animals as they came to the water.

They were indeed astonished to find how cleverly the crafty Jackal had been caught; and Tortoise was much praised, while the unhappy Baboon was again reminded of his misconduct when set to guard the water.

Jackal was at once condemned to death by Lion; and Hyena was to execute the sentence. Jackal pleaded hard for mercy, but finding this useless, he made a last request to Lion (always, as he said, so fair and just in his dealings) that he should not have to suffer a lingering death.

Lion inquired of him in what manner he wished to die; and he asked that his tail might be shaved and rubbed with a little fat, and that Hyena might then swing him round twice and dash his brains out upon a stone. This, being considered sufficiently fair by Lion, was ordered by him to be carried out in his presence.

When Jackal's tail had been shaved and greased, Hyena caught hold of him with great force, and before he had fairly lifted him from the ground, the cunning Jackal had slipped away from Hyena's grasp, and was running for his life, pursued by all the animals.

Lion was the foremost pursuer, and after a great chase Jackal got under an overhanging precipice, and, standing on his hind legs with his shoulders pressed against the rock, called loudly to Lion to help him, as the rock was falling, and would crush them both. Lion put his shoulders to the rock, and exerted himself to the utmost. After some little time Jackal proposed that he should creep slowly out, and fetch a large pole to prop up the rock, so that Lion could get out and save his life. Jackal did creep out, and left Lion there to starve and die.

Writing: Copia

Take the following sentence and play with it. Remember that the point is not necessarily to make the sentence better. The point is to play with the sentence and make it different. Make a new sentence with a change from each of the following categories.

>A Hare was making fun of the Tortoise one day for being so slow.

1. Change the grammar.
   - Change the nouns from common to proper and vice versa.
   - Change the nouns from singular to plural and vice versa.
   - Change the sentence type.
   - Change the adjectives from articles to descriptive to possessive, etc.
   - Change a quotation from direct to indirect and vice versa.
   - Change the verb tense.

2. Condense the sentence.
   - Remove details.
   - Remove modifiers.
   - Remove phrases or clauses.

3. Amplify the sentence.
   - Add details.
   - Add dialogue.
   - Add modifiers.
   - Add phrases or clauses.

4. Use synonyms and antonyms.
   - Substitute synonyms.
   - Say the opposite thing using antonyms.

5. Point of view.
   - Change the point of view.
   - Slant the sentence.

Exercise

Review memory work. Name the part of the verb underlined in the following sentences.

    Peter now <u>begins</u> <u>to call</u> loudly and <u>to whistle</u>.

    Heidi, knowing that something <u>had happened</u>, <u>follows</u> him.

Copy each sentence below. Double underline the predicate, and underline the subject. Put brackets around any prepositional phrases. Label the part of speech of each word. Noun, N; Proper Noun, PN; Pronoun, PRO; Verb, V; Linking Verb, LV; Adjective, ADJ; Article, ART; Conjunction, CJ; Preposition, Prep; Interjection, INJ. Diagram each sentence.

    "Oh, does it really live there?

    "Where is her grandmother?"

    Heidi at last went to the little thing again.

Commonplace Book

With your instructor's approval, add the passage below to your commonplace book, or choose your own passage from a work of fiction. This can be from either school reading or free reading.

    Not taking Heidi in earnest, he hesitated till she put the things on his knees. Then he saw she really meant it, and he seized his prize. Nodding his thanks to her, he ate the most luxurious meal he had ever had in all his life. Heidi was watching the goats in the meantime, and asked Peter for their names.

Dictation

    Heidi at last went to the little thing again, and throwing her arms around its head, she asked, "What is the matter with you, Snowhopper? Why do you always cry for help?" The little goat pressed close to Heidi's side and became perfectly quiet. Peter was still eating, but between the swallows he called to Heidi: "She is so unhappy, because the old goat has left us. She was sold to somebody in Mayenfeld two days ago."

71. Properties of Nouns and Pronouns

• Heidi, Chapter 4

Nouns and pronouns have four properties. They are **number**, **gender**, **person**, and **case**.

Number simply means that nouns and pronouns are either singular or plural.

Gender means that nouns and pronouns can be either masculine—having to do with males; feminine—having to do with females; or neuter—neither male nor female.

Person tells us the identity of the subject—first person, second person, or third person.

Case is a change in form that shows a word's use in a sentence. We'll discuss this more in a future lesson.

Sometimes when speaking or writing, we don't know whether the subject is male or female. Think of the word **someone**. We know **someone** is singular, but the word could refer to either a male or a female person. So how do we add a possessive pronoun to this sentence?

    Someone left _____ book.

The traditional way is to use the masculine pronoun when gender is not known, so the sentence could read:

    Someone left <u>his</u> book.

But nowadays, the feminine pronoun can also be used, so the sentence could read:

    Someone left <u>her</u> book.

Some people prefer to say:

    Someone left <u>his or her</u> book.

Sometimes, we can avoid the whole issue by saying it in a different way.

    Someone left <u>a</u> book.

That won't always work, though, so you should ask your instructor which form you should use.

But under no circumstances may you say:

Someone left ~~their~~ book.

<u>Pronouns</u> and <u>their</u> antecedents must agree in number, gender, and person.

Driving Home the Cows

By Kate Putnam Osgood

Out of the clover and blue-eyed grass
  He turned them into the river lane;
One after another he let them pass,
  Then fastened the meadow bars again.

Under the willows and over the hill,
  He patiently followed their sober pace;
The merry whistle for once was still,
  And something shadowed the sunny face.

Only a boy! And his father had said
  He never could let his youngest go:
Two already were lying dead,
  Under the feet of the trampling foe.

But after the evening work was done,
  And the frogs were loud in the meadow-swamp,
Over his shoulder he slung his gun,
  And stealthily followed the footpath damp.

Across the clover, and through the wheat,
  With resolute heart and purpose grim:
Though the dew was on his hurrying feet,
  And the blind bat's flitting startled him.

Thrice since then had the lanes been white,
  And the orchards sweet with apple-bloom;
And now, when the cows came back at night,
  The feeble father drove them home.

For news had come to the lonely farm
  That three were lying where two had lain;
And the old man's tremulous, palsied arm
  Could never lean on a son's again.

The summer day grew cool and late:
  He went for the cows when the work was done;
But down the lane, as he opened the gate,
  He saw them coming one by one:

Brindle, Ebony, Speckle, and Bess,
  Shaking their horns in the evening wind;
Cropping the buttercups out of the grass,
  But who was it following close behind?

Loosely swung in the idle air
  The empty sleeve of army blue;
And worn and pale, from the crisping hair,
  Looked out a face that the father knew.

For close-barred prisons will sometimes yawn,
  And yield their dead unto life again;
And the day that comes with a cloudy dawn,
  In golden glory at last may wane.

The great tears sprang to their meeting eyes;
  For the heart must speak when the lips are dumb,
And under the silent evening skies
  Together they followed the cattle home.

The Dance for Water or Rabbit's Triumph

From *South-African Folk-Tales* by James A. Honey

    There was a frightful drought. The rivers after a while dried up and even the springs gave no water.
    The animals wandered around seeking drink, but to no avail. Nowhere was water to be found.
    A great gathering of animals was held: Lion, Tiger, Wolf, Jackal, Elephant, all of them came together. What was to be done? That was the question. One had this plan, and another had that; but no plan seemed of value.
    Finally one of them suggested: "Come, let all of us go to the dry river bed and dance; in that way we can tread out the water."
    Good! Everyone was satisfied and ready to begin instantly, excepting Rabbit, who said, "I will not go and dance. All of you are mad to attempt to get water from the ground by dancing."
    The other animals danced and danced, and ultimately danced the water to the surface. How glad they were. Everyone drank as much as he could, but Rabbit did not dance with them. So it was decided that Rabbit should have no water.
    He laughed at them: "I will nevertheless drink some of your water."
    That evening he proceeded leisurely to the river bed where the dance had been, and drank as much as he wanted. The following morning the animals saw the footprints of Rabbit in the ground, and Rabbit shouted to them: "Aha! I did have some of the water, and it was most refreshing and tasted fine."
    Quickly all the animals were called together. What were they to do? How were they to get Rabbit in their hands? All had some means to propose; the one suggested

this, and the other that.

Finally old Tortoise moved slowly forward, foot by foot: "I will catch Rabbit."

"You? How? What do you think of yourself?" shouted the others in unison.

"Rub my shell with pitch, and I will go to the edge of the water and lie down. I will then resemble a stone, so that when Rabbit steps on me his feet will stick fast."

"Yes! Yes! That's good."

And in a one, two, three, Tortoise's shell was covered with pitch, and foot by foot he moved away to the river. At the edge, close to the water, he lay down and drew his head into his shell.

Rabbit during the evening came to get a drink. "Ha!" he chuckled sarcastically, "they are, after all, quite decent. Here they have placed a stone, so now I need not unnecessarily wet my feet."

Rabbit trod with his left foot on the stone, and there it stuck. Tortoise then put his head out. "Ha! Old Tortoise! And it's you, is it, that's holding me. But here I still have another foot. I'll give you a good clout." Rabbit gave Tortoise what he said he would with his right fore foot, hard and straight; and there his foot remained.

"I have yet a hind foot, and with it I'll kick you." Rabbit drove his hind foot down. This also rested on Tortoise where it struck.

"But still another foot remains, and now I'll tread you." He stamped his foot down, but it stuck like the others.

He used his head to hammer Tortoise, and his tail as a whip, but both met the same fate as his feet, so there he was tight and fast down to the pitch.

Tortoise now slowly turned himself round and foot by foot started for the other animals, with Rabbit on his back.

"Ha! Ha! Ha! Rabbit! How does it look now? Insolence does not pay after all," shouted the animals.

Now advice was sought. What should they do with Rabbit? He certainly must die. But how? One said, "Behead him"; another, "Some severe penalty."

"Rabbit, how are we to kill you?"

"It does not affect me," Rabbit said. "Only a shameful death please do not pronounce."

"And what is that?" they all shouted.

"To take me by my tail and dash my head against a stone; that I pray and beseech you don't do."

"No, but just so you'll die. That is decided."

It was decided Rabbit should die by taking him by his tail and dashing his head to pieces against some stone. But who is to do it?

Lion, because he is the most powerful one.

Good! Lion should do it. He stood up, walked to the front, and poor Rabbit was brought to him. Rabbit pleaded and beseeched that he couldn't die such a miserable death.

Lion took Rabbit firmly by the tail and swung him around. The white skin slipped off from Rabbit, and there Lion stood with the white bit of skin and hair in his paw. Rabbit was free.

Exercise

Review memory work. Copy each sentence below. Double underline the predicate, and underline the subject. Put brackets around any prepositional phrases. Label the part of speech of each word. Noun, N; Proper Noun, PN; Pronoun, PRO; Verb, V; Linking Verb, LV; Adjective, ADJ; Article, ART; Conjunction, CJ; Preposition, Prep; Interjection, INJ. Diagram each sentence.

"How is it possible?"

"Why, grandmother, can't you see the shutter?"

Heidi would talk about her life.

Writing: Commonplace Book

Add the passage below from your model story to your commonplace book.

The Tortoise meanwhile kept goingly slowly but steadily, and, after a time, passed the place where the Hare was sleeping. But the Hare slept on very peacefully; and when at last he did wake up, the Tortoise was near the goal. The Hare now ran his swiftest, but he could not overtake the Tortoise in time.

Dictation

Use part of today's poem for dictation.

72. Slant Narrative: The Hare and the Tortoise

- Heidi, Chapter 5

Today, use your outline to write "The Hare and the Tortoise" as a slant narrative. Write it in the first person. Who are you—the tortoise or the hare? Remember to watch your pronouns. And don't be objective! Cast blame, make accusations, and show how **you** were not at fault!

The Wreck of the Hesperus

By Henry Wadsworth Longfellow

It was the schooner *Hesperus*,
  That sailed the wintry sea;
And the skipper had taken his little daughter,
  To bear him company.

Blue were her eyes as the fairy-flax,
  Her cheeks like the dawn of day,
And her bosom white as the hawthorn buds
  That ope in the month of May.

The skipper he stood beside the helm,
  His pipe was in his mouth,
And he watched how the veering flaw did blow
  The smoke now west, now south.

Then up and spake an old sailor,
  Had sailed the Spanish Main,
"I pray thee put into yonder port,
  For I fear a hurricane.

"Last night the moon had a golden ring,
  And to-night no moon we see!"
The skipper he blew a whiff from his pipe,
  And a scornful laugh laughed he.

Colder and louder blew the wind,
  A gale from the northeast,
The snow fell hissing in the brine,
  And the billows frothed like yeast.

Down came the storm, and smote amain
  The vessel in its strength;
She shuddered and paused, like a frighted steed,
  Then leaped her cable's length.

  "Come hither! Come hither! My little daughter,
    And do not tremble so;
For I can weather the roughest gale
  That ever wind did blow."

He wrapped her warm in his seaman's coat
  Against the stinging blast;
He cut a rope from a broken spar,
  And bound her to the mast.

  "O father! I hear the church-bells ring,
  O say, what may it be?"
  "'Tis a fog-bell on a rock-bound coast!"—
And he steered for the open sea.

  "O father! I hear the sound of guns,
  O say, what may it be?"
"Some ship in distress, that cannot live
In such an angry sea!"

  "O father! I see a gleaming light,
  O say, what may it be?"
But the father answered never a word,
  A frozen corpse was he.

Lashed to the helm, all stiff and stark,
  With his face turned to the skies,
The lantern gleamed through the gleaming snow
  On his fixed and glassy eyes.

Then the maiden clasped her hands and prayed
  That saved she might be;
And she thought of Christ, who stilled the wave
  On the Lake of Galilee.

And fast through the midnight dark and drear,
  Through the whistling sleet and snow,
Like a sheeted ghost the vessel swept
  Toward the reef of Norman's Woe.

And ever the fitful gusts between
  A sound came from the land;
It was the sound of the trampling surf
  On the rocks and the hard sea-sand.

The breakers were right beneath her bows,
  She drifted a dreary wreck,
And a whooping billow swept the crew
  Like icicles from her deck.

She struck where the white and fleecy waves
  Looked soft as carded wool,
But the cruel rocks they gored her side
  Like the horns of an angry bull.

Her rattling shrouds all sheathed in ice,
  With the masts went by the board;
Like a vessel of glass she stove and sank,—
  Ho! Ho! The breakers roared!

At daybreak on the bleak sea-beach
  A fisherman stood aghast,
To see the form of a maiden fair
  Lashed close to a drifting mast.

The salt sea was frozen on her breast,
  The salt tears in her eyes;
And he saw her hair, like the brown sea-weed,
  On the billows fall and rise.

Such was the wreck of the *Hesperus*,
  In the midnight and the snow!
Christ save us all from a death like this,
  On the reef of Norman's Woe!

Editing

• Did you meet the goal of this writing exercise?

• Look at your word choice. Is there a good mixture of nouns and pronouns? Is the antecedent of each pronoun clear?

• Look at your paragraphs. Are all the sentences related? Does each paragraph focus on a single topic?

73. Collective Nouns

• Heidi, Chapter 6

Definition: A collective noun is a noun which refers to a group of individuals.

A collective noun is a group of nouns. **Family**, **team**, and **orchestra** are all collective nouns. Each is made up of a group of people.

Although there can be many members of a group, the group itself is singular in nature. This leads to an important question: Do we use singular or plural verbs and pronouns with collective nouns?

The answer is that it depends on whether we're speaking of the group as a unit acting altogether, or a bunch of individuals who are all doing their own thing. Consider the following two sentences.

My family lives in the white house.

My family are all traveling to different places this summer.

In the first sentence, **family** is a group acting in unison. It is not many members doing different things. It is a single entity doing the same thing, so the verb is singular. However, in the second sentence, we're talking about the **family members**, not the family as a group. The **family** is not acting in unison. Instead, each member is acting separately, so the verb is plural.

The same rule tells whether to use singular or plural pronouns.

The team takes its vacation time seriously.

The team prefer to take their vacations separately.

In the first sentence, the **team** acting in unison has a singular verb and pronoun. In the second sentence, the **team** acting separately as individuals have a plural verb and pronoun.

Look at these sentences. Is the collective noun singular or plural?

The class (meets/meet) each Monday morning.

The theater troupe (is/are) playing *Macbeth* this fall.

The jury (disagrees/disagree) about the guilt of the defendant.

In the first sentence, the **class** acting in unison is singular. In the second sentence, the **troupe** acting in unison is singular. In the third sentence, the **jury** acting separately is plural.

Some other common collective nouns are: army, audience, board, cabinet, committee, company, corporation, council, department, faculty, firm, group, jury, majority, minority, navy, public, school, senate, society.

John Anderson

By Robert Burns

John Anderson, my jo, John,
When we were first acquent
Your locks were like the raven,
Your bonnie brow was brent;
But now your brow is bald, John,
Your locks are like the snow;
But blessings on your frosty pow,
John Anderson, my jo.

John Anderson, my jo, John,
We clamb the hill thegither,
And mony a canty day, John,
We've had wi' ane anither;
Now we maun totter down, John,
But hand in hand we'll go,
And sleep thegither at the foot,
John Anderson, my jo.

Writing: Oral Narration

Read your new model story below, and then give your instructor an oral narration of it.

Snow

From *The Secret of Everyday Things* by Jean Henri Fabre

"Snow has the same origin as rain: it comes from vapor in the atmosphere, especially from vapor rising from the surface of the sea. When a sudden cooling-off takes place in clouds at a high elevation, the condensation of vapor is immediately followed by freezing, which turns water into ice.

"I have already told you that cirrus clouds, which are the highest of all clouds and hence more exposed to cold than the others, are composed of extremely fine needles of ice. Lower clouds, too, if subjected to a sufficient degree of cold, undergo the same transformation. Then there follows a symmetrical grouping of adjacent needles in delicate six-pointed stars which, in greater or less numbers and heaped together at random, make a snowflake. Soon afterward, when it has grown too heavy to float in the air, the flake falls to the ground.

"Examine attentively one that has just fallen on the dark background of your sleeve or cap. You will see a mass of beautiful little starry crystals so graceful in form, so delicate in structure, that the most skilful fingers could never hope to make anything like them. These exquisite formations, which put to shame our poor human artistry, have nevertheless sprung from the haphazard mingling of cloud-masses.

"Such then is the nature of snow, the schoolboy's favorite plaything. From a somber and silent sky it falls softly, almost perpendicularly. The eye follows it in its fall. Above, in the gray depths, it looks like the confused whirling of a swarm of white insects; below it resembles a shower of down, each flake turning round and round and reaching the ground only after considerable hesitation. If the snowfall continues thus for a little while, everything will be hidden under a sheet of dazzling whiteness.

"Now is the time for dusting the back of a schoolmate with a well-directed snowball, which will bring a prompt reply. Now is the time for rolling up an immense snowball which, turning over and over and creaking as it grows, at last becomes too large to move even under our united efforts. On top of this ball a similar one will be hoisted, then another still smaller on that, and the whole will be shaped into a grotesque giant having for mustache two large turkey feathers and for arms an old broomstick. But look out for the hands in modeling this masterpiece! More than one young sculptor will hasten to thrust them, aching with cold, into his pockets. But, though inactive himself, he will none the less give the others plenty of advice on how to finish off the colossus.

"Oh, how glorious is a holiday when there is snow on the ground! If I were to let myself go, how eloquent I could be on the subject! But, after all, what could I say that would be new to you? You know better than I all about the games appropriate to the occasion. You belong to the present, I to the past; you make the snow man now and here; I only tell about it from memory. We shall do better to go on with our modest studies, in which I can be of some help to you.

"From snow to hail is a short step, both being nothing but atmospheric vapor turned to ice by cold. But while snow is in delicate flakes, hail takes the form of hard pellets of ice called hailstones. These vary greatly in size, from that of a tiny pin-head to that of a pea, a plum, a pigeon's egg, and larger.

"Hail often does much harm. The icy pellets, hard as stone, in falling from the clouds gain speed enough to make them break window-panes, bruise the unfortunate person not under cover, and cut to pieces in a few minutes harvests, vineyards, and fruit-crops. It is nearly always in warm weather that hail falls, and as necessary conditions there must be a violent storm with flashes of lightning and peals of thunder.

"If on the one hand a hail-storm is to be regarded as a disaster, on the other a fall of snow if often to be welcomed as a blessing. Snow slowly saturates the earth with moisture that is of more lasting benefit than a rainfall. It also covers the fields with a mantle that affords protection from severe frost, so that the young shoots from seeds recently sown remain green and vigorous instead of being exposed to the deadly sting of the north wind.

"Snow plays still another part, and a very important one, a part having to do with the very existence of our streams. On account of the cold in high regions it snows more often on the mountains than in the plains. In our latitude peaks three thousand meters high, or more, are unvisited by rain. Every cloud borne to them by the wind deposits, instead of a shower of rain, a mantle of snow, and that in all seasons of the year, summer as well as winter.

"Driven by the wind or sliding down the steep slopes, this snow from the mountain-tops, renewed almost daily, collects in the neighboring valleys and piles up there in drifts hundreds of meters deep, which finally turn to ice as hard and clear as that of the pond where we go skating. In this way there are formed and maintained those masses of moving ice known as glaciers, immense reservoirs of frozen water which abound in all the larger mountain systems.

"In its upper reaches, where the mountain peaks pierce the sky, the glacier is continually receiving fresh snow that comes sliding down the neighboring slopes, while in its lower course, farther down the valley, where the warmth is sufficient, the ice melts and gives rise to a stream which is soon added to by others from neighboring glaciers. In this way the largest rivers are started on their courses.

"From the soil saturated with rain-water and snow-water come springs and brooks and larger streams, each but a slender thread at first, a few drops trickling slowly, a tiny streamlet that one could stop with the hand. But, collecting drop by drop from all around, trickling down the mountainside, a little here and a little there, one thimbleful added to another, one tiny streamlet uniting with its neighbor, at last we have, first, the little brook babbling over its smooth pebbles, then the larger brook that drives the mill-wheel, then the stream on which rides the rowboat, and finally the majestic river carrying to the sea all the drainage of an immense watershed.

"Every drop of water that irrigates the soil comes from the sea, and every drop returns to the sea. The heat of the sun draws the water up in the form of vapor; this vapor goes to make clouds, which the wind scatters in all directions; from these clouds fall rain and snow; and from this rain and snow are formed rivers and other streams which all combine to return to the sea the water thus distributed.

"The water of every spring, well, fountain, lake, pond, marsh, and ditch—all, absolutely all, even to the tiniest mud-puddle and the moisture that bedews a sprig of moss—comes from the sea and returns to it.

"If water cannot run because it is held back in the hollow of some rock, or in a depression in the ground, or in a leaf that has drunk its fill of sap, no matter: the great journey will be accomplished all the same. The sun will turn it to vapor, which will be dissipated in the atmosphere; and, having once started on this broad highway that leads everywhere, sooner or later it must return to the sea.

"I hope now you are beginning to understand all this, except one puzzling detail that must certainly have occurred to you. You wonder how it can be that, sea-water being so salt and so disagreeable to drink, rain-water, snow-water, spring-water, river-water, and so on, should be so tasteless. The answer is easy. Recall to mind the experiment of the plate of salt water placed in the sun. The part that disappears, evaporated by the heat, is pure water and nothing more. What remains in the plate is the salt that water contained, a substance on which evaporation has no hold.

"The same process of evaporation is constantly going on over all the broad expanse of the sea: the water alone is reduced to vapor, the salt remains. From this vapor, purged of all that made the sea-water so disagreeable to the taste, only tasteless water can result."

Exercise

Review memory work. Name the part of the verb underlined in the following sentences.

> She is sitting in a comfortable rolling-chair.

> "That's not my business," grumbled the coachman.

Copy each sentence below. Double underline the predicate, and underline the subject. Put brackets around any prepositional phrases. Label the part of speech of each word. Noun, N; Proper Noun, PN; Pronoun, PRO; Verb, V; Linking Verb, LV; Adjective, ADJ; Article, ART; Conjunction, CJ; Preposition, Prep; Interjection, INJ. Diagram each sentence.

> Sebastian, the butler, soon stood before her.

> "Miss Deta, how could you bring this child?"

> "I have never heard the name before."

Commonplace Book

With your instructor's approval, add the passage below to your commonplace book, or choose your own passage from a work of fiction. This can be from either school reading or free reading.

> "What a curious child you are," said Clara. "You have come to Frankfurt to stay with me, don't you know that? We shall have our lessons together, and I think it will be great fun when you learn to read. Generally the morning seems to have no end, for Mr. Candidate comes at ten and stays till two."

Dictation

> When Miss Rottenmeier found that she was unable to recall Deta, she came back to the children. She was in a very excited mood, for she felt responsible for Heidi's coming and did not know how to cancel this unfortunate step. She soon got up again to go to the dining-room, criticizing the butler and giving orders to the maid. Sebastian, not daring to show his rage otherwise, noisily opened the folding doors. When he went up to Clara's chair, he saw Heidi watching him intently. At last she said: "You look like Peter."

74. Subject-Verb Agreement

• Heidi, Chapter 7

Nouns, pronouns, and verbs all possess the property **number**.

Sentences can have more than one verb, and each verb has a subject. Each subject must agree with its verb in number. You've probably already noticed this. In your Copia exercises, you may have tried to change the number of a noun or verb, and found that you had to change other words in the sentence, too.

Look at the following sentences from *Heidi*. Change the subject's number without changing the verb's, and see how that sounds. Change the verb's number without changing the subject's, and see how that sounds.

> She was sitting in a comfortable rolling-chair.

> Clara's father leaves the management of the house to this lady.

Subjects and verbs must agree in number.

Each subject must agree with its verb in number. In most cases, this is somewhat automatic for native speakers of a language. However, there are four situations which can cause confusion. We'll discuss two of these situations today. In all cases, the solution is to determine the subject of the verb.

The first situation occurs when the subject is separated from the verb by modifiers. Look at these sentences:

> Heidi, Clara, and Mr. Candidate were in the study.

> The group was in the study.

> The group of people was in the study.

In the first sentence, we have a compound subject. This plural subject requires a plural verb, so we use **were**. In the second sentence, the subject is **group**. **Group** is a **collective noun**. While there may be many in a group, the group, when acting together as a unit, is singular. This singular subject requires a singular verb, so we use **was**.

In the last sentence, the subject and the verb are divided by a prepositional phrase, and the object of the preposition is plural. Remember, though, that the verb must agree with its subject, and the subject of that sentence is still **group**, a singular noun.

A second situation occurs with conjunctions. When **and** joins two or more subjects, the subject combines to be more than one and needs a plural verb. However, when **or** or **nor** join singular subjects, the subject is not combining. Instead, the conjunction shows a choice, one **or** the other. The subject remains singular, and the sentence needs a singular verb. These rules make perfect sense when you think about it.

> Both Heidi and Clara were in the study.

> Neither Heidi nor Clara was in the kitchen.

The God of Music

By Edith M. Thomas

The God of Music dwelleth out of doors.
All seasons through his minstrelsy we meet,
Breathing by field and covert haunting-sweet
From organ-lofts in forests old he pours:
A solemn harmony: on leafy floors
To smooth autumnal pipes he moves his feet,
Or with the tingling plectrum of the sleet
In winter keen beats out his thrilling scores.
Leave me the reed unplucked beside the stream.
And he will stoop and fill it with the breeze;
Leave me the viol's frame in secret trees,
Unwrought, and it shall wake a druid theme;
Leave me the whispering shell on Nereid shores.
The God of Music dwelleth out of doors.

Jackal and Monkey

From *South-African Folk-Tales* by James A. Honey

Every evening Jackal went to the Boer's kraal. He crept through the sliding door and stole a fat young lamb. This, clever Jackal did several times in succession. Boer set a wip for him at the door. Jackal went again and zip—there he was caught around the body by the noose. He swung and swayed high in the air and couldn't touch ground. The day began to dawn and Jackal became uneasy.

On a stone kopje, Monkey sat. When it became light he could see the whole affair, and descended hastily for the purpose of mocking Jackal. He went and sat on the wall. "Ha, ha, good morning. So there you are hanging now, eventually caught."

"What? I caught? I am simply swinging for my pleasure; it is enjoyable."

"You fibber. You are caught in the wip."

"If you but realized how nice it was to swing and sway like this, you wouldn't hesitate. Come, try it a little. You feel so healthy and strong for the day, and you never tire afterwards."

"No, I won't. You are caught."

After a while Jackal convinced Monkey. He sprang from the kraal wall, and freeing Jackal, adjusted the noose around his own body. Jackal quickly let go and began to laugh, as Monkey was now swinging high in the air.

"Ha, ha, ha," he laughed. "Now Monkey is in the wip."

"Jackal, free me," he screamed.

"There, Boer is coming," shouted Jackal.

"Jackal, free me of this, or I'll break your playthings."

"No, there Boer is coming with his gun; you rest a while in the noose."

"Jackal, quickly make me free."

"No, here's Boer already, and he's got his gun. Good morning." And with these parting words he ran away as fast as he could. Boer came and saw Monkey in the wip.

"So, so, Monkey, now you are caught. You are the fellow who has been stealing my lambs, hey?"

"No, Boer, no," screamed Monkey, "not I, but Jackal."

"No, I know you; you aren't too good for that."

"No, Boer, no, not I, but Jackal," Monkey stammered.

"Oh, I know you. Just wait a little," and Boer, raising his gun, aimed and shot poor Monkey dead.

Writing: Outline

Write or type an outline of the new model story which you read in the last lesson.

Exercise

Review memory work. Name the part of the verb underlined in the following sentences.

"This child <u>brings</u> nothing but misfortunes on us."

"I <u>hear</u> the fir-trees rustle."

Copy each sentence below. Double underline the predicate, and underline the subject. Put brackets around any prepositional phrases. Label the part of speech of each word. Noun, N; Proper Noun, PN; Pronoun, PRO; Verb, V; Linking Verb, LV; Adjective, ADJ; Article, ART; Conjunction, CJ; Preposition, Prep; Interjection, INJ. Diagram each sentence.

Where has she gone?

"Where is the tower with the golden dome?"

"Can you open a window for me?"

Commonplace Book

With your instructor's approval, add the poem below to your commonplace book, or choose your own poem.

> Heidi immediately stepped down from the stool and ran down-stairs. Opening the door, she found herself in the street, but she could not see the tower any more. She wandered on from street to street, not daring to accost any of the busy people. Passing a corner, she saw a boy who had a barrel-organ on his back and a curious animal on his arm.

Dictation

Luke 2:39-40

When they had performed everything according to the Law of the Lord, they returned to Galilee, to their own city of Nazareth. The Child continued to grow and become strong, increasing in wisdom; and the grace of God was upon Him.

Street of the Bavolle at Honfleur by Claude Monet

Picture Study

1. Read the title and the name of the artist. Study the picture for several minutes, then put the picture away.

2. Describe the picture.

3. Look at the picture again. Do you notice any details that you missed before? What do you like or dislike about this painting? Does it remind you of anything?

75. Literary Analysis

- Heidi, Chapter 8

Writing: Literary Analysis

Today you have another literary analysis assignment. Now that you've had some practice, this should be a written assignment, though it can be helpful to discuss your ideas before writing.

With your instructor's approval, choose *Heidi*, or one of the other books you're currently reading, and answer the following questions.

What is the book about? Give a brief summary, just a few sentences. Has any part of the book seemed particularly real, or particularly unlikely?

A Musical Instrument

By Elizabeth Barrett Browning

"The great god sighed for the cost and the pain."

What was he doing, the great god Pan,
  Down in the reeds by the river?
Spreading ruin and scattering ban,
Splashing and paddling with hoofs of a goat,
And breaking the golden lilies afloat
  With the dragon-fly on the river.

He tore out a reed, the great god Pan,
  From the deep cool bed of the river:
The limpid water turbidly ran,
And the broken lilies a-dying lay,
And the dragon-fly had fled away,
  Ere he brought it out of the river.

High on the shore sat the great god Pan,
  While turbidly flow'd the river;
And hack'd and hew'd as a great god can,

With his hard bleak steel at the patient reed,
Till there was not a sign of a leaf indeed
  To prove it fresh from the river.

He cut it short, did the great god Pan
  (How tall it stood in the river!),
Then drew the pith, like the heart of a man,
Steadily from the outside ring,
And notched the poor dry empty thing
  In holes, as he sat by the river.

"This is the way," laugh'd the great god Pan
  (Laugh'd while he sat by the river),
"The only way, since gods began
To make sweet music, they could succeed."
Then, dropping his mouth to a hole in the reed
  He blew in power by the river.

Sweet, sweet, sweet, O Pan!
  Piercing sweet by the river!
Blinding sweet, O great god Pan!
The sun on the hill forgot to die,
And the lilies reviv'd, and the dragon-fly
  Came back to dream on the river.

Yet half a beast is the great god Pan,
  To laugh as he sits by the river,
Making a poet out of a man:
The true gods sigh for the cost and pain,—
For the reed which grows nevermore again
  As a reed with the reeds in the river.

The Man and Snake

From *South-African Folk-Tales* by James A. Honey

    A Dutchman was walking by himself and saw Snake lying under a large stone. Snake implored his help; but when she had become free she said, "Now I shall eat you."
    The Man answered, "That is not right. Let us first go to Hare."
    When Hare had heard the affair, he said, "It is right."
    "No," said the Man, "let us ask Hyena."
    Hyena declared the same, saying, "It is right."
    "Now let us ask Jackal," said the Man in his despair.
    Jackal answered very slowly and considerately, doubting the whole affair, and demanding to see first the place, and whether the Man was able to lift the stone. Snake lay down, and the Man, to prove the truth of his account, put the stone again over her.
    When she was fast, Jackal said, "Now let her lie there."

Exercise

Review memory work. Punctuate the following sentence.

Oh please Mr. Candidate can't we just peep in

Identify each group of words below as either a phrase or a clause. If it is a clause, double underline the predicate and underline the subject. Remember to find the verb first! Then ask who or what did the action.

the furious lady proceeded

whispered the frightened child

for mercy's sake

Copy each sentence below. Double underline the predicate, and underline the subject. Put brackets around any prepositional phrases. Label the part of speech of each word. Noun, N; Proper Noun, PN; Pronoun, PRO; Verb, V; Linking Verb, LV; Adjective, ADJ; Article, ART; Conjunction, CJ; Preposition, Prep; Interjection, INJ. Diagram each sentence.

Sebastian obediently pulled the boy after him.

Clara, on the contrary, enjoyed her companion's society.

"Bring the unlucky child up!"

Commonplace Book

With your instructor's approval, add the passage below to your commonplace book, or choose your own passage from a work of non-fiction. This can be from the Bible, a biography, or one of your history or science books.

> "Stop! Stop!" she called, but in vain, for the music drowned her voice. Suddenly she made a big jump, for there, between her feet, crawled a black turtle. Only when she shrieked for Sebastian could her voice be heard. The butler came straight in, for he had seen everything behind the door, and a great scene it had been!

76. Comparatives

• Heidi, Chapter 9

Definition: Comparative adjectives and adverbs compare two things.

We use **comparative adjectives** to compare two nouns and **comparative adverbs** to compare two adjectives or verbs.

To make comparatives of one-syllable words, we add the ending **er**. Look at the following examples:

Adjectives: cold, colder; dry, drier; hot, hotter,.
Adverbs: hard, harder; fast, faster; early, earlier.

In two-syllable adjectives which end in *y*, we also add *er*, after changing the *y* to *i*.

Adjectives: wavy, wavier; happy, happier.
Adverbs: early, earlier.

For other words with two or more syllables, adjectives and adverbs, we don't change the form. Instead, we add the word **more**.

Adjectives: radiant, more radiant; comfortable, more comfortable
Adverbs: carefully, more carefully; horribly, more horribly.

Look at the following sentences from *Heidi*.

They will be much softer than those stale ones you have kept.

The grandmother exclaimed every time more joyfully.

But the teacher had more serious troubles still.

The Harp That Once Through Tara's Halls

By Thomas Moore

The harp that once through Tara's halls
  The soul of music shed,
Now hangs as mute on Tara's walls
  As if that soul were fled.
So sleeps the pride of former days,
  So glory's thrill is o'er,
And hearts, that once beat high for praise,
  Now feel that pulse no more.

No more to chiefs and ladies bright
  The harp of Tara swells;
The chord alone, that breaks at night,
  Its tale of ruin tells.
Thus Freedom now so seldom wakes,
  The only throb she gives
Is when some heart indignant breaks,
  To show that still she lives.

Lion's Share

From *South-African Folk-Tales* by James A. Honey

Lion and Jackal went together a-hunting. They shot with arrows. Lion shot first, but his arrow fell short of its aim; but Jackal hit the game, and joyfully cried out, "It has hit."

Lion looked at him with his two large eyes; Jackal, however, did not lose his countenance, but said, "No, uncle, I mean to say that you have hit." Then they followed the game, and Jackal passed the arrow of Lion without drawing the latter's attention to it. When they arrived at a crossway, Jackal said: "Dear uncle, you are old and tired; stay here." Jackal went then on a wrong track, beat his nose, and, in returning, let the blood drop from it like traces of game. "I could not find anything," he said, "but I met with traces of blood. You had better go yourself to look for it. In the meantime I shall go this other way."

Jackal soon found the killed animal, crept inside of it, and devoured the best portion; but his tail remained outside, and when Lion arrived, he got hold of it, pulled Jackal out, and threw him on the ground with these words: "You rascal!"

Jackal rose quickly again, complained of the rough handling, and asked, "What have I now done, dear uncle? I was busy cutting out the best part."

"Now let us go and fetch our wives," said Lion, but Jackal entreated his dear uncle to remain at the place because he was old. Jackal then went away, taking with him two portions of the flesh, one for his own wife, but the best part for the wife of Lion. When Jackal arrived with the flesh, the children of Lion, seeing him, began to jump, and clapping their hands, cried out: "There comes cousin with flesh!" Jackal threw, grumbling, the worst portion to them, and said, "There, you brood of the big-eyed one!" Then he went to his own house and told his wife immediately to break up the house, and to go where the killed game was. Lioness wished to do the same, but he forbade her, and said that Lion would himself come to fetch her.

When Jackal, with his wife and children, arrived in the neighborhood of the killed animal, he ran into a thorn bush, scratched his face so that it bled, and thus made his appearance before Lion, to whom he said, "Ah! What a wife you have got. Look here, how she scratched my face when I told her that she should come with us. You must fetch her yourself; I cannot bring her." Lion went home very angry. Then Jackal said, "Quick, let us build a tower." They heaped stone upon stone, stone upon stone, stone upon stone; and when it was high enough, everything was carried to the top of it. When Jackal saw Lion approaching with his wife and children, he cried out to him:

"Uncle, whilst you were away we have built a tower, in order to be better able to see game."

"All right," said Lion; "but let me come up to you."

"Certainly, dear uncle; but how will you manage to come up? We must let down a thong for you."

Lion tied the thong around his body and Jackal began drawing him up, but when nearly to the top Jackal cried to Lion, "My, uncle, how heavy you are!" Then, unseen by Lion, he cut the thong. Lion fell to the ground, while Jackal began loudly and angrily to scold his wife, and then said, "Go, wife, fetch me a new thong"—"an old one," he said aside to her.

Lion again tied himself to the thong, and, just as he was near the top, Jackal cut the thong as before; Lion fell heavily to the bottom, groaning aloud, as he had been seriously hurt.

"No," said Jackal, "that will never do: you must, however, manage to come up high enough so that you may get a mouthful at least." Then aloud he ordered his wife to prepare a good piece, but aside he told her to make a stone hot, and to cover it with fat. Then he drew Lion up once more, and complaining how heavy he was to hold, told him to open his mouth, and thereupon threw the hot stone down his throat. Lion fell to the ground and lay there pleading for water, while Jackal climbed down and made his escape.

Writing: Copia

Take the following sentence and play with it. Remember that the point is not necessarily to make the sentence better. The point is to play with the sentence and make it different. Make a new sentence with a change from each of the following categories.

> "Snow has the same origin as rain: it comes from vapor in the atmosphere, especially from vapor rising from the surface of the sea."

1. Change the grammar.
   - Change the nouns from common to proper and vice versa.
   - Change the nouns from singular to plural and vice versa.
   - Change the sentence type.
   - Change the adjectives from articles to descriptive to possessive, etc.
   - Change a quotation from direct to indirect and vice versa.
   - Change the verb tense.

2. Condense the sentence.
   - Remove details.
   - Remove modifiers.
   - Remove phrases or clauses.

3. Amplify the sentence.
   - Add details.
   - Add dialogue.
   - Add modifiers.
   - Add phrases or clauses.

4. Use synonyms and antonyms.
   - Substitute synonyms.
   - Say the opposite thing using antonyms.

5. Point of view.
   - Change the point of view.
   - Slant the sentence.

Exercise

Review memory work. Copy each sentence below. Double underline the predicate, and underline the subject. Put brackets around any prepositional phrases. Label the part of speech of each word. Noun, N; Proper Noun, PN; Pronoun, PRO; Verb, V; Linking Verb, LV; Adjective, ADJ; Article, ART; Conjunction, CJ; Preposition, Prep; Interjection, INJ. Diagram each sentence.

"How do you mean?"

"Oh, Mr. Sesemann, we have been terribly disappointed."

"I thought of this Swiss child."

Commonplace Book

With your instructor's approval, add the passage below to your commonplace book, or choose your own passage from a work of fiction. This can be from either school reading or free reading.

> Clara now began to relate to her father all the incidents with the kittens and the turtle, and explained Heidi's speeches that had so frightened the lady. Mr. Sesemann laughed heartily and asked Clara if she wished Heidi to remain.

Dictation

> But this was impossible for Mr. Candidate, who had to greet Mr. Sesemann first. Then he began to reassure his host about the child, pointing out to him that her education had been neglected till then, and so on. But poor Mr. Sesemann, unfortunately, did not get his answer, and had to listen to very long-winded explanations of the child's character. At last Mr. Sesemann got up, saying: "Excuse me, Mr. Candidate, but I must go over to Clara now."

77. Superlatives

• Heidi, Chapter 10

Definition: Superlative adjectives and adverbs compare three or more things.

We use **superlative adjectives** to compare three or more nouns and **superlative adverbs** to compare three or more adjectives or verbs.

To make superlatives of one-syllable words, we add the ending *est*. Look at the following examples:

Adjectives: cold, coldest; dry, driest; hot, hottest.
Adverbs: hard, hardest; fast, fastest.

In two-syllable adjectives, but not adverbs, which end in *y*, we also add *est*, after changing the *y* to *i*.

Adjectives: wavy, waviest; happy, happiest.
Adverbs: early, earliest.

For other words with two or more syllables, adjectives and adverbs, we don't change the form. Instead, we add the word **most**.

Adjectives: radiant, most radiant; comfortable, most comfortable
Adverbs: carefully, most carefully; horribly, most horribly.

Some adjectives and adverbs are **irregular**, meaning they don't follow the normal form. Here are a few irregular adjectives:

Adjective	Comparative	Superlative
good	better	best
bad	worse	worst
little	less	least
many	more	most

And here are a few irregular adverbs:

Adverb	Comparative	Superlative
well	better	best
badly	worse	worst
much	more	most

Look at the following sentences from *Heidi*.

He found Miss Rottenmeier surveying the table with a <u>most tragic</u> face.

"This child has brought the most frightful animals into the house."

"She has not the <u>slightest</u> desire to do something useful."

L'Envoi

By Rudyard Kipling

When Earth's last picture is painted, and the tubes are
twisted and dried,
When the oldest colors have faded, and the youngest critic has died,
We shall rest, and, faith, we shall need it—lie down
for an æon or two,
Till the Master of All Good Workmen shall set us to work anew!

And those who were good shall be happy: they shall sit
in a golden chair;
They shall splash at a ten-league canvas with brushes of comet's hair;
They shall find real saints to draw from—Magdalene, Peter, and Paul;
They shall work for an age at a sitting and never be tired at all!

And only the Master shall praise us, and only the Master shall blame;
And no one shall work for money, and no one shall work for fame;
But each for the joy of the working, and each, in his separate star,
Shall draw the Thing as he sees It for the God of Things as They Are!

Jackal, Dove, and Heron

From *South-African Folk-Tales* by James A. Honey

Jackal, it is said, came once to Dove, who lived on the top of a rock, and said, "Give me one of your little ones."

Dove answered, "I shall not do anything of the kind."

Jackal said, "Give me it at once! Otherwise, I shall fly up to you." Then she threw one down to him.

He came back another day and demanded another little one, and she gave it to him. After Jackal had gone, Heron came, and asked, "Dove, why do you cry?"

Dove answered him, "Jackal has taken away my little ones; it is for this that I cry." He asked her, "In what manner did he take them?" She answered him, "When he asked me I refused him; but when he said, 'I shall at once fly up, therefore give me it,' I threw it down to him."

Heron said, "Are you such a fool as to give your young ones to Jackal, who cannot fly?" Then, with the admonition to give no more, he went away.

Jackal came again, and said, "Dove, give me a little one." Dove refused, and told him that Heron had told her that he could not fly up. Jackal said, "I shall catch him."

So when Heron came to the banks of the water, Jackal asked him: "Brother Heron, when the wind comes from this side, how will you stand?" He turned his neck towards him and said, "I stand thus, bending my neck on one side." Jackal asked him again, "When a storm comes and when it rains, how do you stand?" He said to him: "I stand thus, indeed, bending my neck down."

Then Jackal beat him on his neck, and broke his neck in the middle.

Since that day Heron's neck is bent.

Exercise

Review memory work. Name the part of the verb underlined in the following sentences.

"What <u>have</u> you <u>learned</u>, child, tell me?"

"I <u>am going</u> to tell you something, Heidi."

Copy each sentence below. Double underline the predicate, and underline the subject. Put brackets around any prepositional phrases. Label the part of speech of each word. Noun, N; Proper Noun, PN; Pronoun, PRO; Verb, V; Linking Verb, LV; Adjective, ADJ; Article, ART; Conjunction, CJ; Preposition, Prep; Interjection, INJ. Diagram each sentence.

"Rottenmeier, where is the child?"

"When I am going home?" [Hint: **home** tells where.]

Heidi was looking with wondering eyes at the splendid pictures.

Writing: Commonplace Book

Add the passage below from your model story to your commonplace book.

> "I have already told you that cirrus clouds, which are the highest of all clouds and hence more exposed to cold than the others, are composed of extremely fine needles of ice. Lower clouds, too, if subjected to a sufficient degree of cold, undergo the same transformation. Then there follows a symmetrical grouping of adjacent needles in delicate six-pointed stars which, in greater or less numbers and heaped together at random, make a snowflake."

Dictation

Use part of today's poem for dictation.

78. Scientific Narration: Snow

- Heidi, Chapter 11

Your next three narrations will be on scientific topics. The model stories are from Jean Henri Fabre's *The Secret of Everyday Things*. In his book, the character of Uncle Paul is explaining these scientific concepts to a group of children. The stories are written in the first person with frequent use of the second person as he speaks directly to the children.

Use your outline to write a narration on this topic. Don't include references to the children or Uncle Paul; just write about the topic. Your narration should be in the third person. You may use other sources for more details if desired. You'll need to decide which details are important to your narration and which ones should be left out.

The Lye

By Sir Walter Raleigh

Goe, soule, the bodie's guest,
  Upon a thanklesse arrant;
Feare not to touche the best—
  The truth shall be thy warrant!
Goe, since I needs must dye,
And give the world the lye.

Goe tell the court it glowes
  And shines like rotten wood;
Goe tell the church it showes
  What's good, and doth no good;
If church and court reply,
Then give them both the lye.

Tell potentates they live
  Acting by others' actions—
Not loved unlesse they give,
  Not strong but by their factions;
If potentates reply,
Give potentates the lye.

Tell men of high condition,
   That rule affairs of state,
Their purpose is ambition,
   Their practice only hate;
And if they once reply,
Then give them all the lye.

Tell zeale it lacks devotion;
   Tell love it is but lust;
Tell time it is but motion;
   Tell flesh it is but dust;
And wish them not reply,
For thou must give the lye.

Tell wit how much it wrangles
   In tickle points of nicenesse;
Tell wisdome she entangles
   Herselfe in over-wisenesse;
And if they do reply,
Straight give them both the lye.

Tell physicke of her boldnesse;
   Tell skill it is pretension;
Tell charity of coldnesse;
   Tell law it is contention;
And as they yield reply,
So give them still the lye.

Tell fortune of her blindnesse;
   Tell nature of decay;
Tell friendship of unkindnesse;
   Tell justice of delay;
And if they dare reply,
Then give them all the lye.

Tell arts they have no soundnesse,
   But vary by esteeming;
Tell schooles they want profoundnesse,
   And stand too much on seeming;
If arts and schooles reply,
Give arts and schooles the lye.

So, when thou hast, as I
   Commanded thee, done blabbing—
Although to give the lye
   Deserves no less than stabbing—
Yet stab at thee who will,
No stab the soule can kill.

Editing

• Did you meet the goal of this writing exercise?

• Look at your word choice. Is there a good mixture of nouns and pronouns? Is the antecedent of each pronoun clear?

• Look at your paragraphs. Are all the sentences related? Does each paragraph focus on a single topic?

79. Irregular Verbs

• Heidi, Chapter 12

There are many common verbs which are irregular. Irregular verbs do not have principal parts which follow the normal pattern, and they sometimes have irregular conjugations.

Participle just means a word formed from a verb. Participles can act as other parts of speech. To act as a verb, a participle requires a helping verb.

"Something secret and horrible has happened in this house."

"Tell me honestly if you have played the ghost for Miss Rottenmeier's pastime?"

With regular verbs, the past participle is made up of the past tense form. You will see it used without a helping verb. It is the past tense then, not the past participle.

When the doctor laughed, Mr. Sesemann continued.

This becomes more important with irregular verbs. Irregular verbs have irregular past participles, and some of these words are never used as verbs without a helping verb, such as **gone**, **done**, and **seen**.

I have gone; she has done; they have seen.

"Because I have prayed for the same thing many, many weeks and God has not done what I have asked Him to."

Infinitive	Present	Present Participle	Past	Past Participle
to go	go	going	went	gone
to do	do	doing	did	done
to see	see	seeing	saw	seen
to come	come	coming	came	come
to have	have	having	had	had

Contentment

By Edward Dyer

My mind to me a kingdom is;
  Such perfect joy therein I find
As far excels all earthly bliss
  That God or Nature hath assigned;
Though much I want that most would have,
Yet still my mind forbids to crave.

Content I live; this is my stay,—
  I seek no more than may suffice.
I press to bear no haughty sway;
  Look, what I lack my mind supplies.
Lo, thus I triumph like a king,
Content with that my mind doth bring.

I laugh not at another's loss,
  I grudge not at another's gain;
No worldly wave my mind can toss;
  I brook that is another's bane.
I fear no foe, nor fawn on friend;
I loathe not life, nor dread mine end.

My wealth is health and perfect ease;
  My conscience clear my chief defense;
I never seek by bribes to please
  Nor by desert to give offense.
Thus do I live, thus will I die;
Would all did so as well as I!

Writing: Oral Narration

Read your new model story below, and then give your instructor an oral narration of it.

Silk

From *The Secret of Everyday Things* by Jean Henri Fabre

    The culture of the silkworm having been explained by Uncle Paul in one of his previous talks, he now confined himself chiefly to the structure of the cocoon and the unwinding of the delicate silk thread composing it.

    "The cocoon of the silkworm," he began, "is composed of two envelops: an outer one of very coarse gauze, and an inner one of very fine fabric. This latter is the cocoon properly so called, and from it alone is obtained the silk thread so highly valued in manufacture and commerce, whereas the other, owing to its irregular structure, cannot be unwound and furnishes only an inferior grade of silk suitable for carding.

    "The outer envelop is fastened by some of its threads to the little twigs amid which the worm has taken its position, and forms merely a sort of scaffolding or openwork hammock wherein the worm seeks seclusion and establishes itself for the serious and delicate task of spinning its inner envelop. When, accordingly, the hammock is ready the worm fixes its hind feet in the threads and proceeds to raise and bend its body, carrying its head from one side to the other and emitting from its spinneret as it does so a tiny thread which, by its sticky quality, immediately adheres to the points touched. Without change of position the caterpillar thus lays one thickness of its web over that portion of the enclosure which it faces. Then it turns to another part and carpets that in the same manner. After the entire enclosure has thus been lined, other layers are added, to the number of five or six or even more. In fact, the process goes on until the store of silk-making material is exhausted and the thickness of the wall is sufficient for the security of the future chrysalis.

"From the way the caterpillar works you will see that the thread of silk is not wound in circles, as it is in a ball of cotton, but is arranged in a series of zigzags, back and forth, and to right and left. Yet in spite of these abrupt changes in direction and notwithstanding the length of the thread—from three hundred to five hundred meters—there is never any break in its continuity. The silkworm gives it forth uninterruptedly without suspending for a moment the work of its spinneret until the cocoon is finished. This cocoon has an average weight of a decigram and a half, and it would take only fifteen or twenty kilograms of the silk thread to extend ten thousand leagues, or once around the earth.

"Examined under the microscope, the thread is seen to be an exceedingly fine tube, flattened and with an irregular surface, and composed of three distinct concentric layers, of which the innermost one is pure silk. Over this is laid a varnish that resists the action of warm water, but dissolves in a weak alkaline solution. Finally, on the outside there is a gummy coating which serves to bind the zigzag courses firmly together and thus to make of them a substantial envelop.

"As soon as the caterpillars have completed their tasks, the cocoons are gathered from the sprigs of heather. A few of these cocoons, selected from those that show the best condition, are set aside and left for the completion of the metamorphosis. The resulting butterflies furnish the eggs or 'seeds' whence, next year, will come the new litter of worms. The rest of the cocoons are immediately subjected to the action of very hot steam, which kills the chrysalis in each just when the tender flesh is beginning slowly to take form. Without this precaution the butterfly would break through the cocoon, which, no longer capable of being unwound, because of its broken strands, would lose all its value.

"The cocoons are unwound in workrooms fitted up for the purpose. First the cocoons are put into a pan of boiling water to dissolve the gum which holds together the several courses of thread. An operator equipped with a small broom of heather twigs stirs the cocoons in the water in order to find and seize the end of the thread, which is then attached to a reel in motion. Under the tension thus exerted by the machine, the thread of the silk unwinds while the cocoon jumps up and down in the warm water like a ball of worsted when you pull at the loose end of the yarn. In the heart of the unwound cocoon there remains a chrysalis, inert, killed by the steam.

"Since a single strand would not be strong enough for the purpose of weaving, it is usual to unwind all at once a number of cocoons, from three to fifteen and even more, according to the thickness of the fabric for which the silk is destined; and these united strands are used later as one thread in the weaving machines.

"As it comes from the pan the raw silk of the cocoon is found to have shed its coating of gum, which has become dissolved in the hot water; but it is still coated with its natural varnish, which gives it its firmness, its elasticity, its color, often of a golden yellow. In this state it is called raw silk and has a yellow or white appearance according to the color of the cocoons from which it came. In order to take in the dye that is to enhance its brilliance and add to its value, the silk must first be cleansed of its varnish by a gentle washing in a solution of lye and soap in warm water. This process causes it to lose about a quarter of its weight and to become of a beautiful white, whatever may have been its original color. After this purifying process it is called washed silk or finished silk. Finally, if perfect whiteness is desired, the silk is exposed to the action of sulphur, as I will explain to you when we come to the subject of wool.

"Cocoons that have been punctured by the butterfly, together with all scraps and remnants that cannot be disentangled and straightened out, are carded and thus reduced to a sort of fluff known as floss-silk, which is spun on the distaff or the spinning-wheel very much as wool is treated; but even with the utmost pains the thread thus obtained never has the beautiful regularity and the soft fineness of that which is furnished by unwinding the cocoon. It is used for fabrics of inferior quality, for stockings, shoe-laces, and corset-laces.

"The silkworm and the tree that feeds it, the mulberry, are indigenous to China, where silk-weaving has been practiced for some four or five thousand years. Today, when the highly prized caterpillar is dying out in our part of the world, China and its neighbor Japan are called upon to furnish healthy silkworm eggs. Silk-culture was introduced into Europe from Asia in the year 555 by two monks who came to Constantinople with mulberry plants and silkworm eggs concealed in a hollow cane; for it was strictly forbidden to disseminate abroad an industry that yielded such immense riches."

Exercise

Review memory work. Name the part of the verb underlined in the following sentences.

"I want to speak to him alone."

"Come here, Sebastian, and tell me honestly, if you have played the ghost for Miss Rottenmeier's pastime?"

Copy each sentence below. Double underline the predicate, and underline the subject. Put brackets around any prepositional phrases. Label the part of speech of each word. Noun, N; Proper Noun, PN; Pronoun, PRO; Verb, V; Linking Verb, LV; Adjective, ADJ; Article, ART; Conjunction, CJ; Preposition, Prep; Interjection, INJ. Diagram each sentence.

His eyes were lively and kind.

"Have patience, my old friend."

A few bottles of wine stood on the table.

Commonplace Book

With your instructor's approval, add the passage below to your commonplace book, or choose your own passage from a work of fiction. This can be from either school reading or free reading.

> "Who is there?" thundered the doctor, approaching the figure. It turned and uttered a low shriek. There stood Heidi, with bare feet and in her white nightgown, looking bewildered at the bright light and the weapons. She was shaking with fear, while the two men were looking at her in amazement.

Dictation

> "Really! Tell me, what did you dream?"
> "Oh, I have the same dream every night. I always think I am with my grandfather again and can hear the fir-trees roar. I always think how beautiful the stars must be, and then I open the door of the hut, and oh, it is so wonderful! But when I wake up I am always in Frankfurt." Heidi had to fight the sobs that were rising in her throat.

80. Tenses: Negatives and Questions

- Heidi, Chapter 13

The simple past tense is formed by adding **ed** to regular verbs. The simple future tense is formed by adding the word **will** to the base verb.

The helping verb **will** makes it easy to form negatives and questions in the future tense. Look at the following sentence from *Heidi*.

"If you show my card they, will give you good accommodations."

We can easily change it to a negative by adding the word **not**:

"If you show my card, they will not give you good accommodations."

And we can easily change it into a question by changing the word order:

"If you show my card, will they give you good accommodations?"

But how can we form negatives and questions from sentences in the past tense like this one?

He stepped into the cottage.

We use the helping verb **did** and drop the **ed** ending. It allows us to form negatives in the past tense:

He did not step into the cottage.

And we can ask questions in the past tense like this one:

Did he step into the cottage?

The Old Oaken Bucket

By Samuel Woodworth

How dear to this heart are the scenes of my childhood,
  When fond recollection presents them to view!
The orchard, the meadow, the deep-tangled wild-wood,

And every loved spot which my infancy knew!
The wide-spreading pond, and the mill that stood by it,
  The bridge, and the rock where the cataract fell,
The cot of my father, the dairy-house nigh it,
  And e'en the rude bucket that hung in the well—
The old oaken bucket, the iron-bound bucket,
The moss-covered bucket which hung in the well.

That moss-covered vessel I hailed as a treasure,
  For often at noon, when returned from the field,
I found it the source of an exquisite pleasure,
  The purest and sweetest that nature can yield.
How ardent I seized it, with hands that were glowing,
  And quick to the white-pebbled bottom it fell;
Then soon, with the emblem of truth overflowing,
  And dripping with coolness, it rose from the well—
The old oaken bucket, the iron-bound bucket,
The moss-covered bucket arose from the well.

How sweet from the green mossy brim to receive it
  As poised on the curb it inclined to my lips!
Not a full blushing goblet could tempt me to leave it,
  The brightest that beauty or revelry sips.
And now, far removed from the loved habitation,
  The tear of regret will intrusively swell.
As fancy reverts to my father's plantation,
  And sighs for the bucket that hangs in the well—
The old oaken bucket, the iron-bound bucket,
The moss-covered bucket that hangs in the well!

Elephant and Tortoise

From *South-African Folk-Tales* by James A. Honey

    Two powers, Elephant and Rain, had a dispute. Elephant said, "If you say that you nourish me, in what way is it that you say so?" Rain answered, "If you say that I do not nourish you, when I go away, will you not die?" And Rain then departed.
    Elephant said, "Vulture! Cast lots to make rain for me."
    Vulture said, "I will not cast lots."
    Then Elephant said to Crow, "Cast lots!" who answered, "Give the things with which I may cast lots." Crow cast lots and rain fell. It rained at the lagoons, but they dried up, and only one lagoon remained.
    Elephant went a-hunting. There was, however, Tortoise, to whom Elephant said, "Tortoise, remain at the water!" Thus Tortoise was left behind when Elephant went a-hunting.
    There came Giraffe, and said to Tortoise, "Give me water!" Tortoise answered, "The water belongs to Elephant."
    There came Zebra, who said to Tortoise, "Give me water!" Tortoise answered, "The water belongs to Elephant."
    There came Gemsbok, and said to Tortoise, "Give me water!" Tortoise answered, "The water belongs to Elephant."

There came Wildebeest, and said, "Give me water!" Tortoise said, "The water belongs to Elephant."

There came Roodebok, and said to Tortoise, "Give me water!" Tortoise answered, "The water belongs to Elephant."

There came Springbok, and said to Tortoise, "Give me water!" Tortoise said, "The water belongs to Elephant."

There came Jackal, and said to Tortoise, "Give me water!" Tortoise said, "The water belongs to Elephant."

There came Lion, and said, "Little Tortoise, give me water!" When little Tortoise was about to say something, Lion got hold of him and beat him; Lion drank of the water, and since then the animals drink water.

When Elephant came back from the hunting, he said, "Little Tortoise, is there water?" Tortoise answered, "The animals have drunk the water." Elephant asked, "Little Tortoise, shall I chew you or swallow you down?" Little Tortoise said, "Swallow me, if you please!" and Elephant swallowed him whole.

After Elephant had swallowed Little Tortoise, and he had entered his body, he tore off his liver, heart, and kidneys. Elephant said, "Little Tortoise, you kill me."

So Elephant died; but little Tortoise came out of his dead body, and went wherever he liked.

Writing: Outline

Write or type an outline of the new model story which you read in the last lesson.

Exercise

Review memory work. Name the part of the verb underlined in the following sentences.

Mr. Sesemann <u>called</u> her now.

Sebastian <u>is feeling</u> ashamed.

Copy each sentence below. Double underline the predicate, and underline the subject. Put brackets around any prepositional phrases. Label the part of speech of each word. Noun, N; Proper Noun, PN; Pronoun, PRO; Verb, V; Linking Verb, LV; Adjective, ADJ; Article, ART; Conjunction, CJ; Preposition, Prep; Interjection, INJ. Diagram each sentence.

Heidi looked up to him in amazement. [Hint: **up to** is a two word preposition.]

Heidi was dressed in her Sunday frock.

"Why don't you give it to me?"

Commonplace Book

With your instructor's approval, add the poem below to your commonplace book, or choose your own poem.

> How dear to this heart are the scenes of my childhood,
>   When fond recollection presents them to view!
> The orchard, the meadow, the deep-tangled wild-wood,
>   And every loved spot which my infancy knew!
> The wide-spreading pond, and the mill that stood by it,
>   The bridge, and the rock where the cataract fell,
> The cot of my father, the dairy-house nigh it,
>   And e'en the rude bucket that hung in the well—
> The old oaken bucket, the iron-bound bucket,
> The moss-covered bucket which hung in the well.

Dictation

John 1:14-15

And the Word became flesh, and dwelt among us, and we saw His glory, glory as of the only begotten from the Father, full of grace and truth. John testified about Him and cried out, saying, "This was He of whom I said, 'He who comes after me has a higher rank than I, for He existed before me.'"

A Farmyard in Normandy by Claude Monet

Picture Study

1. Read the title and the name of the artist. Study the picture for several minutes, then put the picture away.

2. Describe the picture.

3. Look at the picture again. Do you notice any details that you missed before? What do you like or dislike about this painting? Does it remind you of anything?

81. Descriptive Writing

- Heidi, Chapter 14

Writing: Descriptive Writing

In the first chapter of *Heidi*, we're given a brief description of the town of Mayenfeld and the footpath that leads up the Alps, of Heidi, and of Deta taking Heidi to her grandfather. Read the opening paragraphs below, paying close attention to the details that make a vivid picture in your mind, and then write a narration of it. What is the landscape like? How is Heidi described? What is the weather like, and how does it affect the little girl?

Add details if you wish. Remember, the point of this exercise is to write as descriptively as possible, not just to narrate the passage exactly.

Heidi

The little old town of Mayenfeld is charmingly situated. From it a footpath leads through green, well-wooded stretches to the foot of the heights which look down imposingly upon the valley. Where the footpath begins to go steeply and abruptly up the Alps, the heath, with its short grass and pungent herbage, at once sends out its soft perfume to meet the wayfarer.

One bright sunny morning in June, a tall, vigorous maiden of the mountain region climbed up the narrow path, leading a little girl by the hand. The youngster's cheeks were in such a glow that it showed even through her sun-browned skin. Small wonder though! For in spite of the heat, the little one, who was scarcely five years old, was bundled up as if she had to brave a bitter frost. Her shape was difficult to distinguish, for she wore two dresses, if not three, and around her shoulders a large red cotton shawl. With her feet encased in heavy hob-nailed boots, this hot and shapeless little person toiled up the mountain.

The pair had been climbing for about an hour when they reached a hamlet half-way up the great mountain named the Alm. This hamlet was called "Im Dörfli" or "The Little Village." It was the elder girl's home town, and therefore she was greeted from nearly every house; people called to her from windows and doors, and very often from the road. But, answering questions and calls as she went by, the girl did not loiter on her way and only stood still when she reached the end of the hamlet. There a few cottages lay scattered about, from the furthest of which a voice called out to her through an open door: "Deta, please wait one moment! I am coming with you, if you are going further up."

The Skylark

By Thomas Hogg

Bird of the wilderness,
Blithesome and cumberless,
Sweet be thy matin o'er moorland and lea!
Emblem of happiness,
Blest is thy dwelling-place—
Oh, to abide in the desert with thee!

Wild is thy lay and loud,
Far in the downy cloud,
Love gives it energy, love gave it birth.
Where, on thy dewy wing,
Where art thou journeying?
Thy lay is in heaven, thy love is on earth.

O'er fell and fountain sheen,
O'er moor and mountain green,
O'er the red streamer that heralds the day,
Over the cloudlet dim,
Over the rainbow's rim,
Musical cherub, soar, singing, away!

Then, when the gloaming comes,
Low in the heather blooms
Sweet will thy welcome and bed of love be!
Emblem of happiness,
Blest is thy dwelling-place—
Oh, to abide in the desert with thee!

The Man and Snake

From *South-African Folk-Tales* by James A. Honey

A Man, it is said, met Snake upon whom a large stone had fallen and covered her so that she could not rise. The Man lifted the stone off Snake, but when he had done so, she wanted to bite him. The Man said, "Stop! Let us both go first to some wise people." They went to Hyena, and the Man asked him, "Is it right that Snake should want to bite me, when I helped her as she lay under a stone and could not rise?"

Hyena (who thought he would get his share of the Man's body) said, "If you were bitten what would it matter?"

Then Snake wanted to bite him, but the Man said again, "Wait a little, and let us go to other wise people, that I may hear whether this is right."

They went and met Jackal. The Man said to Jackal, "Is it right for Snake to want to bite me, when I lifted up the stone which lay upon her?"

Jackal replied, "I do not believe that Snake could be covered by a stone so she could not rise. Unless I saw it with my two eyes, I would not believe it. Therefore, come let us go and see the place where you say it happened whether it can be true."

They went, and arrived at the place where it had happened. Jackal said, "Snake, lie down, and let thyself be covered."

Snake did so, and the Man covered her with the stone; but although she exerted herself very much, she could not rise. Then the Man wanted again to release Snake, but Jackal interfered, and said, "Do not lift the stone. She wanted to bite you, therefore she may rise by herself."

Then they both went away and left Snake under the stone.

Exercise

Review memory work. Identify each group of words below as either a phrase or a clause. If it is a clause, double underline the predicate and underline the subject.

to mar the happiness of the child

after she had carefully wiped it off

shall I read you a song from your book now

Copy each sentence below. Double underline the predicate, and underline the subject. Put brackets around any prepositional phrases. Label the part of speech of each word. Noun, N; Proper Noun, PN; Pronoun, PRO; Verb, V; Linking Verb, LV; Adjective, ADJ; Article, ART; Conjunction, CJ; Preposition, Prep; Interjection, INJ. Diagram each sentence.

"Have you come again, child?"

Grandmother's face changed to a joyous expression.

God Our Father had not answered her prayer immediately.

Commonplace Book

With your instructor's approval, add the passage below to your commonplace book, or choose your own passage from a work of non-fiction. This can be from the Bible, a biography, or one of your history or science books.

Heidi's face suddenly shone. "Oh, grandmother, I have an awful lot of money," she cried. "Now I know what I'll do with it. Every day you must have a fresh roll and two on Sundays. Peter can bring them up from the village."

"No, no, child," the grandmother implored. "That must not be. You must give it to grandfather and he'll tell you what to do with it."

82. To Be

- Heidi, Chapter 15

The verb **to be** is the basic verb form of the state of being verbs. It is probably the most common irregular verb.

The principal parts of **to be** are:

Infinitive	Simple Present	Present Participle	Simple Past	Past Participle
to be	am/is/are	being	was/were	been

In the simple present, we conjugate **to be** like this:

to be	Singular	Plural
1st Person	I am	we are
2nd Person	you are	you are
3rd Person	he, she, or it is	they are

To be is an irregular verb in all of its tenses, and it has an irregular past participle. The future tense is just **will**. I will, you will, he will, etc. Its past tense form, however, must be conjugated, like this:

to be (past tense)	Singular	Plural
1st Person	I was	we were
2nd Person	you were	you were
3rd Person	he, she, or it was	they were

Now that you can conjugate **to be**, it's probably obvious why **be, being,** and **been** are also part of our state of being verbs. These are also forms of the verb **to be**.

Remember that when we use **to be** as a linking verb, it can include helping verbs. Look at the following sentences from *Heidi*.

"God has been good to me."

"That would have been ungrateful."

All of the above verb forms are linking verbs because they end in a form of **to be**; **to be** is the main verb. What does that make the nouns and adjectives which follow the linking verbs?

Subject complements follow the linking verbs. The nouns are predicate nominatives, and the adjectives are predicate adjectives.

The Choir Invisible

By George Eliot

O, may I join the choir invisible
Of those immortal dead who live again
In minds made better by their presence; live
In pulses stirred to generosity,
In deeds of daring rectitude, in scorn
Of miserable aims that end with self,
In thoughts sublime that pierce the night like stars,
And with their mild persistence urge men's minds
To vaster issues.
 May I reach
That purest heaven,—be to other souls
The cup of strength in some great agony,
Enkindle generous ardour, feed pure love,
Beget the smiles that have no cruelty,
Be the sweet presence of good diffused,
And in diffusion ever more intense!

So shall I join the choir invisible,
Whose music is the gladness of the world.

The Judgment of Baboon

From *South-African Folk-Tales* by James A. Honey

One day, it is said, the following story happened:

Mouse had torn the clothes of Itkler (the tailor), who then went to Baboon, and accused Mouse with these words:

"In this manner I come to thee: Mouse has torn my clothes, but will not know anything of it, and accuses Cat; Cat protests likewise her innocence, and says, 'Dog must have done it'; but Dog denies it also, and declares Wood has done it; and Wood throws the blame on Fire, and says, 'Fire did it'; Fire says, 'I have not, Water did it'; Water says, 'Elephant tore the clothes'; and Elephant says, 'Ant tore them.' Thus a dispute has arisen among them. Therefore, I, Itkler, come to thee with this proposition: Assemble the people and try them in order that I may get satisfaction."

Thus he spake, and Baboon assembled them for trial. Then they made the same excuses which had been mentioned by Itkler, each one putting the blame upon the other.

So Baboon did not see any other way of punishing them, save through making them punish each other; he therefore said,

"Mouse, give Itkler satisfaction."

Mouse, however, pleaded not guilty. But Baboon said, "Cat, bite Mouse." She did so.

He then put the same question to Cat, and when she exculpated herself, Baboon called to Dog, "Here, bite Cat."

In this manner Baboon questioned them all, one after the other, but they each denied the charge. Then he addressed the following words to them, and said,

"Wood, beat Dog.

Fire, burn Wood.

Water, quench Fire.

Elephant, drink Water.

Ant, bite Elephant in his most tender parts."

They did so, and since that day they cannot any longer agree with each other.

Ant enters into Elephant's most tender parts and bites him.

Elephant swallows Water.

Water quenches Fire.

Fire consumes Wood.

Wood beats Dog.

Dog bites Cat.

And Cat bites Mouse.

Through this judgment Itkler got satisfaction and addressed Baboon in the following manner:

"Yes! Now I am content, since I have received satisfaction, and with all my heart I thank thee, Baboon, because thou hast exercised justice on my behalf and given me redress."

Then Baboon said, "From today I will not any longer be called Jan, but Baboon shall be my name."

Since that time Baboon walks on all fours, having probably lost the privilege of walking erect through this foolish judgment.

Writing: Copia

Take the following sentence and play with it. Remember that the point is not necessarily to make the sentence better. The point is to play with the sentence and make it different. Make a new sentence with a change from each of the following categories.

> "The cocoon of the silkworm," he began, "is composed of two envelops: an outer one of very coarse gauze, and an inner one of very fine fabric."

1. Change the grammar.
   - Change the nouns from common to proper and vice versa.
   - Change the nouns from singular to plural and vice versa.
   - Change the sentence type.
   - Change the adjectives from articles to descriptive to possessive, etc.
   - Change a quotation from direct to indirect and vice versa.
   - Change the verb tense.

2. Condense the sentence.
   - Remove details.
   - Remove modifiers.
   - Remove phrases or clauses.

3. Amplify the sentence.
   - Add details.
   - Add dialogue.
   - Add modifiers.
   - Add phrases or clauses.

4. Use synonyms and antonyms.
   - Substitute synonyms.
   - Say the opposite thing using antonyms.

5. Point of view.
   - Change the point of view.
   - Slant the sentence.

Exercise

Review memory work. Copy each sentence below. Double underline the predicate, and underline the subject. Put brackets around any prepositional phrases. Label the part of speech of each word. Noun, N; Proper Noun, PN; Pronoun, PRO; Verb, V; Linking Verb, LV; Adjective, ADJ; Article, ART; Conjunction, CJ; Preposition, Prep; Interjection, INJ. Diagram each sentence.

> "Oh please, doctor, do go to Heidi."

> With shrugging shoulders the doctor replied.

> Clara's eyes had filled with tears.

Commonplace Book

With your instructor's approval, add the passage below to your commonplace book, or choose your own passage from a work of fiction. This can be from either school reading or free reading.

> "Oh please, doctor, do go to Heidi; then you can tell me all about her, and can describe her grandfather to me, and Peter, with his goats,—I seem to know them all so well. Then you can take all the things to her that I had planned to take myself. Oh, please doctor, go, and then I'll be good and take as much cod-liver oil as ever you want me to."

Dictation

The doctor had to laugh. "Why don't you chide me for being here still? I shall go as quickly as I can, Sesemann."

Clara gave many messages to him for Heidi. She also told him to be sure to observe everything closely, so that he would be able to tell her all about it when he came back. The things for Heidi were to be sent to him later, for Miss Rottenmeier, who had to pack them, was out on one of her lengthy wanderings about town.

83. To Do and To Go

- Heidi, Chapter 16

The principal parts of **to do** are:

Infinitive	Simple Present	Present Participle	Simple Past	Past Participle
to do	do/does	doing	did	done

In the simple present, we conjugate **to do** like this:

to do	Singular	Plural
1st Person	I do	we do
2nd Person	you do	you do
3rd Person	he, she, or it does	they do

To do is an irregular verb in both its present and simple past tenses, and it has an irregular past participle. The future tense is just **will do**. I will do, you will do, he will do, etc. Its past tense form is simply **did**: I did, you did, he did, etc.

Our next irregular verb is **to go**. The principal parts of **to go** are:

Infinitive	Simple Present	Present Participle	Simple Past	Past Participle
to go	go/goes	going	went	gone

In the simple present, we conjugate **to go** like this:

to go	Singular	Plural
1st Person	I go	we go
2nd Person	you go	you go
3rd Person	he, she, or it goes	they go

To go is an irregular verb in both its present and simple past tenses, and it has an irregular past participle. The future tense is just **will go**: I will go, you will go, he will go, etc. Its past tense form is simply **went**: I went, you went, he went, etc.

Remember that the past participle is never used without a helping verb, and the past participles of **to do** and **to go** are irregular. You should never use their past participles, **done** and **gone**, without a helping verb.

The Dwarf

By Walter De La Mare

'Now, Jinnie, my dear, to the dwarf be off,
That lives in Barberry Wood,
And fetch me some honey, but be sure you don't laugh,—
He hates little girls that are rude, are rude,
He hates little girls that are rude.'
Jane tapped at the door of the house in the wood,
And the dwarf looked over the wall,
He eyed her so queer, 'twas as much as she could
To keep from laughing at all, at all,
To keep from laughing at all.
His shoes down the passage came clod, clod, clod,
And when he opened the door,
He croaked so harsh, 'twas as much as she could
To keep from laughing the more, the more,
To keep from laughing the more.
As there, with his bushy red beard, he stood,
Pricked out to double its size,

He squinted so cross, 'twas as much as she could
To keep the tears out of her eyes, her eyes,
To keep the tears out of her eyes.
He slammed the door, and went clod, clod, clod,
But while in the porch she bides,
He squealed so fierce, 'twas as much as she could
To keep from cracking her sides, her sides,
To keep from cracking her sides.
He threw a pumpkin over the wall,
And melons and apples beside,
So thick in the air, that to see 'em all fall,
She laughed, and laughed, till she cried, cried, cried,
Jane laughed and laughed till she cried.
Down fell her teardrops a pit-apat-pat,
And red as a rose she grew;—
'Kah! Kah!' said the dwarf, 'is it crying you're at?
It's the very worst thing you could do, do, do,
It's the very worst thing you could do.'
He slipped like a monkey up into a tree,
He shook her down cherries like rain;
'See now,' says he, cheeping, 'a blackbird I be,
Laugh, laugh, little Jinnie, again-gain-gain,
Laugh, laugh, little Jinnie, again.'
Ah me! What a strange, what a gladsome duet
From a house i' the deeps of a wood!
Such shrill and such harsh voices never met yet
A-laughing as loud as they could-could-could,
A-laughing as loud as they could.
Come Jinnie, come dwarf, cocksparrow, and bee,
There's a ring gaudy-green in the dell,
Sing, sing, ye sweet cherubs, that flit in the tree;
La! Who can draw tears from a well-well-well,
Who ever drew tears from a well!

The Zebra Stallion

From *South-African Folk-Tales* by James A. Honey

The Baboons, it is said, used to disturb the Zebra Mares in drinking. But one of the Mares became the mother of a foal. The others then helped her to suckle (the young stallion), that he might soon grow up.

When he was grown up and they were in want of water, he brought them to the water. The Baboons, seeing this, came, as they formerly were used to do, into their way, and kept them from the water.

While the Mares stood thus, the Stallion stepped forward, and spoke to one of the Baboons, "Thou gum-eater's child!"

The Baboon said to the Stallion, "Please open thy mouth, that I may see what thou livest on." The Stallion opened his mouth, and it was milky.

Then the Stallion said to the Baboon, "Please open thy mouth also, that I may see." The Baboon did so, and there was some gum in it. But the Baboon quickly licked some milk off the Stallion's tongue. The Stallion on this became angry, took the Baboon by his shoulders, and pressed him upon a hot, flat rock. Since that day the Baboon has a bald place on his back.

The Baboon said, lamenting, "I, my mother's child, I, the gum-eater, am outdone by this milk-eater!"

Exercise

Review memory work. Name the part of the verb underlined in the following sentences.

> When Heidi at last <u>reached</u> her old friend, he held out his hand.
>
> She <u>caressed</u> them tenderly, and they in their turn nearly <u>crushed</u> her between them.

Copy each sentence below. Double underline the predicate, and underline the subject. Put brackets around any prepositional phrases. Label the part of speech of each word. Noun, N; Proper Noun, PN; Pronoun, PRO; Verb, V; Linking Verb, LV; Adjective, ADJ; Article, ART; Conjunction, CJ; Preposition, Prep; Interjection, INJ. Diagram each sentence.

> "Are your eyes bright already?"
>
> With an old rag she would rub the chairs and table.
>
> The grandfather had been busy in his little shop.

Writing: Commonplace Book

Add the passage below from your model story to your commonplace book.

> "The cocoon of the silkworm," he began, "is composed of two envelops: an outer one of very coarse gauze, and an inner one of very fine fabric. This latter is the cocoon properly so called, and from it alone is obtained the silk thread so highly valued in manufacture and commerce, whereas the other, owing to its irregular structure, cannot be unwound and furnishes only an inferior grade of silk suitable for carding.

Dictation

Use part of today's poem for dictation.

84. Scientific Narration: Silk

• Heidi, Chapter 17

Your model story, "Silk," is from Jean Henri Fabre's *The Secret of Everyday Things*. In his book, the character of Uncle Paul is explaining these scientific concepts to a group of children. The stories are written in the first person with frequent use of the second person as he speaks directly to the children.

Use your outline to write a narration on this topic. Don't include references to the children or Uncle Paul; just write about the topic. Your narration should be in the third person. You may use other sources for more details if desired. You'll need to decide which details are important to your narration and which ones should be left out.

Recessional

By Rudyard Kipling

"Reverence is the master-key of knowledge."

God of our fathers, known of old—
  Lord of our far-flung battle-line—
Beneath whose awful Hand we hold
  Dominion over palm and pine—
Lord God of Hosts, be with us yet,
Lest we forget—lest we forget!

The tumult and the shouting dies—
  The captains and the kings depart—
Still stands Thine ancient Sacrifice,
  An humble and a contrite heart.
Lord God of Hosts, be with us yet,
Lest we forget—lest we forget!

Far-called our navies melt away—
  On dune and headland sinks the fire—
Lo, all our pomp of yesterday
  Is one with Nineveh and Tyre!

Judge of the Nations, spare us yet,
Lest we forget—lest we forget!

If, drunk with sight of power, we loose
  Wild tongues that have not Thee in awe—
Such boasting as the Gentiles use
  Or lesser breeds without the Law—
Lord God of Hosts, be with us yet,
Lest we forget—lest we forget!

For heathen heart that puts her trust
  In reeking tube and iron shard—
All valiant dust that builds on dust,
  And guarding calls not Thee to guard—
For frantic boast and foolish word,
Thy mercy on Thy People, Lord! Amen.

Editing

- Did you meet the goal of this writing exercise?

- Look at your word choice. Is there a good mixture of nouns and pronouns? Is the antecedent of each pronoun clear?

- Look at your paragraphs. Are all the sentences related? Does each paragraph focus on a single topic?

85. To See and To Come

• Heidi, Chapter 18

The principal parts of **to see** are:

Infinitive	Simple Present	Present Participle	Simple Past	Past Participle
to see	see(s)	seeing	saw	seen

In the simple present, we conjugate **to see** like this:

to see	Singular	Plural
1st Person	I see	we see
2nd Person	you see	you see
3rd Person	he, she, or it sees	they see

To do is an irregular verb in simple past tense, and it has an irregular past participle. The future tense is just **will see**. I will see, you will see, he will see, etc. Its past tense form is simply **saw**: I saw, you saw, he saw, etc.

Our next irregular verb is **to come**. The principal parts of **to come** are:

Infinitive	Simple Present	Present Participle	Simple Past	Past Participle
to come	come(s)	coming	came	come

In the simple present, we conjugate **to come** like this:

to come	Singular	Plural
1st Person	I come	we come
2nd Person	you come	you come
3rd Person	he, she, or it comes	they come

To come is an irregular verb in its simple past tense, and it has an irregular past participle. The future tense is just **will come**: I will come, you will come, he will come, etc. Its past tense form is simply **came**: I came, you came, he came, etc.

Remember that the past participle is never used without a helping verb. This means that you should never use the words **seen** without a helping verb. Notice, however, that the past participle for **to come** is the same as its simple present.

Ozymandias of Egypt

By Percy Bysshe Shelley

I met a traveler from an antique land
Who said: "Two vast and trunkless legs of stone
Stand in the desert. Near them on the sand,
Half sunk, a shattered visage lies, whose frown
And wrinkled lip and sneer of cold command
Tell that its sculptor well those passions read
Which yet survive, stamped on these lifeless things,
The hand that mock'd them and the heart that fed;
And on the pedestal these words appear:
  'My name is Ozymandias, king of kings:
Look on my works, ye Mighty, and despair!'
Nothing beside remains. Round the decay
Of that colossal wreck, boundless and bare,
The lone and level sands stretch far away;"

Writing: Oral Narration

Read your new model story below, and then give your instructor an oral narration of it.

Sound

From The Secret of Everyday Things *by Jean Henri Fabre*

"Give a light blow to a wine-glass. The glass will ring, giving forth a sound, weaker or stronger, lower or higher, according to the quality and size of the glass. The sound lasts but a moment, and then ceases. Strike the glass once more and while it is still ringing touch the rim with your finger. Instantly all is still again; not a sound from the glass. Why does it ring when struck, and why does it stop ringing at the touch of a finger? Before replying let us experiment with other resonant objects.

"A violin-string twangs on being scraped by the bow or plucked with the finger, and while it thus gives forth its note it is seen to vibrate rapidly. So rapid, indeed, is its vibration that it appears to fill the entire space between its extreme positions, with the result that it presents a swollen appearance in the middle, after the manner of a spindle. With the cessation of its vibration it becomes silent. It also falls silent immediately at the touch of a finger.

"A bell rings on being struck by its clapper, and if observed closely the substance of the bell will be seen to tremble in an unmistakable manner. Place your hand on the bronze and you will experience a disagreeable sensation almost amounting to pain, due to the vibration of the metal. Finally, if your hand continues to rest on the bell, the vibration will cease and with it the sound.

"Let us try something still more remarkable. Take a pin by its pointed end and bring the head very close to a ringing wine-glass or bell. You will hear a rapid succession of little taps. Whence do they come? From the glass or the bell-metal striking the pin a series of quick blows as long as the ringing continues. They come from the lively trembling of the sonorous object.

"It is unnecessary to cite other examples; these three will suffice. They show that, in order to give forth sound, a wine-glass or a bell or a violin-string—in short, any object whatever—must be made to tremble or vibrate with great rapidity. The sound is heard as long as the vibration continues, and ceases when the vibrating object returns to a state of rest. That explains why the wine-glass and the violin-string stop sounding at the touch of a finger, and why the bell will not ring if you rest your hand against it. The finger in the one instance, the hand in the other, stop the resonant trembling, and in so doing arrest the sound. Motion causes the sound; rest brings silence.

"To this rapid motion back and forth is given the name I have already used, vibration. An object from which comes a sound is in vibration; it vibrates. Each of its backward and forward movement, too rapid for the eye to follow, is a vibration; and the quicker these vibrations, the higher the note sounded; the slower they are, the lower the note. In a word, sound is motion and its place in the scale measures the rapidity of that motion.

"In order to be heard, this sound, this motion, must reach us. The hand detects it in its own way when, resting on the vibrating bell, it experiences a very disagreeable thrill; the finger becomes conscious of it in a peculiar manner when, touching the violin-string, it feels a ticking sensation. But how does the ear contrive to receive the sound when it is at a distance from the resonant object and apparently in no sort of communication with it?

"At this point let me invite you to join me in a sport very familiar to you all. We will take a big stone and drop it into a calm sheet of water. Around the place where the stone struck the water there is instantly formed a circle, then another and another, and so on indefinitely; and all these circles, described about the same center and as regular as if drawn with a pair of compasses, grow larger and larger, in successive rings, until they die out at a long distance from their common center, if the sheet of water is large enough.

"Now, do those circles really chase one another over the water's surface as they appear to? One would certainly think so. You remember how fast they go, one ring after another, each in apparent haste to catch up with its predecessor. But the pursued always keep clear of the pursuers, and the distance between the rings remains the same. And so the fact is they are not really chasing one another; they are not, in fact, moving at all; but they have that deceptive appearance, and it will not be hard for us to understand why.

"Let us drop a straw or a dry leaf upon the surface of the water. When one of these concentric circles passes like a wave, the straw or leaf is lifted up, after which the wave goes on and leaves it, and it sinks down again, remaining exactly where it was in the first place. Thus it is proved that the water does not move forward at all, for if it did it would carry with it the straw or leaf on its surface.

"What, then, are those waves? Mere palpitations of the water as, without changing its place, it gently rises and falls, thus producing a succession of alternate billows and furrows which appear to go chasing after one another. Watch a field of wheat when the wind blows. Its surface undulates in waves that seem to move forward although the wheat-stalks remain firmly rooted in the ground. Of like sort is the apparent movement of a sheet of smooth water when disturbed by the fall of a stone.

"The circles of the water and the undulations of the wheat-field explain to us the nature of sound. Every object emitting a sound is in rapid vibration, and each of these vibrations causes a shock to the surrounding air and produces a wave which spreads out in all directions, immediately followed by a second, a third, and countless others, all resulting from as many successive vibrations.

"In the air thus shocked by the vibrating body there takes place exactly what we see in the sheet of smooth water disturbed by a falling stone and in the wheat-field ruffled by the wind. Without changing its place the air undergoes an undulatory movement which is transmitted to great distances. In other words, air-waves are formed which propagate themselves in every direction at once through the atmosphere, thus taking the form, not of circles, but rather of hollow spheres, all having a common center.

"These air-waves are not visible to us, because air itself is invisible; but they are none the less real, just as real as waves of water and undulations of a wheat-field. If the eye cannot see them, the ear can hear them, for it is from them that sound comes. Hence they are called sound-waves. The ear hears when sound-waves reach it from any vibrating object."

Exercise

Review memory work. Punctuate the following sentence.

Oh grandfather I have found my bedroom

Copy each sentence below. Double underline the predicate, and underline the subject. Put brackets around any prepositional phrases. Label the part of speech of each word. Noun, N; Proper Noun, PN; Pronoun, PRO; Verb, V; Linking Verb, LV; Adjective, ADJ; Article, ART; Conjunction, CJ; Preposition, Prep; Interjection, INJ. Diagram each sentence.

"Now come and look at mine."

Heidi slept very well in her chimney corner.

Was she away from home? [Hint: **away from** is a two word preposition.]

Commonplace Book

With your instructor's approval, add the passage below to your commonplace book, or choose your own passage from a work of fiction. This can be from either school reading or free reading.

But the grandfather shook his head and said: "You can't go yet, child. The snow is fathoms deep up there and is still falling. Peter can hardly get through. A little girl like you would be snowed up and lost in no time. Wait a while till it freezes and then you can walk on top of the crust."

Dictation

With that the grandfather led her into his bed-room. From there a door led into the hugest kitchen Heidi had ever seen. With a great deal of trouble the grandfather had fitted up this place. Many boards were nailed across the walls and the door had been fastened with heavy wires, for beyond, the building lay in ruins. Thick underbrush was growing there, sheltering thousands of insects and lizards. Heidi was delighted with her new home, and when Peter arrived next day, she did not rest till he had seen every nook and corner of the curious dwelling-place.

86. To Have

- Heidi, Chapter 19

The principal parts of **to have** are:

Infinitive	Simple Present	Present Participle	Simple Past	Past Participle
to have	have/has	having	had	had

In the simple present, we conjugate **to have** like this:

to see	Singular	Plural
1st Person	I have	we have
2nd Person	you have	you have
3rd Person	he, she, or it has	they have

To have is an irregular verb in simple past tense, and it has an irregular past participle. The future tense is just **will have**. I will have, you will have, he will have, etc. Its past tense form is simply **had**: I had, you had, he had, etc.

Remember that the past participle is never used without a helping verb. Notice, however, that the past participle for **to have** is the same as its simple past.

I Remember, I Remember

By Thomas Hood

I remember, I remember
The house where I was born,
The little window where the sun
Came peeping in at morn;
He never came a wink too soon
Nor brought too long a day;
But now, I often wish the night
Had borne my breath away.

I remember, I remember
The roses, red and white,
The violets, and the lily-cups—
Those flowers made of light!
The lilacs where the robin built,
And where my brother set
The laburnum on his birthday,—
The tree is living yet!

I remember, I remember
Where I was used to swing,
And thought the air must rush as fresh
To swallows on the wing;
My spirit flew in feathers then
That is so heavy now,
And summer pools could hardly cool
The fever on my brow.

I remember, I remember
The fir trees dark and high;
I used to think their slender tops
Were close against the sky:
It was a childish ignorance,
But now 'tis little joy
To know I'm farther off from Heaven
Than when I was a boy.

Lion Who Thought Himself Wiser Than His Mother

From *South-African Folk-Tales* by James A. Honey

It is said that when Lion and Gurikhoisip (the Only man), together with Baboon, Buffalo, and other friends, were playing one day at a certain game, there was a thunderstorm and rain at Aroxaams. Lion and Gurikhoisip began to quarrel. "I shall run to the rain-field," said Lion. Gurikhoisip said also, "I shall run to the rain-field." As neither would concede this to the other, they separated (angrily). After they had parted, Lion went to tell his Mother those things which they had both said.

His Mother said to him, "My son! That Man whose head is in a line with his shoulders and breast, who has pinching weapons, who keeps white dogs, who goes about wearing the tuft of a tiger's tail, beware of him!" Lion, however, said, "Why need I be on my guard against those whom I know?" Lioness answered, "My Son, take care of him who has pinching weapons!" But Lion would not follow his Mother's advice, and the same morning, when it was still pitch dark, he went to Aroxaams, and laid himself in ambush. Gurikhoisip went also that morning to the same place. When he had arrived he let his dogs drink, and then bathe. After they had finished they wallowed. Then also Man drank; and, when he had done drinking, Lion came out of the bush. Dogs surrounded him as his Mother had foretold, and he was speared by Gurikhoisip. Just as he became aware that he was speared, the Dogs drew him down again. In this manner he grew faint. While he was in this state, Gurikhoisip said to the Dogs, "Let him alone now, that he may go and be taught by his Mother." So the Dogs let him go. They left him, and went home as he lay there. The same night he walked towards home, but whilst he was on the way his strength failed him, and he lamented:

"Mother! Take me up!
Grandmother! Take me up! Oh me! Alas!"
At the dawn of day his Mother heard his wailing, and said—
"My Son, this is the thing which I have told thee:
"'Beware of the one who has pinching weapons,
Who wears a tuft of tiger's tail,
Of him who has white dogs!
Alas! Thou son of her who is short-eared,
Thou, my short-eared child!
Son of her who eats raw flesh,
Thou flesh-devourer;
Son of her whose nostrils are red from the prey,
Thou with blood-stained nostrils!
Son of her who drinks pit-water,
Thou water-drinker!'"

Writing: Outline

Write or type an outline of the new model story which you read in the last lesson.

Exercise

Review memory work. Name the part of the verb underlined in the following sentences.

Peter <u>began</u> and <u>read</u> three lines without stopping.

"I shall not say <u>to read</u>, but <u>to stammer</u> through a line?"

Copy each sentence below. Double underline the predicate, and underline the subject. Put brackets around any prepositional phrases. Label the part of speech of each word. Noun, N; Proper Noun, PN; Pronoun, PRO; Verb, V; Linking Verb, LV; Adjective, ADJ; Article, ART; Conjunction, CJ; Preposition, Prep; Interjection, INJ. Diagram each sentence.

"Hurry up and learn the three letters."

He came daily to her for his lesson.

"What, is it possible?"

Commonplace Book

With your instructor's approval, add the poem below to your commonplace book, or choose your own poem.

> I remember, I remember
> The house where I was born,
> The little window where the sun
> Came peeping in at morn;
> He never came a wink too soon
> Nor brought too long a day;
> But now, I often wish the night
> Had borne my breath away.
>
> I remember, I remember
> The roses, red and white,
> The violets, and the lily-cups—
> Those flowers made of light!
> The lilacs where the robin built,
> And where my brother set
> The laburnum on his birthday,—
> The tree is living yet!

Dictation

Acts 2:17

> "And it shall be in the last days," God says,
> "That I will pour forth of My Spirit on all mankind;
> And your sons and your daughters shall prophesy,
> And your young men shall see visions,
> And your old men shall dream dreams,"

Garden at Sainte Adresse by Claude Monet

Picture Study

1. Read the title and the name of the artist. Study the picture for several minutes, then put the picture away.

2. Describe the picture.

3. Look at the picture again. Do you notice any details that you missed before? What do you like or dislike about this painting? Does it remind you of anything?

87. Literary Analysis

- Heidi, Chapter 20

Writing: Literary Analysis

Today you have another literary analysis assignment. Now that you've had some practice, this should be a written assignment, though it can be helpful to discuss your ideas before writing.

With your instructor's approval, choose *Heidi*, or one of the other books you're currently reading, and answer the following questions.

What is the book about? Give a brief summary, just a few sentences. Who is this book about? What does she want? Who or what prevents her from getting it?

A Modest Wit

By Selleck Osborne

A supercilious nabob of the East—
  Haughty, being great—purse-proud, being rich—
A governor, or general, at the least,
  I have forgotten which—
Had in his family a humble youth,
  Who went from England in his patron's suit,
An unassuming boy, in truth
  A lad of decent parts, and good repute.

This youth had sense and spirit;
  But yet with all his sense,
  Excessive diffidence
Obscured his merit.

One day, at table, flushed with pride and wine,
  His honor, proudly free, severely merry,
Conceived it would be vastly fine
  To crack a joke upon his secretary.

"Young man," he said, "by what art, craft, or trade,
Did your good father gain a livelihood?"—
"He was a saddler, sir," Modestus said,
"And in his time was reckon'd good."

"A saddler, eh! And taught you Greek,
Instead of teaching you to sew!
Pray, why did not your father make
A saddler, sir, of you?"

Each parasite, then, as in duty bound,
The joke applauded, and the laugh went round.
At length Modestus, bowing low,
Said (craving pardon, if too free he made),
"Sir, by your leave, I fain would know
Your father's trade!"

"My father's trade! By heaven, that's too bad!
My father's trade? Why, blockhead, are you mad?
My father, sir, did never stoop so low—
He was a gentleman, I'd have you know."

"Excuse the liberty I take,"
Modestus said, with archness on his brow,
"Pray, why did not your father make
A gentleman of you?"

Rooster and Jackal

From *South-African Folk-Tales* by James A. Honey

Rooster, it is said, was once overtaken by Jackal, and caught. Rooster said to Jackal, "Please, pray first (before you kill me), as the man does."

Jackal asked, "In what manner does he pray? Tell me."

"He folds his hands in praying," said Rooster. Jackal folded his hands and prayed. Then Rooster spoke again; "You ought not to look about you as you do. You had better shut your eyes." He did so; and Rooster flew away, upbraiding at the same time Jackal with these words, "You rogue! Do you also pray?"

There sat Jackal, speechless, because he had been outdone.

Exercise

Review memory work. Identify each group of words below as either a phrase or a clause. If it is a clause, double underline the predicate and underline the subject.

thoughtfully looking at the backless chairs

what the grandfather had meant

but not with us

Copy each sentence below. Double underline the predicate, and underline the subject. Put brackets around any prepositional phrases. Label the part of speech of each word. Noun, N; Proper Noun, PN; Pronoun, PRO; Verb, V; Linking Verb, LV; Adjective, ADJ; Article, ART; Conjunction, CJ; Preposition, Prep; Interjection, INJ. Diagram each sentence.

"Did you get a letter for me on the pasture?"

The letter had been given to Peter.

Clara, her true friend, wrote a letter.

Commonplace Book

With your instructor's approval, add the passage below to your commonplace book, or choose your own passage from a work of non-fiction. This can be from the Bible, a biography, or one of your history or science books.

>   Heidi visited the grandmother next day, for she had to tell her the good news. Sitting up in her corner, the old woman was spinning as usual. Her face looked sad, for Peter had already announced the near visit of Heidi's friends, and she dreaded the result.
>   After having poured out her full heart, Heidi looked at the old woman. "What is it, grandmother?" said the child. "Are you not glad?"

88. Other Irregular Verbs

- Heidi, Chapter 21

Regular verbs form the simple past with the ending ***ed***. The past participle is the same, and it uses a helping verb when it acts as a verb.

"I have often wished that I should never have to eat."

"Grandfather has promised to let us come up with you once."

Irregular verbs do not follow this pattern. The simple past and past participles of irregular verbs can end in a variety of ways, following no pattern at all. The simple past tense has just one part, while the past participle must have a helping verb when acting as a verb.

"All my life I have only eaten because I had to."

Clara had many things to relate of all the people that Heidi knew.

But the uncle had known how to help himself.

In her dreams Clara saw before her a field that was thickly strewn with light-blue flowers.

In truth she had never seen them before.

Use the chart on the following pages to become familiar with common irregular verbs. But when in doubt, use the dictionary. It will list the various forms of the verb.

Infinitive	Simple Present	Present Participle	Simple Past	Past Participle
to arise	arise(s)	arising	arose	arisen
to awake	awake(s)	awaking	awoke or awaked	awaked or awoken
to be	am, is, are	being	was, were	been
to bear	bear(s)	bearing	bore	borne or born
to beat	beat(s)	beating	beat	beaten
to become	become(s)	becoming	became	become
to begin	begin(s)	beginning	began	begun
to bend	bend(s)	bending	bent	bent
to bet	bet(s)	betting	bet	bet
to bid	bid(s)	bidding	bid	bid
to bid	bid(s)	bidding	bade	bidden
to bind	bind(s)	binding	bound	bound
to bite	bite(s)	biting	bit	bitten or bit
to blow	blow(s)	blowing	blew	blown
to break	break(s)	breaking	broke	broken
to bring	bring(s)	bringing	brought	brought
to build	build(s)	building	built	built
to burst	burst(s)	bursting	burst	burst
to buy	buy(s)	buying	bought	bought
to cast	cast(s)	casting	cast	cast
to catch	catch(es)	catching	caught	caught
to choose	choose(s)	choosing	chose	chosen
to cling	cling(s)	clinging	clung	clung
to come	come(s)	coming	came	come
to cost	cost(s)	costing	cost	cost
to creep	creep(s)	creeping	crept	crept
to cut	cut(s)	cutting	cut	cut
to deal	deal(s)	dealing	dealt	dealt
to dig	dig(s)	digging	dug	dug
to dive	dive(s)	diving	dived or dove	dived
to do	do(es)	doing	did	done
to draw	draw(s)	drawing	drew	drawn
to dream	dream(s)	dreaming	dreamed or dreamt	dreamed or dreamt
to drink	drink(s)	drinking	drank	drunk
to drive	drive(s)	driving	drove	driven

to eat	eat(s)	eating	ate	eaten
to fall	fall(s)	falling	fell	fallen
to feed	feed(s)	feeding	fed	fed
to feel	feel(s)	feeling	felt	felt
to fight	fight(s)	fighting	fought	fought
to find	find(s)	finding	found	found
to flee	flee(s)	fleeing	fled	fled
to fling	fling(s)	flinging	flung	flung
to fly	flies, fly	flying	flew	flown
to forbid	forbid(s)	forbidding	forbade	forbidden
to forget	forget(s)	forgetting	forgot	forgotten or forgot
to forgive	forgive(s)	forgiving	forgave	forgiven
to forsake	forsake(s)	forsaking	forsook	forsaken
to freeze	freeze(s)	freezing	froze	frozen
to get	get(s)	getting	got	got or gotten
to give	give(s)	giving	gave	given
to go	go(es)	going	went	gone
to grow	grow(s)	growing	grew	grown
to hang	hang(s)	hanging	hung	hung
to have	has, have	having	had	had
to hear	hear(s)	hearing	heard	heard
to hide	hide(s)	hiding	hid	hidden
to hit	hit(s)	hitting	hit	hit
to hurt	hurt(s)	hurting	hurt	hurt
to keep	keep(s)	keeping	kept	kept
to know	know(s)	knowing	knew	known
to lay	lay(s)	laying	laid	laid
to lead	lead(s)	leading	led	led
to leap	leap(s)	leaping	leaped or leapt	leaped or leapt
to leave	leave(s)	leaving	left	left
to lend	lend(s)	lending	lent	lent
to let	let(s)	letting	let	let
to lie	lie(s)	lying	lay	lain
to light	light(s)	lighting	lighted or lit	lighted or lit
to lose	lose(s)	losing	lost	lost
to make	make(s)	making	made	made
to mean	mean(s)	meaning	meant	meant
to pay	pay(s)	paying	paid	paid

to prove	prove(s)	proving	proved	proved or proven
to quit	quit(s)	quitting	quit	quit
to read	read(s)	reading	read	read
to rid	rid(s)	ridding	rid	rid
to ride	ride(s)	riding	rode	ridden
to ring	ring(s)	ringing	rang	rung
to rise	rise(s)	rising	rose	risen
to run	run(s)	running	ran	run
to say	say(s)	saying	said	said
to see	see(s)	seeing	saw	seen
to seek	seek(s)	seeking	sought	sought
to send	send(s)	sending	sent	sent
to set	set(s)	setting	set	set
to shake	shake(s)	shaking	shook	shaken
to shine	shine(s)	shining	shone	shone
to shoot	shoot(s)	shooting	shot	shot
to show	show(s)	showing	showed	shown or showed
to shrink	shrink(s)	shrinking	shrank	shrunk
to sing	sing(s)	singing	sang	sung
to sink	sink(s)	sinking	sank or sunk	sunk
to sit	sit(s)	sitting	sat	sat
to slay	slay(s)	slaying	slew	slain
to sleep	sleep(s)	sleeping	slept	slept
to sling	sling(s)	slinging	slung	slung
to sneak	sneak(s)	sneaking	sneaked or snuck	sneaked or snuck
to speak	speak(s)	speaking	spoke	spoken
to spend	spend(s)	spending	spent	spent
to spin	spin(s)	spinning	spun	spun
to spring	spring(s)	springing	sprang or sprung	sprung
to stand	stand(s)	standing	stood	stood
to steal	steal(s)	stealing	stole	stolen
to sting	sting(s)	stinging	stung	stung
to stink	stink(s)	stinking	stank or stunk	stunk
to stride	stride(s)	striding	strode	stridden
to strike	strike(s)	striking	struck	struck
to strive	strive(s)	striving	strove	striven

to swear	swear(s)	swearing	swore	sworn
to sweep	sweep(s)	sweeping	swept	swept
to swim	swim(s)	swimming	swam	swum
to swing	swing(s)	swinging	swung	swung
to take	take(s)	taking	took	taken
to teach	teach(es)	teaching	taught	taught
to tear	tear(s)	tearing	tore	torn
to tell	tell(s)	telling	told	told
to think	think(s)	thinking	thought	thought
to throw	throw(s)	throwing	threw	thrown
to understand	understand(s)	understanding	understood	understood
to wake	wake(s)	waking	woke or waked	waked or woken
to wear	wear(s)	wearing	wore	worn
to weave	weave(s)	weaving	wove or weaved	woven or wove
to weep	weep(s)	weeping	wept	wept
to wring	wring(s)	wringing	wrung	wrung
to write	write(s)	writing	wrote	written

The Burial of Sir John Moore

By C. Wolfe

Not a drum was heard, not a funeral note,
  As his corse to the rampart we hurried;
Not a soldier discharged his farewell shot
  O'er the grave where our hero we buried.

We buried him darkly at dead of night,
  The sods with our bayonets turning;
By the struggling moonbeam's misty light,
  And the lantern dimly burning.

No useless coffin enclosed his breast,
  Not in sheet nor in shroud we wound him;
But he lay like a warrior taking his rest,
  With his martial cloak around him.

Few and short were the prayers we said,
  And we spoke not a word of sorrow;
But we steadfastly gazed on the face that was dead,
  And we bitterly thought of the morrow.

We thought, as we hollowed his narrow bed,
  And smoothed down his lonely pillow,
That the foe and the stranger would tread o'er his head,
  And we far away on the billow!

Lightly they'll talk of the spirit that's gone,
  And o'er his cold ashes upbraid him,—
But little he'll reck, if they let him sleep on
  In the grave where a Briton has laid him.

But half of our heavy task was done
  When the clock struck the hour for retiring;
And we heard the distant and random gun
  That the foe was sullenly firing.

Slowly and sadly we laid him down,
  From the field of his fame fresh and gory;
We carved not a line, and we raised not a stone—
  But we left him alone with his glory!

Why Has Jackal a Long Black Stripe On His Back?

From *South-African Folk-Tales* by James A. Honey

The Sun, it is said, was one day on earth, and the men who were traveling saw him sitting by the wayside, but passed him without notice. Jackal, however, who came after them, and saw him also sitting, went to him and said, "Such a fine little child is left behind by the men." He then took Sun up, and put it into his awa-skin (on his back). When it burnt him, he said, "Get down," and shook himself; but Sun stuck fast to his back, and burnt Jackal's back black from that day.

Writing: Copia

Take the following sentence and play with it. Remember that the point is not necessarily to make the sentence better. The point is to play with the sentence and make it different. Make a new sentence with a change from each of the following categories.

  The sound lasts but a moment, and then ceases.

1. Change the grammar.
    - Change the nouns from common to proper and vice versa.
    - Change the nouns from singular to plural and vice versa.
    - Change the sentence type.
    - Change the adjectives from articles to descriptive to possessive, etc.
    - Change a quotation from direct to indirect and vice versa.
    - Change the verb tense.

2. Condense the sentence.
    - Remove details.
    - Remove modifiers.
    - Remove phrases or clauses.

3. Amplify the sentence.
    - Add details.
    - Add dialogue.
    - Add modifiers.
    - Add phrases or clauses.

4. Use synonyms and antonyms.
    - Substitute synonyms.
    - Say the opposite thing using antonyms.

5. Point of view.
    - Change the point of view.
    - Slant the sentence.

Exercise

Review memory work. Punctuate the following sentence.

> The grandfather Heidi and Clara were all in the mountain home.

Copy each sentence below. Double underline the predicate, and underline the subject. Put brackets around any prepositional phrases. Label the part of speech of each word. Noun, N; Proper Noun, PN; Pronoun, PRO; Verb, V; Linking Verb, LV; Adjective, ADJ; Article, ART; Conjunction, CJ; Preposition, Prep; Interjection, INJ. Diagram each sentence.

> "How did you sleep?"

> The grandfather was just coming out of the shed with two full bowls of milk. [Hint: **out of** is a two word preposition.]

> Heidi merrily came running with her message.

Commonplace Book

With your instructor's approval, add the passage below to your commonplace book, or choose your own passage from a work of fiction. This can be from either school reading or free reading.

> The children had just resolved to stay awake all night to talk about the coming day, when their conversation suddenly ceased and they were both peacefully slumbering. In her dreams Clara saw before her a field that was thickly strewn with light-blue flowers, while Heidi heard the eagle scream to her from above, "Come, come, come!"

Dictation

> This evening Clara fell asleep the moment she lay down. Two or three days passed in this pleasant way. The next brought a surprise. Two strong porters came up the Alp, each carrying on his back a fresh, white bed. They also brought a letter from grandmama, in which she thanked the children for their faithful writing, and told them that the beds were meant for them. When they went to sleep that night, they found their new beds in exactly the same position as their former ones had been.

89. Subordinate Conjunctions

• Heidi, Chapter 22

The subordinate conjunctions are: after, although, as, because, before, even if, even though, if, in order that, once, provided that, rather than, since, so that, than, that, though, unless, until, when, whenever, where, whereas, wherever, whether, while.

Some clauses express a complete thought and stand alone as sentences. But some clauses do not express a complete thought, even though they have both a subject and a predicate.

Certain words which can begin clauses prevent them from being complete sentences. When a clause begins with a word like **when**, **while**, or **before**, it leaves us wondering, "And then what?" We need more information to have a complete thought expressed.

One type of word which prevents clauses from being sentences is the **subordinate conjunction**. A list of all the subordinate conjunctions is above. This is an important list to memorize.

Consider the following clauses from *Heidi*.

when, arriving on top, they saw Peter already lying on the ground

when dinner time had come

Even though the sentences above each have a subject and a predicate, they are not complete sentences because of the subordinate conjunction which begins each clause. Look at those same clauses without the subordinate conjunctions.

Arriving on top, they saw Peter already lying on the ground.

Dinner time had come.

When I took away that beginning word, I also took away the expectation for the rest of the story. Now these clauses can stand alone as complete sentences.

A clause which can stand alone as a complete sentence is called an **independent clause**. A clause which cannot stand as a complete sentence is a **dependent clause**; it **depends** on another clause to express a complete thought. Subordinate conjunctions make clauses dependent.

The Well of St. Keyne

By Robert Southey

A well there is in the west country,
  And a clearer one never was seen;
There is not a wife in the west-country
  But has heard of the Well of St. Keyne.

An oak and an elm tree stand beside,
  And behind does an ash tree grow,
And a willow from the bank above
  Droops to the water below.

A traveler came to the Well of St. Keyne:
  Pleasant it was to his eye,
For from cock-crow he had been traveling
  And there was not a cloud in the sky.

He drank of the water so cool and clear,
  For thirsty and hot was he,
And he sat down upon the bank,
  Under the willow tree.

There came a man from the neighboring town
  At the well to fill his pail;
On the well-side he rested it,
  And bade the stranger hail.

  "Now, art thou a bachelor, stranger?" quoth he,
"For an if thou hast a wife,
The happiest draught thou hast drunk this day
  That ever thou didst in thy life.

  "Or has your good woman, if one you have,
  In Cornwall ever been?
For an if she have, I'll venture my life
  She has drunk of the Well of St. Keyne."

  "I have left a good woman who never was here,"
The stranger he made reply;
  "But that my draught should be better for that,
I pray you answer me why,"

  "St. Keyne," quoth the countryman, "many a time
  Drank of this crystal well,
And before the angel summoned her
  She laid on the water a spell.

  "If the husband of this gifted well
  Shall drink before his wife,

A happy man thenceforth is he,
  For he shall be master for life.

  "But if the wife should drink of it first,
    God help the husband then!"
The stranger stoop'd to the Well of St. Keyne,
  And drank of the waters again.

  "You drank of the well, I warrant, betimes?"
    He to the countryman said;
But the countryman smiled as the stranger spake,
  And sheepishly shook his head.

  "I hastened as soon as the wedding was done,
    And left my wife in the porch,
But i' faith she had been wiser than me,
  For she took a bottle to church,"

The Lamplighter

By Walter De La Mare

When the light of day declineth,
And a swift angel through the sky
Kindleth God's tapers clear,
With ashen staff the lamplighter
Passeth along the darkling streets
To light our earthly lamps;
Lest, prowling in the darkness,
The thief should haunt with quiet tread,
Or men on evil errands set;
Or wayfarers be benighted;
Or neighbors bent from house to house
Should need a guiding torch.
He is like a needlewoman
Who deftly on a sable hem
Stitches in gleaming jewels;
Or, haply, he is like a hero,
Whose bright deeds on the long journey
Are beacons on our way.
And when in the East cometh morning,
And the broad splendour of the sun,
Then, with the tune of little birds
Ringing on high, the lamplighter
Passeth by each quiet house,
And putteth out the lamps.

Horse Cursed by Sun

From *South-African Folk-Tales* by James A. Honey

It is said that once Sun was on earth, and caught Horse to ride it. But it was unable to bear his weight, and therefore Ox took the place of Horse, and carried Sun on its back. Since that time Horse is cursed in these words, because it could not carry Sun's weight:

"From today thou shalt have a (certain) time of dying.
This is thy curse, that thou hast a (certain) time of dying.
And day and night shalt thou eat,
But the desire of thy heart shall not be at rest,
Though thou grazest till morning and again until sunset.
Behold, this is the judgment which I pass upon thee," said Sun.

Since that day Horse's (certain) time of dying commenced.

Exercise

Review memory work. Punctuate the following sentence.

Grandfather the wind has done it exclaimed Heidi eagerly

Copy each sentence below. Double underline the predicate, and underline the subject. Put brackets around any prepositional phrases. Label the part of speech of each word. Noun, N; Proper Noun, PN; Pronoun, PRO; Verb, V; Linking Verb, LV; Adjective, ADJ; Article, ART; Conjunction, CJ; Preposition, Prep; Interjection, INJ. Diagram each sentence.

Heidi had told Clara of the flowers on the pasture.

"Have you seen the chair?"

"Oh, Clara, would you be angry?"

Writing: Commonplace Book

Add the passage below from your model story to your commonplace book.

"Give a light blow to a wine-glass. The glass will ring, giving forth a sound, weaker or stronger, lower or higher, according to the quality and size of the glass. The sound lasts but a moment, and then ceases. Strike the glass once more and while it is still ringing touch the rim with your finger. Instantly all is still again; not a sound from the glass. Why does it ring when struck, and why does it stop ringing at the touch of a finger? Before replying let us experiment with other resonant objects.

Dictation

Use part of today's poem for dictation.

90. Scientific Narration: Sound

- Heidi, Chapter 23

Your model story, "Sound," is from Jean Henri Fabre's *The Secret of Everyday Things*. In his book, the character of Uncle Paul is explaining these scientific concepts to a group of children. The stories are written in the first person with frequent use of the second person as he speaks directly to the children.

Use your outline to write a narration on this topic. Don't include references to the children or Uncle Paul; just write about the topic. Your narration should be in the third person. You may use other sources for more details if desired. You'll need to decide which details are important to your narration and which ones should be left out.

The Planting of the Apple-Tree

By William Cullen Bryant

  Come, let us plant the apple-tree.
Cleave the tough greensward with the spade;
Wide let its hollow bed be made;
There gently lay the roots, and there
Sift the dark mould with kindly care,
  And press it o'er them tenderly,
As round the sleeping infant's feet
We softly fold the cradle sheet;
  So plant we the apple-tree.

  What plant we in this apple-tree?
Buds, which the breath of summer days
Shall lengthen into leafy sprays;
Boughs where the thrush, with crimson breast,
Shall haunt, and sing, and hide her nest;
  We plant, upon the sunny lea,
A shadow for the noontide hour,
A shelter from the summer shower,
  When we plant the apple-tree.

What plant we in this apple-tree?
Sweets for a hundred flowery springs,
To load the May wind's restless wings,
When, from the orchard row, he pours
Its fragrance through our open doors;
  A world of blossoms for the bee,
Flowers for the sick girl's silent room,
For the glad infant sprigs of bloom,
  We plant with the apple-tree.

What plant we in this apple-tree?
Fruits that shall swell in sunny June,
And redden in the August noon,
And drop, when gentle airs come by,
That fan the blue September sky,
  While children come, with cries of glee,
And seek them where the fragrant grass
Betrays their bed to those who pass,
  At the foot of the apple-tree.

  And when, above this apple-tree,
The winter stars are quivering bright,
The winds go howling through the night,
Girls, whose eyes o'erflow with mirth,
Shall peel its fruit by cottage hearth,
  And guests in prouder homes shall see,
Heaped with the grape of Cintra's vine,
And golden orange of the line,
  The fruit of the apple-tree.

  The fruitage of this apple-tree,
Winds and our flag of stripe and star
Shall bear to coasts that lie afar,
Where men shall wonder at the view,
And ask in what fair groves they grew;
  And sojourners beyond the sea
Shall think of childhood's careless day,
And long, long hours of summer play,
  In the shade of the apple-tree.

  Each year shall give this apple-tree
A broader flush of roseate bloom,
A deeper maze of verdurous gloom,
And loosen, when the frost-clouds lower,
The crisp brown leaves in thicker shower.
  The years shall come and pass, but we
Shall hear no longer, where we lie,
The summer's songs, the autumn's sigh,
  In the boughs of the apple-tree.

And time shall waste this apple-tree.
Oh, when its aged branches throw
Thin shadows on the ground below,
Shall fraud and force and iron will
Oppress the weak and helpless still!
  What shall the tasks of mercy be,
Amid the toils, the strifes, the tears
Of those who live when length of years
  Is wasting this apple-tree?

"Who planted this old apple-tree?"
The children of that distant day
Thus to some aged man shall say;
And, gazing on its mossy stem,
The gray-haired man shall answer them:
"A poet of the land was he,
Born in the rude but good old times;
  'Tis said he made some quaint old rhymes
  On planting the apple-tree."

Editing

- Did you meet the goal of this writing exercise?

- Look at your word choice. Is there a good mixture of nouns and pronouns? Is the antecedent of each pronoun clear?

- Look at your paragraphs. Are all the sentences related? Does each paragraph focus on a single topic?

91. Compound Sentences

- This Week: Tanglewood Tales, The Minotaur

In grammar, we use the word **compound** to show that we have two or more of something. A compound subject is two or more subjects. A compound predicate is two or more predicates. What do you think a **compound sentence** is?

A **compound sentence** is one which has two or more independent clauses. Consider this sentence from "The Minotaur."

"Be patient, and we shall see."

Notice that in the sentence above, there are two subject-predicate pairs, which means two clauses. The first clause is a command, so it has the understood **you** as its subject. Both clauses are independent. Remember that an independent clause is one which can stand alone as a complete sentence.

There are three ways to correctly punctuate between two independent clauses. When proper punctuation is not used, it creates a run-on sentence. These are known as run-on sentences because they continue running on even when they should have stopped. In the following examples from *Tanglewood Tales*, I've taken liberties with Hawthorne's writing to produce a **fused sentence** and a **comma splice**.

A **fused sentence** occurs when two or more independent clauses are joined with no punctuation at all. Have you ever known someone who talked really fast and never seemed to pause for breath? That is what a fused sentence is like.

X "You be patient we shall see."

A **comma splice** occurs when two or more independent clauses are joined with only a comma.

X "You be patient, we shall see."

In the example above, the clauses seem to go together. They seem to be part of the same thought. However, each is an independent clause, so they need more than just a comma between them.

Each independent clause can stand as a sentence in its own right. Therefore, the first way to punctuate two or more independent clauses is to allow them to do precisely that. This method of punctuation produces two separate simple sentences.

"You be patient. We shall see."

No wonder he could not move it. It would have taken all the force of a very strong man to lift it out of its earthy bed.

The other ways to punctuate between independent clauses result in compound sentences.

The second way to punctuate two or more independent clauses is to use a comma with a coordinating conjunction. When we join two or more independent clauses with a coordinating conjunction, the FANBOYS, both the comma and the coordinating conjunction are required. Only using a comma would produce a comma splice, and only using a conjunction would produce a run-on sentence.

"You be patient**, and** we shall see."

No wonder he could not move it**, for** it would have taken all the force of a very strong man to lift it out of its earthy bed.

The third way to punctuate two or more independent clauses is to use a semicolon. The semicolon can be used alone. Since it does not end the sentence, the word following the semicolon is not capitalized unless it is a proper noun or adjective.

"You be patient**;** we shall see."

No wonder he could not move it**;** it would have taken all the force of a very strong man to lift it out of its earthy bed.

The Homes of England

By Felicia Hemans

The stately homes of England!
  How beautiful they stand,
Amidst their tall ancestral trees,
  O'er all the pleasant land!
The deer across their greensward bound
  Through shade and sunny gleam,
And the swan glides past them with the sound
  Of some rejoicing stream.

The merry homes of England!
  Around their hearths by night
What gladsome looks of household love
  Meet in the ruddy light!
There woman's voice flows forth in song,
  Or childish tale is told,
Or lips move tunefully along
  Some glorious page of old.

The blessed homes of England!
  How softly on their bowers
Is laid the holy quietness
  That breathes from Sabbath hours!
Solemn, yet sweet, the church-bell's chime
  Floats through their woods at morn;
All other sounds, in that still time,
  Of breeze and leaf are born.

The cottage homes of England!
  By thousands on her plains,
They are smiling o'er the silvery brooks,
  And round the hamlets' fanes.
Through glowing orchards forth they peep,
  Each from its nook of leaves;
And fearless there the lowly sleep,
  As the bird beneath their eaves.

The free, fair homes of England!
  Long, long, in hut and hall
May hearts of native proof be reared
  To guard each hallowed wall!
And green forever be the groves,
  And bright the flowery sod,
Where first the child's glad spirit loves
  Its country and its God!

Writing: Oral Narration

Read your new model story below, and then give your instructor an oral narration of it.

Hieroglyphics

From *The Story of Mankind* by Hendrik Van Loon

These earliest ancestors of ours who lived in the great European wilderness were rapidly learning many new things. It is safe to say that in due course of time they would have given up the ways of savages and would have developed a civilization of their own. But suddenly there came an end to their isolation. They were discovered.

A traveler from an unknown southland who had dared to cross the sea and the high mountain passes had found his way to the wild people of the European continent. He came from Africa. His home was in Egypt.

The valley of the Nile had developed a high stage of civilization thousands of years before the people of the west had dreamed of the possibilities of a fork or a wheel or a house. And we shall therefore leave our great-great-grandfathers in their caves, while we visit the southern and eastern shores of the Mediterranean, where stood the earliest school of the human race.

The Egyptians have taught us many things. They were excellent farmers. They knew all about irrigation. They built temples which were afterwards copied by the Greeks and which served as the earliest models for the churches in which we worship nowadays. They had invented a calendar which proved such a useful instrument for the purpose of measuring time that it has survived with a few changes until today. But most important of all, the Egyptians had learned how to preserve speech for the benefit of future generations. They had invented the art of writing.

We are so accustomed to newspapers and books and magazines that we take it for granted that the world has always been able to read and write. As a matter of fact, writing, the most important of all inventions, is quite new. Without written documents we would be like cats and dogs, who can only teach their kittens and their puppies a few simple things and who, because they cannot write, possess no way in which they can make use of the experience of those generations of cats and dogs that have gone before.

In the first century before our era, when the Romans came to Egypt, they found the valley full of strange little pictures which seemed to have something to do with the history of the country. But the Romans were not interested in "anything foreign" and did not inquire into the origin of these queer figures which covered the walls of the temples and the walls of the palaces and endless reams of flat sheets made out of the papyrus reed. The last of the Egyptian priests who had understood the holy art of making such pictures had died several years before. Egypt deprived of its independence had become a store-house filled with important historical documents which no one could decipher and which were of no earthly use to either man or beast.

Seventeen centuries went by and Egypt remained a land of mystery. But in the year 1798 a French general by the name of Bonaparte happened to visit eastern Africa to prepare for an attack upon the British Indian Colonies. He did not get beyond the Nile, and his campaign was a failure. But, quite accidentally, the famous French expedition solved the problem of the ancient Egyptian picture-language.

One day a young French officer, much bored by the dreary life of his little fortress on the Rosetta river (a mouth of the Nile) decided to spend a few idle hours rummaging among the ruins of the Nile Delta. And behold! He found a stone which greatly puzzled him. Like everything else in Egypt it was covered with little figures. But this particular slab of black basalt was different from anything that had ever been discovered. It carried three inscriptions. One of these was in Greek. The Greek language was known. "All that is necessary," so he reasoned, "is to compare the Greek text with the Egyptian figures, and they will at once tell their secrets."

The plan sounded simple enough but it took more than twenty years to solve the riddle. In the year 1802 a French professor by the name of Champollion began to compare the Greek and the Egyptian texts of the famous Rosetta stone. In the year 1823 he announced that he had discovered the meaning of fourteen little figures. A short time later he died from overwork, but the main principles of Egyptian writing had become known. Today the story of the valley of the Nile is better known to us than the story of the Mississippi River. We possess a written record which covers four thousand years of chronicled history.

As the ancient Egyptian hieroglyphics (the word means "sacred writing") have played such a very great role in history, (a few of them in modified form have even found their way into our own alphabet,) you ought to know something about the ingenious system which was used fifty centuries ago to preserve the spoken word for the benefit of the coming generations.

Of course, you know what a sign language is. Every Indian story of our western plains has a chapter devoted to strange messages writer in the form of little pictures which tell how many buffaloes were killed and how many hunters there were in a certain party. As a rule it is not difficult to understand the meaning of such messages.

Ancient Egyptian, however, was not a sign language. The clever people of the Nile had passed beyond that stage long before. Their pictures meant a great deal more than the object which they represented, as I shall try to explain to you now.

Suppose that you were Champollion, and that you were examining a stack of papyrus sheets, all covered with hieroglyphics. Suddenly you came across a picture of a man with a saw. "Very well," you would say, "that means of course that a farmer went out to cut down a tree." Then you take another papyrus. It tells the story of a queen who had died at the age of eighty-two. In the midst of a sentence appears the picture of the man with the saw. Queens of eighty-two do not handle saws. The picture therefore must mean something else. But what?

That is the riddle which the Frenchman finally solved. He discovered that the Egyptians were the first to use what we now call "phonetic writing"—a system of characters which reproduce the "sound" (or phone) of the spoken word and which make it possible for us to translate all our spoken words into a written form, with the help of only a few dots and dashes and pothooks.

Let us return for a moment to the little fellow with the saw. The word "saw" either means a certain tool which you will find in a carpenter's shop, or it means the past tense of the verb "to see."

This is what had happened to the word during the course of centuries. First of all it had meant only the particular tool which it represented. Then that meaning had been lost and it had become the past participle of a verb. After several hundred years, the Egyptians lost sight of both these meanings and the picture came to stand for a single letter, the letter S. A short sentence will show you what I mean. Here is a modern English sentence as it would have been written in hieroglyphics.

The either means one of these two round objects in your head, which allow you to see or it means "I," the person who is talking.

A is either an insect which gathers honey, or it represents the verb "to be" which means to exist. Again, it may be the first part of a verb like "be-come" or "be-have." In this particular instance it is followed by which means a "leaf" or "leave" or "lieve" (the sound of all three words is the same).

The "eye" you know all about.

Finally you get the picture of a . It is a giraffe It is part of the old sign-language out of which the hieroglyphics developed.

You can now read that sentence without much difficulty.

"I believe I saw a giraffe."

Having invented this system the Egyptians developed it during thousands of years until they could write anything they wanted, and they used these "canned words" to send messages to friends, to keep business accounts and to keep a record of the history of their country, that future generations might benefit by the mistakes of the past.

Exercise

Review memory work. Below are two independent clauses. Show the three ways to join them.

> she began to be conscious that her son was no longer a child

> she must soon send him forth among the perils and troubles of the world

Copy each sentence below. Double underline the predicate, and underline the subject. Put brackets around any prepositional phrases. Label the part of speech of each word. Noun, N; Proper Noun, PN; Pronoun, PRO; Verb, V; Linking Verb, LV; Adjective, ADJ; Article, ART; Conjunction, CJ; Preposition, Prep; Interjection, INJ. Diagram each sentence.

> "Be patient and see."

> "Why can not I go to this famous city of Athens?"

> The eyes of Theseus glowed with enthusiasm.

Commonplace Book

With your instructor's approval, add the passage below to your commonplace book, or choose your own passage from a work of fiction. This can be from either school reading or free reading.

> Often and often, after this, did Theseus ask his mother whether it was yet time for him to go to Athens; and still his mother pointed to the rock, and told him that, for years to come, he could not be strong enough to move it. And again and again the rosy-cheeked and curly-headed boy would tug and strain at the huge mass of stone, striving, child as he was, to do what a giant could hardly have done without taking both of his great hands to the task.

Dictation

> Meanwhile the rock seemed to be sinking farther and farther into the ground. The moss grew over it thicker and thicker, until at last it looked almost like a soft green seat, with only a few gray knobs of granite peeping out. The overhanging trees, also, shed their brown leaves upon it, as often as the autumn came; and at its base grew ferns and wild flowers, some of which crept quite over its surface. To all appearance, the rock was as firmly fastened as any other portion of the earth's substance.

92. Review: Phrases and Clauses

- This Week: Tanglewood Tales, The Minotaur

Definition: A phrase is a group of related words which does not include a subject-predicate pair.

Definition: A clause is a group of words which contains a subject-predicate pair.

A subject-predicate pair is simply a verb and its subject. Remember that the defining characteristic of both phrases and clauses is whether or not they have a subject-predicate pair. Phrases never have a subject-predicate pair, but clauses must have a subject-predicate pair.

Phrases can be short or long. Some phrases have specific names based on the main word or usage of the phrase. A noun phrase consists of a noun and its modifiers. A verb phrase consists of the helping verbs, main verb, and any ending the main verb needs. A prepositional phrase consists of the preposition, its object, and any modifiers of the object.

Look at the following sentences from "The Minotaur." The first has a noun phrase and a prepositional phrase, both of which are underlined. The second has a verb phrase.

"Only admit this evil-minded young man to your presence."

He must have had a very sorrowful dream.

Unlike a phrase, a clause must have a subject and a predicate. Look at these clauses. The predicate is double underlined and the subject is underlined in each clause.

when the king asked what he should do with Theseus

this naughty woman had an answer ready at her tongue's end

because he might thus arrive within fifteen miles of Athens

unless his sinews were made of brass

Some clauses express a complete thought. That makes them independent clauses.

Independent clauses express a complete thought and can therefore stand alone as complete sentences. In the above list, only one clause is independent. Which one is it?

Some clauses do not express a complete thought even though they possess both a subject and a predicate. That's because certain words which can begin clauses set up the expectation for more information. These words that tell us that there is more to the thought. When a clause begins with a **subordinate conjunction**, a word like **when**, **while**, or **before**, it leaves us wondering, "And then what?" We need more information to have a complete thought expressed. Look at those clauses again, this time with the subordinate conjunction removed.

> The king asked what he should do with Theseus.
>
> He might thus arrive within fifteen miles of Athens.
>
> His sinews were made of brass.

When I took away that beginning word, I also took away the expectation for the rest of the story. Now these clauses can stand alone as complete, if sometimes rather odd, sentences.

Remember that coordinating conjunctions, the FANBOYS, do *not* make clauses dependent. They can still stand as complete sentences.

> But the king asked what he should do with Theseus.
>
> And he might thus arrive within fifteen miles of Athens.

A Psalm of Life

By Henry Wadsworth Longfellow

Tell me not, in mournful numbers,
  Life is but an empty dream!—
For the soul is dead that slumbers,
  And things are not what they seem.

Life is real! Life is earnest!
  And the grave is not its goal;
Dust thou art, to dust returnest,
  Was not spoken of the soul.

Not enjoyment, and not sorrow,
  Is our destined end or way;
But to act, that each tomorrow
  Find us farther than today.

Art is long, and Time is fleeting,
  And our hearts, though stout and brave,
Still, like muffled drums, are beating
  Funeral marches to the grave.

In the world's broad field of battle,
  In the bivouac of Life,
Be not like dumb, driven cattle!
  Be a hero in the strife!

Trust no Future, howe'er pleasant!
  Let the dead Past bury its dead!
Act,—act in the living Present!
  Heart within, and God o'erhead!

Lives of great men all remind us
  We can make our lives sublime,
And, departing, leave behind us
  Footprints on the sands of time;

Footprints, that perhaps another,
  Sailing o'er life's solemn main,
A forlorn and shipwrecked brother,
  Seeing, shall take heart again.

Let us, then, be up and doing,
  With a heart for any fate;
Still achieving, still pursuing,
  Learn to labor and to wait.

Lion's Defeat

From *South-African Folk-Tales* by James A. Honey

    The wild animals, it is said, were once assembled at Lion's. When Lion was asleep, Jackal persuaded Little Fox to twist a rope of ostrich sinews, in order to play Lion a trick. They took ostrich sinews, twisted them, and fastened the rope to Lion's tail, and the other end of the rope they tied to a shrub. When Lion awoke, and saw that he was tied up, he became angry, and called the animals together. When they had assembled, Lion said (using this form of conjuration)—
    "What child of his mother and father's love,
    Whose mother and father's love has tied me?"
    Then answered the animal to whom the question was first put—
    "I, child of my mother and father's love,
    I, mother and father's love, I have not done it."
    All answered the same; but when he asked Little Fox, Little Fox said—
    "I, child of my mother and father's love,
    I, mother and father's love, have tied thee!"
    Then Lion tore the rope made of sinews, and ran after Little Fox. But Jackal said:
    "My boy, thou son of lean Mrs. Fox, thou wilt never be caught."
    Truly Lion was thus beaten in running by Little Fox.

Writing: Outline

Write or type an outline of the new model story which you read in the last lesson.

Exercise

Review memory work. Below are two independent clauses. Show the three ways to join them.

   it was not more than a year afterwards

   they were again sitting on the moss-covered stone.

Copy each sentence below. Double underline the predicate, and underline the subject. Put brackets around any prepositional phrases. Label the part of speech of each word. Noun, N; Proper Noun, PN; Pronoun, PRO; Verb, V; Linking Verb, LV; Adjective, ADJ; Article, ART; Conjunction, CJ; Preposition, Prep; Interjection, INJ. Diagram each sentence.

   Theseus had done many valiant deeds with his father's golden-hilted sword.

   "Admit Theseus, this evil-minded young man, to your presence."

   "Why, he must be a very wicked young fellow indeed!" [Hint: **indeed** tells **to what extent** he is a wicked young fellow.]

Commonplace Book

With your instructor's approval, add the poem below to your commonplace book, or choose your own poem.

   Tell me not, in mournful numbers,
      Life is but an empty dream!—
   For the soul is dead that slumbers,
      And things are not what they seem.

   Life is real! Life is earnest!
      And the grave is not its goal;
   Dust thou art, to dust returnest,
      Was not spoken of the soul.

Dictation

   Acts 2:23-24

This Man, delivered over by the predetermined plan and foreknowledge of God, you nailed to a cross by the hands of godless men and put Him to death. But God raised Him up again, putting an end to the agony of death, since it was impossible for Him to be held in its power.

Hauling a Boat Ashore at Honfleur by Claude Monet

Picture Study

1. Read the title and the name of the artist. Study the picture for several minutes, then put the picture away.

2. Describe the picture.

3. Look at the picture again. Do you notice any details that you missed before? What do you like or dislike about this painting? Does it remind you of anything?

93. Descriptive Writing

- This Week: Tanglewood Tales, The Minotaur

Writing: Descriptive Writing

The purpose of descriptive writing is to describe a person, place, thing, or event so well that an image forms in the mind of the reader.

In "The Minotaur," Theseus travels through the labyrinth to discover the minotaur. Read that passage below, paying close attention to the details that make a vivid picture in your mind, and then write a narration of it. What did the minotaur look like? How did it behave? What helped to give Theseus courage?

Add details if you wish. Remember, the point of this exercise is to write as descriptively as possible, not just to narrate the passage exactly.

The Minotaur

He followed the dreadful roar of the Minotaur, which now grew louder and louder, and finally so very loud that Theseus fully expected to come close upon him, at every new zigzag and wriggle of the path. And at last, in an open space, at the very centre of the labyrinth, he did discern the hideous creature.

Sure enough, what an ugly monster it was! Only his horned head belonged to a bull; and yet, somehow or other, he looked like a bull all over, preposterously waddling on his hind legs; or, if you happened to view him in another way, he seemed wholly a man, and all the more monstrous for being so. And there he was, the wretched thing, with no society, no companion, no kind of a mate, living only to do mischief, and incapable of knowing what affection means. Theseus hated him, and shuddered at him, and yet could not but be sensible of some sort of pity; and all the more, the uglier and more detestable the creature was. For he kept striding to and fro in a solitary frenzy of rage, continually emitting a hoarse roar, which was oddly mixed up with half-shaped words; and, after listening awhile, Theseus understood that the Minotaur was saying to himself how miserable he was, and how hungry, and how he hated everybody, and how he longed to eat up the human race alive.

Ah, the bull-headed villain! And O, my good little people, you will perhaps see, one of these days, as I do now, that every human being who suffers anything evil to get into his nature, or to remain there, is a kind of Minotaur, an enemy of his fellow-creatures, and separated from all good companionship, as this poor monster was.

Was Theseus afraid? By no means, my dear auditors. What! A hero like Theseus afraid! Not had the Minotaur had twenty bull heads instead of one. Bold as he was, however, I rather fancy that it strengthened his valiant heart, just at this crisis, to feel a tremulous twitch at the silken cord, which he was still holding in his left hand. It was as if Ariadne were giving him all her might and courage; and, much as he already had, and little as she had to give, it made his own seem twice as much. And to confess the honest truth, he needed the whole; for now the Minotaur, turning suddenly about, caught sight of Theseus, and instantly lowered his horribly sharp horns, exactly as a mad bull does when he means to rush against an enemy. At the same time, he belched forth a tremendous roar, in which there was something like the words of human language, but all disjointed and shaken-to pieces by passing through the gullet of a miserably enraged brute.

Lullaby

By Walter De La Mare

Sleep, sleep, lovely white soul!
The singing mouse sings plaintively,
The sweet night-bird in the chesnut-tree—
They sing together, bird and mouse,
In starlight, in darkness, lonely, sweet,
The wild notes and the faint notes meet—
Sleep, sleep, lovely white soul!
Sleep, sleep, lovely white soul!
Amid the lilies floats the moth,
The mole along his galleries goeth
In the dark earth; the summer moon
Looks like a shepherd through the pane
Seeking his feeble lamb again—
Sleep, sleep, lovely white soul!
Sleep, sleep, lovely white soul!
Time comes to keep night-watch with thee
Nodding with roses; and the sea
Saith 'Peace! Peace!' amid his foam
White as thy night-clothes; 'O be still!'
The wind cries up the whisp'ring hill—
Sleep, sleep, lovely white soul!

Tortoises Hunting Ostriches

From *South-African Folk-Tales* by James A. Honey

One day, it is said, the Tortoises held a council how they might hunt Ostriches, and they said, "Let us, on both sides, stand in rows near each other, and let one go to hunt the Ostriches, so that they must flee along through the midst of us." They did so, and as they were many, the Ostriches were obliged to run along through the midst of them. During this they did not move, but, remaining always in the same places, called each to the other, "Are you there?" and each one answered, "I am here." The Ostriches hearing this, ran so tremendously that they quite exhausted their strength, and fell down. Then the Tortoises assembled by-and-by at the place where the Ostriches had fallen, and devoured them.

Exercise

Review memory work. Below are two independent clauses. Show the three ways to join them.

>do but let me put a single drop into the goblet

>let the young man taste it

Copy each sentence below. Double underline the predicate, and underline the subject. Put brackets around any prepositional phrases. Label the part of speech of each word. Noun, N; Proper Noun, PN; Pronoun, PRO; Verb, V; Linking Verb, LV; Adjective, ADJ; Article, ART; Conjunction, CJ; Preposition, Prep; Interjection, INJ. Diagram each sentence.

>"How came you by it?"

>He drew back the goblet.

>His eyes had fallen on the gold-hilted sword.

Commonplace Book

With your instructor's approval, add the passage below to your commonplace book, or choose your own passage from a work of non-fiction. This can be from the Bible, a biography, or one of your history or science books.

>I have quite forgotten what became of the king's nephews. But when the wicked Medea saw this new turn of affairs, she hurried out of the room, and going to her private chamber, lost no time in setting her enchantments at work. In a few moments, she heard a great noise of hissing snakes outside of the chamber window; and, behold! There was her fiery chariot, and four huge winged serpents, wriggling and twisting in the air, flourishing their tails higher than the top of the palace, and all ready to set off on an aerial journey.

Editing

• Did you meet the goal of this writing exercise?

• Look at your word choice. Is there a good mixture of nouns and pronouns? Is the antecedent of each pronoun clear?

• Look at your paragraphs. Are all the sentences related? Does each paragraph focus on a single topic?

94. Complex Sentences

- This Week: Tanglewood Tales, The Pygmies

The subordinate conjunctions are: after, although, as, because, before, even if, even though, if, in order that, once, provided that, rather than, since, so that, than, that, though, unless, until, when, whenever, where, whereas, wherever, whether, while.

You've learned that clauses can be either dependent or independent. One way to make a clause dependent is to begin it with a subordinate conjunction. I hope you've been memorizing this list because it's an important one to know.

Definition: A complex sentence is a sentence with one independent clause and at least one dependent clause.

An independent clause is one which can stand alone as a complete sentence. A dependent clause needs more information to express a complete thought. Where do we get this additional information?

A dependent clause needs an independent clause! It relies on the independent clause to make sense. Without the independent clause, the reader is left wondering, "And then what?" The independent clause works with the dependent clause by answering that question.

Look at these sentences from "The Pygmies." Notice that each sentence is made up of at least two clauses. These are **complex sentences**. Complex sentences have one independent clause and at least one dependent clause.

Dependent Independent

When the world was full of wonders, Antæus the Giant lived.

Independent Dependent

The very breath of his life would depart from him **unless** the Giant touched Mother Earth as often as once in five minutes.

Look closely at the punctuation in those sentences. Punctuating a complex sentence is simple and straightforward. When the dependent clause comes first, use a comma to separate it from the main clause. However, when the dependent clause comes after the main clause, no comma is necessary. Below are the same sentences, but I've switched the order of the clauses. Notice how the punctuation changed.

Antæus the Giant lived **when** the world was full of wonders.

Unless the Giant touched Mother Earth as often as once in five minutes, the very breath of his life would depart from him.

June

By James Russell Lowell

What is so rare as a day in June?
Then, if ever, come perfect days;
Then Heaven tries the earth if it be in tune,
   And over it softly her warm ear lays:
Whether we look, or whether we listen,
We hear life murmur, or see it glisten;
Every clod feels a stir of might,
   An instinct within it that reaches and towers,
And, groping blindly above it for light,
   Climbs to a soul in grass and flowers;
The flush of life may well be seen
   Thrilling back over hills and valleys;
The cowslip startles in meadows green.
   The buttercup catches the sun in its chalice,
And there's never a leaf nor a blade too mean
   To be some happy creature's palace;
The little bird sits at his door in the sun,
   Atilt like a blossom among the leaves,
And lets his illumined being o'errun
   With the deluge of summer it receives;
His mate feels the eggs beneath her wings,
And the heart in her dumb breast flutters and sings;
He sings to the wide world, and she to her nest,—
In the nice ear of Nature which song is the best?

Crocodile's Treason

From *South-African Folk-Tales* by James A. Honey

Part 1.

   Crocodile was, in the days when animals still could talk, the acknowledged foreman of all water creatures and if one should judge from appearances one would say that he still is. But in those days it was his especial duty to have a general care of all water animals, and when one year it was exceedingly dry, and the water of the river where they had lived dried up and became scarce, he was forced to make a plan to trek over to another river a short distance from there.
   He first sent Otter out to spy. He stayed away two days and brought back a report

that there was still good water in the other river, real sea-cow holes, that not even a drought of several years could dry up.

After he had ascertained this, Crocodile called to his side Tortoise and Alligator.

"Look here," said he, "I need you two to-night to carry a report to Lion. So then get ready; the veldt is dry, and you will probably have to travel for a few days without any water. We must make peace with Lion and his subjects, otherwise we utterly perish this year. And he must help us to trek over to the other river, especially past the Boer's farm that lies in between, and to travel unmolested by any of the animals of the veldt, so long as the trek lasts. A fish on land is sometimes a very helpless thing, as you all know." The two had it mighty hard in the burning sun, and on the dry veldt, but eventually they reached Lion and handed him the treaty.

"What is going on now?" thought Lion to himself, when he had read it. "I must consult Jackal first," said he. But to the commissioners he gave back an answer that he would be the following evening with his advisers at the appointed place, at the big vaarland willow tree, at the farther end of the hole of water, where Crocodile had his headquarters.

When Tortoise and Alligator came back, Crocodile was exceedingly pleased with himself at the turn the case had taken.

He allowed Otter and a few others to be present and ordered them on that evening to have ready plenty of fish and other eatables for their guests under the vaarland willow.

That evening as it grew dark Lion appeared with Wolf, Jackal, Baboon, and a few other important animals, at the appointed place, and they were received in the most open-hearted manner by Crocodile and the other water creatures.

Crocodile was so glad at the meeting of the animals that he now and then let fall a great tear of joy that disappeared into the sand. After the other animals had done well by the fish, Crocodile laid bare to them the condition of affairs and opened up his plan. He wanted only peace among all animals; for they not only destroyed one another, but the Boer, too, would in time destroy them all.

The Boer had already stationed at the source of the river no less than three steam pumps to irrigate his land, and the water was becoming scarcer every day. More than this, he took advantage of their unfortunate position by making them sit in the shallow water and then, one after the other, bringing about their death. As Lion was, on this account, inclined to make peace, it was to his glory to take this opportunity and give his hand to these peace-making water creatures, and carry out their part of the contract, namely, escort them from the dried-up water, past the Boer's farm and to the long sea-cow pools.

"And what benefit shall we receive from it?" asked Jackal.

"Well," answered Crocodile, "the peace made is of great benefit to both sides. We will not exterminate each other. If you desire to come and drink water, you can do so with an easy mind, and not be the least bit nervous that I, or any one of us will seize you by the nose; and so also with all the other animals. And from your side we are to be freed from Elephant, who has the habit, whenever he gets the opportunity, of tossing us with his trunk up into some open and narrow fork of a tree and there allowing us to become biltong."

Lion and Jackal stepped aside to consult with one another, and then Lion wanted to know what form of security he would have that Crocodile would keep to his part of the contract.

"I stake my word of honor," was the prompt answer from Crocodile, and he let drop a few more long tears of honesty into the sand.

Writing: Copia

Take the following sentence and play with it. Remember that the point is not necessarily to make the sentence better. The point is to play with the sentence and make it different. Make a new sentence with a change from each of the following categories.

> In the first century before our era, when the Romans came to Egypt, they found the valley full of strange little pictures which seemed to have something to do with the history of the country.

1. Change the grammar.
   - Change the nouns from common to proper and vice versa.
   - Change the nouns from singular to plural and vice versa.
   - Change the sentence type.
   - Change the adjectives from articles to descriptive to possessive, etc.
   - Change a quotation from direct to indirect and vice versa.
   - Change the verb tense.

2. Condense the sentence.
   - Remove details.
   - Remove modifiers.
   - Remove phrases or clauses.

3. Amplify the sentence.
   - Add details.
   - Add dialogue.
   - Add modifiers.
   - Add phrases or clauses.

4. Use synonyms and antonyms.
   - Substitute synonyms.
   - Say the opposite thing using antonyms.

5. Point of view.
   - Change the point of view.
   - Slant the sentence.

Exercise

Review memory work. Below are two clauses, one dependent and one independent. Show the two ways to join them.

> I shall probably have to teach you a little civility

> before we part

Copy each sentence below. Double underline the predicate, and underline the subject. Put brackets around any prepositional phrases. Label the part of speech of each word. Noun, N; Proper Noun, PN; Pronoun, PRO; Verb, V; Linking Verb, LV; Adjective, ADJ; Article, ART; Conjunction, CJ; Preposition, Prep; Interjection, INJ. Diagram each sentence.

Here the Pygmies planted wheat and other kinds of grain.

These funny Pygmies had a Giant for their neighbor.

"How are you, my good fellow?"

Commonplace Book

With your instructor's approval, add the passage below to your commonplace book, or choose your own passage from a work of fiction. This can be from either school reading or free reading.

> Among the Pygmies, I suppose, if one of them grew to the height of six or eight inches, he was reckoned a prodigiously tall man. It must have been very pretty to behold their little cities, with streets two or three feet wide, paved with the smallest pebbles, and bordered by habitations about as big as a squirrel's cage. The king's palace attained to the stupendous magnitude of Periwinkle's baby-house, and stood in the centre of a spacious square, which could hardly have been covered by our hearth-rug.

Dictation

> Their principal temple, or cathedral, was as lofty as yonder bureau, and was looked upon as a wonderfully sublime and magnificent edifice. All these structures were built neither of stone nor wood. They were neatly plastered together by the Pygmy workmen, pretty much like bird's-nests, out of straw, feathers, eggshells, and other small bits of stuff, with stiff clay instead of mortar; and when the hot sun had dried them, they were just as snug and comfortable as a Pygmy could desire.

95. Indirect Objects

- This Week: Tanglewood Tales, The Pygmies

A transitive verb is one which has a direct object. Intransitive verbs do not have direct objects.

Occasionally, transitive verbs have an additional type of object.

> Definition: An indirect object is a noun or pronoun that tells **to whom** or **what**, or **for whom** or **what**, the action of the verb is performed.

The direct object receives the action of the verb. It answers the question **whom** or **what** following a transitive verb. Sometimes, a transitive verb is performed for someone or something.

　He <u>wrote</u> a letter.

He wrote what? A **letter**. Letter is the direct object. But **to whom** did he write a letter?

　He <u>wrote</u> me a letter.

Now, the sentence tells **to whom** he wrote the letter: **me**. **Me** is the **indirect object**. Notice the position of the indirect object. It sits between the verb and the direct object. To have an indirect object, a sentence must have a direct object, and the indirect object will always be between it and the verb.

The indirect object answers the question **to whom or what**, or **for whom or what**, the action of the verb is performed.

Look at the following sentence from "The Pygmies."

　His one vast eye gave the whole <u>nation</u> a friendly wink.

The transitive verb **gave** has a direct object, **wink**. His eye gave a wink to whom? To the whole **nation**. **Nation** is the indirect object.

Note that this information could also be part of a prepositional phrase, using the preposition **to** or **for**.

　His one vast eye gave a friendly wink <u>to the whole nation</u>.

With the preposition, **nation** is the object of the preposition **to**. The prepositional phrase modifies **gave**. In either case, the purpose is the same: to identify the recipient of the direct object. In other words, the indirect object tells who or what gets the direct object. You'll find indirect objects with verbs such as build, buy, do, get, give, make, read, save, send, show, and tell.

Look at the following two diagrams. The first diagrams the sentence with **nation** as the indirect object. The second digrams the sentence with **nation** as the object of the preposition **to**. In both cases, the word identifies the recipient of the direct object. Who received the wink? The whole **nation**. In both cases, it appears in the same position on the diagram.

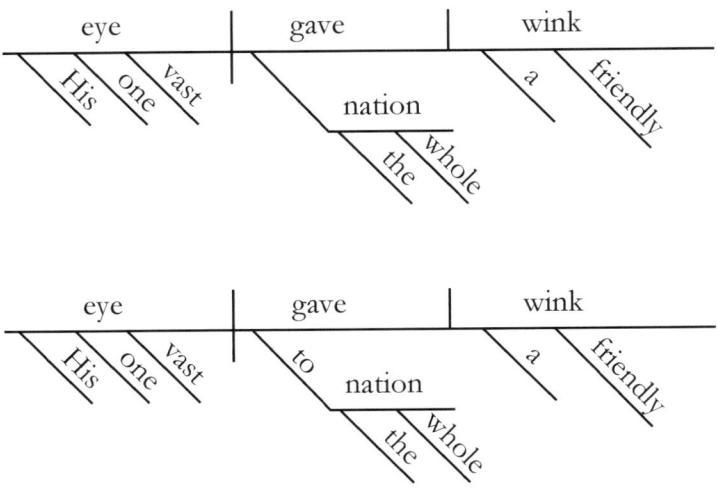

Remember that only a sentence which has a direct object can have an indirect object. Follow this procedure for analyzing sentences.

Put brackets around prepositional phrases.

What is the predicate? The main verb is often easier to find than its subject, so find it first. Double underline it. Is it an action verb or a linking verb?

What is the subject? Underline it once.

For action verbs, is there a direct object which receives the action of the verb by answering the question **whom** or **what**? IF THERE IS A DIRECT OBJECT, is there an indirect object between the DO and the verb which identifies the recipient of the direct object by answering the question **to whom or what**, or **for whom or what**, the action of the verb is performed?

For linking verbs, is there a subject complement—a predicate nominative or a predicate adjective—which renames or modifies the subject?

You can also have a compound indirect object.

He wrote mother and me a letter.

He wrote what? A **letter**; **letter** is the direct object. Who receives the letter? **Mother** and **me**. **Mother** and **me** is the compound indirect object.

A compound indirect object is diagrammed like this:

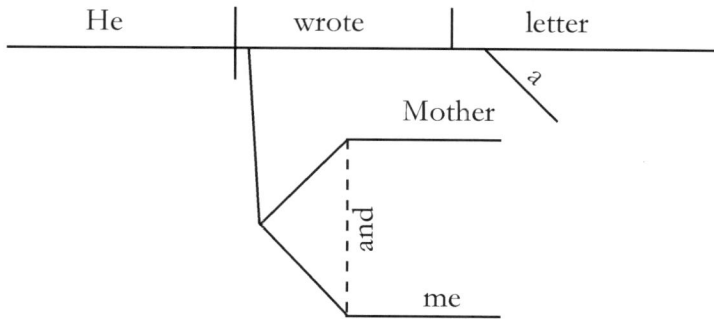

Barnacles

By Sidney Lanier

My soul is sailing through the sea,
But the Past is heavy and hindereth me.
The Past hath crusted cumbrous shells
That hold the flesh of cold sea-mells
About my soul.
The huge waves wash, the high waves roll,
Each barnacle clingeth and worketh dole
And hindereth me from sailing!

Old Past, let go, and drop i' the sea
Till fathomless waters cover thee!
For I am living, but thou art dead;
Thou drawest back, I strive ahead
The Day to find.
Thy shells unbind! Night comes behind;
I needs must hurry with the wind
And trim me best for sailing.

Crocodile's Treason

From *South-African Folk-Tales* by James A. Honey

Part 2.

"I stake my word of honor," was the prompt answer from Crocodile, and he let drop a few more long tears of honesty into the sand.

Baboon then said it was all square and honest as far as he could see into the case. He thought it was nonsense to attempt to dig pitfalls for one another; because he personally was well aware that his race would benefit somewhat from this contract of peace and friendship. And more than this, they must consider that use must be made of the fast disappearing water, for even in the best of times it was an unpleasant thing to be always carrying your life about in your hands. He would, however, like to suggest to the King that it would be well to have everything put down in writing, so that there would be nothing to regret in case it was needed.

Jackal did not want to listen to the agreement. He could not see that it would benefit the animals of the veldt. But Wolf, who had fully satisfied himself with the fish, was in an exceptionally peace-loving mood, and he advised Lion again to close the agreement.

After Lion had listened to all his advisers, and also the pleading tones of Crocodile's followers, he held forth in a speech in which he said that he was inclined to enter into the agreement, seeing that it was clear that Crocodile and his subjects were in a very tight place.

There and then a document was drawn up, and it was resolved, before midnight, to begin the trek. Crocodile's messengers swam in all directions to summon together the water animals for the trek.

Frogs croaked and crickets chirped in the long water grass. It was not long before all the animals had assembled at the vaarland willow. In the meantime Lion had sent out a few despatch riders to his subjects to raise a commando for an escort, and long ere midnight these also were at the vaarland willow in the moonlight.

The trek then was regulated by Lion and Jackal. Jackal was to take the lead to act as spy, and when he was able to draw Lion to one side, he said to him:

"See here, I do not trust this affair one bit, and I want to tell you straight out, I am going to make tracks! I will spy for you until you reach the sea-cow pool, but I am not going to be the one to await your arrival there."

Elephant had to act as advance guard because he could walk so softly and could hear and smell so well. Then came Lion with one division of the animals, then Crocodile's trek with a flank protection of both sides, and Wolf received orders to bring up the rear.

Meanwhile, while all this was being arranged, Crocodile was smoothly preparing his treason. He called Yellow Snake to one side and said to him: "It is to our advantage to have these animals, who go among us every day, and who will continue to do so, fall into the hands of the Boer. Listen, now! You remain behind unnoticed, and when you hear me shout you will know that we have arrived safely at the sea-cow pool. Then you must harass the Boer's dogs as much as you can, and the rest will look out for themselves."

Thereupon the trek moved on. It was necessary to go very slowly as many of the water animals were not accustomed to the journey on land; but they trekked past the Boer's farm in safety, and toward break of day they were all safely at the sea-cow pool. There most of the water animals disappeared suddenly into the deep water, and Crocodile also began to make preparations to follow their example. With tearful eyes he said to Lion that he was, oh, so thankful for the help, that, from pure relief and joy, he must first give vent to his feelings by a few screams. Thereupon he suited his words to actions so that even the mountains echoed, and then thanked Lion on behalf of his subjects, and purposely continued with a long speech, dwelling on all the benefits both sides would derive from the agreement of peace.

Lion was just about to say good day and take his departure, when the first shot fell, and with it Elephant and a few other animals.

"I told you all so!" shouted Jackal from the other side of the sea-cow pool. "Why did you allow yourselves to be misled by a few Crocodile tears?"

Crocodile had disappeared long ago into the water. All one saw was just a lot of bubbles; and on the banks there was an actual war against the animals. It simply crackled the way the Boers shot them.

But most of them, fortunately, came out of it alive.

Shortly after, they say, Crocodile received his well-earned reward, when he met a driver with a load of dynamite. And even now when the Elephant gets the chance he pitches them up into the highest forks of the trees.

Exercise

Review memory work. Below are two clauses, one dependent and one independent. Show the two ways to join them.

> the figure looked all the more terrible
>
> because it carried an enormous brass club on its shoulder

Copy each sentence below. Double underline the predicate, and underline the subject. Put brackets around any prepositional phrases. Label the part of speech of each word. Noun, N; Proper Noun, PN; Pronoun, PRO; Verb, V; Linking Verb, LV; Adjective, ADJ; Article, ART; Conjunction, CJ; Preposition, Prep; Interjection, INJ. Diagram each sentence.

> The Giant gave them his brotherly kindness.
>
> He gave the Pygmies a breeze with his breath.
>
> The Pymies built themselves structures of clay.

Writing: Commonplace Book

Add the passage below from your model story to your commonplace book.

> In the first century before our era, when the Romans came to Egypt, they found the valley full of strange little pictures which seemed to have something to do with the history of the country. But the Romans were not interested in "anything foreign" and did not inquire into the origin of these queer figures which covered the walls of the temples and the walls of the palaces and endless reams of flat sheets made out of the papyrus reed. The last of the Egyptian priests who had understood the holy art of making such pictures had died several years before.

Dictation

Use part of today's poem for dictation.

96. Historical Narration: Hieroglyphics

- This Week: Tanglewood Tales, The Pygmies

Your next three narrations will be on history topics. When you write about fictional stories, it's acceptable to get creative with the story, adding details and perhaps even new characters and events. However, with a historical topic, you should report the facts without making up new content.

The **purpose** of your paper is what you wish to accomplish with your writing. Your purpose is to **inform** your reader about this topic.

Home, Sweet Home

By John Howard Payne

'Mid pleasures and palaces though we may roam,
Be it ever so humble, there's no place like home;
A charm from the sky seems to hallow us there,
Which, seek through the world, is ne'er met with elsewhere.
  Home! Home! Sweet, sweet Home!
There's no place like Home! There's no place like Home!

An exile from Home, splendor dazzles in vain;
O, give me my lowly thatched cottage again!
The birds singing gaily, that came at my call,—
Give me them,—and the peace of mind, dearer than all!
  Home! Home! Sweet, sweet Home!
There's no place like Home! There's no place like Home!

How sweet 'tis to sit 'neath a fond father's smile,
And the cares of a mother to soothe and beguile!
Let others delight 'mid new pleasures to roam,
But give me, oh, give me, the pleasures of Home!
  Home! Home! Sweet, sweet Home!
There's no place like Home! There's no place like Home!

To thee I'll return, overburdened with care;
The heart's dearest solace will smile on me there;
No more from that cottage again will I roam;
Be it ever so humble, there's no place like Home.
   Home! Home! Sweet, sweet Home!
There's no place like Home! There's no place like Home!

Editing

- Did you meet the goal of this writing exercise?

- Look at your word choice. Is there a good mixture of nouns and pronouns? Is the antecedent of each pronoun clear?

- Look at your paragraphs. Are all the sentences related? Does each paragraph focus on a single topic?

97. Review: Compound and Complex Sentences

• This Week: Tanglewood Tales, The Dragon's Teeth

Remember that we use the word **compound** to show that we have two or more of something. A compound subject is two or more subjects. A compound predicate is two or more predicates. A compound sentence is one which has two or more independent clauses. Consider this sentence from "The Dragon's Teeth."

> <u>Europa</u> <u>screamed</u> with delight**, and** <u>Phœnix</u>, <u>Cilix</u>, and <u>Cadmus</u> <u>gaped</u> at their sister mounted on a white bull.

In the sentence above, there are two subject-predicate pairs, which means two clauses. Both clauses are independent. Remember that an independent clause is one which can stand alone as a complete sentence. This means that there are three correct ways to punctuate this sentence. Above, the two clauses are joined with a comma and a coordinating conjunction.

The next way to join the two clauses is to let them stand alone as two separate sentences.

> Europa screamed with delight**.** Phœnix, Cilix, and Cadmus gaped at their sister mounted on a white bull.

The final way to join the two clauses is to separate them with a semicolon.

> Europa screamed with delight**;** Phœnix, Cilix, and Cadmus gaped at their sister mounted on a white bull.

These are the only three correct ways to join independent clauses. When proper punctuation is not used, it creates a run-on sentence. These are known as run-on sentences because they continue running on even when they should have stopped.

A **fused sentence** occurs when two or more independent clauses are joined with no punctuation at all, like a person who never seems to pause for breath.

> **X** Europa screamed with delight Phœnix, Cilix, and Cadmus gaped at their sister mounted on a white bull.

A **comma splice** occurs when two or more independent clauses are joined with only a comma. The sentences are **spliced** together with a comma.

> **X** Europa screamed with delight**,** Phœnix, Cilix, and Cadmus gaped at their sister mounted on a white bull.

Definition: A complex sentence is a sentence with one independent clause and at least one dependent clause.

Independent / Dependent

"You shall never see my face again **unless** you bring me back my little Europa."

Dependent / Independent

When they reached the margin of the sand**,** the treacherous animal was already far away in the wide blue sea.

Remember, punctuating a complex sentence is simple and straightforward. When the dependent clause comes first, use a comma to separate it from the main clause. However, when the dependent clause comes after the main clause, no comma is necessary. Below are the same sentences, but I've switched the order of the clauses. Notice how the punctuation changed.

"**Unless** you bring me back my little Europa**,** you shall never see my face again."

The treacherous animal was already far away in the wide blue sea **when** they reached the margin of the sand.

A Happy Life
By Sir Henry Wotton

How happy is he born and taught
  That serveth not another's will;
Whose armour is his honest thought,
  And simple truth his utmost skill!

Whose passions not his master's are,
  Whose soul is still prepared for death,
Not tied unto the world with care
  Of public fame, or private breath.

Writing: Oral Narration
Read your new model story below, and then give your instructor an oral narration of it.

The Nile Valley

From *The Story of Mankind* by Hendrik Van Loon

The history of man is the record of a hungry creature in search of food. Wherever food was plentiful, thither man has traveled to make his home.

The fame of the Valley of the Nile must have spread at an early date. From the interior of Africa and from the desert of Arabia and from the western part of Asia people had flocked to Egypt to claim their share of the rich farms. Together these invaders had formed a new race which called itself "Remi" or "the Men" just as we sometimes call America "God's own country." They had good reason to be grateful to a Fate which had carried them to this narrow strip of land. In the summer of each year the Nile turned the valley into a shallow lake and when the waters receded all the grainfields and the pastures were covered with several inches of the most fertile clay.

In Egypt a kindly river did the work of a million men and made it possible to feed the teeming population of the first large cities of which we have any record. It is true that all the arable land was not in the valley. But a complicated system of small canals and well-sweeps carried water from the river-level to the top of the highest banks and an even more intricate system of irrigation trenches spread it throughout the land.

While man of the prehistoric age had been obliged to spend sixteen hours out of every twenty-four gathering food for himself and the members of his tribe, the Egyptian peasant or the inhabitant of the Egyptian city found himself possessed of a certain leisure. He used this spare time to make himself many things that were merely ornamental and not in the least bit useful.

More than that. One day he discovered that his brain was capable of thinking all kinds of thoughts which had nothing to do with the problems of eating and sleeping and finding a home for the children. The Egyptian began to speculate upon many strange problems that confronted him. Where did the stars come from? Who made the noise of the thunder which frightened him so terribly? Who made the River Nile rise with such regularity that it was possible to base the calendar upon the appearance and the disappearance of the annual floods? Who was he, himself, a strange little creature surrounded on all sides by death and sickness and yet happy and full of laughter?

He asked these many questions and certain people obligingly stepped forward to answer these inquiries to the best of their ability. The Egyptians called them "priests" and they became the guardians of his thoughts and gained great respect in the community. They were highly learned men who were entrusted with the sacred task of keeping the written records. They understood that it is not good for man to think only of his immediate advantage in this world and they drew his attention to the days of the future when his soul would dwell beyond the mountains of the west and must give an account of his deeds to Osiris, the mighty God who was the Ruler of the Living and the Dead and who judged the acts of men according to their merits. Indeed, the priests made so much of that future day in the realm of Isis and Osiris that the Egyptians began to regard life merely as a short preparation for the Hereafter and turned the teeming valley of the Nile into a land devoted to the Dead.

In a strange way, the Egyptians had come to believe that no soul could enter the realm of Osiris without the possession of the body which had been its place of residence in this world. Therefore as soon as a man was dead his relatives took his corpse and had it embalmed. For weeks it was soaked in a solution of natron and then it was filled with pitch. The Persian word for pitch was "Mumiai" and the embalmed body was called a "Mummy." It was wrapped in yards and yards of specially prepared linen and it was placed in a specially prepared coffin ready to be removed to its final home. But an Egyptian grave was a real home where the body was surrounded by pieces of furniture and musical instruments (to while away the dreary hours of waiting) and by little statues of cooks and bakers and barbers (that the occupant of this dark home might be decently provided with food and need not go about unshaven).

Originally these graves had been dug into the rocks of the western mountains but as the Egyptians moved northward they were obliged to build their cemeteries in the desert. The desert however is full of wild animals and equally wild robbers and they broke into the graves and disturbed the mummy or stole the jewelry that had been buried with the body. To prevent such unholy desecration the Egyptians used to build small mounds of stones on top of the graves. These little mounds gradually grew in size, because the rich people built higher mounds than the poor and there was a good deal of competition to see who could make the highest hill of stones. The record was made by King Khufu, whom the Greeks called Cheops and who lived thirty centuries before our era. His mound, which the Greeks called a pyramid (because the Egyptian word for high was pir-em-us) was over five hundred feet high.

It covered more than thirteen acres of desert which is three times as much space as that occupied by the church of St. Peter, the largest edifice of the Christian world.

During twenty years, over a hundred thousand men were busy carrying the necessary stones from the other side of the river—ferrying them across the Nile (how they ever managed to do this, we do not understand), dragging them in many instances a long distance across the desert and finally hoisting them into their correct position. But so well did the King's architects and engineers perform their task that the narrow passage-way which leads to the royal tomb in the heart of the stone monster has never yet been pushed out of shape by the weight of those thousands of tons of stone which press upon it from all sides.

Exercise

Review memory work. Below are two clauses, one dependent and one independent. Show the two ways to join them.

he ate them out of her hand

because he wanted to be friends with the child

Copy each sentence below. Double underline the predicate, and underline the subject. Put brackets around any prepositional phrases. Label the part of speech of each word. Noun, N; Proper Noun, PN; Pronoun, PRO; Verb, V; Linking Verb, LV; Adjective, ADJ; Article, ART; Conjunction, CJ; Preposition, Prep; Interjection, INJ. Diagram each sentence.

"Where are you?"

"Come back, pretty creature!"

"Bring me back my little Europa."

Commonplace Book

With your instructor's approval, add the passage below to your commonplace book, or choose your own passage from a work of fiction. This can be from either school reading or free reading.

> Never before did a bull have such bright and tender eyes, and such smooth horns of ivory, as this one. And the bull ran little races, and capered sportively around the child; so that she quite forgot how big and strong he was, and, from the gentleness and playfulness of his actions, soon came to consider him as innocent a creature as a pet lamb.

Dictation

> Nevertheless, it was the suddenness with which she had perceived the bull, rather than anything frightful in his appearance, that caused Europa so much alarm. On looking at him more attentively, she began to see that he was a beautiful animal, and even fancied a particularly amiable expression in his face. As for his breath,— the breath of cattle, you know, is always sweet,—it was as fragrant as if he had been grazing on no other food than rosebuds, or, at least, the most delicate of clover-blossoms.

98. Commas After Introductory Elements

- This Week: Tanglewood Tales, The Dragon's Teeth

Phrases and clauses which introduce sentences often need commas to separate them from the rest of the sentence. These elements include several which you've already learned to punctuate, such as nouns of direct address:

"Dear child, let me give you a ride on my back."

Interjections:

"Alas, that is only another reason why I should go with you."

And even the speaker tag, the small clause which identifies the speaker of a quotation:

The three brothers and Thasus answered, "Never! Never! Never! Never!"

These elements need commas because they disturb the flow of the main part of the sentence. At the beginning of the sentence, they are known as introductory elements.

Other types of words, phrases, and clauses can also be introductory elements in sentences, including prepositional phrases and adverbs. These elements need to be separated from the rest of the sentence by commas when they create a strong break from the rest of the sentence. Look at the following sentences from "The Dragon's Teeth." In the first sentence, the introductory element is an adverb.

<u>Indeed</u>, his motion was as light as if he were flying through the air.

In this next sentence, the introductory element is a series of prepositional phrases.

<u>At the first thought of such a thing</u>, Europa drew back.

An introductory element can also be a participle phrase, which is a phrase which begins with either a past or present participle.

<u>Frightened as she at first was</u>, you might by and by have seen Europa stroking the bull's forehead with her small white hand.

A-Tishoo

By Walter De La Mare

"Sneeze, Pretty, sneeze, Dainty,
Else the Elves will have you sure,
Sneeze, Light-of-Seven-Bright-Candles,
See they're tippeting at the door;
Their wee feet in measure falling,
All their little voices calling,
Calling, calling, calling, calling—
Sneeze, or never come no more!"
"A-tishoo!"

Elephant and Tortoise

From *South-African Folk-Tales* by James A. Honey

Giraffe and Tortoise, they say, met one day. Giraffe said to Tortoise, "At once I could trample you to death." Tortoise, being afraid, remained silent. Then Giraffe said, "At once I could swallow you." Tortoise said, in answer to this, "Well, I just belong to the family of those whom it has always been customary to swallow." Then Giraffe swallowed Tortoise; but when the latter was being gulped down, he stuck in Giraffe's throat, and as the latter could not get it down, he was choked to death.

When Giraffe was dead, Tortoise crawled out and went to Crab (who is considered as the mother of Tortoise), and told her what had happened. Then Crab said:

"The little Crab! I could sprinkle it under its arm with Boochoo,
The crooked-legged little one, I could sprinkle under its arm."

Tortoise answered its mother and said:

"Have you not always sprinkled me,
That you want to sprinkle me now?"

Then they went and fed for a whole year on the remains of Giraffe.

Writing: Outline

Write or type an outline of the new model story which you read in the last lesson.

Exercise

Review memory work. Below are two independent clauses. Show the three ways to join them.

it was delightful to witness the gratitude of this amiable bull

he capered higher than ever

Copy each sentence below. Double underline the predicate, and underline the subject. Put brackets around any prepositional phrases. Label the part of speech of each word. Noun, N; Proper Noun, PN; Pronoun, PRO; Verb, V; Linking Verb, LV; Adjective, ADJ; Article, ART; Conjunction, CJ; Preposition, Prep; Interjection, INJ. Diagram each sentence.

"Come and drive away this bull!"

Where did the bull take Europa?

King Agenor, Europa's father, said this. [Hint: **this** is a pronoun in this sentence.]

Commonplace Book

With your instructor's approval, add the poem below to your commonplace book, or choose your own poem.

> "Sneeze, Pretty, sneeze, Dainty,
> Else the Elves will have you sure,
> Sneeze, Light-of-Seven-Bright-Candles,
> See they're tippeting at the door;
> Their wee feet in measure falling,
> All their little voices calling,
> Calling, calling, calling, calling—
> Sneeze, or never come no more!"
> "A-tishoo!"

Dictation

Genesis 1:26-27

Then God said, "Let Us make man in Our image, according to Our likeness; and let them rule over the fish of the sea and over the birds of the sky and over the cattle and over all the earth, and over every creeping thing that creeps on the earth." God created man in His own image, in the image of God He created him; male and female He created them.

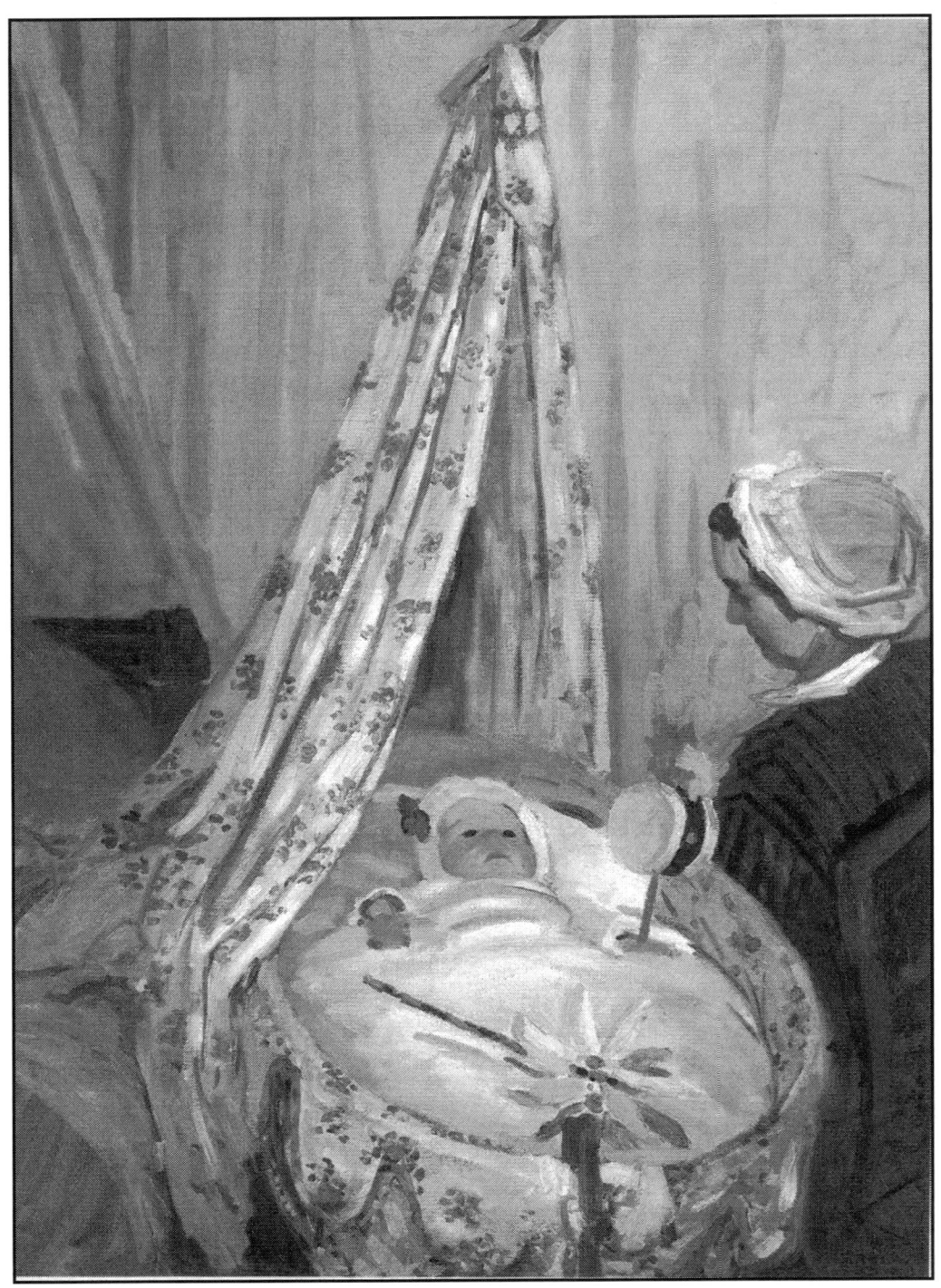

Jean Monet in the Cradle by Claude Monet

Picture Study

1. Read the title and the name of the artist. Study the picture for several minutes, then put the picture away.

2. Describe the picture.

3. Look at the picture again. Do you notice any details that you missed before? What do you like or dislike about this painting? Does it remind you of anything?

99. Literary Analysis

- This Week: Tanglewood Tales, The Dragon's Teeth

Writing: Literary Analysis

Today you have another literary analysis assignment. Now that you've had some practice, this should be a written assignment, though it can be helpful to discuss your ideas before writing.

With your instructor's approval, choose a story from *Tanglewood Tales*, or one of the other books you're currently reading, and answer the following questions.

What is the book about? Give a brief summary, just a few sentences. Was there a character that you didn't like? Why? If you liked all the characters, choose one, and tell about what you liked about him. Give examples from the story.

Annie Laurie

By William Douglas

Maxwelton braes are bonnie
Where early fa's the dew,
And it's there that Annie Laurie
Gie'd me her promise true—
Gie'd me her promise true,
Which ne'er forgot will be;
And for bonnie Annie Laurie
I'd lay me doune and dee.

Her brow is like the snawdrift,
Her throat is like the swan,
Her face it is the fairest
That e'er the sun shone on—
That e'er the sun shone on;
And dark blue is her e'e;
And for bonnie Annie Laurie
I'd lay me doune and dee.

Like dew on the gowan lying
Is the fa' o' her fairy feet;
Like the winds in summer sighing,
Her voice is low and sweet—
Her voice is low and sweet;
And she's a' the world to me;
And for bonnie Annie Laurie
I'd lay me doune and dee.

Lion and Baboon

From *South-African Folk-Tales* by James A. Honey

Baboon, it is said, once worked bamboos, sitting on the edge of a precipice, and Lion stole upon him. Baboon, however, had fixed some round, glistening, eye-like plates on the back of his head. When, therefore, Lion crept upon him, he thought, when Baboon was looking at him, that he sat with his back towards him, and crept with all his might upon him. When, however, Baboon turned his back towards him, Lion thought that he was seen, and hid himself. Thus, when Baboon looked at him, he crept upon him. When he was near him Baboon looked up, and Lion continued to creep upon him. Baboon said (aside), "Whilst I am looking at him he steals upon me, whilst my hollow eyes are on him."

When at last Lion sprung at him, he lay (quickly) down upon his face, and Lion jumped over him, falling down the precipice, and was dashed to pieces.

Exercise

Review memory work. Below are two clauses, one dependent and one independent. Show the two ways to join them.

Telephassa threw away her crown

because it chafed her forehead

Copy each sentence below. Double underline the predicate, and underline the subject. Put brackets around any prepositional phrases. Label the part of speech of each word. Noun, N; Proper Noun, PN; Pronoun, PRO; Verb, V; Linking Verb, LV; Adjective, ADJ; Article, ART; Conjunction, CJ; Preposition, Prep; Interjection, INJ. Diagram each sentence.

"Do not seek her!"

"Stop, my good cow."

"I am pretty well acquainted with the ways of cattle."
[Hint: **pretty** shows **to what extent**.]

Commonplace Book

With your instructor's approval, add the passage below to your commonplace book, or choose your own passage from a work of non-fiction. This can be from the Bible, a biography, or one of your history or science books.

> Then what a scream of terror did the poor child send forth! The three brothers screamed manfully, likewise, and ran to the shore as fast as their legs would carry them, with Cadmus at their head. But it was too late. When they reached the margin of the sand, the treacherous animal was already far away in the wide blue sea, with only his snowy head and tail emerging, and poor little Europa between them, stretching out one hand towards her dear brothers, while she grasped the bull's ivory horn with the other.

Editing

• Did you meet the goal of this writing exercise?

• Look at your word choice. Is there a good mixture of nouns and pronouns? Is the antecedent of each pronoun clear?

• Look at your paragraphs. Are all the sentences related? Does each paragraph focus on a single topic?

100. Relative Pronouns

- This Week: Tanglewood Tales, Circe's Palace

You've learned that dependent clauses can begin with subordinate conjunctions. They can also begin with **relative pronouns**. Clauses which begin with relative pronouns are called **relative clauses**.

>The relative pronouns are: that, which, whichever, who, whoever, whom, whomever, whose, whosever.

Just like clauses which begin with subordinate conjunctions, seeing a relative pronoun at the beginning of a clause is a signal that the clause cannot stand alone as a sentence. Alone, it does not express a complete thought.

The function of conjunctions, including subordinate conjunctions, is to join words and groups of words together. Pronouns, on the other hand, stand in for nouns (he, she, we), or they modify nouns (his, her, our). When a relative pronoun begins a dependent clause, the relative pronoun will either be the subject of the clause or it will modify the subject of the clause.

>This misfortune was entirely owing to the foolish curiosity of his shipmates <u>who had untied</u> some very bulky leathern bags.

>It was the same pretty little bird **whose** <u>behavior</u> had so much <u>surprised</u> Ulysses.

In the first sentence above, **who** is the subject of the relative clause. In the second sentence, **whose** is an adjective which modifies behavior.

Don't confuse relative pronouns with interrogative pronouns! Although most of the words are the same, the purpose is different. Interrogative pronouns introduce a question. Relative pronouns introduce a dependent clause, not a question.

>ature <u>Who</u> <u>sent</u> you hither?

Dream-Song

By Walter De La Mare

Sunlight, moonlight,
Twilight, starlight—
Gloaming at the close of day,
And an owl calling,
Cool dews falling
In a wood of oak and may.
Lantern-light, taper-light,
Torchlight, no-light:
Darkness at the shut of day,
And lions roaring,
Their wrath pouring
In wild waste places far away.
Elf-light, bat-light,
Touchwood-light and toad-light,
And the sea a shimmering gloom of grey,
And a small face smiling
In a dream's beguiling
In a world of wonders far away.

Lion Who Took a Woman's Shape

From *South-African Folk-Tales* by James A. Honey

Part 1.

    Some Women, it is said, went out to seek roots and herbs and other wild food. On their way home they sat down and said, "Let us taste the food of the field." Now they found that the food picked by one of them was sweet, while that of the others was bitter. The latter said to each other, "Look here! This Woman's herbs are sweet." Then they said to the owner of the sweet food, "Throw it away and seek for other." So she threw away the food, and went to gather more. When she had collected a sufficient supply, she returned to join the other Women, but could not find them. She went therefore down to the river, where Hare sat lading water, and said to him, "Hare, give me some water that I may drink." But he replied, "This is the cup out of which my uncle (Lion) and I alone may drink."

    She asked again: "Hare, draw water for me that I may drink." But Hare made the same reply. Then she snatched the cup from him and drank, but he ran home to tell his uncle of the outrage which had been committed.

    The Woman meanwhile replaced the cup and went away. After she had departed Lion came down, and, seeing her in the distance, pursued her on the road. When she turned round and saw him coming, she sang in the following manner:

    "My mother, she would not let me seek herbs,
     Herbs of the field, food from the field. Hoo!"

    When Lion at last came up with the Woman, they hunted each other round a shrub. She wore many beads and arm-rings, and Lion said, "Let me put them on!" So she lent them to him, but he afterwards refused to return them to her.

    They then hunted each other again round the shrub, till Lion fell down, and the Woman jumped upon him, and kept him there. Lion (uttering a form of conjuration) said:

"My Aunt! It is morning, and time to rise;
  Pray, rise from me!"

She then rose from him, and they hunted again after each other round the shrub, till the Woman fell down, and Lion jumped upon her. She then addressed him:

"My Uncle! It is morning, and time to rise;
  Pray, rise from me!"

He rose, of course, and they hunted each other again, till Lion fell a second time. When she jumped upon him he said:

"My Aunt! It is morning, and time to rise;
  Pray, rise from me!"

They rose again and hunted after each other. The Woman at last fell down. But this time when she repeated the above conjuration, Lion said:

"He Kha! Is it morning, and time to rise?"

He then ate her, taking care, however, to leave her skin whole, which he put on, together with her dress and ornaments, so that he looked quite like a woman, and then went home to her kraal.

When this counterfeit woman arrived, her little sister, crying, said, "My sister, pour some milk out for me." She answered, "I shall not pour you out any." Then the Child addressed their Mother: "Mama, do pour out some for me." The Mother of the kraal said, "Go to your sister, and let her give it to you!" The little Child said again to her sister, "Please, pour out for me!" She, however, repeated her refusal, saying, "I will not do it." Then the Mother of the kraal said to the little One, "I refused to let her (the elder sister) seek herbs in the field, and I do not know what may have happened; go therefore to Hare, and ask him to pour out for you."

So then Hare gave her some milk; but her elder sister said, "Come and share it with me." The little Child then went to her sister with her bamboo (cup), and they both sucked the milk out of it. Whilst they were doing this, some milk was spilt on the little one's hand, and the elder sister licked it up with her tongue, the roughness of which drew blood; this, too, the Woman licked up.

The little Child complained to her Mother: "Mama, sister pricks holes in me and sucks the blood." The Mother said, "With what Lion's nature your sister went the way that I forbade her, and returned, I do not know."

Now the Cows arrived, and the elder sister cleansed the pails in order to milk them. But when she approached the Cows with a thong (in order to tie their forelegs), they all refused to be milked by her.

Hare said, "Why do not you stand before the Cow?" She replied, "Hare, call your brother, and do you two stand before the Cow." Her husband said, "What has come over her that the Cows refuse her? These are the same Cows she always milks." The Mother (of the kraal) said, "What has happened this evening? These are Cows which she always milks without assistance. What can have affected her that she comes home as a woman with a Lion's nature?"

Writing: Copia

Take the following sentence and play with it. Remember that the point is not necessarily to make the sentence better. The point is to play with the sentence and make it different. Make a new sentence with a change from each of the following categories.

> The Egyptian began to speculate upon many strange problems that confronted him.

1. Change the grammar.
   - Change the nouns from common to proper and vice versa.
   - Change the nouns from singular to plural and vice versa.
   - Change the sentence type.
   - Change the adjectives from articles to descriptive to possessive, etc.
   - Change a quotation from direct to indirect and vice versa.
   - Change the verb tense.

2. Condense the sentence.
   - Remove details.
   - Remove modifiers.
   - Remove phrases or clauses.

3. Amplify the sentence.
   - Add details.
   - Add dialogue.
   - Add modifiers.
   - Add phrases or clauses.

4. Use synonyms and antonyms.
   - Substitute synonyms.
   - Say the opposite thing using antonyms.

5. Point of view.
   - Change the point of view.
   - Slant the sentence.

Exercise

Review memory work. Below are two clauses, one dependent and one independent. Show the two ways to join them.

> when they bade him farewell

> Phœnix shed tears

Copy each sentence below. Double underline the predicate, and underline the subject. Put brackets around any prepositional phrases. Label the part of speech of each word. Noun, N; Proper Noun, PN; Pronoun, PRO; Verb, V; Linking Verb, LV; Adjective, ADJ; Article, ART; Conjunction, CJ; Preposition, Prep; Interjection, INJ. Diagram each sentence.

"That smoke comes from the kitchen!"

A gush of smoke came from a chimney.

The palace kitchen was now very perceptible.

Commonplace Book

With your instructor's approval, add the passage below to your commonplace book, or choose your own passage from a work of fiction. This can be from either school reading or free reading.

> At length they came within full sight of the palace, which proved to be very large and lofty, with a great number of airy pinnacles upon its roof. Though it was now midday, and the sun shone brightly over the marble front, yet its snowy whiteness, and its fantastic style of architecture, made it look unreal, like the frostwork on a window-pane, or like the shapes of castles which one sees among the clouds by moonlight.

Dictation

> But, just then, a puff of wind brought down the smoke of the kitchen chimney among them, and caused each man to smell the odor of the dish that he liked best; and, after scenting it, they thought everything else moonshine, and nothing real save this palace, and save the banquet that was evidently ready to be served up in it.

101. A Poem and a Fable

- This Week: Tanglewood Tales, Circe's Palace

The Ship of State

By Henry Wadsworth Longfellow

Sail on, sail on, O Ship of State!
Sail on, O Union, strong and great!
Humanity, with all its fears,
With all the hopes of future years,
Is hanging breathless on thy fate!
We know what Master laid thy keel,
What Workmen wrought thy ribs of steel,
Who made each mast, and sail, and rope;
What anvils rang, what hammers beat,
In what a forge and what a heat
Were forged the anchors of thy hope!
Fear not each sudden sound and shock—
   'Tis of the wave, and not the rock;
   'Tis but the flapping of the sail,
And not a rent made by the gale!
In spite of rock, and tempest roar,
In spite of false lights on the shore,
Sail on, nor fear to breast the sea!
Our hearts, our hopes, are all with thee.
Our hearts, our hopes, our prayers, our tears,
Our faith, triumphant o'er our fears,
Are all with thee, are all with thee!

Lion Who Took a Woman's Shape

From *South-African Folk-Tales* by James A. Honey

Part 2.

The elder daughter then said to her Mother, "I shall not milk the Cows." With these words she sat down. The Mother said therefore to Hare, "Bring me the bamboos, that I may milk. I do not know what has come over the girl."

So the Mother herself milked the cows, and when she had done so, Hare brought the bamboos to the young wife's house, where her husband was, but she (the wife) did not give him (her husband) anything to eat. But when at night time she fell asleep, they saw some of the Lion's hair, which was hanging out where he had slipped on the Woman's skin, and they cried, "Verily! This is quite another being. It is for this reason that the Cows refused to be milked."

Then the people of the kraal began to break up the hut in which Lion lay asleep. When they took off the mats, they said (conjuring them), "If thou art favorably inclined to me, O Mat, give the sound 'sawa'" (meaning, making no noise).

To the poles (on which the hut rested) they said, "If thou art favorably inclined to me, O Pole, thou must give the sound 'gara.'"

They addressed also the bamboos and the bed-skins in a similar manner.

Thus gradually and noiselessly they removed the hut and all its contents. Then they took bunches of grass, put them over the Lion, and lighting them, said, "If thou art favorably inclined to me, O Fire, thou must flare up, 'boo boo,' before thou comest to the heart."

So the Fire flared up when it came towards the heart, and the heart of the Woman jumped upon the ground. The Mother (of the kraal) picked it up, and put it into a calabash.

Lion, from his place in the fire, said to the Mother (of the kraal), "How nicely I have eaten your daughter." The Woman answered, "You have also now a comfortable place!"

Now the Woman took the first milk of as many Cows as had calves, and put it into the calabash where her daughter's heart was; the calabash increased in size, and in proportion to this the girl grew again inside it.

One day, when the Mother (of the kraal) went out to fetch wood, she said to Hare, "By the time that I come back you must have everything nice and clean." But during her Mother's absence, the girl crept out of the calabash, and put the hut in good order, as she had been used to do in former days, and said to Hare, "When Mother comes back and asks, 'Who has done these things?' you must say, 'I, Hare, did them.'" After she had done all, she hid herself on the stage.

When the Mother of the kraal came home, she said, "Hare, who has done these things? They look just as they used when my daughter did them." Hare said, "I did the things." But the Mother would not believe it, and looked at the calabash. Seeing it was empty, she searched the stage and found her daughter. Then she embraced and kissed her, and from that day the girl stayed with her Mother, and did everything as she was wont in former times; but she now remained unmarried.

Exercise

Review memory work. Below are two independent clauses. Show the three ways to join them.

> they could think of nothing but their greedy appetite
>
> they resembled those vilest of animals far more than they did kings

Copy each sentence below. Double underline the predicate, and underline the subject. Put brackets around any prepositional phrases. Label the part of speech of each word. Noun, N; Proper Noun, PN; Pronoun, PRO; Verb, V; Linking Verb, LV; Adjective, ADJ; Article, ART; Conjunction, CJ; Preposition, Prep; Interjection, INJ. Diagram each sentence.

> They saw their own figures in different colored threads.
>
> "Ha! Do you smell the feast?"
>
> Serving men brought them dishes of the richest food.

Writing: Commonplace Book

Add the passage below from your model story to your commonplace book.

> The Egyptian began to speculate upon many strange problems that confronted him. Where did the stars come from? Who made the noise of the thunder which frightened him so terribly? Who made the River Nile rise with such regularity that it was possible to base the calendar upon the appearance and the disappearance of the annual floods? Who was he, himself, a strange little creature surrounded on all sides by death and sickness and yet happy and full of laughter?

Dictation

Use part of today's poem for dictation.

102. Historical Narration: The Nile Valley

- This Week: Tanglewood Tales, Circe's Palace

Remember that with a historical topic, you should report the facts without making up new content or adding details.

The **purpose** of your paper is what you wish to accomplish with your writing. Your purpose is to **inform** your reader about this topic.

The Landing of the Pilgrims

By Felicia Hemans

The breaking waves dashed high
  On a stern and rock-bound coast,
And the woods against a stormy sky
  Their giant branches tossed.

And the heavy night hung dark
  The hills and waters o'er,
When a band of exiles moored their bark
  On the wild New England shore.

Not as the conqueror comes,
  They, the true-hearted, came;
Not with the roll of the stirring drums,
  And the trumpet that sings of fame.

Not as the flying come,
  In silence and in fear;
They shook the depths of the desert gloom
  With their hymns of lofty cheer.

Amid the storm they sang,
  And the stars heard, and the sea,
And the sounding aisles of the dim woods rang
  To the anthem of the free!

The ocean eagle soared
  From his nest by the white wave's foam;
And the rocking pines of the forest roared,—
  This was their welcome home!

There were men with hoary hair,
  Amid that pilgrim band;
Why had *they* come to wither there,
  Away from their childhood's land?

There was woman's fearless eye,
  Lit by her deep love's truth;
There was manhood's brow serenely high,
  And the fiery heart of youth.

What sought they thus afar?
  Bright jewels of the mine?
The wealth of seas, the spoils of war?—
  They sought a faith's pure shrine!

Ay! Call it holy ground,
  The soil where first they trod:
They have left unstained what there they found,
  Freedom to worship God.

Editing

• Did you meet the goal of this writing exercise?

• Look at your word choice. Is there a good mixture of nouns and pronouns? Is the antecedent of each pronoun clear?

• Look at your paragraphs. Are all the sentences related? Does each paragraph focus on a single topic?

103. Sit and Set

- This Week: Tanglewood Tales, The Pomegranate Seeds

Today we're going to talk about the verbs **to sit** and **to set**. Because these words are so similar, many people get them confused.

To sit means to place oneself in a seated position. You **sit** on your chair or couch. The verb **sit** never has a direct object. It's something that a subject does to himself.

To sit is an irregular verb. Look at the five principal parts of **sit**:

Infinitive	Present	Present Participle	Past	Past Participle
to sit	sit	sitting	sat	sat

Look at the following examples of **sit** from "The Pomegranate Seeds."

"I will sit on the footstool."

"What, the young man that always sits in the sunshine?

In the chariot sat the figure of a man.

Still she continued her search without sitting down to rest.

To set means to place, arrange, or leave something. The verb **set** always has a direct object. It's something the subject does to the direct object.

Look at the five principal parts of **set**:

Infinitive	Present	Present Participle	Past	Past Participle
to set	set	setting	set	set

Look at the following examples of **set** from "The Pomegranate Seeds." Notice how you could replace the form of **set** in these sentences with a form of **place** or another of its synonyms.

"I shall never smile again till you <u>set</u> me down at my mother's door."

She <u>set</u> forth resolving never to come back until Proserpina was discovered.

He immediately set up a grievous cry.

Pluto bade them lose no time in preparing a most sumptuous banquet, and not to fail of <u>setting</u> a golden beaker of the water of Lethe by Proserpina's plate.

America

By Samuel Francis Smith

My country, 'tis of thee,
Sweet land of liberty,
Of thee I sing;
Land where my fathers died,
Land of the Pilgrims' pride;
From every mountain side,
Let freedom ring.

My native country, thee—
Land of the noble free—
Thy name I love;
I love thy rocks and rills,
Thy woods and templed hills;
My heart with rapture thrills,
Like that above.

Let music swell the breeze,
And ring from all the trees
Sweet freedom's song;
Let mortal tongues awake;
Let all that breathe partake;
Let rocks their silence break—
The sound prolong.

Our fathers' God, to Thee,
Author of liberty,
To Thee we sing:

Long may our land be bright
With freedom's holy light:
Protect us by Thy might,
Great God, our King.

Writing: Oral Narration

Read your new model story below, and then give your instructor an oral narration of it.

Greek Life

From *The Story of Mankind* by Hendrik Van Loon

But how, you will ask, did the ancient Greeks have time to look after their families and their business if they were forever running to the market-place to discuss affairs of state? In this chapter I shall tell you.

In all matters of government, the Greek democracy recognized only one class of citizens—the freemen. Every Greek city was composed of a small number of free born citizens, a large number of slaves and a sprinkling of foreigners.

At rare intervals (usually during a war, when men were needed for the army) the Greeks showed themselves willing to confer the rights of citizenship upon the "barbarians" as they called the foreigners. But this was an exception. Citizenship was a matter of birth. You were an Athenian because your father and your grandfather had been Athenians before you. But however great your merits as a trader or a soldier, if you were born of non-Athenian parents, you remained a "foreigner" until the end of time.

The Greek city, therefore, whenever it was not ruled by a king or a tyrant, was run by and for the freemen, and this would not have been possible without a large army of slaves who outnumbered the free citizens at the rate of six or five to one and who performed those tasks to which we modern people must devote most of our time and energy if we wish to provide for our families and pay the rent of our apartments. The slaves did all the cooking and baking and candlestick making of the entire city. They were the tailors and the carpenters and the jewelers and the school-teachers and the bookkeepers and they tended the store and looked after the factory while the master went to the public meeting to discuss questions of war and peace or visited the theatre to see the latest play of AEschylus or hear a discussion of the revolutionary ideas of Euripides, who had dared to express certain doubts upon the omnipotence of the great god Zeus.

Indeed, ancient Athens resembled a modern club. All the freeborn citizens were hereditary members and all the slaves were hereditary servants, and waited upon the needs of their masters, and it was very pleasant to be a member of the organization.

But when we talk about slaves, we do not mean the sort of people about whom you have read in the pages of "Uncle Tom's Cabin." It is true that the position of those slaves who tilled the fields was a very unpleasant one, but the average freeman who had come down in the world and who had been obliged to hire himself out as a farm hand led just as miserable a life. In the cities, furthermore, many of the slaves were more prosperous than the poorer classes of the freemen. For the Greeks, who loved moderation in all things, did not like to treat their slaves after the fashion which afterward was so common in Rome, where a slave had as few rights as an engine in a modern factory and could be thrown to the wild animals upon the smallest pretext.

The Greeks accepted slavery as a necessary institution, without which no city could possibly become the home of a truly civilized people.

The slaves also took care of those tasks which nowadays are performed by the business men and the professional men. As for those household duties which take up so much of the time of your mother and which worry your father when he comes home from his office, the Greeks, who understood the value of leisure, had reduced such duties to the smallest possible minimum by living amidst surroundings of extreme simplicity.

To begin with, their homes were very plain. Even the rich nobles spent their lives in a sort of adobe barn, which lacked all the comforts which a modern workman expects as his natural right. A Greek home consisted of four walls and a roof. There was a door which led into the street but there were no windows. The kitchen, the living rooms and the sleeping quarters were built around an open courtyard in which there was a small fountain, or a statue and a few plants to make it look bright. Within this courtyard the family lived when it did not rain or when it was not too cold. In one corner of the yard the cook (who was a slave) prepared the meal and in another corner, the teacher (who was also a slave) taught the children the alpha beta gamma and the tables of multiplication and in still another corner the lady of the house, who rarely left her domain (since it was not considered good form for a married woman to be seen on the street too often) was repairing her husband's coat with her seamstresses (who were slaves,) and in the little office, right off the door, the master was inspecting the accounts which the overseer of his farm (who was a slave) had just brought to him.

When dinner was ready the family came together but the meal was a very simple one and did not take much time. The Greeks seem to have regarded eating as an unavoidable evil and not a pastime, which kills many dreary hours and eventually kills many dreary people. They lived on bread and on wine, with a little meat and some green vegetables. They drank water only when nothing else was available because they did not think it very healthy. They loved to call on each other for dinner, but our idea of a festive meal, where everybody is supposed to eat much more than is good for him, would have disgusted them. They came together at the table for the purpose of a good talk and a good glass of wine and water, but as they were moderate people they despised those who drank too much.

The same simplicity which prevailed in the dining room also dominated their choice of clothes. They liked to be clean and well groomed, to have their hair and beards neatly cut, to feel their bodies strong with the exercise and the swimming of the gymnasium, but they never followed the Asiatic fashion which prescribed loud colors and strange patterns. They wore a long white coat and they managed to look as smart as a modern Italian officer in his long blue cape.

They loved to see their wives wear ornaments but they thought it very vulgar to display their wealth (or their wives) in public and whenever the women left their home they were as inconspicuous as possible.

In short, the story of Greek life is a story not only of moderation but also of simplicity. "Things," chairs and tables and books and houses and carriages, are apt to take up a great deal of their owner's time. In the end they invariably make him their slave and his hours are spent looking after their wants, keeping them polished and brushed and painted. The Greeks, before everything else, wanted to be "free," both in mind and in body. That they might maintain their liberty, and be truly free in spirit, they reduced their daily needs to the lowest possible point.

Exercise

Review memory work. Below are two clauses, one dependent and one independent. Show the two ways to join them.

> I will not taste a morsel of food
>
> even if you keep me forever in your palace

Copy each sentence below. Double underline the predicate, and underline the subject. Put brackets around any prepositional phrases. Label the part of speech of each word. Noun, N; Proper Noun, PN; Pronoun, PRO; Verb, V; Linking Verb, LV; Adjective, ADJ; Article, ART; Conjunction, CJ; Preposition, Prep; Interjection, INJ. Diagram each sentence.

> They prepared her a sumptuous banquet.
>
> "You are a spoiled child, my little Proserpina."
>
> "Will the dog bite me?"

Commonplace Book

With your instructor's approval, add the passage below to your commonplace book, or choose your own passage from a work of fiction. This can be from either school reading or free reading.

> King Pluto had taken a road which now began to grow excessively gloomy. It was bordered on each side with rocks and precipices, between which the rumbling of the chariot-wheels was reverberated with a noise like rolling thunder. The trees and bushes that grew in the crevices of the rocks had very dismal foliage; and by and by, although it was hardly noon, the air became obscured with a gray twilight.

Dictation

> The black horses had rushed along so swiftly, that they were already beyond the limits of the sunshine. But the duskier it grew, the more did Pluto's visage assume an air of satisfaction. After all, he was not an ill-looking person, especially when he left off twisting his features into a smile that did not belong to them. Proserpina peeped at his face through the gathering dusk, and hoped that he might not be so very wicked as she at first thought him.

104. Lie and Lay

- This Week: Tanglewood Tales, The Pomegranate Seeds

Today we're going to talk about the verbs **to lie** and **to lay**. These are very similar to **sit** and **set**, both in meaning and confusion.

To lie means to place oneself in a prone, lying down position. You **lie** on your bed. The verb **lie** never has a direct object. It's something that a subject does to himself, not something the subject does to something.

To lie is an irregular verb. Look at the five principal parts of **lie**:

Infinitive	Present	Present Participle	Past	Past Participle
to lie	lie	lying	lay	lain

Lay is the past tense of this irregular verb.

Look at the following examples of **lie** from *Tanglewood Tales*.

"We may as well <u>lie</u> down on a bank of soft sponge, under the water."

She could perceive no token of the child's being injured by the hot fire in which he had <u>lain</u>.

All the pleasure she had, you know, <u>lay</u> in being miserable.

The cow was staring leisurely about her, as other cows do when on the point of <u>lying</u> down.

To lay means to place, arrange, set, or leave something. The verb **lay** always has a direct object. It's something the subject does to the direct object.

Look at the five principal parts of **lay**:

Infinitive	Present	Present Participle	Past	Past Participle
to lay	lay	laying	laid	laid

Lay is the present tense of this irregular verb.

Look at the following examples of **lay** from *Tanglewood Tales*. Notice how you could replace the form of **lay** in these sentences with a form of **place** or another of its synonyms.

> Medea stayed only long enough to take her son with her, and to steal whatever valuable things she could lay hands on.

> They were talking of these schemes, and beguiling the tediousness of the way with laying out the plan of the new city.

> Ceres suddenly laid him, all naked as he was, in the hollow among the red-hot embers.

The Lotos-Eaters

By Alfred Tennyson

"Courage!" he said, and pointed toward the land,
"This mounting wave will roll us shoreward soon."
In the afternoon they came unto a land
In which it seemed always afternoon.
All round the coast the languid air did swoon,
Breathing like one that hath a weary dream.
Full-faced above the valley stood the moon;
And like a downward smoke, the slender stream
Along the cliff to fall and pause and fall did seem.

A land of streams! Some, like a downward smoke,
Slow-dropping veils of thinnest lawn, did go;
And some thro' wavering lights and shadows broke,
Rolling a slumbrous sheet of foam below.
They saw the gleaming river seaward flow
From the inner land: far off, three mountain-tops,
Three silent pinnacles of aged snow,
Stood sunset-flush'd: and, dew'd with showery drops,
Up-clomb the shadowy pine above the woven copse.

The charmed sunset linger'd low adown
In the red West: thro' mountain clefts the dale
Was seen far inland, and the yellow down
Border'd with palm, and many a winding vale
And meadow, set with slender galingale;

A land where all things always seem'd the same!
And round about the keel with faces pale,
Dark faces pale against that rosy flame,
The mild-eyed melancholy Lotos-eaters came.

Branches they bore of that enchanted stem,
Laden with flower and fruit, whereof they gave
To each, but whoso did receive of them,
And taste, to him the gushing of the wave
Far, far away did seem to mourn and rave
On alien shores; and if his fellow spake,
His voice was thin, as voices from the grave;
And deep-asleep he seem'd, yet all awake,
And music in his ears his beating heart did make.

They sat them down upon the yellow sand,
Between the sun and moon upon the shore;
And sweet it was to dream of Fatherland,
Of child, and wife, and slave; but evermore
Most weary seem'd the sea, weary the oar,
Weary the wandering fields of barren foam.
Then some one said, "We will return no more;"
And all at once they sang, "Our island home
Is far beyond the wave; we will no longer roam."

How Wisdom Became the Property of the Human Race

From *West African Folk-Tales* by William H. Barker

There once lived, in Fanti-land, a man named Father Anansi. He possessed all the wisdom in the world. People came to him daily for advice and help.

One day the men of the country were unfortunate enough to offend Father Anansi, who immediately resolved to punish them. After much thought he decided that the severest penalty he could inflict would be to hide all his wisdom from them. He set to work at once to gather again all that he had already given. When he had succeeded, as he thought, in collecting it, he placed all in one great pot. This he carefully sealed, and determined to put it in a spot where no human being could reach it.

Now, Father Anansi had a son, whose name was Kweku Tsin. This boy began to suspect his father of some secret design, so he made up his mind to watch carefully. Next day he saw his father quietly slip out of the house, with his precious pot hung round his neck. Kweku Tsin followed. Father Anansi went through the forest till he had left the village far behind. Then, selecting the highest and most inaccessible-looking tree, he began to climb. The heavy pot, hanging in front of him, made his ascent almost impossible. Again and again he tried to reach the top of the tree, where he intended to hang the pot. There, he thought, Wisdom would indeed be beyond the reach of every one but himself. He was unable, however, to carry out his desire. At each trial the pot swung in his way.

For some time Kweku Tsin watched his father's vain attempts. At last, unable to contain himself any longer, he cried out: "Father, why do you not hang the pot on your back? Then you could easily climb the tree."

Father Anansi turned and said: "I thought I had all the world's wisdom in this pot. But I find you possess more than I do. All my wisdom was insufficient to show me what to do, yet you have been able to tell me." In his anger he threw the pot down. It struck on a great rock and broke. The wisdom contained in it escaped and spread throughout the world.

Writing: Outline

Write or type an outline of the new model story which you read in the last lesson.

Exercise

Review memory work. Copy each sentence below. Double underline the predicate, and underline the subject. Put brackets around any prepositional phrases. Label the part of speech of each word. Noun, N; Proper Noun, PN; Pronoun, PRO; Verb, V; Linking Verb, LV; Adjective, ADJ; Article, ART; Conjunction, CJ; Preposition, Prep; Interjection, INJ. Diagram each sentence.

"Where is Proserpina?"

"Tell me, you naughty sea-nymphs."

"I once had a child of my own."

Commonplace Book

With your instructor's approval, add the poem below to your commonplace book, or choose your own poem.

"Courage!" he said, and pointed toward the land,
"This mounting wave will roll us shoreward soon."
In the afternoon they came unto a land
In which it seemed always afternoon.
All round the coast the languid air did swoon,
Breathing like one that hath a weary dream.
Full-faced above the valley stood the moon;
And like a downward smoke, the slender stream
Along the cliff to fall and pause and fall did seem.

Dictation

Ephesians 1:3-4

Blessed be the God and Father of our Lord Jesus Christ, who has blessed us with every spiritual blessing in the heavenly places in Christ, just as He chose us in Him before the foundation of the world, that we would be holy and blameless before Him.

Madame Monet and Child by Claude Monet

Picture Study

1. Read the title and the name of the artist. Study the picture for several minutes, then put the picture away.

2. Describe the picture.

3. Look at the picture again. Do you notice any details that you missed before? What do you like or dislike about this painting? Does it remind you of anything?

105. Descriptive Writing

- This Week: Tanglewood Tales, The Pomegranate Seeds

Writing: Descriptive Writing

Remember that the purpose of descriptive writing is to describe a person, place, thing, or event so well that an image forms in the mind of the reader.

Your last six picture studies have been on paintings by Claude Monet. Today, choose one of his paintings, either one from this book or one from another source, and write a description of it. Imagine that you're describing the picture to someone who has never seen it before. Get creative if you wish. Write a description for a museum catalog, or as part of a police report describing stolen merchandise. Or get really creative. Imagine that the painting is a window to another dimension, and you've just been pulled in. Describe the environment in which you find yourself. Or, write a story about the picture, or about your experiences within it. Be as creative as you want. Just don't forget to describe the picture

Moly

By Edith M. Thomas

Traveler, pluck a stem of moly,
If thou touch at Circe's isle,—
Hermes' moly, growing solely
To undo enchanter's wile!
When she proffers thee her chalice,—
Wine and spices mixed with malice,—
When she smites thee with her staff
To transform thee, do thou laugh!
Safe thou art if thou but bear
The least leaf of moly rare.
Close it grows beside her portal,
Springing from a stock immortal,
Yes! And often has the Witch
Sought to tear it from its niche;
But to thwart her cruel will
The wise God renews it still.
Though it grows in soil perverse,

Heaven hath been its jealous nurse,
And a flower of snowy mark
Springs from root and sheathing dark;
Kingly safeguard, only herb
That can brutish passion curb!
Some do think its name should be
Shield-Heart, White Integrity.
Traveler, pluck a stem of moly,
If thou touch at Circe's isle,—
Hermes' moly, growing solely
To undo enchanter's wile!

When Lion Could Fly

From *South-African Folk-Tales* by James A. Honey

Lion, it is said, used once to fly, and at that time nothing could live before him. As he was unwilling that the bones of what he caught should be broken into pieces, he made a pair of White Crows watch the bones, leaving them behind at the kraal whilst he went a-hunting. But one day Great Frog came there, broke the bones in pieces, and said, "Why can men and animals live no longer?" And he added these words, "When he comes, tell him that I live at yonder pool; if he wishes to see me, he must come there."

Lion, lying in wait (for game), wanted to fly up, but found he could not fly. Then he got angry, thinking that at the kraal something was wrong, and returned home. When he arrived he asked, "What have you done that I cannot fly?" Then they answered and said, "Some one came here, broke the bones into pieces, and said, 'If he want me, he may look for me at yonder pool!'" Lion went, and arrived while Frog was sitting at the water's edge, and he tried to creep stealthily upon him. When he was about to get hold of him, Frog said, "Ho!" and, diving, went to the other side of the pool, and sat there. Lion pursued him; but as he could not catch him he returned home.

From that day, it is said, Lion walked on his feet, and also began to creep upon (his game); and the White Crows became entirely dumb since the day that they said, "Nothing can be said of that matter."

Exercise

Review memory work. Identify each group of words below as either a phrase or a clause. If it is a clause, double underline the predicate and underline the subject.

which I may judge proper for him

what the nurse did to her child

flinging a warm and ruddy light upon the walls

Copy each sentence below. Double underline the predicate, and underline the subject. Put brackets around any prepositional phrases. Label the part of speech of each word. Noun, N; Proper Noun, PN; Pronoun, PRO; Verb, V; Linking Verb, LV; Adjective, ADJ; Article, ART; Conjunction, CJ; Preposition, Prep; Interjection, INJ. Diagram each sentence.

Queen Metanira, his mother, shrieked.

The little damsel was not so unhappy.

"Hasten home to your dear mother." [Hint: **home** tells where.]

Commonplace Book

With your instructor's approval, add the passage below to your commonplace book, or choose your own passage from a work of non-fiction. This can be from the Bible, a biography, or one of your history or science books.

> So she took up the pomegranate, and applied it to her nose; and, somehow or other, being in such close neighborhood to her mouth, the fruit found its way into that little red cave. Dear me! What an everlasting pity! Before Proserpina knew what she was about, her teeth had actually bitten it, of their own accord. Just as this fatal deed was done, the door of the apartment opened, and in came King Pluto, followed by Quicksilver, who had been urging him to let his little prisoner go.

Editing

• Did you meet the goal of this writing exercise?

• Look at your word choice. Is there a good mixture of nouns and pronouns? Is the antecedent of each pronoun clear?

• Look at your paragraphs. Are all the sentences related? Does each paragraph focus on a single topic?

106. Well and Good

- This Week: Tanglewood Tales, The Golden Fleece

Good is an adjective. That means it modifies nouns and pronouns.

Well is usually an adverb. That means it can modify verbs, adjectives, and other adverbs. But sometimes, it acts as an adjective. When it's used as an adjective, it means to be in good health.

When you need to decide whether to describe something as **good** or **well**, determine what part of speech the word you're describing is. In the following examples, I've underlined **good** or **well** and the word it modifies in the sentence.

The hot cocoa was good this morning. You made it well.

How are you today? I am good. I am doing well.
(Note: In the second sentence, **good** modifies the pronoun **I**. In the third sentence, **well** modifies the verb **am doing**.)

Are you feeling ill? No, I am well.
(Note: In the second sentence, **well** modifies the pronoun **I**; it is acting as the adjective that means good health.)

Few have gotten a good look at a Sasquatch. The Sasquatch hides well.

Your behavior was good. You behaved well.

The Stranger

By Walter De La Mare

In the nook of a wood where a pool freshed with dew
Glassed, daybreak till evening, blue sky glimpsing through
Then a star; or a slip of May-moon silver-white,
Thridding softly aloof the quiet of night,
Was a thicket of flowers.
Willow herb, mint, pale speedwell and rattle
Water hemlock and sundew—to the wind's tittle-tattle

They nodded, dreamed, swayed in jocund delight,
In beauty and sweetness arrayed, still and bright.
By turn scampered rabbit; trotted fox; bee and bird
Paused droning, sang shrill, and the fair water stirred.
Plashed green frog, or some brisk little flickering fish—
Gudgeon, stickleback, minnow—set the ripples a-swish.
A lone pool, a pool grass-fringed, crystal-clear:
Deep, placid, and cool in the sweet of the year;
Edge-parched when the sun to the Dog Days drew near;
And with winter's bleak rime hard as glass, robed in snow,
The whole wild-wood sleeping, and nothing a-blow
But the wind from the North—bringing snow.
That is all. Save that one long, sweet, June night-tide straying,
The harsh hemlock's pale umbelliferous bloom
Tenting nook, dense with fragrance and secret with gloom,
In a beaming of moon-colored light faintly raying,
On buds orbed with dew phosphorescently playing,
Came a Stranger—still-footed, feat-fingered, clear face
Unhumanly lovely: ... and supped in that place.

How We Got the Name "Spider Tales"

From *West African Folk-Tales* by William H. Barker

In the olden days all the stories which men told were stories of Nyankupon, the chief of the gods. Spider, who was very conceited, wanted the stories to be told about him.

Accordingly, one day he went to Nyankupon and asked that, in future, all tales told by men might be Anansi stories, instead of Nyankupon stories. Nyankupon agreed, on one condition. He told Spider (or Anansi) that he must bring him three things: the first was a jar full of live bees, the second was a boa-constrictor, and the third a tiger. Spider gave his promise.

He took an earthen vessel and set out for a place where he knew were numbers of bees. When he came in sight of the bees he began saying to himself, "They will not be able to fill this jar"—"Yes, they will be able"—"No, they will not be able," until the bees came up to him and said, "What are you talking about, Mr. Anansi?" He thereupon explained to them that Nyankupon and he had had a great dispute. Nyankupon had said the bees could not fly into the jar—Anansi had said they could. The bees immediately declared that of course they could fly into the jar—which they at once did. As soon as they were safely inside, Anansi sealed up the jar and sent it off to Nyankupon.

Next day he took a long stick and set out in search of a boa-constrictor. When he arrived at the place where one lived he began speaking to himself again. "He will just be as long as this stick"—"No, he will not be so long as this"—"Yes, he will be as long as this." These words he repeated several times, till the boa came out and asked him what was the matter. "Oh, we have been having a dispute in Nyankupon's town about you. Nyankupon's people say you are not as long as this stick. I say you are. Please let me measure you by it." The boa innocently laid himself out straight, and Spider lost no time in tying him on to the stick from end to end. He then sent him to Nyankupon.

The third day he took a needle and thread and sewed up his eye. He then set out for a den where he knew a tiger lived. As he approached the place he began to shout and sing so loudly that the tiger came out to see what was the matter. "Can you not see?" said Spider. "My eye is sewn up and now I can see such wonderful things that I must sing about them." "Sew up my eyes," said the tiger, "then I too can see these surprising sights." Spider immediately did so. Having thus made the tiger helpless, he led him straight to Nyankupon's house. Nyankupon was amazed at Spider's cleverness in fulfilling the three conditions. He immediately gave him permission for the future to call all the old tales Anansi tales.

Writing: Copia

Take the following sentence and play with it. Remember that the point is not necessarily to make the sentence better. The point is to play with the sentence and make it different. Make a new sentence with a change from each of the following categories.

> When dinner was ready the family came together but the meal was a very simple one and did not take much time.

1. Change the grammar.
    - Change the nouns from common to proper and vice versa.
    - Change the nouns from singular to plural and vice versa.
    - Change the sentence type.
    - Change the adjectives from articles to descriptive to possessive, etc.
    - Change a quotation from direct to indirect and vice versa.
    - Change the verb tense.

2. Condense the sentence.
    - Remove details.
    - Remove modifiers.
    - Remove phrases or clauses.

3. Amplify the sentence.
    - Add details.
    - Add dialogue.
    - Add modifiers.
    - Add phrases or clauses.

4. Use synonyms and antonyms.
    - Substitute synonyms.
    - Say the opposite thing using antonyms.

5. Point of view.
    - Change the point of view.
    - Slant the sentence.

Exercise

Review memory work. Identify each group of words below as either a phrase or a clause. If it is a clause, double underline the predicate and underline the subject.

> when the old dame and her peacock were out of sight
>
> over her shoulder as she departed
>
> after traveling a pretty long distance

Copy each sentence below. Double underline the predicate, and underline the subject. Put brackets around any prepositional phrases. Label the part of speech of each word. Noun, N; Proper Noun, PN; Pronoun, PRO; Verb, V; Linking Verb, LV; Adjective, ADJ; Article, ART; Conjunction, CJ; Preposition, Prep; Interjection, INJ. Diagram each sentence.

> Argus, the ship builder, built him a galley with fifty oars.
>
> "We are the subjects of King Pelias."
>
> Jason the one-sandaled man had come.

Commonplace Book

With your instructor's approval, add the passage below to your commonplace book, or choose your own passage from a work of fiction. This can be from either school reading or free reading.

> "You will get a handsomer pair of sandals by and by," said the old woman, with a kindly look out of her beautiful brown eyes. "Only let King Pelias get a glimpse of that bare foot, and you shall see him turn as pale as ashes, I promise you. There is your path. Go along, my good Jason, and my blessing go with you. And when you sit on your throne, remember the old woman whom you helped over the river."

Dictation

> With these words, she hobbled away, giving him a smile over her shoulder as she departed. Whether the light of her beautiful brown eyes threw a glory round about her, or whatever the cause might be, Jason fancied that there was something very noble and majestic in her figure, after all, and that, though her gait seemed to be a rheumatic hobble, yet she moved with as much grace and dignity as any queen on earth. Her peacock, which had now fluttered down from her shoulder, strutted behind her in prodigious pomp, and spread out its magnificent tail on purpose for Jason to admire it.

107. A Poem and a Fable

- This Week: Tanglewood Tales, The Golden Fleece

A Name in the Sand

By Hannah Flagg Gould

Alone I walked the ocean strand;
A pearly shell was in my hand:
I stooped and wrote upon the sand
  My name—the year—the day.
As onward from the spot I passed,
One lingering look behind I cast;
A wave came rolling high and fast,
  And washed my lines away.

And so, methought, 'twill shortly be
With every mark on earth from me:
A wave of dark oblivion's sea
  Will sweep across the place
Where I have trod the sandy shore
Of time, and been, to be no more,
Of me—my day—the name I bore,
  To leave nor track nor trace.

And yet, with Him who counts the sands
And holds the waters in His hands,
I know a lasting record stands
  Inscribed against my name,
Of all this mortal part has wrought,
Of all this thinking soul has thought,
And from these fleeting moments caught
  For glory or for shame.

The Squirrel and the Spider

From *West African Folk-Tales* by William H. Barker

A hard-working squirrel had, after much labor, succeeded in cultivating a very fine farm. Being a skilful climber of trees, he had not troubled to make a roadway into his farm. He used to reach it by the trees.

One day, when his harvests were very nearly ripe, it happened that Spider went out hunting in that neighborhood. During his travels, he arrived at Squirrel's farm. Greatly pleased at the appearance of the fields, he sought for the roadway to it. Finding none, he returned home and told his family all about the matter. The very next day they all set out for this fine place, and set to work immediately to make a road. When this was completed Spider—who was very cunning—threw pieces of earthenware pot along the pathway. This he did to make believe that his children had dropped them while working to prepare the farm.

Then he and his family began to cut down and carry away such of the corn as was ripe. Squirrel noticed that his fields were being robbed, but could not at first find the thief. He determined to watch. Sure enough Spider soon reappeared to steal more of the harvest. Squirrel demanded to know what right he had on these fields. Spider immediately asked him the same question. "They are my fields," said Squirrel. "Oh, no! They are mine," retorted Spider. "I dug them and sowed them and planted them," said poor Squirrel. "Then where is your roadway to them?" said crafty Spider. "I need no roadway. I come by the trees," was Squirrel's reply. Needless to say, Spider laughed such an answer to scorn, and continued to use the farm as his own.

Squirrel appealed to the law, but the court decided that no one had ever had a farm without a road leading to it, therefore the fields must be Spider's.

In great glee Spider and his family prepared to cut down all the harvest that remained. When it was cut they tied it in great bundles and set off to the nearest market-place to sell it. When they were about half-way there, a terrible storm came on. They were obliged to put down their burdens by the roadside and run for shelter. When the storm had passed they returned to pick up their loads.

As they approached the spot they found a great, black crow there, with his broad wings outspread to keep the bundles dry. Spider went to him and very politely thanked him for so kindly taking care of their property. "Your property!" replied Father Crow. "Who ever heard of any one leaving bundles of corn by the roadside? Nonsense! These loads are mine." So saying, he picked them up and, went off with them, leaving Spider and his children to return home sorrowful and empty-handed. Their thieving ways had brought them little profit.

Writing: Commonplace Book

Add the passage below from your model story to your commonplace book.

> When dinner was ready the family came together but the meal was a very simple one and did not take much time. The Greeks seem to have regarded eating as an unavoidable evil and not a pastime, which kills many dreary hours and eventually kills many dreary people. They lived on bread and on wine, with a little meat and some green vegetables. They drank water only when nothing else was available because they did not think it very healthy.

Dictation

Use part of today's poem for dictation.

108. Historical Narration: Greek Life

- This Week: Tanglewood Tales, The Golden Fleece

Remember that with a historical topic, you should report the facts without making up new content or adding details.

The **purpose** of your paper is what you wish to accomplish with your writing. Your purpose is to **inform** your reader about this topic.

The Three Beggars

By Walter De La Mare

'Twas autumn daybreak gold and wild,
While past St. Ann's grey tower they shuffled,
Three beggars spied a fairy-child
In crimson mantle muffled.
The daybreak lighted up her face
All pink, and sharp, and emerald-eyed;
She looked on them a little space,
And shrill as hautboy cried:—
"O three tall footsore men of rags
Which walking this gold morn I see,
What will ye give me from your bags
For fairy kisses three?"
The first, that was a reddish man,
Out of his bundle takes a crust:
"La, by the tombstones of St. Ann,
There's fee, if fee ye must!"
The second, that was a chestnut man,
Out of his bundle draws a bone:
"Lo, by the belfry of St. Ann,
And all my breakfast gone!"
The third, that was a yellow man,
Out of his bundle picks a groat,
"La, by the Angel of St. Ann,
And I must go without."

That changeling, lean and icy-lipped,
Touched crust, and bone, and groat, and lo!
Beneath her finger taper-tipped
The magic all ran through.
Instead of crust a peacock pie,
Instead of bone sweet venison,
Instead of groat a white lily
With seven blooms thereon.
And each fair cup was deep with wine:
Such was the changeling's charity,
The sweet feast was enough for nine,
But not too much for three.
O toothsome meat in jelly froze!
O tender haunch of elfin stag!
O rich the odour that arose!
O plump with scraps each bag!
There, in the daybreak gold and wild,
Each merry-hearted beggar man
Drank deep unto the fairy child,
And blessed the good St. Ann.

Editing

- Did you meet the goal of this writing exercise?

- Look at your word choice. Is there a good mixture of nouns and pronouns? Is the antecedent of each pronoun clear?

- Look at your paragraphs. Are all the sentences related? Does each paragraph focus on a single topic?

Exercise Answers

Exercise 2

Common nouns: present, dragon, child, happiness, niece, pleasure, dragon, home, friends

Exercise 3

Common nouns: frock, stuff, curtains, poison, hands, joy
Proper nouns: Harry, Effie, Harry, St. George

Exercise 4

Linking verbs and verbals are not included in my list, though it's fine if the student included them.
Verbs: tumble, cried, fell, fell, crawled, dressed, had

Exercise 5

Linking verbs and verbals are not included in my list, though it's fine if the student included them.
Verbs: boiled, sent, poured, set

Exercise 7

It, the creature; she, Sabrinetta; me, Sabrinetta; I, Sabrinetta

Exercise 8

he, Edmund; it, the new lantern

Exercise 9

me, Black Beauty; they, the six colts; I, Black Beauty; them, the six colts; we, Beauty and the other colts

Exercise 10

I, Black Beauty; me, Black Beauty; he, Squire Gordon; my, Black Beauty's; him, Squire Gordon
In the quote from Squire Gordon, Black Beauty is the antecedent of he.

Exercise 11

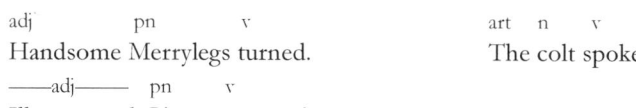

adj   pn   v
Handsome Merrylegs turned.
——adj—— pn   v
Ill-tempered Ginger snapped.

art   n   v
The colt spoke.

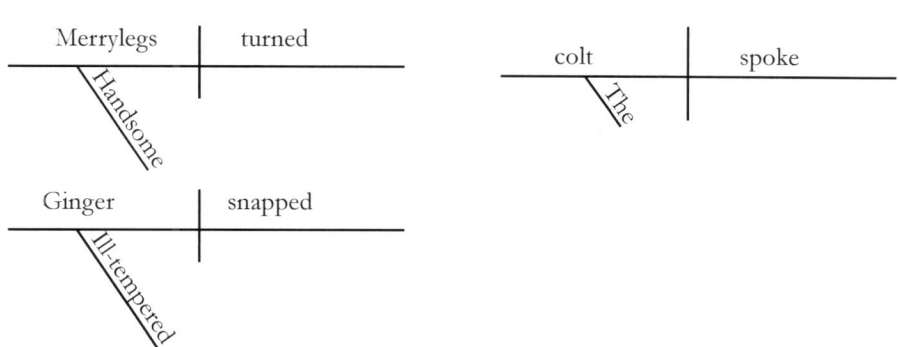

Exercise 13

adj　　adj　adj　　pn　　　v
Strong, tall, bold Samson boasted.

adj　　　adj　　pn　　v
Steady, thoughtful Job trained.

art　adj　　adj　　n　　v
The kindly old master helped.

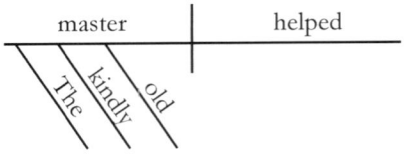

Exercise 14

pro　lv　art　adj　　──n──
"I am the best riding-master."

pro　lv　art　adj　　n
"He was a good master."

pro　lv　　n
"We were colts."

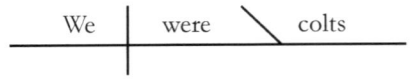

Exercise 15

pro　lv　art　adj　　　n
"They were a valuable kind."

n　　lv　　adj　　n
"Blinkers are dangerous things."

n　　lv　　n
"Men are blockheads."

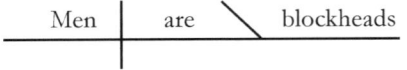

Exercise 16

pro　lv　art　adj　　　n
"They are a handsome pair."

pro　lv　art　adj　　n
"You are a military man."

adj　n　　v
My master rode.

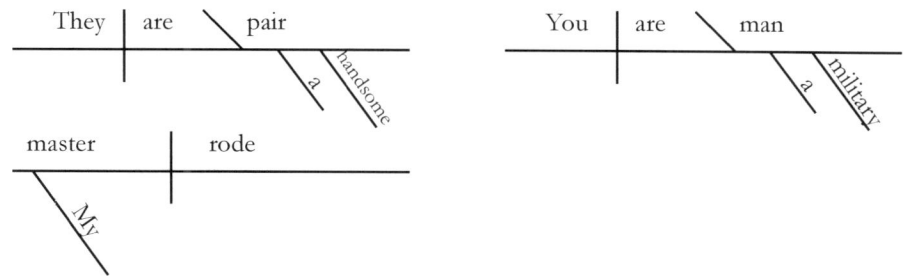

Exercise 17

art n lv adj
"The horse is fresh."

art n lv adj
"The bridge is broken."

adj adj n lv art n
"That young fellow is a liar."

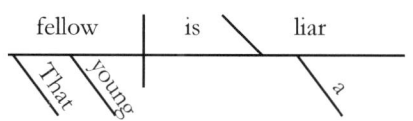

Exercise 19

pro lv art adj n
"He is a brave lad."

art adj n ——v——
A fine horse had died.

adj n ——lv—— adj
Our mistress had been alarmed.

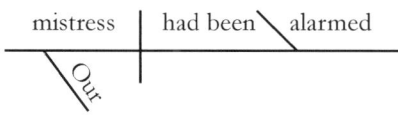

Exercise 20

kerchiefs, reefs, bluffs; scarves according to the rules, but scarfs is also correct

pro —lv— adj
"I will be ready."

——pn—— ——v——
"Black Beauty will go."

pro ——v——
We had left.

Exercise 21

lives, cliffs, roofs; dwarves according the rules, but dwarfs is also correct

art   n   lv ———adj———
"The boy is broken-hearted."

pro lv   adj   n
"It was only ignorance."

pro lv   adj
He was better.

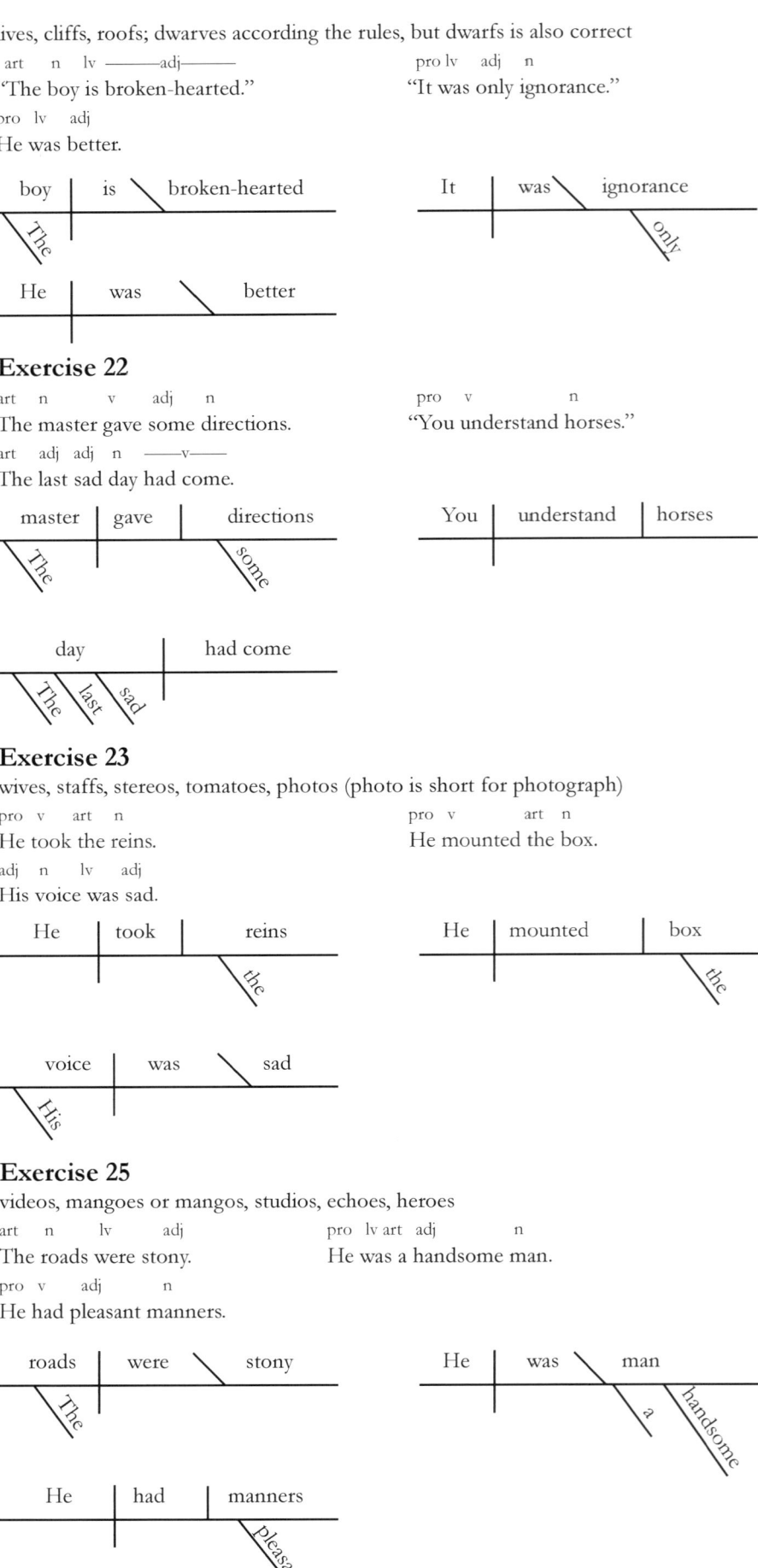

Exercise 22

art   n   v   adj   n
The master gave some directions.

pro   v   n
"You understand horses."

art adj adj n ———v———
The last sad day had come.

Exercise 23

wives, staffs, stereos, tomatoes, photos (photo is short for photograph)

pro v art n
He took the reins.

pro v   art n
He mounted the box.

adj n lv adj
His voice was sad.

Exercise 25

videos, mangoes or mangos, studios, echoes, heroes

art n   lv adj
The roads were stony.

pro lv art adj   n
He was a handsome man.

pro v adj   n
He had pleasant manners.

Exercise 26

hv pn v art adj n
Did Beauty enjoy the sweet grass?

lv pn adj
Was Beauty lonely?

hv pro v adj n
Had they become fast friends?

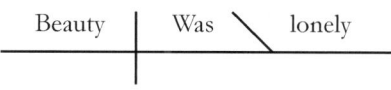

Exercise 27

adj n lv adj
These drivers are careless.

hv pro v art n
Did he have a stone?

pro v adj n
He lifted his hat.

Exercise 28

hv pro lv adj
"Has he been well?"

pn art pn v art n
Beauty and Peggy pulled the carriage.

art n v cj v adj n
The farmer dismounted and held his rein.

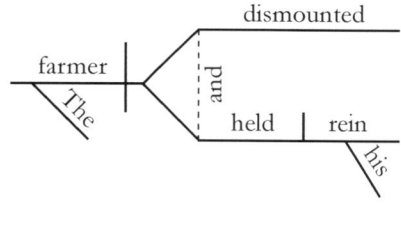

Exercise 29

pro v art n cj v adj n
"I will attend the hoof and direct your man."

art n v cj v adj n
The bricklayer came and pulled many bricks.

pro lv adj cj adj
He was ignorant and conceited.

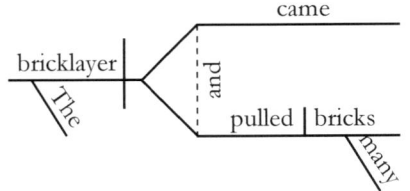

Exercise 31

pro lv art ———adj——— adj   n
He was a good-humored, sensible man.

adj n   cj pro v   ——pro——
My master and I understood each other.

v   art n
"Open the gates."

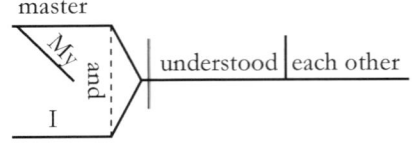

Exercise 32

pro adv v art adj   n
I never knew a better man.

pro hv adv v
"I do not believe."

pro lv adv adj
"They are not religious."

Exercise 33

adj   n   lv adv   adj
"Her mother is dangerously ill."

pro ——lv—— art adj n
"It would be a rare treat."

pro ——v—— adv
"She must go directly."

Exercise 34

 n   v   adv
Winter came early.

adj   n   v   adv
Dinah's family lived there.

art ——adj—— n v adv
The high-wheeled gig ran easily.

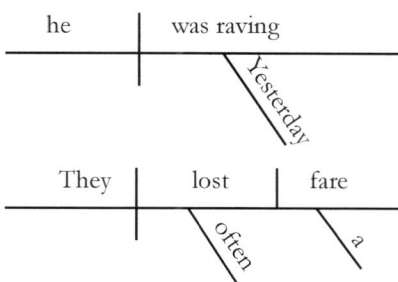

Exercise 35

adv   pro   ——v——
"Yesterday he was raving."

adv   pro   v   adj   n   adv
Now he took his handkerchief out.

pro   adv   v   art   n
They often lost a fare.

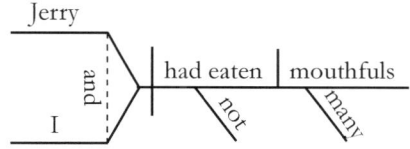

Exercise 37

pn   cj   pro   hv   adv   v   adj   n
Jerry and I had not eaten many mouthfuls.

adv   pro   v   pn
Presently she approached Jerry.

hv   pro   lv   adj   n
Had she been Polly's mistress?

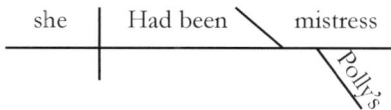

Exercise 38

art   n   ——lv——   adv   adj
The wind had been very changeable.

adv   n   cj   n   ——v——
Sometimes driver and horse must wait.

hv'adv pro v   pro
"Can't I do something?"

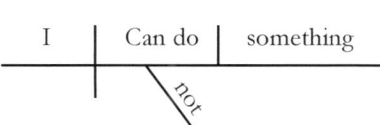

Exercise 39

pn   ——v——   cj   v   pro   adv
Dolly was crying and kissed me too.

lv   pro   art   adj   n
"Is it a heavy load?"

pro ——v—— art n adv
He was raising the whip again.

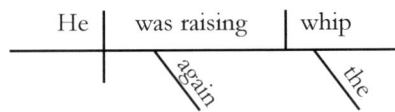

Exercise 40

pro v adj n cj art adj n
He had black eyes and a hooked nose.

hv adj n v pro
"Can your horse do it?"

——v—— art adj n
"Do take a second cab."

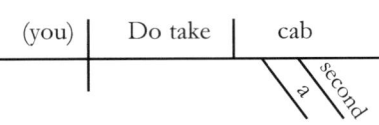

Exercise 41

art n hv adv v adj n
The boy could hardly control his delight.

art n v cj v pro
The groom cleaned and dressed me.

v adj n
"Check his mouth."

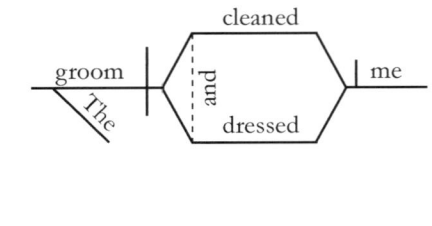

Exercise 43

phrase, in his little sleeping-berth
clause, the <u>wind</u> <u>blew</u> hard and <u>joggled</u> the water of the ocean
clause, <u>she</u> <u>sat</u> down in a corner of the coop

hv pro lv adv adv
"Have you been here, too?"

hv pro v adv adv
"Do I speak quite properly?"

pro ——v—— adj n
"You may have my egg."

Exercise 44
clause, while she was speaking
clause, when Billina suddenly cried
phrase, upon all fours

"Can I tell metal?"   "Run!"
The Wheeler gave a sharp, wild cry and chased her.

Exercise 45
phrase, that crack in the rock
clause, so I think
clause, don't be frightened [understood you is the subject!]

"We could unlock it."   "Try it and see."
"Don't be frightened."

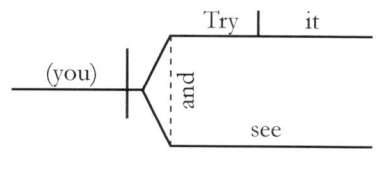

Exercise 46
clause, until suddenly he became motionless
phrase, that low bow to you
clause, she ran around the copper man

"Haven't you a club?"   "He must have been a great loss."
"The best thinker was a scarecrow."

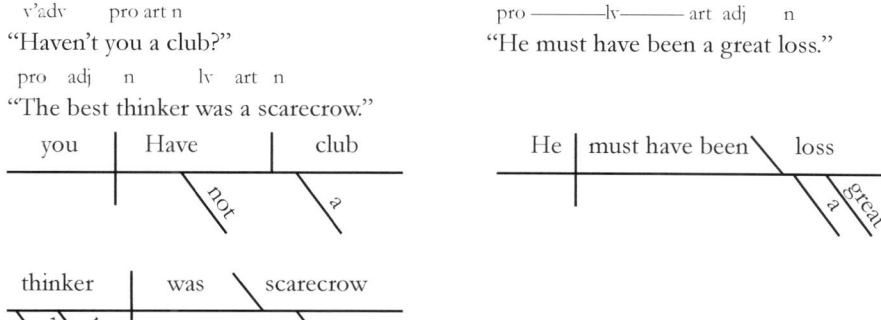

Exercise 47
phrase, from those ugly creatures
clause, and the copper fingers closed firmly over the stout handle
clause, the yellow hen gave a cackle of delight

```
        hv    pro      v       n                              v     pro adv  adv
    "Will you exchange heads?"                          "Wind me up, quick."
         pro  v      n              ————pn————
    "You have company, Your Highness."
```

Exercise 49
Dorothy was guided to the chicken house by a loud cackling, crowing, and distracting hubbub of sounds.

phrase, as cowardly as ever
clause, but suddenly the <u>bunch</u> of feathers <u>stopped</u> whirling
clause, which <u>Dorothy</u> <u>unlatched</u>

```
     inj     pn    hv   pro  ———v———                hv'adv   v
    "Why, Billina! Have you been fighting?"       "Don't worry."
     art  ————pn————  v      adj   n     art  ————pn————
    The Cowardly Lion introduced his friend the Hungry Tiger.
```

Exercise 50
[In these exercises, the quotation marks around obvious quotations are optional.]
"Please to get me about thirty pounds of tenderloin steak, a peck of boiled potatoes, and five gallons of ice-cream for dessert."

phrase, a queen mother and her ten children
phrase, for the sake of the poor prisoners
clause, <u>I</u> <u>will</u> now <u>retire</u> to my cabinet

```
      lv   pro adv adv  adj                  pro  v    adv    cj   v    adj  n
    "Are you so very hungry?"              He bowed politely and blinked his eyes.
     adj  n     pn     lv art adv  adj    n
    "My uncle, Evoldo, was a very wicked man."
```

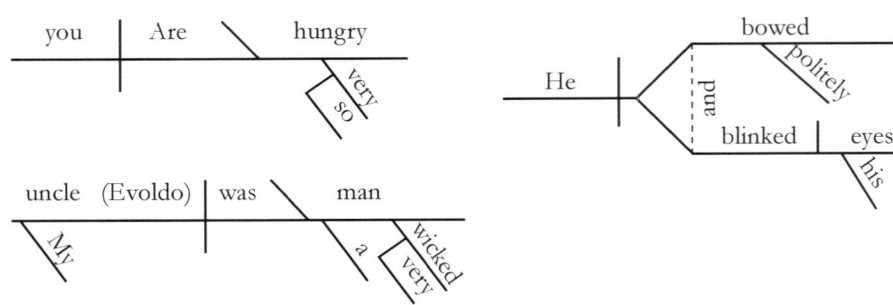

Exercise 51
clause, <u>she</u> <u>lays</u> one every morning
phrase, about this time
clause, although <u>all</u> <u>were</u> restless and anxious

```
     inj    pn    ——v——  adj   n               pn   hv'adv lv  adv
    "Why, Billina is laying her egg."         "Billina won't be long."
```

art ———pn——— lv   adv   adj
The Cowardly Lion was dreadfully nervous.

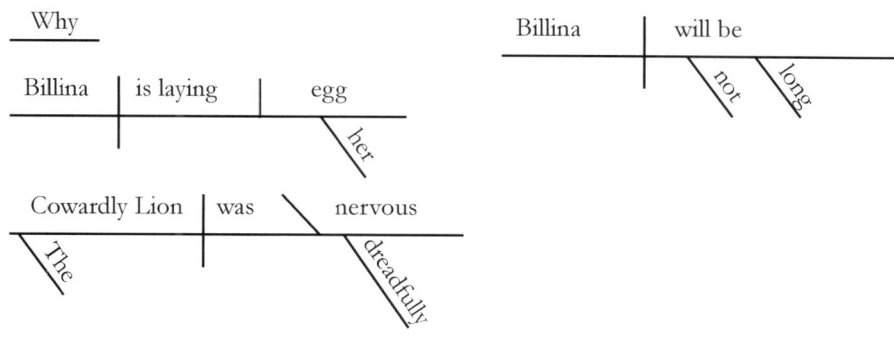

Exercise 52

                             ph   ph
Ozma and Dorothy were a little awed by the silence.
     gr   ph
We will dig him out of his hole, like a fox.

inj   ———pn———   v   adv cj v pro   lv'adv pro art n
"PLEASE Mr. Nome King, come here and see us."   "Isn't it a trick?"
art ———pn——— art adj   n   v
The Nome King, the underground monarch, answered.

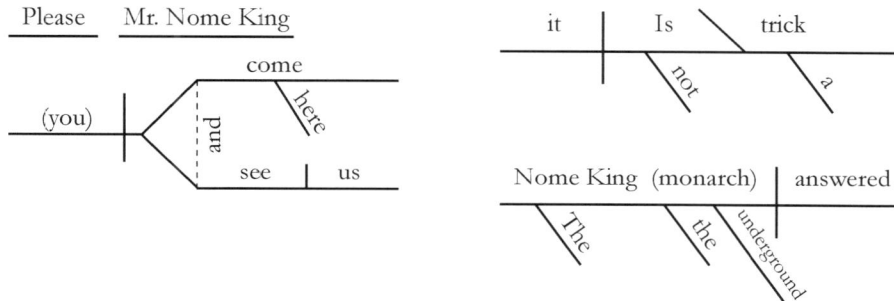

Exercise 53

Dorothy, the Scarecrow, and the Tin Woodman each gave a start of dismay and stared into one another's eyes.

ph ph   ph   ph   ph
"Surely I ought to guess one object in eleven correctly."
  ph   ph ph   ph   ph
"It would be weak and cowardly in us to abandon the adventure."

pn art adj   n   lv art n   hv pro v
Ozma the pretty grasshopper was an emerald.   "Has she failed?"
art ———pn——— adv   v   adv cj   v
The Nome King suddenly looked up and smiled. [In this sentence, it could be argued that the verb modified both verbs, or only the first, so either diagram is acceptable.]

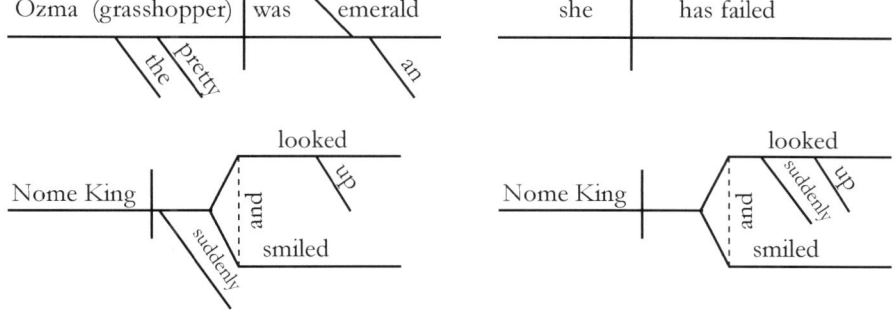

Exercise 55

Dorothy, the Lion, and Tiger were given their breakfast in their rooms.

clause, where <u>he</u> <u>said</u> to the King
phrase, in so enraged a voice
phrase, squatting under the throne

   hv   pn   v   adv
Had Billina listened carefully?

  inj   v   adj   adj   n
"Oh, cease your tiresome chatter!"

    adj   pn   pro lv art n
"Your Majesty, you are a fool."

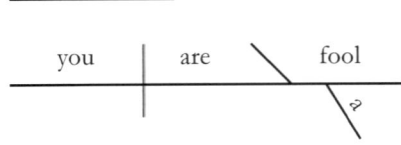

Exercise 56

The Scarecrow, Billina, and the Nome King were in the throne room.
"Why, it's Billina."

        ph   ph   ph
"I've got a right to cackle, I guess."

  gr   ph ph ph gr   ph
"Well, you'll have to bear this one around."

  v pro adv prep n
"Take it away [at once]!"
              WHEN

           hv pro adv v   prep pro prep n
"Will she now return [to us] [in safety]?"
                          WHERE HOW

  pn   v art adj ——pn—— prep art   n
Dorothy led the little Prince Evring [by the hand].
                               HOW

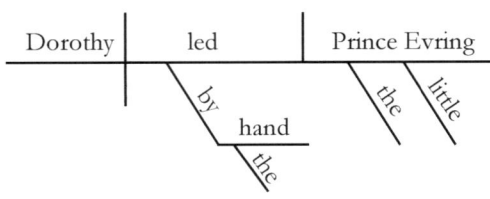

Exercise 57

phrase, with an air of vast importance
clause, then <u>I</u> <u>thank</u> you for the gracious favor
clause, <u>don't</u> <u>worry</u>

  inj   adj n   lv pn prep n
"Why, my name is Bill, [by rights]."
                        HOW

            lv pro art adj   n   ——pn——
"Am I a good guesser, Mr. Nome King?"

  pn   art ——adj—— n   v   prep   pro
Evanna, a sweet-faced girl, stood [beside them].
                              WHERE

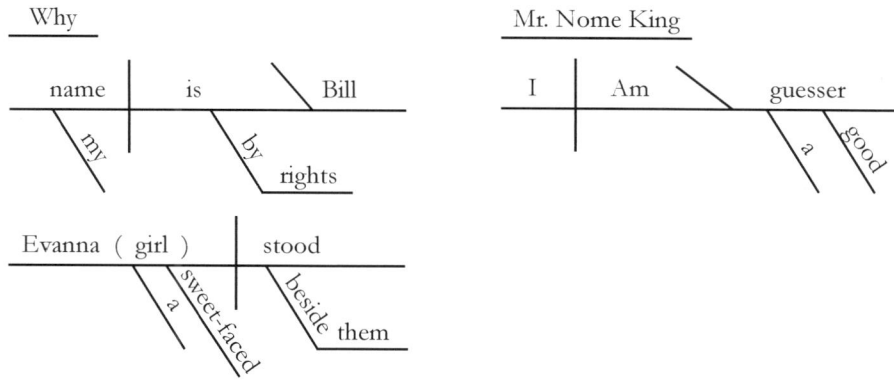

Exercise 58

The generals, the colonels, the majors, and the captains all commanded, "Forward, march!" [Either a period or an exclamation mark is acceptable.]

                  ph   ph
"The creature is made of wood."

                         ph ph   ph ph
At once the army filed out in great numbers, led by their captain.

art   n   —v— prep n   hv'adv v   pro
"The creature is made [of wood]."   "Don't mind them!"
                        HOW

hv pro v
"Do you surrender?"

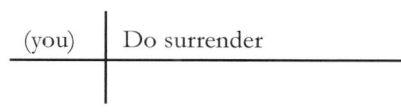

Exercise 59

clause, although <u>I wonder</u> why
clause, so the <u>King stopped</u> and <u>looked</u> at them in surprise
clause, where the <u>king jeered</u> at Dorothy

inj   pro hv adv v   adj   adj   n
"Why, you are not wearing your magic belt."

pn   v   adv   pn   cj art   pn   prep pn
Dorothy welcomed back Ozma and the Queen [of Ev].

art   n   v   prep   pn
The others went [with Dorothy].
            WHERE

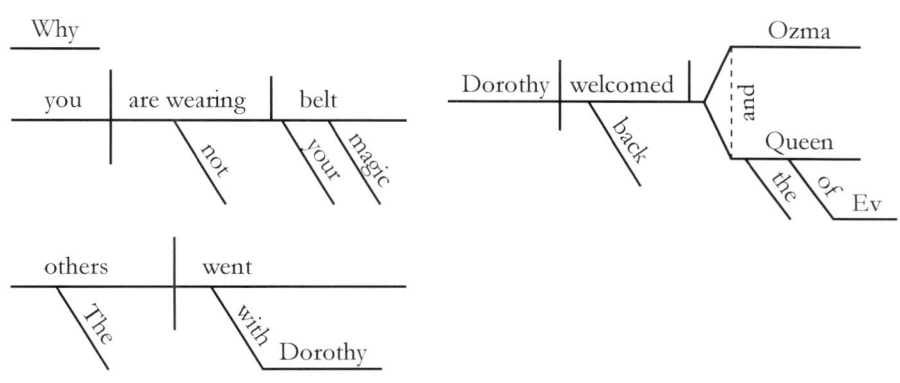

Exercise 61

For Ozma of Oz ruled the King of the Munchkins, the King of the Winkies, the King of the Quadlings, and the King of the Gillikins.

   gr ph   ph ph   ph
She lives in the Emerald City, which is in the exact center of the four kingdoms of the Land of Oz.

  ph   gr
"Now I am happy and contented and willing to lead a quiet life and mind my own business."

  v pro adv adj n   prep art n   —pn— pro v pro
"Have we any other privates [in the armies]?" "Omby Amby, I promote you."
            WHERE

pn art pn prep pn v   prep art ——pn——
Ozma, the Ruler [of Oz], returned [to the Emerald City].
    WHAT KIND WHERE

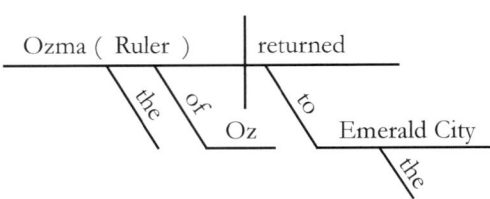

Exercise 62

"The belt has magical powers only while it is in some fairy country, my little friend."

——pn—— ——v—— prep art adj n
Uncle Henry was seated [in an easy chair].
        WHERE
adv art n   v prep art n
Instantly the farmhouse appeared [in the picture].
pn art adj adj n ——v——
Dorothy, the little Kansas girl, might visit.

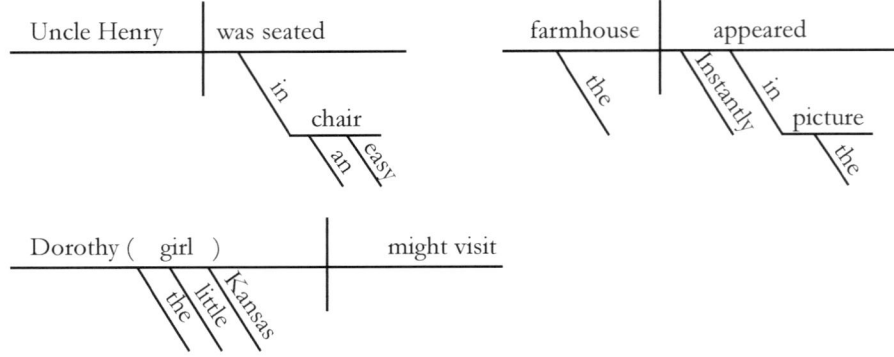

Exercise 63

 inj inj pro lv art adj   n prep n   v pro prep pro adv
"Oh, yes, he was a peaceable sort [of beast]." "Tell us [about it] first."
           WHAT KIND   HOW
adj n lv adv adj prep pro
His parents were very fond [of him].
        HOW

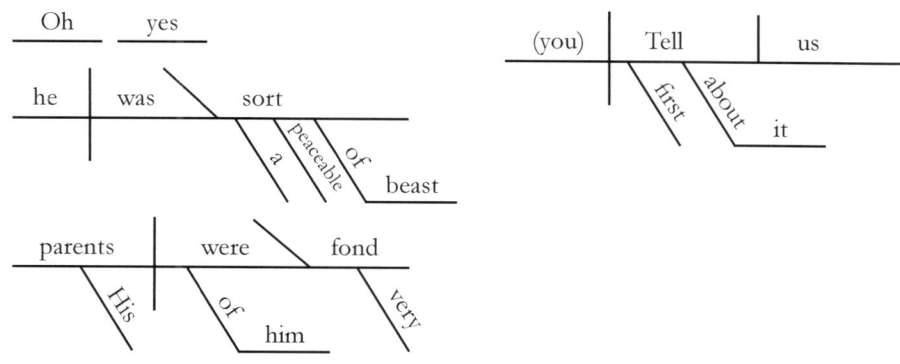

Exercise 64

adv hv'adv v pro   adv   hv pro v   art   n
"Now don't hit me."   Where did he see the dragon?

art adj n   v   prep art   n   prep art n
A cool breeze played [over the surface] [of the grass].
                 HOW/WHERE   WHAT KIND

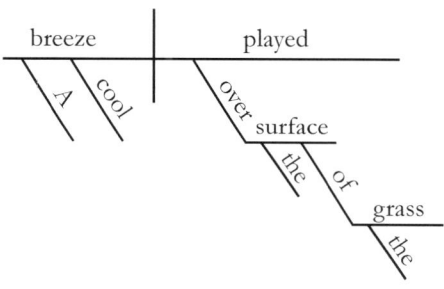

Exercise 65

simple present, hear
simple past, tired
inf., to work

adv lv ——pn——   adj adj adj   n   adv v
Where is St. George?   "My dear little man, just understand."

art pn   v   adv   prep adj   n
The Boy jumped round [in sheer delight].
             HOW

 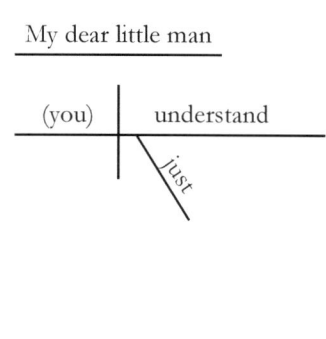

Exercise 67

pres. part., are going
pres. part., am going
inf., to make

art pn ——v—— art adj adj n
The Boy had secured a good front place.

pn hv'adv pro v art pn
"Boy, can't you arrange a Princess?"

adv hv ——pn—— art adj n v
When did St. George the dragon slayer arrive?

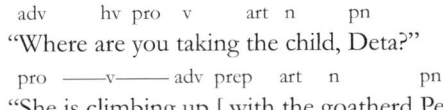

Exercise 68

simple past, looked
past participle, have noticed
inf., to see

adv hv pro v art n pn
"Where are you taking the child, Deta?"

adv lv adj n adv adj
"Why are his eyes so fierce?"

pro ——v—— adv prep art n pn
"She is climbing up [with the goatherd Peter]."

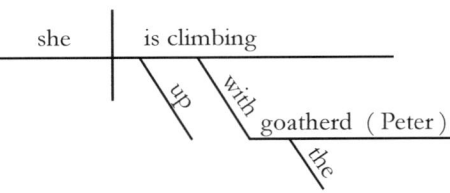

Exercise 69

phrase, after looking around attentively in the room
clause, Heidi followed him into a fairly spacious room
clause, when he opened it

adv hv'adv pro v pro
"Why don't you need them?"

v adv
"Come then."

prep art adj adj n pro v art n
[Beside the old man's bed] she saw a ladder.

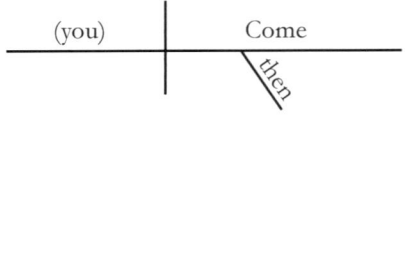

Exercise 70

simple present, begins   inf., to call   inf., to whistle.
past part., had happened   simple present, follows

inj hv pro adv v adv   adv   lv adj   n
"Oh, does it really live there?"   "Where is her grandmother?"
pn   prep n   v   prep art adj n   adv
Heidi [at last] went [to the little thing] again.
        WHEN   WHERE

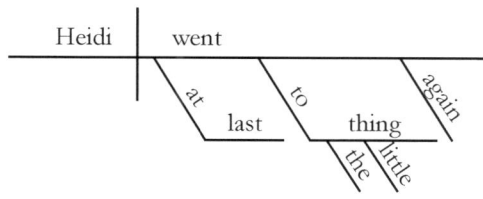

Exercise 71

adv lv pro adj   inj   n   hv'adv pro v art   n
"How is it possible?"   "Why, grandmother, can't you see the shutter?"
pn   ——v—— prep adj n
Heidi would talk [about her life].
           HOW

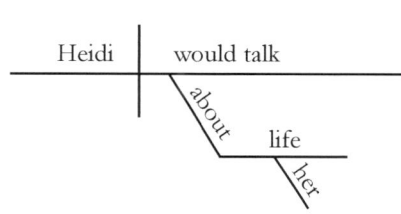

Exercise 73

pres. part., is sitting   simple past, grumbled

pn   art n   adv   v   prep pro
Sebastian, the butler, soon stood [before her].
——pn—— adv hv   pro v   adj n
"Miss Deta, how could you bring this child?"
pro hv adv   v   art n   adv
"I have never heard the name before."

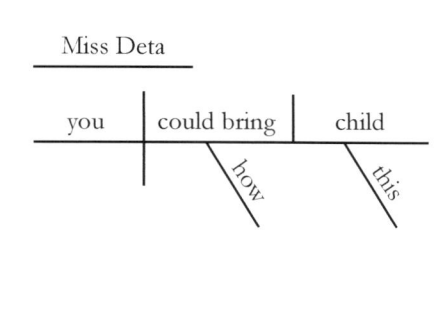

Exercise 74

simple pres., brings   simple pres., hear

adv   hv pro v   adv   lv art n   prep art adj   n
Where has she gone?   "Where is the tower [with the golden dome]?"
                                                        WHAT KIND

hv pro v   art n   prep pro
"Can you open a window [for me]?"
                                HOW

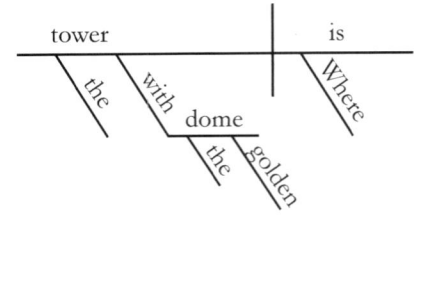

Exercise 75
"Oh, please, Mr. Candidate, can't we just peep in?"

clause, the furious <u>lady</u> <u>proceeded</u>
clause, <u>whispered</u> the frightened <u>child</u>
phrase, for mercy's sake

pn   adv   v   art n   prep pro
Sebastian obediently pulled the boy [after him].
                                        WHERE
pn   prep art   n   v   adj adj   n
Clara, [on the contrary], enjoyed her companion's society.
        HOW
v   art adj   n   adv
"Bring the unlucky child up!"

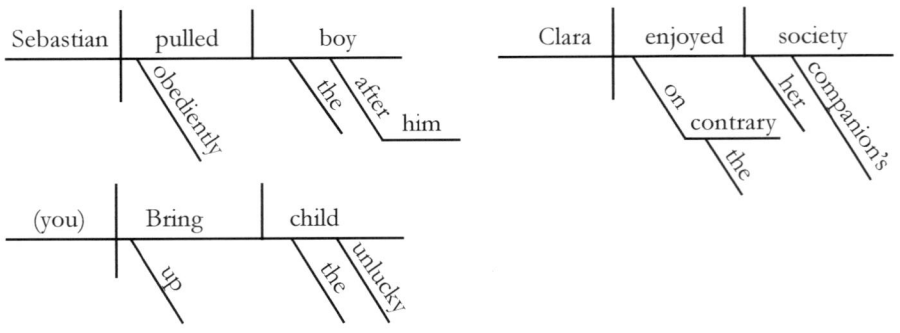

Exercise 76

adv hv pro v   pro v   prep adj   adj   n
"How do you mean?"   "I thought [of this Swiss child]."
                                                HOW

inj ——pn—— pro ——lv—— adj   adj
"Oh, Mr. Sesemann, we have been terribly disappointed."

Exercise 77

past part., have learned   pres. part., am going

```
  pn         adv  lv  art  n              adv  pro ——v—— adv
"Rottenmeier, where is the child?"       "When I am going home?"
  pn   ——v——  prep  adj     n    prep art   adj       n
Heidi was looking [ with wondering eyes ] [ at the splendid pictures ].
                         HOW                      WHERE
```

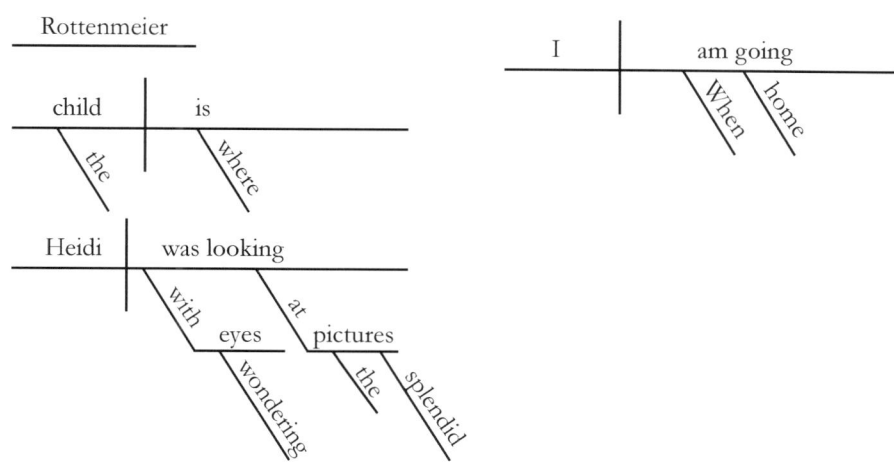

Exercise 79

inf., to speak   simple present, tell   past part., have played

```
 adj   n   lv  adj  cj  adj                 v     n    adj adj   n
His eyes were lively and kind.          "Have patience, my old friend."
art adj   n   prep  n    v   prep art   n
A few bottles [ of wine ] stood [ on the table ].
                WHAT KIND     WHERE
```

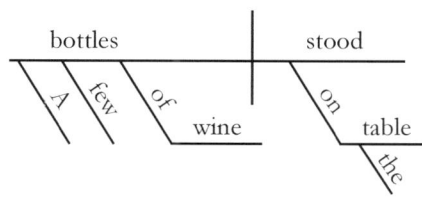

Exercise 80

simple past, called   pres. part., is feeling

```
  pn    v   –prep– pro  prep   n
Heidi looked [ up to him ] [ in amazement ].
 pro  ——v——  prep adj   adj     n
Heidi was dressed [ in her Sunday frock ].
                        HOW
```

adv hv'adv pro v   pro prep pro
"Why don't you give it [to me]?"

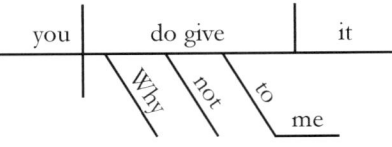

Exercise 81

phrase, to mar the happiness of the child
clause, after she had carefully wiped it off
clause, shall I read you a song from your book now

hv   pro v   adv   n
"Have you come again, child?"
adj   n   v   prep art adj   n
Grandmother's face changed [to a joyous expression].
pn   adj   pn   hv adv v   adj n   adv
God Our Father had not answered her prayer immediately.

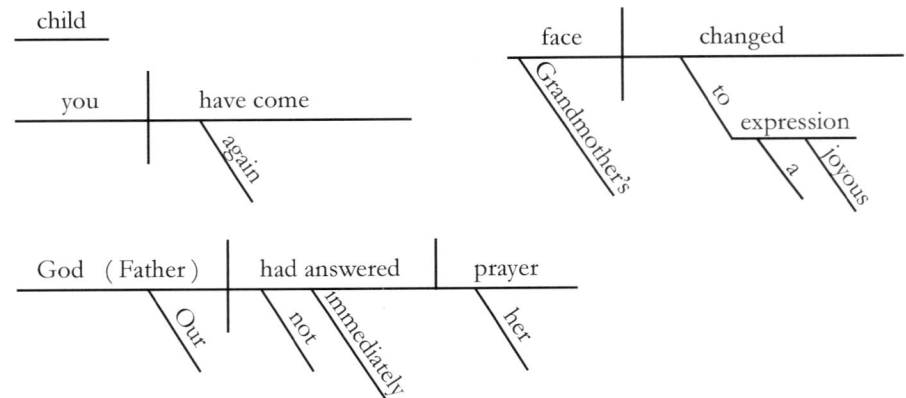

Exercise 82

——inj—— n   —v— prep pn
"Oh please, doctor, do go [to Heidi]."
prep   adj   n   art n   v
[With shrugging shoulders] the doctor replied.
adj   n   —v— prep n
Clara's eyes had filled [with tears].

460

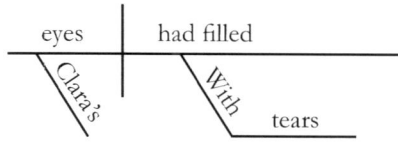

Exercise 83
simple past, reached   simple past, caressed   simple past, crushed

   lv   adj   n   adj   adv
"Are your eyes bright already?"
 prep art adj   n   pro ——v—— art   n   cj   n
[With an old rag] she would rub the chairs and table.
HOW
art   n   ——v—— adj prep adj adj   n
The grandfather had been busy [in his little shop].
                                WHERE

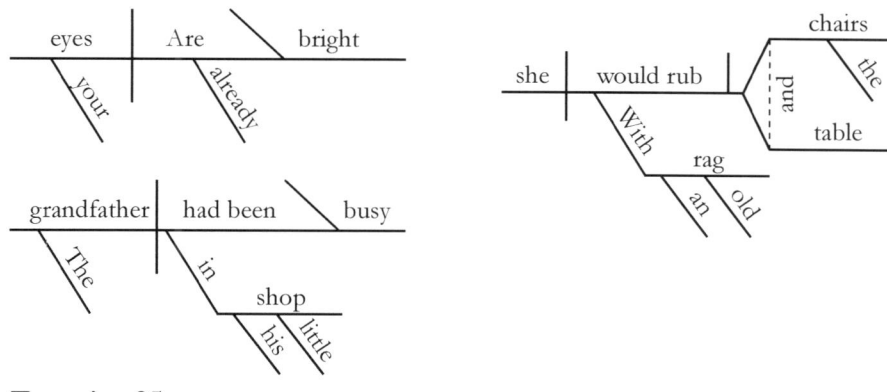

Exercise 85
"Oh, grandfather, I have found my bedroom."
[An exclamation point would also be acceptable.]

 adv v   cj v prep pro   pn   v   adv adj prep adj adj   n
"Now come and look [at mine]."   Heidi slept very well [in her chimney corner].
                HOW/WHERE   WHERE
lv   pro adv prep n
Was she away [from home]?
        WHERE

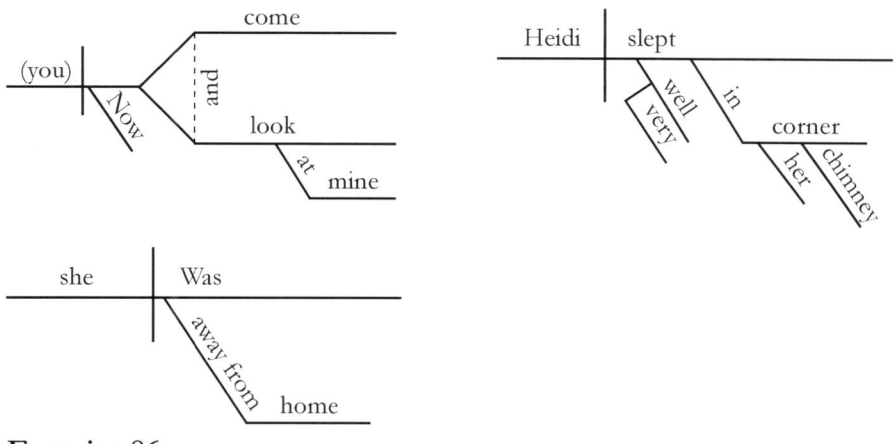

Exercise 86
simple past, began   simple past, read
inf., to read,   inf., to stammer

   v   adv cj   v   art adj   n   pro v   adv prep pro prep adj   n
"Hurry up and learn the three letters."   He came daily [to her] [for his lesson].
                                                          WHERE HOW

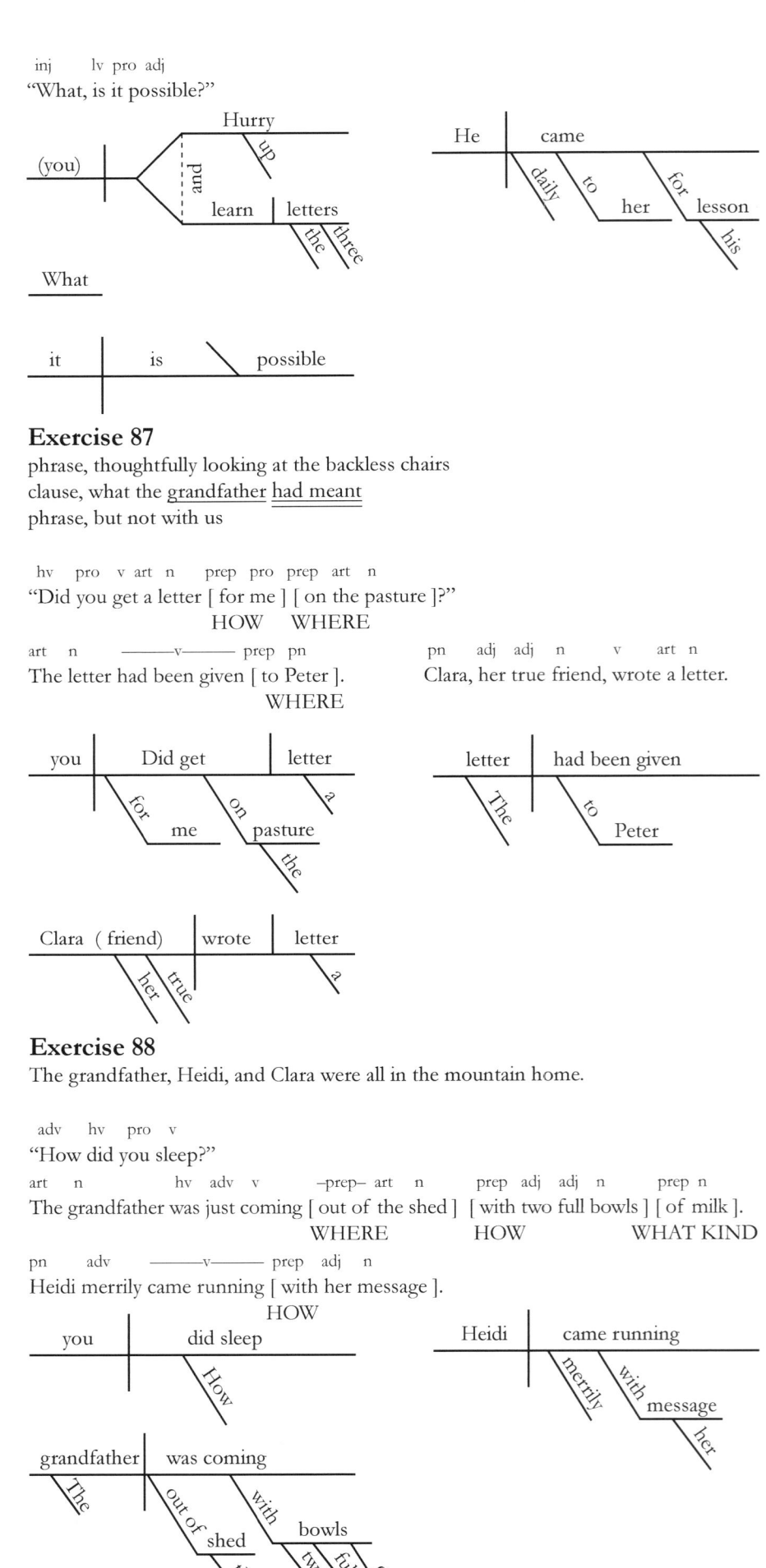

Exercise 87

phrase, thoughtfully looking at the backless chairs
clause, what the <u>grandfather</u> <u>had meant</u>
phrase, but not with us

hv pro v art n   prep pro prep art n
"Did you get a letter [for me] [on the pasture]?"
                         HOW   WHERE
art n   ———v——— prep pn   pn adj adj n   v   art n
The letter had been given [to Peter].   Clara, her true friend, wrote a letter.
                                WHERE

Exercise 88

The grandfather, Heidi, and Clara were all in the mountain home.

adv hv pro v
"How did you sleep?"
art n   hv adv v —prep— art n   prep adj adj n prep n
The grandfather was just coming [out of the shed] [with two full bowls] [of milk].
                                      WHERE   HOW   WHAT KIND
pn adv   ———v——— prep adj n
Heidi merrily came running [with her message].
                         HOW

Exercise 89
Grandfather the wind has done it exclaimed Heidi eagerly

pn   —v—   pn   prep art n   prep art n
Heidi had told Clara [of the flowers] [on the pasture].
                      HOW   WHAT KIND

[This sentence might be a little tricky. In some sentences, "on the pasture" could tell where. However, we know it's modifying the flowers because if we take out the phrase "of the flowers," "on the pasture" no longer makes sense: Heidi had told Clara on the pasture. What kind of flowers? The ones on the pasture.]

hv   pro v art n   inj pn   hv   pro lv adj
"Have you seen the chair?"   "Oh, Clara, would you be angry?"

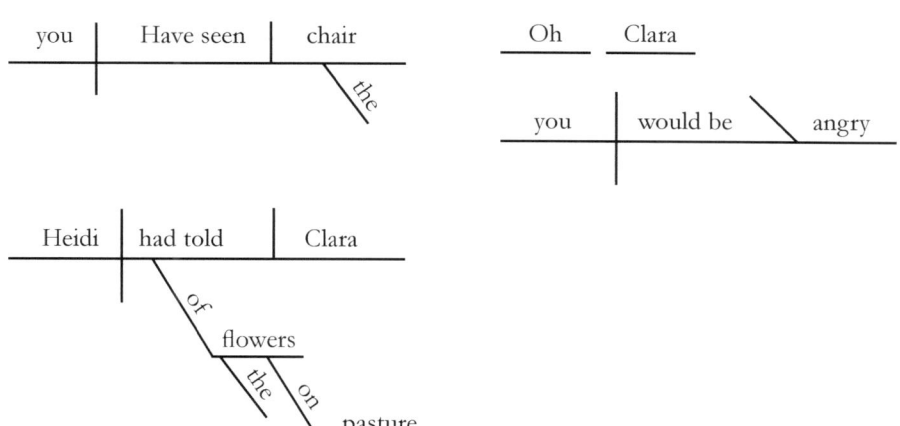

Exercise 91
In this first sentence, any coordinating conjunction is technically correct, though some would produce an odd sentence. In my household, making the sentence odd would be a bonus.

She began to be conscious that her son was no longer a child, <u>so</u> she must soon send him forth among the perils and troubles of the world.

She began to be conscious that her son was no longer a child. She must soon send him forth among the perils and troubles of the world.

She began to be conscious that her son was no longer a child; she must soon send him forth among the perils and troubles of the world.

lv adj cj v
"Be patient and see."

adv hv adv pro v prep adj adj   n   prep pn
"Why can not I go [to this famous city] [of Athens]?"
                       WHERE   WHICH ONE

art n prep pn   v   prep n
The eyes [of Theseus] glowed [with enthusiasm].
     WHICH ONES   HOW

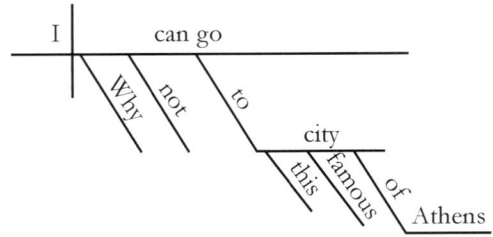

Exercise 92

It was not more than a year afterwards. They were again sitting on the moss-covered stone.

It was not more than a year afterwards, and they were again sitting on the moss-covered stone.

It was not more than a year afterwards; they were again sitting on the moss-covered stone.

pn   ——v——   adj   adj   n   prep   adj   adj   adj   n
Theseus had done many valiant deeds [with his father's golden-hilted sword].
  v   pn   adj   adj   adj   n   prep   adj   n
"Admit Theseus, this evil-minded young man, [to your presence]."
 inj   pro ——lv—— art   adv   adj   adj   n   adv
"Why, he must be a very wicked young fellow indeed!"

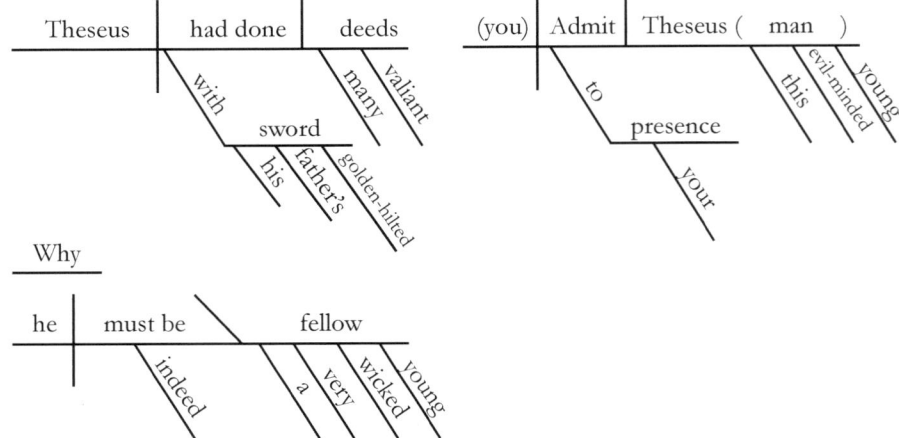

Exercise 93

Do but let me put a single drop into the goblet. Let the young man taste it.

Do but let me put a single drop into the goblet; let the young man taste it.

Do but let me put a single drop into the goblet, and let the young man taste it.

 adv   v   pro prep pro   pro v   adv   art   n
"How came you [by it]?"   He drew back the goblet.
adj n   ——v—— prep art   adj   n
His eyes had fallen [on the gold-hilted sword].

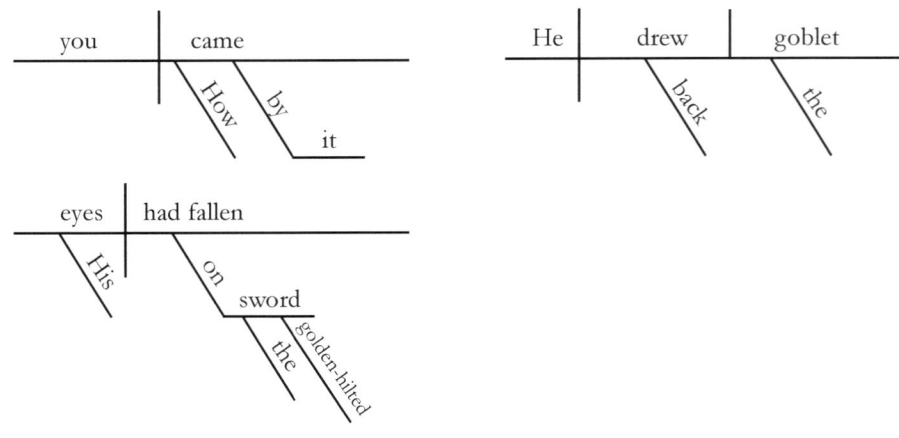

Exercise 94

I shall probably have to teach you a little civility before we part.
Before we part, I shall probably have to teach you a little civility.

adv art pn   v   n   cj adj   n   prep n
Here the Pygmies planted wheat and other kinds [of grain].
                                                      WHAT KIND

adj   adj   pn   v art pn   prep adj   n
These funny Pygmies had a Giant [for their neighbor].
                                        HOW

adv   lv pro adj adj   n
"How are you, my good fellow?"

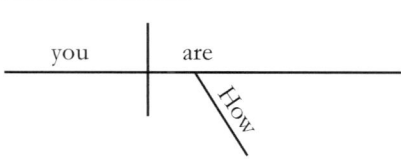

Exercise 95

The figure looked all the more terrible because it carried an enormous brass club on its shoulder.
Because it carried an enormous brass club on its shoulder, the figure looked all the more terrible.

art pn   v   pro adj   adj   n
The Giant gave them his brotherly kindness.
pro v art   pn   art n   prep adj   n
He gave the Pygmies a breeze [with his breath].
                               HOW
art   pn   v   pro   n   prep n
The Pymies built themselves structures [of clay].
                                 WHAT KIND

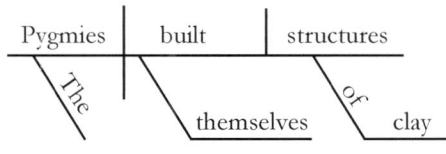

Exercise 97

Because he wanted to be friends with the child, he ate them out of her hand.
He ate them out of her hand because he wanted to be friends with the child.

adv   lv pro
"Where are you?"
 v   adv   adj   n
"Come back, pretty creature!"

```
        v   pro adv  adj adj   pn
```
"Bring me back my little Europa."

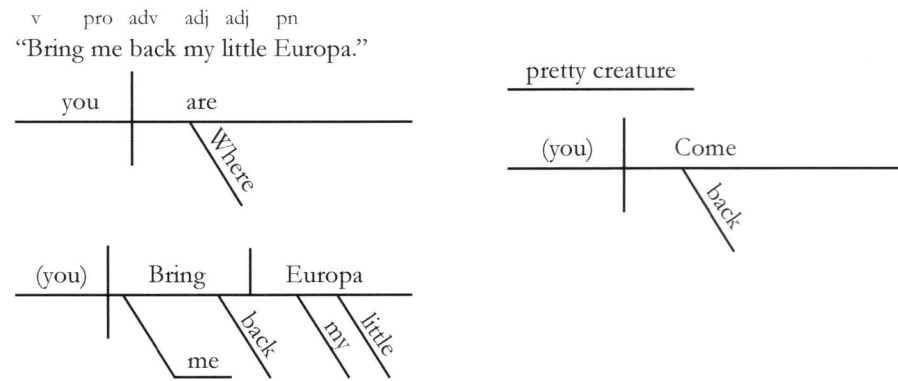

Exercise 98

It was delightful to witness the gratitude of this amiable bull; he capered higher than ever.

It was delightful to witness the gratitude of this amiable bull. He capered higher than ever.

It was delightful to witness the gratitude of this amiable bull, for he capered higher than ever.

```
    v   cj   v   adv  adj  n
```
"Come and drive away this bull!"

```
adv   hv  art  n    v   pn
```
Where did the bull take Europa?

```
─────pn─────   adj   n    v   pro
```
King Agenor, Europa's father, said this.

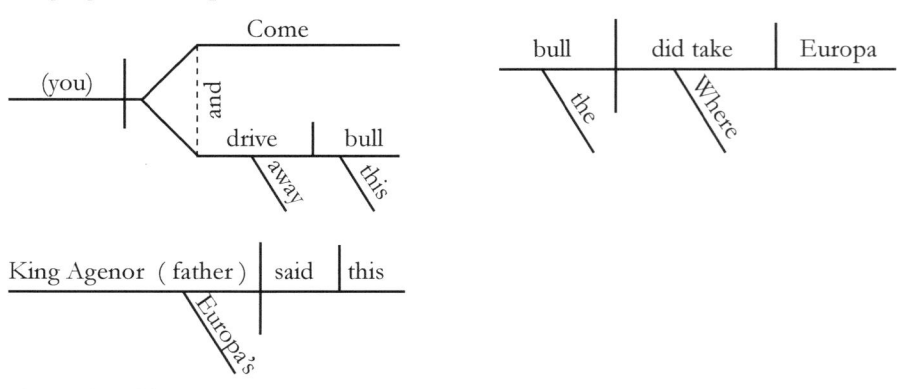

Exercise 99

Telephassa threw away her crown because it chafed her forehead.

Because it chafed her forehead, Telephassa threw away her crown.

```
      hv  adv  v  pro
```
"Do not seek her!"

```
   v   adj  adj  n
```
"Stop, my good cow."

```
pro hv  adv  adv   v       prep  art  n   prep  n
```
"I am pretty well acquainted [with the ways] [of cattle]."
          HOW   WHAT KIND

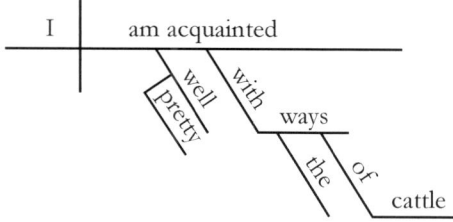

Exercise 100

When they bade him farewell, Phœnix shed tears.
Phœnix shed tears when they bade him farewell.

       adj   n   v   prep   art n
"That smoke comes [from the kitchen]!"
                     WHERE

art n   prep n   v   prep art n
A gush [of smoke] came [from a chimney].
       WHAT KIND   WHERE

art adj   n   lv adv adv adj
The palace kitchen was now very perceptible.

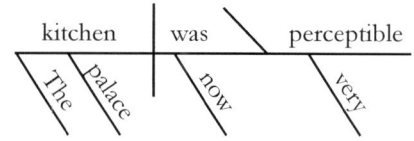

Exercise 101

They could think of nothing but their greedy appetite; they resembled those vilest of animals far more than they did kings.

They could think of nothing but their greedy appetite. They resembled those vilest of animals far more than they did kings.

They could think of nothing but their greedy appetite, and they resembled those vilest of animals far more than they did kings.

pro v   adj   adj   n   prep adj   adj   n
They saw their own figures [in different colored threads].
                    WHERE

inj hv pro v   art n
"Ha! Do you smell the feast?"

adj   n   v   pro   n   prep art adj   n
Serving men brought them dishes [of the richest food].
                             WHAT KIND

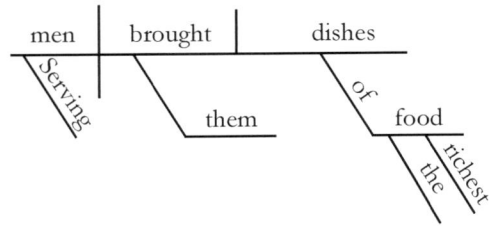

Exercise 103

I will not taste a morsel of food even if you keep me forever in your palace.
Even if you keep me forever in your palace, I will not taste a morsel of food.

pro   v   pro art adj   n
They prepared her a sumptuous banquet.
  adj lv art adj   n   adj adj pn
"You are a spoiled child, my little Proserpina."
  hv art n v pro
"Will the dog bite me?"

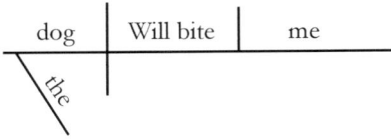

Exercise 104

  adv   lv pn
"Where is Proserpina?"
  v   pro pro adj   ——n——
"Tell me, you naughty sea-nymphs."
pro adv v art n prep adj n
"I once had a child [of my own]."

WHAT KIND

Exercise 105

clause, which I <u>may judge</u> proper for him
clause, what the <u>nurse did</u> to her child
phrase, flinging a warm and ruddy light upon the walls

     ——pn—— adj n   v
Queen Metanira, his mother, shrieked.
art adj   n   lv adv adv adj
The little damsel was not so unhappy.
  v   adv prep adj adj   n
"Hasten home [to your dear mother]."

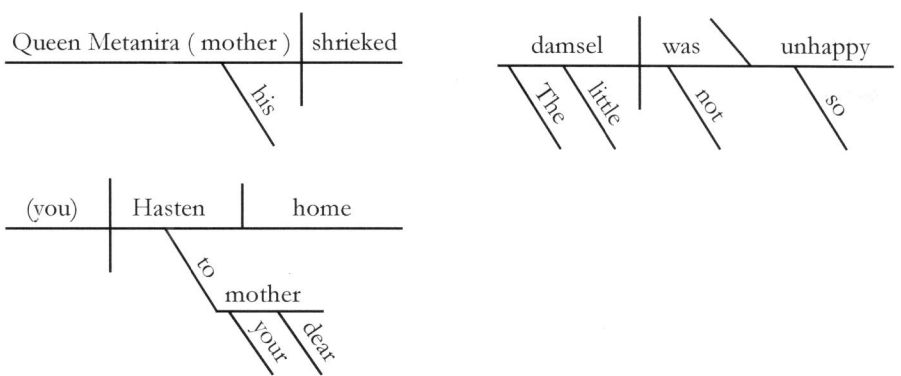

Exercise 106

clause, when the old <u>dame</u> and her <u>peacock</u> <u>were</u> out of sight
phrase, over her shoulder as she departed
phrase, after traveling a pretty long distance

```
pn       art  adj  n       v    pro art  n     prep  adj   n
```
Argus, the ship builder, built him a galley [with fifty oars].
                              WHAT KIND

```
pro  lv   art   n        prep ——pn——
```
"We are the subjects [of King Pelias]."
                     WHAT KIND

```
pn    art ———adj——  n    ——v——
```
Jason the one-sandaled man had come.

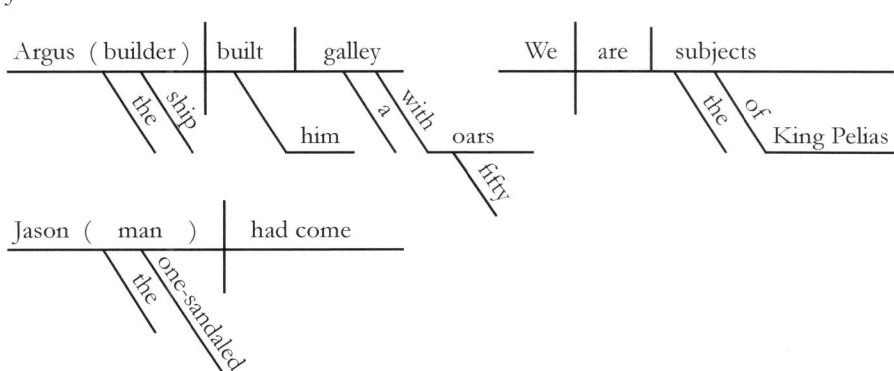

Appendix A: Memory Work

A noun is the name of a person, place, thing, or idea.

A pronoun is a word used in the place of a noun.

>The first person pronouns are: I, me, my, mine, we, us, our, ours.

>The second person pronouns are: you, your, yours.

>The third person pronouns are: he, him, his, she, her, hers, it, its, they, them, their, theirs.

An antecedent is the noun that a pronoun replaces.

A verb is a word that shows action or a state of being.

>The state of being verbs are: am, are, is, was, were, be, being, been.

>The linking verbs are: am, are, is, was, were, be, being, been, become, seem.

>The helping verbs are:
>am, are, is,   was, were,   be, being, been,
>do, does, did,   have, has, had,   may, might, must,
>can, could,   shall, should,   will, would

A conjunction is a word that joins words or groups of words together. The three types of conjunctions are: coordinating, subordinating, and correlative.

A sentence is a group of words that expresses a complete thought.

The Four Types of Sentences:

>A declarative sentence makes a statement. It ends with a period.

>An interrogative sentence asks a question. It ends with a question mark.

>An exclamatory sentence shows sudden or strong feeling. It ends with an exclamation mark.

>An imperative sentence gives a command or makes a request. It ends with a period.

An adjective is a word that modifies a noun or a pronoun. Adjectives tell what kind, how many, which one, and whose.

The articles are: a, an, the. Articles are adjectives.

A predicate nominative is a noun or pronoun which follows a linking verb and renames the subject.

A predicate adjective is an adjective which follows a linking verb and modifies the subject.

Predicate nominatives and predicate adjectives are called subject complements because they complete the subject.

A direct object is the noun or pronoun that follows an action verb and receives the action of the verb.

A preposition is a word that shows the relationship between a noun or a pronoun and another word in the sentence.

The object of the preposition is a noun or pronoun which teams up with the preposition and completes its meaning.

An interjection is a word or group of words that shows sudden or strong feeling.

An adverb is a word that modifies a verb, an adjective, or another adverb. Adverbs tell how, when, where, how often, and to what extent.

Synonyms are words that have the same meaning.

Antonyms are words that have opposite meanings.

Homophones are words that sound the same but have different meanings and may have different spellings.

Homographs are words that have the same spelling but have different meanings and may have different pronunciations.

The subject pronouns are: I, we, you, he, she, it, they.

The object pronouns are: me, us, you, him, her, it, them.

The possessive pronouns are: my, mine, our, ours, your, yours, his, her, hers, its, their, theirs.

The interrogative adverbs are when, where, why, how.

Some of the most common prepositions are:
>aboard, about, above, across, after, against, along, among, around, at,
before, behind, below, beneath, beside, between, beyond, by,
down, during, except, for, from, in, inside, into, like, near, of, off,
on, onto, outside, over, past, round, since, through, throughout, till, to, toward,
under, underneath, until, up, upon, with, within, without.

A phrase is a group of related words which does not include a subject-predicate pair.

A clause is a group of words which contains a subject-predicate pair. The four types of clauses are main, subordinate, adjective, and noun.

The four sentence structures are simple, complex, compound, and compound-complex.

A subordinate clause begins with a subordinate conjunction, a relative pronoun, or a relative adverb. It contains a subject-predicate pair, but it does not form a complete sentence.

The seven coordinating conjunctions are: for, and, nor, but, or, yet, so.

The subordinate conjunctions are: after, although, as, because, before, even if, even though, if, in order that, once, provided that, rather than, since, so that, than, that, though, unless, until, when, whenever, where, whereas, wherever, whether, while.

The relative pronouns are: that, which, whichever, who, whoever, whom, whomever, whose, whosever.

An indirect object is a noun or pronoun that tells to whom or what, or for whom or what, the action of the verb is performed.

Nouns and pronouns have four properties. They are number, gender, person, and case.

An appositive is a noun, noun phrase, or series of nouns placed next to another noun to identify or rename it.

The interrogative adverbs are when, where, why, how.

The interrogative pronouns are who, whom, whose, which, what.

The five principal parts of the verb are the infinitive, the present tense, the present participle, the past tense, and the past participle.

The five properties of verbs are: person, number, tense, voice, mood.

The relative adverbs are when, where, why.

Appendix B: Correct Use of Words

This is like copywork in that it is intended to imprint certain grammatical concepts into the child's mind just through repetition. Have you ever said, or heard another say, that something just "sounds" right? Saying these sentences aloud regularly will help the correct forms "sound" right to our children and to ourselves.

My advice is to read these sentences approximately once a week for the school year. That could mean all of them once a week, or it could mean a page a day. By the time you get to the actual lessons on these topics, your child will already know these forms and the lessons will be reviews.

Predicate nominatives are in the subjective/nominative case.

It is I.

This is he.

This is she.

It is we.

It was I.

It was not I; it was she.

I think it was he.

I am sure it is she.

It was we.

It might have been they.

It was he and I.

It was they.

No, it is not she.

Yes, it is he.

Some irregular past participles are never used without a helping verb.

I came.

I saw.

I conquered.

I have come.

I have seen.

I have conquered.

I did my chores.

I am done with chores.

She did her quiz.

He is done with his quiz.

We did the work.

We have done the work.

They did fine.

They have done fine.
I go to the store.
She goes to the store.
He went to the store.
It has gone to the store.
We have gone on vacation.
They went on vacation.
You go on vacation.
I see the bird.
We did see the bird.
They saw the bird.
The bird has seen us.

Sit and Set

I sit in my favorite chair.
He is sitting in my favorite chair.
She sat in my favorite chair yesterday.
You have sat in my favorite chair.
I will sit in my favorite chair today.
They are sitting on the couch.

I set my book on the table.
You set your book on the table yesterday.
He will set his book on the table tomorrow.
They are setting books on the table.
We have set our books on the table.

Lie and Lay

I lie on the couch.
He lay on the ground.
She will lie in the flowers.
They are lying in the field.
I have lain here on the couch.

I lay the book on the table.
He laid the book on the table earlier.
She will lay the book on the table later.
We are laying the books on the table.
They have laid books on the table before.

Objects are in the objective case.

Did you call her?
Did you call me?
Did you call him and me?
Mother bought a ball for you.
Mother bought a ball for me.
Mother bought a ball for you and me.
Between you and me, I really wanted a dinosaur.

Well and Good

The hot cocoa was good this morning. You made it well.
How are you today? I am good. I am doing well.
Are you feeling ill? No, I am well.
Few have gotten a good look at a Sasquatch. The Sasquatch hides well.
Your behavior was good. You behaved well.

Double Negatives: Use only one negative word per sentence.

I have never heard that. I had not ever heard that.
I know nothing about that. I do not know anything about that.
Nobody is home. No one is at home.
None of our relatives live near. Not any of our relatives live near.
The train went nowhere. The train did not go anywhere.

Appendix C: Diagramming Reference

Procedure for analyzing sentences (skip parts you haven't learned yet):

Put brackets around prepositional phrases.

What is the predicate? The main verb is often easier to find than its subject, so find it first. Double underline it. Is it an action verb or a linking verb? Label it.

What is the subject? Underline it once.

For action verbs, is there a direct object which receives the action of the verb by answering the question **whom** or **what**? IF THERE IS A DIRECT OBJECT, is there an indirect object between the DO and the verb which identifies the recipient of the direct object by answering the question **to whom or what**, or **for whom or what**, the action of the verb is performed?

For linking verbs, is there a subject complement—a predicate nominative or a predicate adjective—which renames or modifies the subject?

Basic sentence.

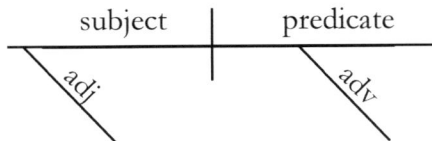

Sentences with subject complements. Note that the predicate nominative can be modified by an adjective, and the predicate adjective can be modified by an adverb.

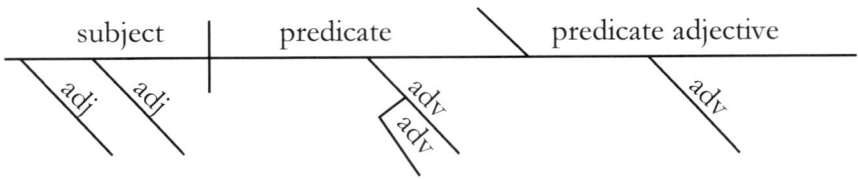

Sentence with a direct object.

Sentences with compound structures.

Compound direct object.

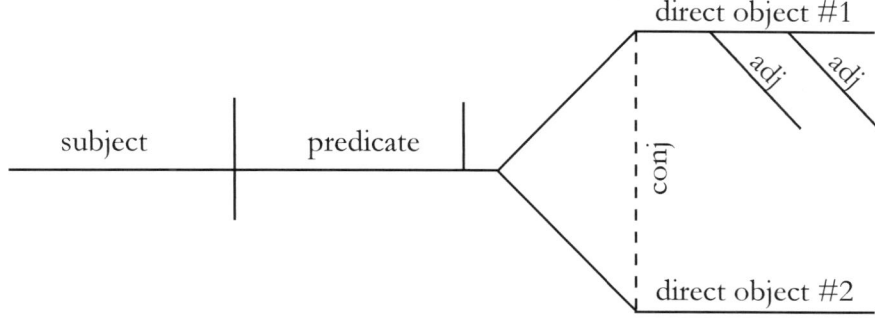

Compound predicate with shared direct object.

Command with understood you.

Prepositional phrases.

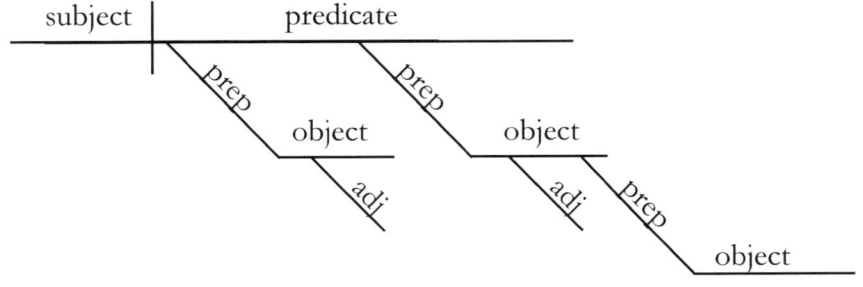

Interjections and nouns of direct address.

Expletive sentences which begin with: There is, There are.

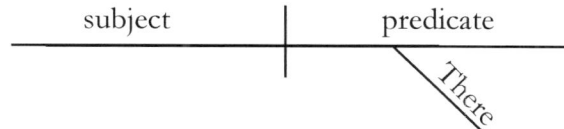

Complex sentence with a subordinate clause which begins with a subordinate conjunction. Subordinate conjunction connects the verbs.

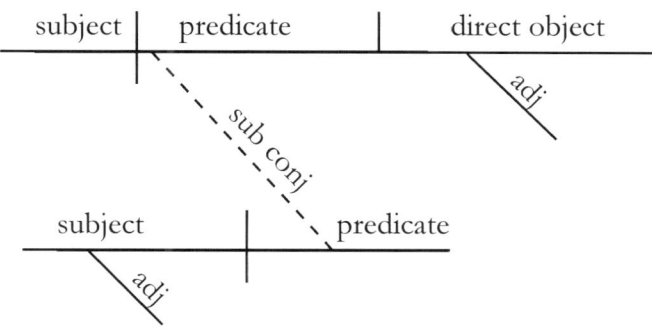

Complex sentence with a relative clause, which begins with a relative pronoun or relative adverb. Dotted line connects the relative clause to the word it modifies. The relative pronoun acts as the subject of the relative clause or it modifies the subject of the relative clause.

Indirect object.

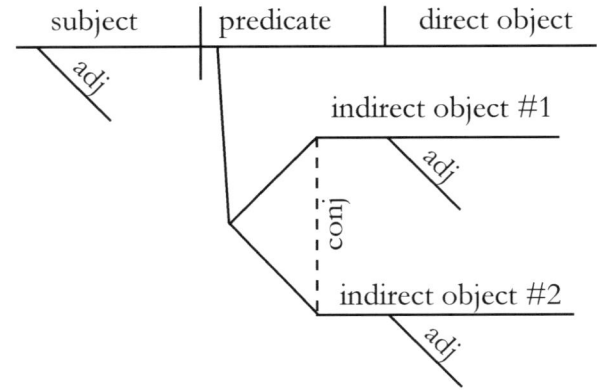

Compound indirect object.

Compound sentence.

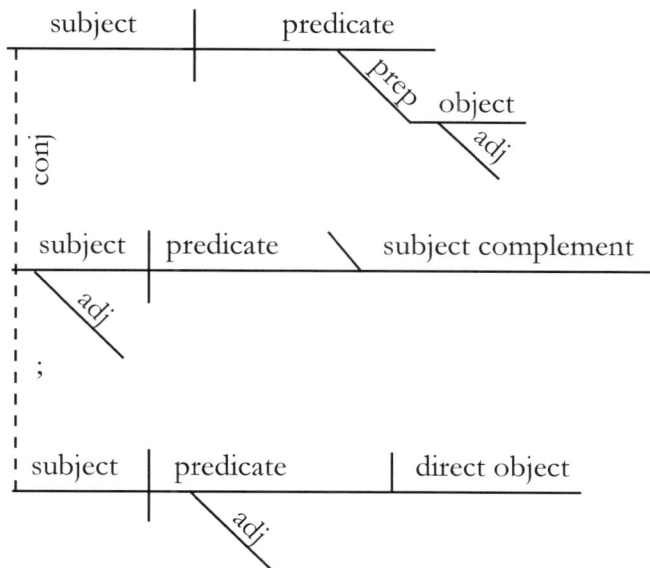

Compound complex sentence. Subordinate clauses are connected to independent clauses in the normal ways, which depend on whether the clause begins with a subordinate conjunction or a relative pronoun.

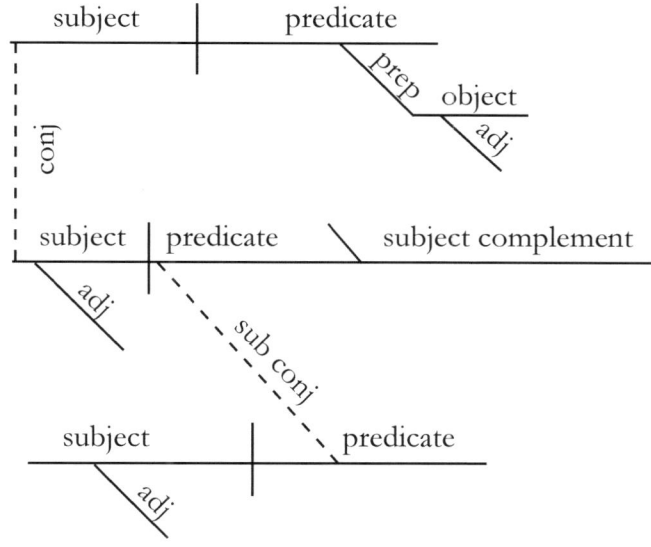

Appositive. Modifiers for the appositive go under it.

Correlative conjunctions.

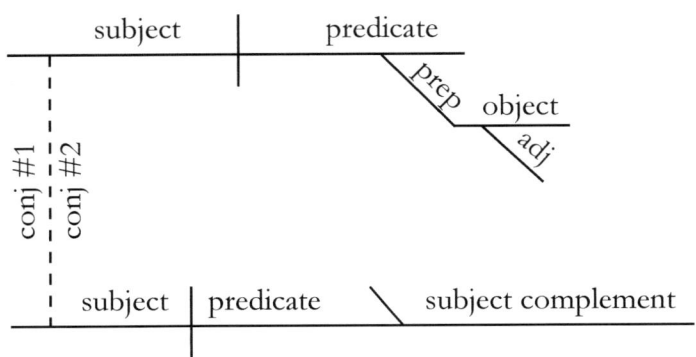

Appendix D: Additional Writing Lessons for Older Students

If you are doing Level 4 with a 4th or 5th grade student, the writing exercises within should be sufficient. However, if your student is older, you can cover these lessons from Level 5 so that he can begin practicing these concepts in his writing. The following three lessons cover introductions and conclusions, and they are copied from Level 5.

I recommend covering Introductions, Part 1, before doing Lesson 51; Introductions, Part 2, before doing Lesson 63; and Conclusions before doing Lesson 75. When you begin Level 5, continue adding introductions and conclusions to the literary analysis assignments even though they're not written into the assignments at first. In fact, once they understand how to write introductions and conclusions, these should be required parts of any paper which would generally have this sort of beginning and ending, such as reports.

Introductions, Part 1

In your literary analysis assignments so far, you've probably started off by just writing the brief summary of the book. Today, you'll learn about **introductions**. The introduction gets the reader's attention by telling something interesting about the subject of the composition. A good introduction makes the reader want to read the paper.

Read the first four paragraphs on Eleanor of Aquitaine from Appendix E, then return to this lesson.

Notice that instead of beginning with the details of Eleanor's life, the author hints at who the woman was. The author mentions her reputation, discusses whether or not it was deserved, and briefly mentions some of the more exciting parts of her life. Only then does she begin giving the details of Eleanor's life.

This is an introduction, written to inspire an interest in the topic. What if the author had skipped the first two paragraphs? Would the passage be as interesting? If a person had no idea who Eleanor of Aquitaine was, is he likely to become interested when he reads, "Eleanor was born in 1122, in Aquitaine, a dukedom in the south-west corner of France"? Probably not. So instead, the author begins by telling us why we should be interested, hinting at exciting events to come.

The introduction also sets the **tone**. The **tone** is the feeling or attitude of a composition. Is it casual, like something written to a friend, or more formal, like something written for a college class? Is it serious, or is it light-hearted? Is it dark and gloomy, or is it pleasant and cheerful? The introduction lets the reader know what to expect.

There are several different types of introductions. Today, we'll discuss **background** and **anecdotal** introductions.

Background: Some introductions give background information. The introduction for "Eleanor of Aquitaine" is a **historical review**. It sets the scene by giving a brief overview of her place in history. Another type of background introduction is the **chronological narrative**. This is a brief story in the order in which the events took place; it can be an interesting way to begin a paper about any subject at all. A composition about Jupiter's moons could begin with either a historical review or a narrative of Galileo discovering the four largest ones. NASA's article, "Our Solar System: Galileo's Observations of the Moon, Jupiter, Venus and the Sun," employs both of these methods. The first paragraph gives a historical review.

> Galileo sparked the birth of modern astronomy with his observations of the Moon, phases of Venus, moons around Jupiter, sunspots, and the news that seemingly countless individual stars make up the Milky Way Galaxy. If Galileo were around today, he would surely be amazed at NASA's exploration of our solar system and beyond.

The following paragraphs from the same article offer a chronological narrative of Galileo's discovery of Jupiter's moons.

> After learning of the newly invented "spyglass," a device that made far objects appear closer, Galileo soon figured out how it worked and built his own, improved version. In 1609, using this early version of the telescope, Galileo became the first person to record observations of the sky made with the help of a telescope....
>
> When Galileo pointed his telescope at Jupiter, the largest planet in our solar system, he made a startling discovery. The planet had four "stars" surrounding it. Within days, Galileo figured out that these "stars" were actually moons in orbit of Jupiter. His discovery challenged common beliefs of his time about the bodies of our solar system. Continuing Galileo's legacy, modern telescopes and space probes observe the wonders of Jupiter's many moons.

A literary analysis composition could begin with a story from the author's life which is relevant to the book. It could also give information about the time period or the setting of the book. For instance, an introduction for a literary analysis composition on *The Adventures of Tom Sawyer* might begin with a discussion of Mark Twain and his views against slavery, or his life growing up in a small town. It could instead discuss the time period. An introduction for a literary analysis composition on *The Emerald City of Oz* could tell of the magical setting of Oz.

Anecdotal: An anecdote is a little story. The story can be personal, from your own life, or it can be a story about someone else. It's not a long story with multiple characters, a setting, and a plot. Think back to your first literary analysis assignment, and consider this anecdote as an introduction:

> I grew up with twin brothers, two of the most mischievous children ever born. Because of this, when I read "The Ransom of Red Chief" by O. Henry, my sympathy was for the kidnappers.

Whichever type of introduction you choose to write, make sure that it is relevant to your topic. It should be connected to the rest of what you have to say. You could use the chronological narrative of Galileo to introduce a composition about Jupiter's moon, or even moons in general, but you wouldn't use it for a composition about comets.

Take a sneak peak at your next lesson, which is a literary analysis assignment. Think about which book and which type of introduction you'd like to use for that assignment.

Introductions, Part 2

The introduction to a paper gets the reader's attention by telling something interesting about the subject of the composition. A good introduction makes the reader want to read the paper.

You've learned about background and anecdotal introductions. A background introduction gives information to put the composition in context. An anecdotal introduction tells a little story to connect the reader to the composition.

Today we're going to discuss other types of introductions: **surprising statement or question**, **quotation**, and **imaginary scenario**. Remember that whichever type of introduction you use, its purpose is to introduce the reader to the topic of your paper. For the examples below, I've included possible introductions to a paper concerning Galileo.

Surprising statement or question: A surprising statement or question can catch your reader's attention and get him interested in reading your paper. A surprising sentence can be surprising for a number of reasons. It could be shocking, disgusting, or happy.

Surprising question:

> Can you imagine publicly calling the most powerful man in the world a simpleton? That's what Galileo did in his book, *Dialogue Concerning the Two Chief World Systems*, when he put the words of the Pope into the mouth of his character Simplicio.

Surprising statement:

> Galileo was an idiot. While he showed brilliance in his scientific discoveries, publicly insulting the Pope—the most powerful man in the world at that time—was not the action of a genius.

Quotation: When you can find one, an interesting quotation related to your subject can be a good way to get your reader's attention.

> "The Bible teaches us how to go to heaven, not how the heavens go." So said Cardinal Caesar Baronius to Galileo concerning the controversies surrounding scientific theories of the time.

Imaginary scenario: An imaginary scenario asks your reader to consider something in a new way. A paper which discusses an endangered species might ask the reader to imagine the planet without them. A paper about a discovery or invention might ask the reader to consider life before the discovery or invention. The following could be an imaginary scenario to introduce a paper on Galileo, his discoveries, or even on the subject of moons in general.

> Imagine that everyone believes that the heavens are made up of perfect spheres, moving around the Earth in perfect circles. One night, you point your new "spyglass" towards Jupiter, and you see something never seen before: satellites obviously orbiting another planet.

Conclusions

A **conclusion** is the end of something or a judgment reached by reasoning. In a composition, it is both. The conclusion is the last paragraph of your paper, and it adds some final thoughts that you have reached on your subject. Just as an introduction of a paper has the purpose of gaining the reader's interest, the conclusion of a paper has the purpose of leaving the reader with an interesting final thought.

The type of final thought will depend on your subject and the **purpose** of your paper. The **purpose** of your paper is what you wish to accomplish with your writing. Do you wish to **entertain** your reader, or do you want to **explain** something to him? Do you wish to **inform** your reader about a topic, or do you want to **persuade** your reader to have the same opinion about the topic that you have?

Let us return once more to the chapter on Eleanor of Aquitaine from *Great Englishwomen* by M. B. Synge (Appendix E). The introduction gave us an overview of the woman and her place in history, and it hinted at exciting things to come. At the end, the author sums up. The paragraph before the conclusion ends with the death of Eleanor. The concluding paragraph gives a few final thoughts on Eleanor from the author.

> Then Eleanor retired to Fonteraux, where she died at the age of eighty-two…
> Sorrow and adversity had taught Eleanor many a stern lesson, and few women have lived to a more honorable old age than "Eleanor, beloved of God and man," as the monks of Canterbury used to address her.

The conclusion should summarize the discussion in your paper. Look at the conclusion to the chapter on Eleanor of Aquitaine again, and notice that "summarize" does not mean "say it all again." In this case, the conclusion restated in general terms something of her life, that she had "[s]orrow and adversity," with a conclusion about this from the author, that they "had taught Eleanor many a stern lesson." She then ended the chapter with a quote about Eleanor from the monks of Canterbury. The concluding paragraph is both short and simple, but it allows the chapter to end on a more interesting note than it would have if it merely said, "Then Eleanor retired to Fonteraux, where she died at the age of eighty-two."

Conclusions can include some of the same elements as introductions, such as the quotation in the one above. Other elements include background information, anecdotes, surprising statements or questions, or imaginary scenarios.

A composition which begins with a story from history or an anecdote can circle around and end with a continuation of the story. Remember the following paragraphs from NASA's article "Our Solar System: Galileo's Observations of the Moon, Jupiter, Venus and the Sun"?

> After learning of the newly invented "spyglass," a device that made far objects appear closer, Galileo soon figured out how it worked and built his own, improved version. In 1609, using this early version of the telescope, Galileo became the first person to record observations of the sky made with the help of a telescope.…

> When Galileo pointed his telescope at Jupiter, the largest planet in our solar system, he made a startling discovery. The planet had four "stars" surrounding it.

Within days, Galileo figured out that these "stars" were actually moons in orbit of Jupiter. His discovery challenged common beliefs of his time about the bodies of our solar system. Continuing Galileo's legacy, modern telescopes and space probes observe the wonders of Jupiter's many moons.

If these paragraphs served as an introduction to a paper about moons in the universe, then the rest of the paper might not mention Galileo at all. Instead, there would be paragraphs on moons within our solar system, perhaps including artificial satellites. There might be a theoretical paragraph discussing the possibility of moons circling planets outside of our solar system. Then the conclusion could return us to Galileo:

> During the time of Galileo, the very idea of moons other than Earth's own seemed not only preposterous, but even blasphemous to some. But Galileo pointed his new device into the night sky, and he saw the impossible. Today, we scan the night sky with "spyglasses" that see even farther than Galileo could have imagined. What new impossible discoveries await us?

The introduction should get the reader's attention. The conclusion should leave the reader thinking.

Appendix E: Eleanor of Aquitaine (1122-1204)

From *Great Englishwomen* by M. B. Synge

Eleanor of Aquitaine, the wife of Henry II., has been handed down to us by popular tradition, as a tyrannical woman, with a great many bad faults and very few good traits of character. This is not entirely the case. Although her early life was marked by wild and reckless freaks, and though we must blame her for helping her sons against their father, yet we must recognize her, as one whose masterful power in ruling the kingdom kept the country at peace, whose last years were marked by very merciful acts, who never spared herself any trouble for her son, even when bowed down with fourscore years—as a great and illustrious woman.

Her energy from early youth to old age was unrivalled; at the age of twenty-five, she went on a crusade, dressed as a pilgrim, with her husband; at the age of seventy she had the energy to go to Italy with a wife for her son, and to Germany with the ransom she had raised to release him from prison.

Eleanor was born in 1122, in Aquitaine, a dukedom in the south-west corner of France. Count William, her father, was a good prince, and so beloved by his people, that when he died, fighting in the Holy Land; he was remembered as "St. William." He died when Eleanor was ten, and her grandfather undertook to provide for her future welfare. He called together his barons, and made them acknowledge Eleanor as his heiress, and further agree to a proposal that Eleanor should marry the future King of France, Louis, and thus unite the north of France with the south.

So it came to pass that, when Eleanor was fifteen, she was married with great pomp, for her grandfather had been one of the most powerful princes in Europe. Then her grandfather left her, laid down his robes, and went off to Spain, where he soon after died. After their marriage, Louis and Eleanor were summoned to the death-bed of Louis VI.

"Remember, royalty is a public trust," were his last words to the future king and queen, and on them the words made a lasting impression.

The new Queen of France was very beautiful; moreover she was musical, and composed songs and poetry; she could read and write, then a rare accomplishment, and was adored by her southern subjects, who always welcomed her with joy, and mourned her absence, when she was obliged to return to her court at Paris. Now it was at this time that St. Bernard was preaching about the Crusades, and the king and queen with all their court went to hear him. He had to preach in the market-place, as no cathedral would hold the crowds that went to listen. Now the king,—urged by Eleanor,—had already been to war in France, and in course of war he had ruthlessly set fire to a cathedral, in which 1,300 people had taken refuge; all had perished, and the king, stirred by St. Bernard, resolved to atone for this heartless deed by going to the Holy Land to fight. Eleanor declared that she would go too, so, dressed as a "gay and courtly pilgrim," and mounted on horseback, she accompanied Louis to the Crusade. But it was not a success. It led to disagreement between Louis and Eleanor, and on their return they obtained a divorce, and Eleanor went back to her own country.

Six weeks after she married Henry, Duke of Normandy, the future King of England. Louis was very angry, because now Aquitaine was united to Normandy; both would soon be joined to England, and Louis foresaw dangerous enemies.

In 1154 Henry became King of England, and he and Eleanor went over to be crowned. Everything looked bright before them; the queen rode by the king's side into Winchester, and the handsome and bravo young Henry with his beautiful wife called forth shouts of joy from the English people.

Soon after her marriage, one day, in the grounds of Woodstock, Eleanor saw the king walking with the end of a ball of silk caught on his spur. Knowing it was not her silk, her suspicions were aroused, and, without letting him see, she took up the ball of silk, and the king walking on, the silk unwound, and the queen traced him to a maze in the park, where he disappeared. Thus runs the story.

Soon after this, the king left Woodstock for a long journey; the queen, remembering the silk, then searched the grounds, and found a low door half hidden by the thicket. She opened it, and went down along a path underground, which at length led out to a lodge in a remote part of the forest, and here in a bower Eleanor found a very beautiful lady busily engaged in work. This was the fair Rosamond, and she could now account for the silk on her husband's spur. Eleanor was very angry, and it has been said that she poisoned her rival. Rosamond, however, retired to a convent, where she lived for the rest of her life.

The king was very often obliged to be in France to look after his vast possessions, but he always left Eleanor to rule in his absence, and she governed well and wisely. But the people in her duchy in the south of France did not like her to leave them so much, and at last they broke into open revolt, and would not be pacified till Eleanor went with her third son Richard to govern them for a time.

Now Henry had four sons, Henry, Richard, Geoffrey, and John, who was ten years younger than his brother Geoffrey. The two eldest, Henry and Richard, had, while quite little boys, been married to two daughters of the King of France, by which Henry hoped to keep peace with France.

Geoffrey was to marry the heiress of Brittany, so by this means the King of England possessed more of France than King Louis himself.

Henry and his little wife Margaret had been sent to Thomas a Becket, the Chancellor, to be educated and brought up in a way befitting the future king and queen of England. The children loved Becket, and when in after years Henry and Margaret were summoned to be crowned—in the lifetime of the king— by the Archbishop of York, Margaret refused to appear, because the guardian of her youth, Becket, was not to perform the coronation.

In 1172, after the murder of Becket, Henry and Margaret were again crowned, and soon after went to the French court to Louis. Now, though they had been crowned, Henry and Margaret could take no share in the government till the king's death, but Louis stirred up his young son-in-law to rebel against this rule.

At his father's death Henry was to have England, Normandy, Anjou, Maine, and Touraine; Richard, Aquitaine and Poitou; and Geoffrey, Brittany. Eleanor encouraged Henry to rebel against his father. "I advise you, king, beware of your wife and sons," were words addressed to Henry, with a warning to look after Aquitaine.

One night the king and his son stopped to sleep a night at Chimon; in the night Henry escaped and fled to the French king, where a few days after he was joined by Richard and Geoffrey. Queen Eleanor attempted to join them, but she was seized—dressed in men's clothes—escaping to the French court, and soon after Henry came over to fetch her and take her back to England, where he kept her as a sort of prisoner, safely guarded in her palace at Winchester, for many years.

Then there was peace for a time. Richard, the darling of his imprisoned mother, was the first to renew the war. On being told to do homage to young Henry for Aquitaine, he refused; whereupon Henry and Geoffrey marched against him. But peace was made. Nevertheless, the people of Aquitaine were more enraged than ever. In their eyes Eleanor was their chief, and Henry had no power over them, except through her and by affectionate treatment of her. Now she was in prison,—Eleanor, the princess of their old stock,—the princess born among them, brought up in their midst.

"Daughter of Aquitaine," sang the troubadours, "thou hast been torn from thy country and led into a strange land. Return, poor prisoner, return to thy faithful cities, if thou canst; if thou canst not, weep and cry, 'Alas, how long is my exile!' Raise thy voice like a trumpet, that thy sons may hear thee; for the day is at hand when thy sons shall deliver thee, and then thou shalt see thy native land again!

In 1183 young Henry the heir died. When he found he could not live much longer, he sent for his father to implore forgiveness for his wrongdoings. Henry, who had always loved his son, forgave him readily, and the prince—almost passionate in his sorrow—died on sackcloth and ashes as an atonement for his sins.

The following year there was a solemn peace making between Henry and his three sons. Eleanor was released from her prison to be present, and "peace and final concord" was established. Soon after Geoffrey was killed, and the King of France at once invited Richard to his court. The oft-repeated risings and rebellions of Henry's sons were making his last days very unhappy. He longed to make peace with Richard, but he could not. The people of the South were against him, his vassals were even forsaking him for Richard. A list was brought of those who had left him; he ordered the names to be read. The first name on the list was John. The king leapt from his bed in agony.

"Is it true," he cried, "that John, the child of my heart, the best beloved of all my sons, has forsaken me?"

He looked at the name, as if to make sure there was no mistake; then, turning his face to the wall, lie groaned: "Now let everything go as it will; I care no more for myself, nor for the world."

Richard's first act as King of England was to release his mother from her captivity, and make her Queen Regent of England. She made a royal progress through England, releasing prisoners throughout the country to pray "for the soul of Henry II.," pardoning offences against the crown, making the forest laws easier, and restoring to their families those who had been put in prison for disobeying them.

Her long captivity and sorrow for her two dead sons had softened her character, and the latter part of her life was kinder, more merciful, and, therefore, more powerful than the former. When Richard had settled a dower on her, she went back to France. Soon after Richard joined the King of France to go to the crusade, leaving a regent to govern England, and that regent was not his brother John. John felt the slight, but waited till Richard had gone before he put in his claims.

Eleanor's next step was to go to Spain to fetch Berengaria, the beautiful daughter of the King of Navarre, and take her to Richard, who had fallen in love with her some years before. The royal ladies set off from the court of Navarre together, crossed the Pyrenees, and went to Naples, where they found ships, and crossed to Messina, where Richard met them.

Now Eleanor had several reasons for taking this long journey to Messina. There was a question who should succeed Richard as King of England, and it was therefore important he should have an heir. Geoffrey's son Arthur was the rightful heir, as matters stood, but Eleanor hated Arthur and Arthur's mother, and was anxious to prevent his ever being king. Again, England was not in a happy state, and Eleanor wanted to talk to Richard about it.

Richard left matters entirely in his mother's hands, and Eleanor returned to England. It required all her efforts to keep the country at peace; it was she who conferred with the barons, she who at last prevailed over her youngest unruly son to remain quiet. After a time came the joyful news that Richard had started for home, but it was followed by the tidings that he had been taken prisoner. Then came a letter from Richard:

"Richard, King of England, to his esteemed lady and dearest mother Eleanor, by the same grace Queen of England, health and all happiness, which a devoted son can wish for his mother. In the first place to God, and afterward to your serene highness, sweetest mother, we send our utmost thanks, although we cannot render enough for the faithfulness which you keep for us, and the faithful care and diligence which you spend so devotedly for the peace and defence of our countries."

Then he tells her that if a ransom can be raised, he will receive his freedom. Eleanor at once held a meeting of the barons, and ordered a tax to be made, and the ransom raised. Then she herself set out for Germany with the ransom, and received back her son Richard.

When John heard through the King of France that Richard was returning, he fled. Then Eleanor and Richard held a council, and decreed that if John did not appear in forty days all his English estates should be forfeited. Then John threw himself at his brother's feet, and implored forgiveness. Richard was loth to forgive, but Eleanor begged him not to refuse, and he always obeyed her.

"I forgive him," he cried, "and I hope I shall as easily forget his injuries as he will forget my pardon."

In 1199 Richard died, leaving the kingdom to John. It was due mostly to Eleanor's influence that Arthur was set aside, and John appointed to reign. But many of the French people hated John, and wanted Arthur to reign over them, and Arthur and his friends marched against a French town where his grandmother Eleanor was staying. On hearing of his mother's danger, John, with unwonted energy, marched to the rescue, and Arthur was taken as prisoner to the castle of Rouen. From this time he disappeared. Some say his uncle drowned him; tradition gives a tragic history of how his eyes were burnt out by Hubert. Our poet Shakespere represents him as throwing him self from a high wall and being killed, but we do not know what the truth really is. Then Eleanor retired to Fonteraux, where she died at the age of eighty-two.

With his mother's death John lost all fear and shame, and relapsed into depths of wickedness. Sorrow and adversity had taught Eleanor many a stern lesson, and few women have lived to a more honorable old age than "Eleanor, beloved of God and man," as the monks of Canterbury used to address her.

Made in the USA
San Bernardino, CA
06 July 2016